JUST A LARGER FAMILY

Life Writing Series

In the **Life Writing Series**, Wilfrid Laurier University Press publishes life writing and new life-writing criticism and theory in order to promote autobiographical accounts, diaries, letters, and testimonials written and/ or told by women and men whose political, literary, or philosophical purposes are central to their lives. The Series features accounts written in English, or translated into English from French or the languages of the First Nations, or any of the languages of immigration to Canada.

From its inception, **Life Writing** has aimed to foreground the stories of those who may never have imagined themselves as writers or as people with lives worthy of being (re)told. Its readership has expanded to include scholars, youth, and avid general readers both in Canada and abroad. The Series hopes to continue its work as a leading publisher of life writing of all kinds, as an imprint that aims for both broad representation and scholarly excellence, and as a tool for both historical and autobiographical research.

As its mandate stipulates, the Series privileges those individuals and communities whose stories may not, under normal circumstances, find a welcoming home with a publisher. **Life Writing** also publishes original theoretical investigations about life writing, as long as they are not limited to one author or text.

Series Editor
Marlene Kadar
Humanities Division, York University

Manuscripts to be sent to
Lisa Quinn, Acquisitions Editor
Wilfrid Laurier University Press
75 University Avenue West
Waterloo, Ontario, Canada N2L 3C5

JUST A LARGER FAMILY

**LETTERS OF MARIE WILLIAMSON
FROM THE CANADIAN HOME FRONT,
1940–1944**

**MARY F. WILLIAMSON
AND TOM SHARP, EDITORS**

Wilfrid Laurier University Press

Wilfrid Laurier University Press acknowledges the support of the Canada Council for the Arts for our publishing program. We acknowledge the financial support of the Government of Canada through the Canada Book Fund for our publishing activities.

 Canada Council Conseil des Arts
for the Arts du Canada

 ONTARIO ARTS COUNCIL
CONSEIL DES ARTS DE L'ONTARIC

Library and Archives Canada Cataloguing in Publication

Williamson, Marie, 1898–1969

Just a larger family : letters of Marie Williamson from the Canadian home front, 1940–1944 / Mary F. Williamson and Tom Sharp, editors.

(Life writing series)
Also issued in electronic format.
ISBN 978-1-55458-323-2 (paperback)

1. Williamson, Marie, 1898–1969—Correspondence. 2. Sharp, Margaret, 1896–1987—Correspondence. 3. World War, 1939–1945—Personal narratives, Canadian. 4. World War, 1939–1945—Evacuation of civilians—Great Britain. 5. World War, 1939–1945—Children—Great Britain. 6. World War, 1939–1945—Children—Canada. 7. Toronto (Ont.) —Biography. I. Williamson, Mary F. II. Sharp, Tom, 1931- III. Title. IV. Series: Life writing series

D810.C4W55 2011   940.53'161   C2010-905602-7

Electronic formats.
ISBN 978-1-55458-322-5 (PDF), ISBN 978-1-55458-346-1 (EPUB)

1. Williamson, Marie, 1898–1969—Correspondence. 2. Sharp, Margaret, 1896–1987—Correspondence. 3. World War, 1939–1945—Personal narratives, Canadian. 4. World War, 1939–1945—Evacuation of civilians—Great Britain. 5. World War, 1939–1945—Children—Great Britain. 6. World War, 1939–1945—Children—Canada. 7. Toronto (Ont.) —Biography. I. Williamson, Mary F. II. Sharp, Tom, 1931- III. Title. IV. Series: Life writing series (Online)

D810.C4W55 2011a   940.53'161   C2010-905603-5

Cover photo from the Williamson family collection. Cover design by Sandra Friesen. Text design by Kathe Gray Design.

This book is printed on FSC recycled paper and is certified Ecologo. It is made from 100% post-consumer fibre, processed chlorine free, and manufactured using bio-gas energy.

Printed in Canada

RECYCLED
Paper made from
recycled material
FSC® C021757
www.fsc.org

In loving memory of
Marie Williamson

CONTENTS

FOREWORD

by Jonathan Vance

WHAT WOULD POSSESS A YOUNG DIVORCED WOMAN TO SEND HER THREE
sons, ages thirteen, eleven, and nine, thousands of miles away across a
submarine-infested ocean, to stay for an indefinite period of time in a city
she had never visited with distant relatives she barely knew? And what
could have convinced another young couple with two children of their own,
a limited household income, and a mother whose health was never especially robust to welcome three young boys they had never met into a home
they knew was not large enough?

The answer lies in a phrase that had assumed a powerful meaning in
Britain and Canada by the time of the Second World War: no longer an
island. The phrase had entered the popular consciousness a generation
earlier, when the airplane made it clear that Britain's splendid isolation
had ended. For centuries, the English Channel and the North Sea had been
formidable barriers to the invader; only the Romans, the Vikings, and the
Normans had succeeded in breaching them, the last nearly a thousand
years ago. Protected by water and the Royal Navy, British civilians could,
as Admiral Sir John Fisher put it, "sleep quiet in your beds" in the relative
certainty that war would not touch them personally.[1] In the first decade
of the twentieth century, the airplane destroyed that comforting security.

The Wright brothers first flew in 1903, and in the few years after that
pioneering flight, other intrepid pilots attempted longer and longer flights.
When Louis Blériot became the first person to fly across the English
Channel (or indeed any substantial body of water) in 1909, a new era began. His flimsy monoplane hardly posed a threat to anything, but the technology quickly improved. Futurist writers had long predicted the advent of
air fleets that could rain death on cities from the skies; now that day was

just around the corner. Developments in aviation meant "aerial chariots of a foe descending on British soil if war comes," predicted the *Daily Mail*. Britain was entering a new era "caused by the virtual annihilation of frontiers and the acquisition of the power to pass readily through the air above the sea. The isolation of the United Kingdom may disappear."[2]

The First World War lasted only four years but it saw breathtaking technological change, especially in aviation. The airplane of 1914 was fragile, slow, clumsy, and weak; the airplane of 1918 was reliable, fast, manoeuvrable, and powerful. There were also flying machines, multi-engine biplane bombers and Jules Verne–ish gas-filled dirigibles, that could carry tons of bombs hundreds of miles. The few miles of water that separated Britain from the European continent now seemed to be of little consequence as a protective barrier.

Germany had developed the first viable airships before the war, and by 1914, commercial Zeppelins were regularly plying tourist routes in central Europe. Germany also boasted the world's largest air force, with over 200 serviceable aircraft. In 1915, as stalemate descended on the Western Front and both sides searched for a way to break the deadlock, the German military came up with a novel idea: Why not use flying machines to bypass the battlefield altogether and take the war directly to the British Isles? On Christmas Eve 1914, the first bombs fell on British soil. The results were sufficiently encouraging that the German airship service decided to extract permission from Kaiser Wilhelm for a limited aerial bombardment of England. The first raid came on January 19, 1915, killing four civilians and injuring sixteen, and by the spring of 1915, the raiders were coming with increasing regularity. On May 31, 1915, bombs fell on east London. Only seven people were killed, but four of them were children, including a little girl and her baby sister, burned to death when incendiary bombs hit their home in Stoke Newington. In 1916, the Germans added large biplane bombers, known as Gothas and Giants, to their arsenal. In a Gotha raid on June 13, 1917, that particularly outraged British opinion, more than 160 Londoners were killed, including eighteen children (sixteen of them under the age of six) who died when the Upper North Street School in Poplar was hit by a bomb.

In the final reckoning, the German air offensive had a negligible impact on the war. The engines of the bulky Zeppelins were notoriously unreliable, and fewer than half of the raiders that left their bases actually reached the target. Furthermore, any damage was purely random. Not only were the airship crews unable to hit specific targets, but they often failed to locate even major cities. The Gothas and Giants were generally more accurate but were no more successful in producing a decisive result. But the psychological impact of the raids was enormous. Compared to the big bombing raids of the Second World War, the Poplar school tragedy was minuscule, but at the time it was a nightmare worse than anything the pre-war futurists could conjure up. The few high-profile downings of Zeppelins could not hide the fact that Britain's air defences were usually powerless to stop the raiders, even in daylight. Panic gripped the British public, and absenteeism skyrocketed as workers decided to stay home with their families. It was a sign of the near hysteria created by even intermittent aerial bombing that in January 1918, fourteen people were killed in panicked crushes at two separate air-raid shelters.

In the 1920s and 1930s, the myth of the bomber took on a life of its own. Newspaper headlines from the war years—"Zeppelin Murder of Tots," "Nursery a Slaughterhouse after the Zeppelin Raid," "20 Baby-Killers Sweep over the British Capital"—were not easily forgotten.[3] Britons recalled how journalists had referred not to the bomb deaths of women and children, but to the "midnight murdering" of non-combatants and air raids that represented "a slaughter of the innocents" and "an organized attempt to murder women in their homes and torture children in their cots."[4] The public firmly believed that the bomber would always get through. There was no means of defence; enemy air fleets would simply fly overhead, out of sight and in complete safety, and release high explosives, incendiaries, chemical weapons, or gas bombs. The horrors that the futurists had predicted in the nineteenth century were now accepted as the true face of the future.

Indeed, futurist horror stories became government policy. In 1924, a British government committee on air-raid precautions predicted that in the first twenty-four hours of a future war, more bombs would be dropped on Britain than the 3,000 tons that fell in the entire First World War. As the years passed, such predictions were refined but not substantially altered. In March 1931, an Air Ministry report predicted that an enemy would drop 100 tons of high explosives on Britain in the first twenty-four hours of a future war, seventy-five tons in the second, and fifty tons each and every day thereafter for a month. One expert held that Britain would be subject to sixty straight days of bombing that would kill 600,000 civilians; another forecast that 100,000 tons of bombs would fall on London in the first two weeks alone, with each ton causing fifty casualties.[5]

These fears were fed by events in the late 1930s. On April 27, 1937, German bombers supporting the Nationalist forces in the Spanish Civil War devastated the Basque town of Guernica, destroyed three-quarters of the city, and killed nearly 1,700 people in a single day of air raids. Over the next few weeks, Madrid and Bilbao also experienced the terror of modern bombing. On the other side of the world, Shanghai and Nanking were both bombed intensively by Japanese aircraft, killing thousands of civilians. In a May 1938 interview, Sir John Moore-Brabazon, who was credited with being the first Englishman to make an airplane flight in Britain, summed up the weary disillusionment of pioneering aviators. When he had first flown, he dreamed "that the age of world peace and internationalism was on the horizon," but now those dreams lay in ruins: "It is bitter to reflect that when I took up an aeroplane for the first time I brought nearer the dark ages of the 20th century."[6]

Since there was no way to stop this aerial onslaught, the only alternative was to evacuate from the danger zone the most vulnerable people: women, children, the elderly, and the infirm. This would achieve a number of ends. Obviously, it offered the best kind of protection, not only from the bombing but from the panic that government officials assumed would grip urban neighbourhoods during air raids (particularly working-class districts and slums, where people were imagined to be more susceptible to hysteria).[7] It would also prevent them from getting in the way of vital military and industrial operations. It would reduce the number of *bouches inutiles,* or useless mouths, in urban Britain; if a major city was devastated by aerial bombing and access to food and water had to be restricted, the fewer mouths to feed, the better. And finally, the government admitted that soldiers might well fight better if they knew that their families were away from target areas and relatively safe from enemy action.

Still, the government seemed reluctant to embrace evacuation as a policy and the Air Raid Precautions Bill that received Royal Assent in December 1937 contained only general provisions for removing civilians from urban areas—and that was because some politicians argued that the policy of shelter construction, the bill's first line of defence, was impractical in the already overcrowded working-class districts.[8] Having made the leap, the government then created the House of Commons Committee on Evacuation, which met for the first time on May 27, 1938. Eventually, the committee divided the country into evacuable areas, reception areas (where evacuees would be billeted), and neutral areas (which could expect neither bombing nor evacuees). The evacuable areas were those deemed to be most in danger of aerial attack: London, the county, and surrounding boroughs; the major cities of the industrial Midlands, including Birmingham, Manchester, and Liverpool; and major port cities, such as Portsmouth, Southampton, and Chatham. It was estimated that there were roughly twelve million people living in those areas who should be evacuated. For administrative purposes, they were divided into four classes: Category A were school-age children who would be evacuated in school groups, under the chaperonage of their teachers; Category B were children under the age of five who had not been through evacuation drills in school and would have to be accompanied by a mother or other female escort; Category C were the blind; and Category D were expectant mothers.[9] Finally, the government also decided that it would determine the date of evacuation, rather than being forced into action by an enemy attack.

In the tense atmosphere of 1938, when Europe seemed on the verge of war until the Munich agreement brought a temporary stay of execution, some 4,000 nursery and disabled children were moved out of London as a precaution. From late 1938 on, British parents were subject to an onslaught of propaganda encouraging them to send their children away from vulnerable urban areas in the event of war. Through 1939 rehearsals were commonplace, involving parents (who were instructed to keep suitcases for their children packed at all times), teachers (who would escort children to reception areas), and the children themselves (who would go to school every morning not knowing if they would return home that afternoon).

If urban Britons were willing to send their children away, many people in Canada were willing to offer them temporary homes. In May 1938, the National Council of Women began collecting the names of people who could take in children evacuated from Britain; by September 1939, it had offers from 100,000 women. Ontario premier Mitch Hepburn endorsed the idea, and Lady Eaton offered her estate as a temporary home to child evacuees. The National Council of Education of Canada, which brought school groups from Britain on exchange programs, supported the notion wholeheartedly and made arrangements for groups to remain in Canada in the event that war broke out.[10] Clearly, there was sympathy with an editorial published in *The Globe and Mail* in July 1939. "In recent months newspaper and newsreel pictures of little children, bewildered faces hidden behind ghoulish masks, being herded into dugouts have filled the gaps in the imagination," the editor observed. "From the little Princesses in the palace to the babies of the slums, whole generations are as vulnerable as the troops in the front lines."[11] Although King George VI and Queen Elizabeth declined to send Princesses Elizabeth and Margaret out of London as a precaution, their decision was intended to provide inspiration rather than an example. For the sake of the Empire's future, British parents had a duty to evacuate their children, and Canadians had a duty to offer them shelter.

But Britain's domestic evacuation planning would be tested first. On September 1, 1939, German troops invaded Poland; it was another two days before Britain's declaration of war, but the Clear-Out Scheme was immediately set in motion and the code word Pied Piper went out across the country. Everything functioned just as it was supposed to, with remarkably few hitches. Parents sent their children to school as usual, but with their luggage and supplies for the journey. Teachers shepherded them to railway stations, where waiting trains carried them to reception areas; once there, volunteers and government employees arranged for their billeting. In the first four days of the program, some 1.4 million people were evacuated from British cities to rural areas; within another week, two million more had been moved. The government assumed that there would be a 100% compliance rate with the voluntary evacuations, so most schools in the affected areas were closed.[12]

Because there was nothing like full compliance, it was just as well that the blow did not immediately fall on Britain. Rather than turning its attentions elsewhere after Poland, the German war machine paused. The *blitzkrieg* was followed by the Phony War, when nothing of substance occurred, and by early 1940, more than half of the domestic evacuees had returned home, with more going every week. Then came the German invasion of Denmark, Norway, the Low Countries, and France in April and May 1940, which brought a second wave of evacuations. The number of cities declared evacuable was expanded, and the government announced a more generous billeting allowance (14 shillings 10 pence for a single child, or 8 shillings 6 pence each for two or more children) to deal with the new exodus. Beginning in late May, some 1.25 million children again left their homes for safe zones. With the Nazis just a few miles across the English Channel and invasion barges being stockpiled in French ports, leaving the cities took on a new urgency. So too did leaving Britain altogether.

Only 253 children under the age of sixteen came to Canada in 1939, most of them from well-to-do families. After all, children being evacuated overseas were charged a £15 transportation fee, which represented about a month's salary for three-quarters of the population, as well as £1 per child per week for maintenance.[13] No matter what the level of threat, this was simply beyond the means of the vast majority of Britons. But with the fall of France, a wave of desperation swept in and more parents began to look for ways to get their children safely away from Europe. In London, Canadian diplomatic officials were deluged with applications from people seeking travel permits to Canada. The first to leave were mostly people with sufficient money and influence to push past the administrative obstacles that had been set up. Because most people in Britain did not have that money or influence, groups began getting involved in private programs of sponsored evacuation. Companies such as Ford, Kodak, and CIL arranged evacuation for the children of their employees, and service clubs like Rotary and interest groups like the Eugenics Society organized group schemes as well. Canadian universities helped to bring over the children of their British faculty colleagues, and some private schools evacuated as groups. In June 1940 alone, some 10,000 civilians (including over 2,300 children) left Britain for the Dominions, most of them from affluent families. One concerned politician referred to the migration as "the rich swarming overseas."[14]

He was not the only critic. The Treasury and the Bank of England were worried about the impact on the pound sterling if large sums of money left Britain with evacuees. As a result, they enacted stringent regulations covering the movement of currency: as of June 1940, each traveller could take only £10 out of Britain, and other transfers of funds were prohibited.[15] Prime Minister Winston Churchill objected to evacuations for different reasons. On July 18, 1940, he told the House of Commons that there was no military need for evacuations, and no physical capacity to carry them out. Later, he stated that "a large movement of this kind encourages a defeatist spirit, which is entirely contrary to the true facts of the [war] position and should sternly be discouraged."[16] The headmaster of Winchester College argued in a letter to *The Times* that evacuation taught all the wrong lessons: "How can we with any consistency speak of training in citizenship and in leadership while at the same time we arrange for them [children] against their will to leave the post of danger? ... I believe it is our duty to encourage those for whom we are responsible to stand fast and carry on."[17]

But the most strident objections were raised against the inequality of current practice: the rich and powerful could easily get their loved ones out of harm's way, the mass of the population could not. And since the government could not ban private evacuation altogether, the only solution was to create a system that made it accessible to everyone. The result was the Children's Overseas Reception Board (CORB), which was established after the fall of France.[18] As its head, Sir Geoffrey Shakespeare, said, the CORB was created to oversee a program of "carefully monitored child evacuation that would ensure that overseas evacuation represented a full cross-section of all classes."[19] There were other benefits as well. Its promoters argued that the evacuation of children could encourage host countries, especially the United States, where a Gallup poll found that half a million Americans were willing to host evacuated British children, to recognize common aims with Britain and join the war against Germany. At the very least, the children might serve as ambassadors overseas. This was so because, as the executive director of Canadian Welfare put it, "It is not, therefore, refugees who we plan to receive, it is not just evacuees, transferred from the range of the menace; it is part of Britain's immortality, part of the greatness of her past, part of all the hope of her future that we take into our keeping."[20]

The Canadian government agreed to accept an unspecified number ("several thousand") of children under the CORB, in very specific categories. They must be medically fit (stringent medical exams were required before a child could leave Britain) and unaccompanied and at least 75% of them had to be of British origin and not Roman Catholic. Sixteen years was the maximum age and most provinces preferred evacuees to be at least ten years old; there were few billets available for children under the age of five.[21] Although all provinces agreed to accept children, the majority of evacuees went to Ontario.

The CORB's first day of business at its London office was June 20, 1940, and by 10 that morning, the corridors were already jammed and thousands of people were lined up along the sidewalks of Berkeley Street. On the 23rd, Shakespeare gave a radio address over the BBC to clarify the CORB's policy and perhaps stem the rush. He stated that the program's aim had never been to cause a mass exodus by sea, but rather to spirit away a limited number of children to safe havens overseas. Most important, he steadfastly refused to offer advice to parents: "You have to weigh the danger to which your child is exposed in this country, whether by invasion, or by air raids, against the risks to which every ship that leaves these shores is subject in war-time by enemy action, whether by air, by submarine, or by mine. The risks of the voyage are obvious and the choice is one for which you alone are responsible."[22] But if Shakespeare hoped his remarks would calm the public, he was wrong. Soon, the CORB had a large and growing backlog of cases. By the end of the month, the Board had expanded its staff to 620 employees and still could not keep up with the demand, which approached 20,000 applications a day. On July 4, 1940, Shakespeare decided to suspend registration, with over 210,000 children enrolled as potential evacuees. By the fall of 1940, some 3,500 CORB evacuees (christened CORB Limeys by some anonymous wit) had left Britain for the Dominions, and thousands more went under private arrangements. In total, some 5,500 children came to Canada under various programs in 1940.[23]

But overseas evacuation was about to be dealt a death blow, before it really got started. In the summer of 1940, two passenger liners, the *Arandora Star* (carrying German and Italian internees to Canada) and the *Volendam* (carrying over 300 child evacuees), were torpedoed by German submarines. Although no children were killed, the willingness of U-boat commanders to attack passenger vessels (both the *Arandora Star* and the *Volendam* were modern, fast vessels that sailed without naval escort—just the sort of ships that the CORB intended to use) set off alarm bells in Britain. Then, on September 17, 1940, the *City of Benares,* four days out of Liverpool, was attacked by a German U-boat. Its first two torpedoes missed, but the third struck the vessel's stern and the *City of Benares* went down in about thirty minutes. A British destroyer arrived to pick up survivors (one lifeboat was overlooked, and the occupants drifted in the North Atlantic for eight days before being rescued), but the loss was heavy: of the 406 passengers and crew, 248 died, including seventy-seven evacuees from the CORB and six of their escorts.[24]

The program never recovered from the sinking of the *City of Benares.* Children who were en route to various ports were sent home, and after October 1940, no more CORB evacuees left the British Isles. Through 1941, the flow of private evacuees dwindled to a trickle until it, too, stopped entirely. Altogether, 1,532 British children travelled to Canada under the auspices of the CORB; in addition, 577 went to Australia, 353 to South Africa, and 202 to New Zealand. There is no reliable count of how many children were evacuated under private schemes, although the total may be as high as 15,000.[25]

The CORB operated on fundamentally different principles than the programs that evacuated children to safe areas in the British Isles. Internal evacuees went in school groups, and generally speaking remained together in school groups. CORB children, on the other hand, were integrated into local schools, the CORB having pledged that the children "would be given the same educational opportunities as those available to Dominion children in the district where an evacuee went to live." Domestic evacuees went to billets arranged by the government, to families that in some cases were not especially interested in hosting young evacuees. Of the CORB evacuees, nearly two-thirds were placed with friends or relatives who had been nominated by their own parents.[26] One matter common to all evacuees and hosts was the question of guardianship: What legal rights and responsibilities did host parents overseas have when it came to important decisions involving discipline, medical care, or education? The British government was unable to resolve this issue until June 1941, when the Temporary Migration of Children Act was passed. It allowed the government in Whitehall to appoint British diplomatic officials in the United States and Canada as legal guardians of children evacuated by the CORB. With this, the British government would be legally responsible for the children's care, on the understanding that the day-to-day issues of child rearing would be addressed by the foster parents.

The question of guardianship returns us to the experiences of the Williamsons and the Sharps. As private evacuees, the three boys were in a slightly different position than children who came to Canada under the banner of the CORB. In the first place, because the boys were unofficial evacuees, the Williamsons were not eligible for the tax relief that went to families under the CORB scheme. As Marie's letter of June 24, 1942, notes, the federal government rejected John Williamson's claim for the two boys then living with the family, leaving him with a back tax bill of $150 for 1941, and another $225 to pay for 1942 (roughly $2,100 and $2,900, respectively, in current values). Although Margaret and Douglas Sharp were eventually able to send a certain amount of money, as well as clothing and other small gifts, to Canada, the bulk of the financial burden for the boys' upbringing fell on the Williamsons.

However, as the letters reveal, the family did benefit from the generosity of relatives, neighbours, and local businesspeople who were keen to do what they could to assist evacuees from Britain. Doctors would provide basic services at no charge, no small matter for a large family in the days before socialized medicine, and senior students at Toronto's dental school were willing to work on evacuees at no charge. The Overseas Children's Committee at the University of Toronto put its resources at the disposal of all host families, not only those who were affiliated with the university, which gave Marie access to everything from health and accident insurance to reading matter from the Institute of Child Study, a research centre that had been established at the university in 1925. At least one summer camp was willing to accept evacuees at the deeply reduced fee of $10 per week, so that British children could experience this Canadian childhood ritual. Schoolmasters did what they could to reduce school fees, and the University of Toronto Schools even opened a special class for evacuees. One local couple who had not been able to find a way to do their bit for evacuees volunteered to pay Tom's fees so he would not have to change schools. But Marie was careful to point out to Margaret that the neighbour's offer was not really charity; it should be seen as "an easing of his obligation, not as incurring one ourselves."

Although guardianship of the three boys was not necessarily a concern in a strictly legal sense, it certainly was in a personal sense. As the letters reveal, Marie was constantly forced to deal with everything that goes along with raising children. In the grand scheme of a world at war, some of the issues seem small: What time should the boys be sent to bed? What should their weekly allowance be? What should Marie and John tell them about Santa Claus? Other matters got to the heart of child-rearing philosophies. In October 1940, Marie sent a long description of the Williamsons' reasoning in taking the boys to church and concluded by saying, "I hope all this lengthy explanation is satisfactory to you." There was much discussion of education, everything from Christopher's difficulties in spelling to the choice of a university for Bill. And the Williamsons were careful to give Margaret as much information as possible. On a number of occasions, John took the boys' report cards into his office and had them photographed, so the copies could be sent to Margaret. More often, Marie either transcribed the reports for Margaret or sent the originals to England.

But it was the boys' health that seems to have caused the greatest concern. All three were generally fit and healthy, but they were still afflicted by the periodic illnesses that any children experience. Any injury or illness made Marie more keenly aware than usual that she was the boys' surrogate mother, because in such situations she usually had to make decisions on her own, without reference to Margaret's opinions. One matter of continuing concern was whether to have the boys' tonsils removed, a popular option among doctors at the time. Marie was steadfastly against the practice and was sure to let Margaret know it, but in July 1942, Bill had his tonsils and adenoids removed. "One feels dreadfully responsible, making decisions for children not one's own," she wrote to Margaret, but in this case, it had been the doctor's decision; he swept aside all objections and insisted that the surgery was medically necessary. Questions like that are difficult enough to answer when they concern one's own children; they are doubly difficult when one is deciding for someone else's children. "On rereading this," Marie wrote at the end of a long letter in October 1943, "I have an uncomfortable feeling that it sounds as though I were trying to dictate what is best for you to do about your own child."

In practice, the vast majority of decisions were left almost entirely to Marie. Sometimes it was possible to get Margaret's input but, given the difficulties involved in transatlantic communication, it was not usually feasible to await parental guidance before making a decision. Letters might take weeks to cross the Atlantic, and Marie was frequently left wondering if any of their correspondence had gone down on a torpedoed merchant ship. And although she was always mindful of the potential delays, there is in Marie's letters a certain impatience at Margaret's apparent reluctance to write, either to her or to the boys. In August 1942, she even had to ask Margaret directly to write more frequently, to ensure that the boys did not forget their real mother.

Reading the letters after seventy years, it is difficult to come to any other conclusion than that Bill, Christopher, and Tom Sharp were extraordinarily fortunate. One does not have to delve very deeply into the literature to find horror stories from the evacuation process, of billets where children were treated as slaves or occasions when evacuees shamefully took advantage of their hosts. In contrast, the distant relatives whom the Sharp boys had never met turned out to be kind, compassionate, and wise substitute parents who gave the boys the best upbringing that it is possible to imagine. Marie and John Williamson were no doubt motivated by many factors, but the desire to help British children in a time of need was always present. As Marie wrote to Margaret in July 1940, when the boys were on their way to Canada, "The more children we can have out of England the better we will be pleased."

ACKNOWLEDGEMENTS

A NUMBER OF INDIVIDUALS WHO HELPED US WITH PRECISE NAMES, DATES, and places, and who shared with us their memories from the war years, are particularly deserving of our gratitude. Their families were of critical support to the Williamsons or acted as ambassadors of Margaret Sharp, who lived far away in Britain. They include Anne Innis Dagg, daughter of Mary and Harold Innis; Peter Williamson, son of Marie and John Williamson; Judy Ratcliffe, daughter of Vivien and Harry Ratcliffe; Joan Grierson and Meredith Saunderson, daughters of Jo and Robbie Robinson; Ann Robson and Margaret Ann Wilkinson, daughter and granddaughter of Edith and Bertie Wilkinson; Andrew Beamish, son of Katharine and George Beamish; Brenda Reid, daughter of Frances Billington Cruikshank; John Tylecote, son of Mabel Tylecote ("Phiz"); and William Anthony, son of Sylvia Anthony.

Julia Williamson and Sally Wilson typed the letters, which luckily was not a daunting task, as Marie's handwriting is always clearly legible. Frances Tout, great-granddaughter of Mary Tout, expertly compiled the family tree.

Our heartfelt thanks to Carlotta Lemieux, who with sensitivity and a keen eye created a book out of an unwieldy mound of letters. That we discovered when we were well into the project that Carlotta had been a student at the same small school in England as the two elder Sharp boys was an extraordinary, and of course hugely welcome, surprise.

Jack Granatstein assured us that the military record of the war years should be balanced by accounts of the struggles to live a "normal" life at home. It is possible that had he not endorsed publication of the letters, this mother's bird's-eye view of how British war evacuees adapted to Canadian life would never have been translated into a book. We are indebted to Charlotte Gray for generously offering her advice and encouragement. Mary McDougall Maude was keenly supportive when at the beginning we sought her ideas and practical suggestions.

We are especially grateful to Jonathan Vance for responding enthusiastically to our proposal for a critical introduction. He has established a context for Marie's letters and given us a little history of how Britain stood up to the threat of German invasion in two world wars by encouraging the mass evacuation of thousands of children.

At Wilfrid Laurier University Press we thank most heartily Rob Kohlmeier, Lisa Quinn, Clare Hitchens, Leslie Macredie, and Penelope Grows. We also thank Life Writing Series editor Marlene Kadar and Wendy Thomas, who has been a scrupulous and empathetic copy editor.

Margaret Sharp (Tom's wife) and Susan Houston have stood up admirably to what seemed a never-ending project, especially when the editors seemed to be lost in remembrances of a time when they were irresponsible children. "Thank you" seems inadequate.

Marie Williamson in 1945

INTRODUCTION

IN LATE JULY 1940, MARIE WILLIAMSON, HER HUSBAND JOHN, AND THEIR children Peter and Mary ordinarily would have escaped the heat of Toronto to go swimming, boating, and camping up north in Haliburton. But this summer they were still at home and, with understandable impatience, were wondering when they would have news of Bill, Christopher, and Tom Sharp, who were due to arrive sometime from England. The official silence imposed by the British government on the departure dates, ports of departure, and even the names of ships carrying British children—occasionally accompanied by their mothers—meant that with other foster parents the Williamsons were kept waiting until they could be told that their new charges had arrived in Canada. They weren't even sure whether the boys' mother, Margaret, had decided to come with them. (See Appendix 1 for Margaret's letter to Marie.) Whether they would land in Halifax or Quebec or Montreal was a secret too. On July 30, they would have read in *The Globe and Mail* a story headed "1,580 Children Arrive on Battle-Grey Liners," describing the excitement of the arrival the previous day of two liners at an unnamed eastern Canadian port. Surely one of the ships was carrying the three boys.[1]

Marie must have been apprehensive. With very little warning, she was taking on the responsibility and added expense of children she had never met. Canada had entered the war in September 1939, and in early June 1940 allied troops had evacuated the beaches of the French town of Dunkirk. For Canadians it was painfully clear that a German invasion of Great Britain was a possibility. Many Anglo-Canadians still had strong ties to the mother country and felt committed to supporting the British

1

cause in any way they could. One way they could help was to accept British children into their homes for the duration of the war.

WE CAN ONLY IMAGINE THE DISCUSSIONS THAT LED THE WILLIAMSONS TO welcome the Sharp boys for who knew how long. Not long before the boys sailed from Liverpool on the *Duchess of Bedford* at the end of July, it had been decided that three boys would be too much for Marie, whose health was never robust. The eldest, Bill, then thirteen years old, would live with her close friends Vivien and Harry Ratcliffe, who had three children of their own in a large house in north Toronto. The Williamsons lived on a smaller scale at 118 Hillsdale Avenue West.

Thousands of British children who were brought to Canada in 1940 under a Canadian government scheme were billeted with families they did not know. But the Sharps and the Williamsons had made a private arrangement. Marie's mother, Florence Peterkin (née Johnstone), had come to Toronto as a small child from Bradford in England with her father and four brothers in 1879. In England Mary Tout (née Johnstone), Florence's first cousin and the grandmother of the Sharp boys, was the vital link, nurturing the transatlantic connection throughout her life.

When Marie began to write to "Dear Margaret" in 1940, she had a shadowy image in her mind of her correspondent. Eighteen years earlier John's employer, the Canada Life Assurance Company, had picked him for an overseas assignment in its London office, and Marie and John, newly married, sailed for England. They found an apartment near Kensington Palace, and in her diary, which she kept during those nine months, the new bride recorded a life of pleasurable activity and few responsibilities: shopping at Barker's and Maple's, visiting picture galleries and choosing paintings to take home, going to concerts and the theatre, playing golf, sightseeing, having lunch and dinner with friends, and from time to time visiting John at his office. It was not until Marie and John were almost ready to sail home—John's mother had just died, which speeded their departure—that they actually met Marie's English cousins. On May 23, 1923, the two arrived in Manchester by train and were welcomed by Mary and Thomas Frederick Tout. T.F. Tout was a distinguished professor of medieval history at Manchester University, and Mary had studied under him and taken a first-class honours degree in history. Within intellectual circles she became well known for her activities on behalf of women's education and women's suffrage.[2] After the visit Marie wrote: "Mr. and Mrs. T. lovely to us—beautiful home. After lunch Mr. T. took us to the Univ. and showed us over the buildings.... Back had tea, and we all four went for a walk to see the Univ. playing fields and club house, around to girls' residence.... Back just in time for dinner, sat and talked all evening, bed.... Cousin M. perfectly lovely and so kind to us."

The Touts' daughter, Margaret Sharp, came from London the next day to visit her parents but missed the Williamsons, who had departed right after breakfast. Fortunately, a meeting did take place in London ten days later on the eve of Marie and John's departure for Canada. Marie set out after lunch for the flat of Margaret and her husband Douglas in Lambolle Road, just south of Hampstead. At the end of the day she noted: "a dear little flat, nice people.... Had tea and stayed until about 6.30."

The afternoon visit over tea was probably the only time that Marie and Margaret met before the war although Marie saw Margaret's mother during visits to Toronto in 1929 and 1933. With the arrival of the Sharp boys, their lives were to become intertwined. From 1940 to 1944, more than 165 letters were mailed from Marie to Margaret and rather fewer from Margaret to Marie. Margaret Sharp carefully kept Marie's letters after they had been circulated to the boys' father, her former husband Douglas, and to her mother. Marie did not keep Margaret's letters, but Margaret had made copies of a few that she knew might be needed as a record. There were stacks of letters written by Douglas Sharp, whose divorce from Margaret was official in 1937, although this did not deter him from keeping her up-to-date on his current preoccupations. Included in the trove also are Marie's letters to "Cousin Mary," Margaret's mother, which tend to be less restrained and franker about problems that had arisen.

Out of this mountain of correspondence we have sought to present in this book a continuous narrative focusing on lives lived in Toronto during the war years, with Marie's letters shorn of much of the minutiae of illnesses, school reports, letters sent and received, Christmas presents, and individuals who are not part of the central story. Marie's letters to Margaret Sharp have been edited to about two-thirds of their original length.

THIS COLLECTION BEGINS JUST TEN DAYS BEFORE THE CHILDREN WERE ON their way to Canada. The letters introduce a cast of friends, family, and acquaintances of both the Williamsons and the Sharps who were scattered across North America and Britain, but the central figure is Marie herself. Marie Curtis Peterkin Williamson was born in the final years of Queen Victoria's reign, and when the Sharp boys came to live with the family in 1940 she had recently turned forty-two. Marie cannot be described as a typical housewife and mother living in the city of Toronto in the first half of the twentieth century. For one, when she graduated in 1915 from high school at age sixteen with her senior matriculation, she was recognized as the second-ranking student in the province of Ontario, winning the

John and Marie, 1922

coveted Edward Blake Double Scholarship in Maths and Moderns (i.e., mathematics and modern literature) at the University of Toronto. In a tribute to "Miss Peterkin" the *Toronto Daily News* declared that she "bears her honors modestly [and] is a general favorite in her set." She entered university while World War I was in full swing, and in the summer of 1918 joined other students in the Farm Service Corps to work on the Government Experimental Farm at Vineland, Ontario. She was elected to the University College Women's Athletic Executive and the Permanent Executive of the Class of 1919, won her athletic "T" as a member of the university women's swimming team, and graduated with a B.A.

In later years Marie recalled that within the family circle the roles of her two sisters and a younger brother, as well as her own, had been predetermined. The eldest, Theresa, was to be domestic; Clare, the youngest, would be social; Robert (or Bob) would do what men do; and Marie was to develop her academic side. In the early twentieth century, for an academic young woman, a career as a university teacher or in one of the higher-paid professions or in business was an unlikely option. It was expected that she would concentrate on finding a suitable husband. On October 9, 1922, Marie married John Dudley Williamson, who was thirteen years older. She and John almost immediately sailed for England to take up John's assignment in the Canada Life London office.

John had been a country boy, growing up on a hundred-acre farm near Burlington, Ontario, just west of Toronto, with six siblings. During the summers of 1907, 1908, and 1912, he taught school in Saskatchewan and helped his homesteading brothers to plant and harvest wheat. But John was not destined to be a teacher or a farmer. In 1907 he set off for the University of Toronto, financially supported by his eldest sister, Emily, who was an accountant. Graduating in mathematics and physics in 1910, he joined the actuarial staff at Canada Life and by 1924 had completed the formidable series of actuarial examinations that led to a Fellowship in the Actuarial Society. As a member of a tiny fraternity of crack mathematicians, he was assured a comfortable living for himself and his future family.

AFTER RETURNING FROM ENGLAND IN 1923, MARIE LED A CONVENTIONAL life as homemaker and attentive wife and daughter. From week to week she saw her many friends from university and the Pi Beta Phi sorority, playing bridge and golf, hosting parties, and volunteering. Marie and John lived at first in apartments, but in 1927 they moved into a new house on Hillsdale Avenue where two years later Peter was born. It was typical of middle-class homes in that the maid had her own room on the third floor, and a nanny was hired to look after Peter as a baby. By choice Marie's leisure time at home was mostly spent reading: Virginia Woolf was a favourite author. She was devoted to the weekly *Saturday Night* and during the war looked forward to issues of the British satirical magazine *Punch*, which Margaret sent her.

Marie had been brought up a Presbyterian and John was a Methodist, but it was perhaps a calculated decision early in their marriage to join the Anglican Church. During the war, Marie put in many hours with the church's Red Cross branch. The church meant more to John, and as a sidesman and later rector's warden at Grace Church on-the-Hill, he rarely missed Sunday morning services. On the subject of religion, Marie wrote to Margaret on October 13, 1941: "We are not particularly religious people but we started going to Church some years ago, after we had the children baptized and we both liked it and found it helpful, especially as we have an extremely good rector who preaches most practical and sincere sermons. We felt that the children should be 'exposed' to religion.... For every reason we decided to take the children to Church with us—I want them to be familiar with the Church service and the beautiful language of the prayer book."

In photographs taken in the early 1920s, Marie looks fashionably slim, aspiring to the flat-chested flapper look, but by the time the Sharp boys arrived she was almost gaunt, having lost weight after a serious brush with death from a bone infection in 1924. Among her friends and close acquaintances she was known as a lively conversationalist and was admired and treasured for her warmth and her interest in people and the world outside the home. To outsiders she appeared reserved, partly out of shyness. Marie was not of Scottish ancestry for nothing. She prized the traditional virtues of frugality, which came in handy during the war. Socks were darned until the holes defeated repairs, and family exchanges of coats and other apparel made it possible to keep children of all ages in clothing that fitted properly. Marie wanted to look her best, but at the same time she held back from spending any more money on herself than was necessary. For everyday print frocks and hats she shopped at the Eaton's and Simpson's department stores while venturing into their upscale boutiques at Eaton's College Street and Simpson's St. Regis Room for clothes to wear at "dress-up" occasions.

Across the Atlantic Ocean in England, Margaret Sharp was a very different sort of woman. In a family that above all prized intellectual gifts, she took on in full measure her father's interest in medieval history, taking her B.A., M.A., and Ph.D. degrees at Manchester and securing a university teaching job in the period before she had children. In photographs of the 1920s, Margaret is a tall, slim, and slightly gawky but fashionably dressed young woman, aware of her attractiveness and intellectual abilities. She and Douglas had married in 1920, but in 1934 Douglas had left the home for another woman. Subsequent efforts to salvage the marriage failed, and in 1937 they divorced. During this time the older boys went to boarding school. After the divorce, Margaret decided she had to tailor her lifestyle to her resources and moved to Ulverston, south of the Lake District, where she was able to rent a house cheaply and send the boys to local state-run schools. It is not clear what motivated Margaret in accepting Marie and John's offer to take the children. There was, however, some advantage in the boys' care being transferred elsewhere, leaving her to concentrate on her own life choices and career. For many years her ambition had been to get back into an academic position, but the offer in early 1941 to teach history at Abbotsholme, a boys boarding school in Staffordshire, must have been welcome. The subsequent wartime years were spent there, with holiday periods at the house in Ulverston where her mother, Mary Tout, widowed in 1929, was now living.

But what of the three Sharp boys themselves? One might expect them to be homesick, landing so far from their parents and torn from familiar surroundings. Detachment is a sound defence, and while at boarding school the older two had been away from home for months at a time. Soon after they arrived in Canada, Marie reported with some astonishment that "as far as can be seen there has not been a sign of homesickness which is remarkable, and they are adapting themselves splendidly to what must be an entirely strange way of life" (August 14, 1940). When they thought about it, the boys would make comparisons in their letters between a Toronto winter and winter in England, or the birds found in the Williamson garden and the birds they were familiar with at home. But the different weather and landscape, birds and flowers, schooling and totally new sports were rapidly absorbed, and in the process the boys became gently North Americanized. Tom was pictured in a newspaper story on English evacuees playing cricket at St. Paul's School, yet he complained in January 1941, "I'm rotten at it, I don't like it much either, if you're not batting or bowling you just have to stand—it's very dull!" Skating and skiing gradually replaced cricket as the sports of choice. Hot dogs were immediate favourites as "super" party food, and for Tom two seasons at summer camp, with swimming, camp craft, archery, and hiking, turned out to be the perfect holidays.

The education of the boys is a persistent theme throughout the correspondence. Margaret and Douglas were convinced that the children would fall behind in Canadian classrooms and have to make up missing subjects when they returned to English schools. In Canada every effort was made by the Williamsons and Ratcliffes to place each child in a school that challenged his academic abilities and provided individual attention. The boys were encouraged to send their school report cards home, but leaving nothing to chance, Marie carefully transcribed Christopher and Tom's marks in letters to their mother along with comments by teachers and explanations of the Toronto system of education.

For Marie it was frustrating not to know whether her letters had actually arrived in England. Not only were ships being sunk—two letters were lost that way—but strangely Margaret did not feel the same pressure to write with equal regularity or even to respond to questions regarding the health and education of the boys to which the Williamsons and Ratcliffes needed answers. While burdened with the care of two extra boys, Marie concluded many of her letters with expressions of sympathy for how busy Margaret must be in her teaching job. But increasingly a hint of sarcasm can be detected. On March 7, 1943, Marie, who had been writing to Margaret every week, addressed part of the problem at some length: "If there is anything important which I particularly want you to know I like to repeat it (though that takes time) as, if I have no acknowledgement from you, I don't know whether my letter was sunk, or your reply. And with letters as slow as they are now, things are uncertain for months."

When the Sharp boys arrived in August 1940, it was immediately apparent to Marie and John that the youngsters were very unlike each other: "They are all three so different we can scarcely believe they're brothers!" Bill was a very self-absorbed adolescent, but he was also brilliant and was well placed to take advantage of scholarship opportunities in high school and later at university. At first, the boys' father was worried that a Canadian school would put too much pressure on Bill to be "athletic." Quite independently, Bill took an interest in ice hockey—but as a spectator, not a player. He must have astounded his mother with his letter of January 24, 1941, when after telling her that "Toronto is mad about hockey," he proceeded to list all the players on the Toronto Maple Leafs ice hockey team, with detailed descriptions of every position in the game. Three years on, the big question for Bill was whether he should enter a North American university or return to England and to Oxford or Cambridge, as his parents hoped.

Christopher was age eleven when he arrived in Canada. He had been away from school with pleurisy for much of the previous year and was behind in his lessons. He couldn't spell even simple words, and his total lack of interest in reading almost defeated his foster parents. It didn't help that in her letters his mother made little effort to simplify her indecipherable handwriting so that he could read them. At least Christopher was a thoroughly relaxed and engaging lad, and outsiders were easily charmed by him. He stayed with the Williamsons through to January 1943, when he went to live with his godparents, Eve and Bobby Burns, in Washington, DC.

AND THEN THERE WAS TOM, THE YOUNGEST OF THE SHARP BOYS. LIVING with the Williamsons for almost four years, he becomes a central figure in the correspondence as he grows from a cautious little boy into a more self-reliant adolescent. He began by exasperating Marie for all sorts of reasons, but in the end her initial assessment set the tone: "Tom is such a sweet child," she wrote from Haliburton, "everyone loves him at sight." But he suffered from a severe case of dependency, reinforced on the voyage over from England when he learned to look to Bill for guidance on what to do about everything. As Marie wrote to Margaret on September 20, 1941, whenever Tom and Bill were together, Tom "would become a shadow of Bill," who treated him "with a sort of indulgent patronage." Two years later, Bill acknowledged that his influence on his youngest brother was not always benign and that being with the Williamsons had been good for Tom. After not seeing Tom for nearly two months, in December, 1943, Bill wrote to his mother: "He seems to be growing up very rapidly. He has changed so much since he came out here that you will hardly recognize him. Largely due to the Williamsons' training and my absence, he has become immeasurably more self confident and is now perfectly capable of standing on his own feet rather than someone else's." In time, Tom found an independent life apart from the family as a member of the boys' choir at the church. And he was interested in the garden. He always noticed the first crocuses coming up in the spring, and he had been given his own small plot where he planted flower seeds. The other children were keen to grow carrots and lettuce, but Marie reported that Tom had no interest in planting vegetables when he could barely tolerate them on his dinner plate.

What to feed the boys proved at once to be a challenge. They were picky eaters. The two older Sharps had attended Hurtwood School in England, where the students were allowed to do and say virtually whatever they liked and reject food that didn't appeal to them. But Marie was a no-nonsense mother. She saw Canada's food rules as a standard to be met in her kitchen, and she insisted on well-balanced meals. On October 29, 1940, she wrote Margaret that "at first there were very few things that Tom would eat," which seemed to her criminal, given all the salad greens and fresh vegetables that had been available in the summer. Early in 1941, Tom still balked at any uncooked fruit or vegetables and at pasta dishes and cheese, but by March, Marie could report that "he eats everything he's given and very rarely even shows that he doesn't like it much. In fact he really has grown to like some of the things he didn't use to." In 1943, Tom resolutely wrote to his mother about planting corn, peas, lettuce, and beets along with the flower seeds. So there had been huge progress.

DEALING WITH SICKNESS, DISEASES, AND ACCIDENTS IS A CONTINUING saga that rolls along from beginning to end of the correspondence. The children suffered from frequent colds, as well as bronchitis, German and regular measles, and chicken pox, and then there were eye troubles, tonsils, and accidents requiring a doctor's and even hospital attention. Universal health care was still many years away, but the family doctor and dentist both helped out by not charging for minor attentions to the children. Marie's seasonal lament—"I do hope we've had all our illness for the winter"—usually turned out to be wishful thinking, doomed by the children's or her own medical problems. "My joy at getting all the beds empty proved premature as I am occupying one myself at present," she wrote in January 1942. She had been felled by a recurrence of an old bone infection, and by February she was in bed again with a bout of lumbago and sciatica. The year before, she had been in hospital for the removal of a tumour. A friend of Christopher's godparents Eve and Arthur Burns of Washington who was visiting Toronto in October 1942 looked up the Williamsons and Ratcliffes and almost at once reported to Margaret that it would be better for Marie if she could be relieved of the care of one boy. This set in motion an arrangement for Christopher to be sent to live with the Burnses in Washington.

However patriotic the gesture, taking in a war guest cost money. A major hurdle was the ineligibility of the guest children to count as income tax deductions if they had been brought out privately rather than under the government scheme. At times British currency regulations prevented

Margaret or Douglas Sharp from sending support money, and at other times neither could put their hands on funds to spare, but eventually a few pounds here and there were sent to Canada. Marie was not shy about detailing her financial difficulties to Margaret. In June 1941, she and John were wrestling with the implications of moving to a new and larger house. The fall of France and the imminent threat to England had depressed the cost of houses, but their income taxes had doubled and were expected to double again in 1942. On hearing of their problems, kind neighbours insisted on financing the boys' summer camp fees as their own modest contribution to the war effort. Towards the end of 1940, Marie's brother-in-law, who had been paying the boys' tuition at St. Paul's School, was struck down with tuberculosis and knocked out of the workforce while he recovered in the Hamilton sanatorium, but Marie's sister Clare picked up the boys' fees after the Easter term. A less expensive alternative was to send Tom and Christopher to public school, and this is what happened with no harm done, once they had moved in 1941.

By mid-1941, they had felt the need for a larger house where each child could have a separate room, and by September they were ensconced at 90 Dunvegan Road, just south of the village of Forest Hill. Now they had a ground-floor library, an enclosed sun porch, a dressing room for John, and a large kitchen and pantry, as well as bedrooms for the children and a maid. At a time when wartime employment beckoned young women into well-paid factory jobs that hadn't existed before, Marie was hard-pressed to find—or afford—a live-in maid to look after the larger house.

While Marie's letters reflect the lives and concerns of a particular family in Toronto and its guest children during the Second World War, perhaps they are even more revealing as a portrait of Canada's largest city during a period that was far from normal. Not much had changed during the Depression years leading up to the war. There were few new buildings or evidence of conspicuous wealth. Milk and bread were still delivered by horse-drawn wagons and streetcar lines ran along major roads. The children were advised not to accept candy from strangers, and families living near Toronto's many ravines fretted about homeless people enticing their offspring to the woods and streams below. Random incidents did occur, but parents did not hesitate to allow their young children to walk to school— even alone—for dozens of blocks, or take the streetcar by themselves.

An early sign on the home front that the country was on a war footing was a campaign to raise $300 million from the sale of war bonds, securing $92 million in subscriptions from the first day's sale. Bill's foster father Harry Ratcliffe was directing the Canadian War Bonds campaign from

Ottawa. Interest in buying the bonds was generated in Toronto by staged air raids in which leaflets were dropped.

In 1941, the first blackout was held in Toronto, lasting half an hour. Essential services were exempted, but anybody who violated the strict regulations was subject to penalties. In order to simulate a real air raid, airplanes swooped over the city. Cars were told to pull over to the side of the road and trains halted. Householders were ordered not to light even a match, and no unnecessary telephone calls were to be made. *The Globe and Mail* newspaper led the way with its outside windows painted black or covered with "special light-proof paper." A second blackout was planned for the following January with the addition of twenty-eight air raid sirens to be installed in the city. Marie shared some of the details of the January blackout with Margaret: "We are having all sorts of blackout instructions and demonstrations of 'refuge rooms' with complete equipment—stirrup pumps and bomb shovels are still not available but are promised soon." She was disinclined to believe the scare stories about possible attacks or an invasion, but while the war in Europe continued to go badly it was a nagging worry. She wrote to Margaret in January 1942 about the stepped-up activities of the local ARP (Air Raid Precautions) wardens: "I believe they are making all preparations and arrangements for the evacuation of Toronto children to the surrounding country in case of air raids. I suppose I don't know much about it but it seems to me that, while raids are <u>possible</u>, they would be 'token' raids—one or two planes would unload incendiaries, then land and give themselves up. It could be very serious—most Toronto houses, though built of brick, have shingle roofs—but I don't think any amount of preparation could have much effect against it—except AA guns, firewatchers with sand & water, etc, which are certainly not being considered on the <u>very</u> 'off' chance of a raid. I think if the Germans (or Japs) sent planes over Ontario they would be far more likely (and more well advised) to aim at power plants and such like vital spots."

In 1942, the Toronto transit authority—the TTC—advertised that it had acquired a large number of new streetcars in the expectation that gas rationing would force Torontonians to lock up their cars in the garage for the duration. Characteristically, Marie was more upset about how gas rationing would affect other people, especially those living in the suburbs without access to public transit. She felt that life in the city had been conditioned during the previous twenty-five years by a dependence on cars. The Williamsons, she asserted to Margaret, were very lucky in that their house was conveniently placed for streetcars and buses, school and church, and for John getting to the office, and the Village shopping area was not so far that in a pinch the children couldn't fetch groceries with their wagon. However, by May 1943, she didn't want to waste the little gas they were allowed to drive a mile to the butcher shop. She outlined the alternative: "I lugged an 8 lb. joint home by street car the other day and expect I'll have to continue—the only consolation is that after rationing starts they won't be 8 lb. ones!"

With food it was a similar story. From the beginning, there were restrictions on American currency exchange, making fresh fruit and vegetables scarce in wintertime. In February 1941, Marie observed, "We are trying to use as little imported goods as possible using our own Canadian canned and quick-frozen vegetables instead of California ones, etc." By Christmas it was even worse: "There are no nuts and very few dried fruits to be had, and no cheese. I have not bought oranges for nearly a year." In place of orange juice she was using canned grapefruit juice from Trinidad and quantities of Canadian tomato juice, explaining to Margaret that "it has the same properties as orange juice but more dilute so that one needs 3 times the quantity." Apparently few other foods were in short supply, although fruit and vegetables were expensive and meat prices were sky-high. At the end of January 1942, sugar rationing had come into force, but Marie didn't think the family would suffer; however, by June, food shortages had become a problem. Voluntary rationing didn't seem to work; the amounts of tea and coffee were restricted, and in August full rationing cut supplies to only four ounces of coffee per person per week—a rather "drastic" reduction in Marie's daily consumption. The family's customary purchases of bacon, pork, and cheese were chopped in half.

"Shopping is getting difficult," she wrote on June 7, "with the shops constantly 'out of' what you want—whether due to hoarding or short supplies, I don't know—probably mostly the latter as all manufacturing and processing of food is pretty strictly controlled." She thought the price control system was working surprisingly well, although the cost of living had gone up a good deal. Ration books were introduced in the same month. Canned food was becoming scarce, and this was a blow. On October 4, 1942, Marie noted, "We are not to have any tinned salmon or tinned meat any more as it's all being sent to Britain." By October, meat was almost unobtainable but was not rationed. The problem all along was food shortages, not rationing, and Marie and her friends prayed for more rationing which would stop people hoarding and would bring more items into the grocery stores, if only in small quantities.

In spite of the war and the shortages, for the children life was almost idyllic as they allowed themselves to be carried from one activity to the next, and rarely becoming bored unless sick in bed. Boys and girls generally played separately, but indoors they joined in games that could be extended through rainy afternoons such as Chinese checkers and croquinole [also spelled crokinole], Parcheesi and Sorry!, Monopoly and Totopoly, and Buccaneer and GHQ. There were construction toys such as Tinkertoy and Minibrix to challenge the ingenuity of both girls and boys, and everybody was welcome to play with Peter's electric train, which ran on rails from the back to the front of the house in his top-floor bedroom. Books were always welcome presents, and both Sharp boys looked forward to the latest war maps from their parents. Mary, who had never expressed any interest in sewing, was thrilled with a sewing kit her "Cousin Mary" in England had sent her for Christmas. It became her dearest unused possession. And there was a "printing press with movable rubber type, ink, and a roller drum, which gave birth to an in-house newsletter, masterminded by Peter. Copies of "The Monthly War Drum" were churned out through 1941 with acceptable—though not monthly—regularity. Plays were written and performed for the family and neighbours. Imaginative games could be devised at a moment's notice: magician shows, detective games, treasure hunts and scavenger hunts. And depending on the season, outdoors there were war games; air rifle competitions using tin cans lined up on the garden fence as targets; building snow forts and leaf forts; playing marbles; skipping rope, which even Tom enjoyed; and bicycle hikes.

Douglas Sharp, the father of the boys and "Mr. Sharp" to Marie, is a shadowy figure in the letters. Because of his divorce from their mother, he occupies the background much of the time until serial crises—instigated by Douglas himself—catapult him into full view. As the boys' letters were passed on to him, Douglas was thrilled. He had seen the first letters written from the ship and soon after their arrival in Canada when he wrote to Margaret: "The letters were just grand. Bill has much to express and knows how to express it; Tom, because he finds writing a nuisance, is a model of conciseness; Christopher is just sweetly characteristic.... I'm just swelling with pride in them."[3] He explained to Margaret that he was writing to the boys in turn once a week on Sundays. By September he had read enough of the letters from Marie to Margaret to make a judgement: "I do find Mrs Williamson's [letters] very satisfying. I feel rather an eavesdropper, or an overlooker, as I read them; for whereas there is always a certain falsity or straining after effect in the letters of a man to a woman or a woman to a man, these letters from a woman to a woman seem as sincere as anything can be. They are very simple and natural, and they reveal a very sensible decent woman. I will never of course reveal that I've read them."

As the war went on, and the weeks became years, Marie reflected on the burden of letter writing. By May 1943 she confessed that had she "foreseen the frustrations and complications of such a voluminous correspondence, in July 1940, [she] should certainly have made an effort to get a typewriter." Often written late in the evening or finished after countless interruptions, the letters contain occasional grammatical and spelling errors that reveal the haste and strain of their composition.

Douglas created a flutter when he indicated to Margaret that while he liked Marie, he was less happy with Bill's foster mother, Vivien Ratcliffe. It seems he had decided that while Marie did command his respect, he couldn't trust Vivien. Hints of this were conveyed to Marie in Margaret's letters, much to Marie's horror. She hastened to step in on behalf of her friend, assuring Margaret on November 25, that "Bill is quite happy there and I don't know any place that would be better for him. They are very sane people and very understanding and above all have a 'live and let live' attitude to everyone and everything and would never dream of trying to alter any of Bill's ideas or interests to theirs."

While Douglas went on writing to his former wife, telling her—perhaps boasting?—of a fling with a waitress and a responsibility-free life, in November 1942 he announced that he was going to be married again. In this letter he described his new wife Agnes: "blonde, Rossetti face, grey-green eyes, long lashes and the tiniest hands you have ever seen." Margaret was herself a handsome woman, but physically Agnes could not have been less like her. There was no pretense about Agnes being intellectual, but Douglas felt he had to explain that she had "a small but very well-picked little library of her own. She writes well & with a pretty wit."

The news of the marriage came as a bombshell in the Williamson home. How to tell the boys, and should they be told? In particular, Marie was worried about Tom, who seemed to have entirely forgotten about his parents' break-up. Could they just *not* be told until after they had returned home? Marie agonized, while Margaret and Douglas seem not to have appreciated that it was she who would have to deal with the fallout if the boys were crushed. In the end, as Marie might have anticipated, the younger boys were not disturbed in the least. Tom was puzzled until he it occurred to him that he could boast to all his friends that he had *two* mothers, and Christopher—now living in Washington—pretended that he already knew and then promptly forgot all about it. Further disruptive intrusions by the boys' father came in 1943 when Douglas doubted the wisdom of Bill pursuing his university education in Toronto, rather than at Oxford or Cambridge, and drew in a Toronto acquaintance to "interview" Bill about his choice. Bill was bewildered—his word—by his father's behaviour and his father's pretense of speaking for his mother. He had made his decision, and he was staying.

The timing of both Christopher's and Tom's return to England caused back and forth discussions as early as February 1943 between Marie and Margaret, and between Marie and Margaret's mother, Mary Tout. Some children Marie and Margaret knew had gone home in 1943, but Marie was reluctant to express an opinion about the Sharp boys. However, she advised Margaret in December 1943 of a "hush-hush" scheme to repatriate British children on warships via Portugal and outlined for Mary Tout other arrangements suggested by the University of Toronto committee. Margaret was particularly concerned about how her boys would fit into English schools once they were back in England, and one senses that she was anxious to have them back even though the war with Germany was far from over. For Marie, it was up to Margaret to make the final decision.[4]

Details of the boys' actual return were as cloaked in secrecy as their arrival in Canada four years earlier. In her last letter on May, 22, 1944, Marie was uncertain as to whether to enroll Tom in Pioneer Camp for the summer. Her "Scotch soul" made her hesitate to send in the registration fee in case he wouldn't be going. She still had no idea when she would send him off. Losing Tom would be like losing a son. However, we sense that she would welcome some relief from the arthritis in her wrists and thumbs once the tyranny of the weekly letter to Margaret was over.

THAT THE LETTERS WRITTEN BY MARIE FROM AUGUST 1940 TO MAY 1944 have survived is a lucky chance. When Marie died in 1969, she had no idea that Margaret had kept them, packed into suitcases in London, along with mountains of other correspondence, photographs, and documents from family and friends. The papers of Thomas F. and Mary Tout, Margaret's parents, had long before been deposited in the Manchester University Archives, and family members were used to keeping everything for the historical record. Marie herself had not kept any of Margaret's letters, but Bill held on to most of the letters he received from his father and from his granny. The London suitcase collection also revealed a harvest of letters, postcards, photographs, report cards, and enclosures sent by the boys and their foster parents. Selected letters from Margaret's friends Eve Burns, Katharine Beamish, and Sylvia Anthony, who visited Toronto during the war to check on the boys and reported to Margaret on their welfare, have been included here as appendices. With Margaret's letters having not survived, the correspondence is necessarily one-sided. But others from Vivien Ratcliffe, from Douglas Sharp to his son Bill and to Margaret, and the boys' letters to their parents, help to round out the narrative and shed light on the same events from different points of view. Often they fill in some of the gaps, especially when, for reasons of delicacy, Marie was not entirely

In 1958 Marie (right) visited Margaret at her country home in the Lake District

forthcoming. In later life, Marie would muse that she had not been inclined to letter-writing before the arrival of the Sharp boys, but the tyranny of the war years took hold, and afterwards one or two letters to family and friends were fitted in as part of each day's routine.

After the war, Marie took a keen pleasure in watching the boys move through adolescence into adulthood and assume satisfying careers. She would never have mentioned it, but she must have sensed that she and John, and those years in Toronto, were more than a little responsible for their successes. She had hoped that her letters would help Margaret imagine from a distance that she was close to her boys and that she was with them as they grew up.

Mary and Tom share the warmest memories of Mary's "Mom" and Tom's "Aunt Marie." In her first letter to the Sharp boys' mother, Marie expressed a determination to "maintain and clothe and look after the boys just as though they were our own," but she went far beyond this early declaration by extending her protective love to all the children equally. Today Tom declares that "Marie was a saint," and her daughter is inclined to agree. What Marie accomplished, and put up with, from 1940 to 1944 is miraculous. Unfortunately sainthood, although worthy of our devotion, is not an endearing trait in a parent. Writing to Margaret in 1944, Marie confessed that "I can only say honestly that I do my best but I know I am often impatient and 'edgy' when I'm tired." And very tired she was, much of the time, although typically we children were oblivious to the edginess and the strain on her. We both loved her, and felt ourselves loved.

Tom recalls the shy and diffident boy he was when he arrived in the Williamson home, and how Marie encouraged him and brought him out, coped with his disdain for most foods and his inclination to feel sorry for himself. And she gave him love, and calmness that perhaps his own mother back in England hadn't been able to provide, given the turbulence in the Sharp household during his parents' separation and divorce.

Mary remembers well—with keen regret—joining with other children in that first year, 1940, to bully Tom by tying him to a lamppost in front of our house while we played hide-and-seek, deaf to his cries of protest. But very soon we were playmates and ultimately "lasting friends," as Tom puts it, to this day.

Peter vividly recalls Tom's farewell when he left to join Christopher for the trip home to England. Marie and Peter saw Tom off on a night train to New York. Both Marie and Tom were in tears, and Peter thought at the time that this scene confirmed his sense that Marie had been more of a mother to Tom than his own mother.

IT WAS A TREMENDOUS THRILL TO FIND MARIE'S LETTERS TO MARGARET in that London suitcase so many years ago. Since then we have talked to several individuals who were mentioned by Marie, read hundreds of associated letters, and looked at dozens of photographs. And now, having edited the collection for publication, we feel that we have given "Mom" and "Aunt Marie" her due, that is to tell her story although she never could have imagined that her letters would be read outside the circles of the two families. Inadvertently she has shared with a wider public a record of the daily life of a Toronto family and its war guests during the Second World War. It was an unusual time in Canada's history, one that might otherwise be misunderstood or have simply lapsed into obscurity.

BIOGRAPHICAL NOTES

An asterisk (*) denotes an entry elsewhere in this list.

ANTHONY, Sylvia (1898–1979), a friend of Margaret Sharp* who was in Canada, 1940–44, with her sons Paul (1928–1971) and William (1932–). She was Jewish, and her family feared the consequences of a German invasion of Britain. As a psychologist she believed that she would be able to get a job, as she did in Ottawa. She visited the Williamsons in Toronto in May 1942 (see Appendix 3). Paul and William were at Pioneer Camp that summer with Christopher and Tom.

BEAMISH, Katharine Isabel Monro (1903–1988) and George G. (1901–1965). Parents of Andrew G. (1931–), Timothy G. (1935–1946), and Simon J. (1940–2000). Before the war they lived in the Hampstead Garden suburb in London where Katharine ran a small nursery class at her house that Tom attended. From October 1940 to December 1941, George was one of two people with the mission of arranging to retrocede the London insurance market's liabilities in the event that Britain was overrun, and George and Katharine spent time in Montreal and the United States. Andrew and Tim had already been evacuated to stay with friends in Ottawa, having travelled on the same crossing of the *Duchess of Bedford* as the Sharp boys. Katharine visited the Williamsons in June 1941 (see Appendix 2). When the mission was completed, George and Katharine returned to England and their sons went to stay with other family friends in New Jersey. Andrew was at Trinity College School, Port Hope, at the same time as Peter Williamson.*

BURNS, Eveline "Eve," née Richardson (1900–1985), and Arthur R. (sometimes "Bobbie") (1895–1981) were English friends of Margaret Sharp;* he was Christopher Sharp's* godfather. Both were economists at the London School of Economics who went to the United States in 1926 on a two-year fellowship and decided to stay. Their careers were spent mainly at Columbia University, where both held professorships, but during the war they worked in Washington for federal agencies. Her report for the National Resources Planning Board on social policy, *Security, Work and Relief,* was presented to Congress to considerable acclaim and was seen as the U.S. equivalent of the Beveridge Report in the United Kingdom. The three Sharp boys stayed with the Burnses at their summer place at North Sanbornton, New Hampshire, in 1941, and Christopher lived with them in Washington from January 1943 until he and Tom returned to England in 1944. Eve visited the Williamson family on May 18, 1943, while in Toronto to speak to the Canadian Welfare Council (see Appendix 4).

INNIS, Mary Emma, née Quayle (1899–1972), and Harold Adams (1894–1952). Mary was a writer and editor. Harold, a political economist at the University of Toronto, pioneered the field of communication theory in Canada. Their children were Donald (1924–1988), Mary (1927–), Hugh (1929–), and Anne (1933–). The Innis family moved next door to the Williamsons in April 1942 and subsequently the lives of the two families became intertwined. Marie commented on Anne's arrival as "a great acquisition."

MURPHY, Mary Ursula (1918–1976). Born in Brechin, Ontario, one of 12 children. She was a live-in maid in the Williamson home between 1939 and 1942. She gave her notice in May 1941, hoping to find better-paid opportunities, but returned in October having found that work in a munitions plant involved less convenient hours than housework. Mary left the Williamsons for the last time in April 1942 to help her mother on the family farm.

PETERKIN, BUSBY, JENNINGS, and MCKAY

PETERKIN, Florence Emmaline, née Johnstone (1874–1946), and her husband Charles Robert, Jr. (1872–1956). They were the parents of Theresa Busby,* Marie Williamson,* Clare Jennings,* and Bob Peterkin.* Florence was a first cousin of Mary Tout.* She was six when her family emigrated from Yorkshire to Toronto.

PETERKIN, Charles Robert "Bob" (1905–1979), brother of Marie, and his wife Besse, née Craig (1915–1993). Janet, their daughter, was born in 1941. Bob served in the Canadian Army, 1942–45, as a sergeant in the Quartermaster Corps. He received his call-up papers in August 1942, was sent for "overseas" duty to Newfoundland in April 1943, and in October came home on leave to see his family.

BUSBY, Theresa Florence, née Peterkin (1896–1972), Marie's elder sister, was a school teacher, and her husband Leslie (1899–1957) was a marine engineer employed with Imperial Oil until the end of 1940. Found to have tuberculosis, Leslie was hospitalized at the sanatorium in Hamilton until March of 1942. He returned to work for the British Admiralty Technical Mission and was over a year in Hamilton superintending the installation of machinery in Algerine Mine Sweepers, which had been built in Toronto. He was then transferred to Marine Industries in Sorel, Quebec, where the company was building landing ships tanks (LSTs) for landing tanks on beaches. Theresa met the Sharp boys on their arrival in Toronto; she funded their costs at St. Paul's School; her chief responsibility while her husband was away was to care for her—and Marie's—parents at 460 Brunswick Avenue.

JENNINGS, Clara "Clare" Ethel, née Peterkin (1903–1960), Marie's younger sister, and her husband George L. (1903–1947). Clare worked at the Manufacturers Life Insurance Co. until her marriage. In 1929 she visited with the Touts* in London. George was a construction engineer who was in business with his father, Harry. Together they developed an area of bungalows at Glengrove P.O., just outside the then Toronto city limits, and the Jennings lived there at 82 Glen Park. In 1942 Clare was persuaded to return to the insurance company full-time. In August 1940 there was talk of Tom going to live with Clare and George. The couple invited the children to stay at their house, often to do chores for pocket money or simply to skate or make a snow fort; took the children to the movies or the circus; or "baby sat" the children when Marie and John had to be away. Clare took the children to do their Christmas shopping, knit mittens and socks, and helped Marie with housework when there was no maid.

MCKAY, Ruby Gordon, née Peterkin (1887–1961), Marie's aunt. A widow, she had been a nurse during World War I in Salonika where she had met her husband, Dr. Hugh Alexander McKay (1884–1936). Ruby was helpful to Marie in various capacities: providing nursing care to the children as well as to Marie herself; making curtains; helping with the Christmas dinner; and entertaining everybody with colour movies of her worldwide travels and of the children.

RATCLIFFE, Vivien, née Chalmers (1900–1965), and John Henry "Harry" (1894–1968). Marie and Vivien were old friends from University of Toronto days as both were members of the Pi Beta Phi sorority. Harry was an investment dealer, from 1921 as vice-president and director of McLeod, Young, & Weir Ltd. He was made a CBE in 1946 for his role as assistant chairman of the National War Finance Committee when for three years he directed the Canadian Victory Loan campaign. Children: John Henry (1925–1985), a student at UTS with Bill Sharp* before joining the RCAF in 1943; Nancy (1929–1999); and Judy (1934–). Bill lived with the Ratcliffes at 76 Glenview Ave., Toronto, during the war.

ROBINSON, Josepha "Jo," née Spence (1898–1995), and her husband George Gates "Robbie" (1891–1957), a civil engineer who was general manager of Standard Paving & Materials Ltd., lived at 15 Strathearn Road. Children: Joan (1924–), John "Jack" (1926–); and Meredith (1935–). Christopher and Tom made short visits to the Robinsons for dinner, tea, holiday fireworks, and city excursions; they stayed with the family for several days at a time when there was illness in the Williamson household.

SHARP and TOUT

SHARP, Margaret, née Tout (1896–1987). Mother of Bill, Christopher, and Tom. Eldest child of Thomas Frederick and Mary Tout.* Educated at Manchester High School for Girls 1910–14 and the University of Manchester: BA (first class) 1918; MA 1919; PhD 1924. Part-time lecturer in history, East London College (later Queen Mary's College), 1925–27. Wrote, with C.W. Prosser, *A Short Constitutional History of England* (1938), contributed the section on the Black Prince to her father's six-volume work on medieval administrative history (1933), and edited *The Accounts of the Constables of Bristol Castle in the Thirteenth Century* (1982). Married William Douglas Sharp* 1920; separated 1934; divorced 1937. In 1938 she moved to Ulverston on the southern fringes of the Lake District. Once her three sons were evacuated to Canada, she shared the house with her mother until 1944. She taught history at Abbotsholme School, Derbyshire, 1941–44. She had a teaching job lined up for the autumn term of 1944 at Ulverston Grammar School, to which Christopher and Tom would go, but that summer she secured a teaching job at Bristol University, where she remained until retirement in 1963.

SHARP, William Douglas (1894–1955), known as "Douglas" to his first wife and "William" to his second. Married Margaret, née Tout, 1920; separated 1934; divorced 1937; married Agnes, née Holden, 1943, and had a fourth son, Richard (1947–2005). Attended Manchester Grammar School and Brasenose College, Oxford, c. 1912–13; volunteered 1914, Lieutenant, South Lancashire regiment, severely wounded on the Somme and invalided out in 1916. A civil servant, largely in the Post Office; active in the civil service association and wrote "The Evolution of the Civil Service," *University of Toronto Quarterly* (1939). During World War II he lived for part of the time in London and part in Manchester. His mother, Mary Sharp (1869–1945), is sometimes referred to in the letters as "Little Granny."

SHARP, William Tout "Bill" (1927–1972), eldest son of Douglas and Margaret. His English schools were Hurtwood and Bedales, both boarding, and Ulverston Grammar School. In Toronto he briefly attended Lawrence Park Collegiate Institute and then went to University of Toronto Schools 1940–43. Lived with the Ratcliffe* family. A mathematician: BA 1947, MA 1948 University of Toronto, PhD Princeton 1950. The Epilogue sketches his career. He died in a climbing accident in British Columbia in 1972. A peak nearby—Mount Sharp—is named in memory of him.

SHARP, Christopher (1929–2007), Margaret and Douglas Sharp's second son. After attending Hurtwood and Ulverston Grammar School in England, he was at St. Paul's School and Brown School, successively, in Toronto. While living with his godfather, Arthur Burns,* in Washington he went to Gordon Junior High School. On his return to England, he went to Clifton College, Bristol, and Bristol University 1950–53, with two years of National Service in between. See the Epilogue for his postwar careers in Malaysia and Singapore. He retired to England and died of Parkinson's disease in 2007.

SHARP, Thomas "Tom" (1931–), third son of Margaret and Douglas. Educated at King Alfred's School in Hampstead and Lightburn Elementary School in Ulverston before attending St. Paul's School and Brown School in Toronto. After his return in 1944, he was at Abbotsholme School 1944–49 before doing his National Service. He was at Jesus College, Oxford, 1951–54 before entering the Board of Trade (subsequently the Department of Trade and Industry). He was made a CBE in 1987. See the Epilogue, written by his wife Margaret, for details of his life after the war.

TOUT, Mary, née Johnstone (1873–1960). Received a First Class Honours degree in history at Manchester University and married her professor, Thomas Frederick Tout (1855–1929), who wrote extensively on the medieval period and especially English medieval administrative history. Mary was a first cousin, through their fathers, of Marie Williamson's mother, Florence Johnstone Peterkin.* T.F. Tout taught many renowned historians, including Bertie Wilkinson* and his wife. Marie and John Williamson* visited them at their Manchester house in 1923 and while on an extensive lecture tour in North America in 1928 they visited Marie and John in Toronto. Now widowed, in 1930 Mary Tout moved to the Hampstead Garden Suburb in north London, and during the next decade made two trips to the United States to visit her son Herbert in Minneapolis. Having shared a house with her daughter, Margaret, during the war, she lived until her death in 1960 in her house in north London together with, for most of the time, her son Herbert and her maid Margaret Burton. Children: Margaret Sharp;* Herbert (1904–1997); and Arthur (1905–1971). Herbert was an economist who taught for some time at the University of Minnesota in Minneapolis in the 1930s where he was visited by his mother and his sister. He visited the Williamsons in Toronto in September 1929.

WILKINSON and BLAND

WILKINSON, Bertie (1898–1981) and Edith, née Provost (1896–1978). He studied at the University of Manchester 1919–26, pupil of T.F. Tout.* Emigrated with his family to Canada in 1938 to take up an appointment as professor of medieval history, University of Toronto. Edith was active as a volunteer and in the evacuation scheme arranged between the universities of Birmingham and Toronto in 1940. Children: John (1927–) and Ann (1931–) who went to Brown School with Tom Sharp.*

BLAND, Ethel, née Provost (1900–1983), sister of Edith Wilkinson.* Supervised children on the *Duchess of Bedford*, which sailed from Liverpool to Montreal in July 1940 and carried her two children, her two nephews Alan and Donald Provost, and the three Sharp boys. She initially stayed with the Wilkinsons. She taught at Havergal College, Toronto (1940–44); returned to England in May 1944. Children: David (1926–2001) attended University of Toronto Schools and in 1943 returned to England to attend Cambridge University—a move discussed as a possible precedent for Bill

Sharp.* Jennifer (1927–2009) attended Havergal College and returned home with her mother.

WILLIAMSON

WILLIAMSON, Marie Curtis, née Peterkin (1898–1969), married 1922 John Dudley (1885–1980). As a child living on Bellevue Place, Toronto, she went to Ryerson Public School. At age 11 she entered the newly established Oakwood Collegiate; when the family moved to High Park Avenue in West Toronto she attended Humberside Collegiate Institute 1911–15, where she gave the valedictory address at the 1915 commencement. Graduating with Honour Matriculation she was awarded three scholarships: 1st Double Scholarship in Mathematics and Moderns, 1st Edward Blake Scholarship in Mathematics and 1st Edward Blake Scholarship in Moderns. She ranked second in Ontario in the matriculation examinations. She attended University College at the University of Toronto 1915–19 where she earned a Senior "T" in swimming and diving, and joined the πβφ (Pi Beta Phi) sorority in which she remained an active member for most of her life. During the summer of 1918 she worked on the Governmental Experimental Farm in Vineland, Ontario, as part of the Canadian Farm Service Corps. Following their wedding in October 1922, Marie and John sailed to England where John had been transferred on an assignment as an actuary at the Great Britain branch of the Canada Life Assurance Co. London. While there they visited T.F. and Mary Tout* in Manchester and met Margaret Sharp* in London. They returned to Toronto in June 1923 and after living in several apartments moved to 118 Hillsdale Ave. W. where Peter and Mary were born and Tom* and Christopher Sharp* lived when they first arrived. In 1941 the family moved to 90 Dunvegan Rd. In 1924 Marie had suffered from a life-threatening infection of the bone of one leg, below the knee, which recurred in the early 1940s and quite probably led to her death from leukemia in 1969. During the war, in addition to managing "just a larger family," Marie did volunteer work with the Canadian Red Cross, packing "ditty bags for the lads on the mine-sweepers," and war work with the Women's Auxiliary of Grace Church-on-the-Hill. By 1951 Marie and John had begun to winter in the south, in Bermuda and then in Florida. They made two trips to Britain, renewing their friendship with Mary Tout and Margaret Sharp—and meeting Tom and his future wife, Margaret Hailstone. They sold the Dunvegan house in 1952 and moved to smaller accommodation. While wintering at Delray Beach in Florida, Marie died on March 17, 1969.

WILLIAMSON, John Dudley (1885–1980), husband of Marie. John was born on a farm at Appleby, near Burlington, Ontario. He attended Hamilton Collegiate 1899–1903 and Milton Model School in 1903, and taught at the Merton School, Bronte, 1904–06. Graduated with a BA in Mathematics and Physics at the University of Toronto in 1910; during the summers of 1907–08 he taught school in Saskatchewan and helped his brothers with harvesting. In 1910 he joined the actuarial staff of the Canada Life Assurance Co. and in 1924 obtained the FAS actuarial degree. He held various positions— president of the Life Insurance Institute of Canada (1939); president of the Home Office Life Underwriters Association of New York (1940); and Fellow of the American Institute of Actuaries (1940)—and wrote a number of papers and articles. He retired in 1950. John was a serious bridge player and golfer, and in his eighties took up lawn bowling with enthusiasm.

WILLIAMSON, John Peterkin "Peter" (1929–), son of Marie and John, brother of Mary. He moved on from St. Paul's School 1935–40 (where Christopher and Tom also went) to University of Toronto Schools 1940–41 and then on scholarship to Trinity College School (TCS), Port Hope, Ontario (1941–48). University of Toronto BA 1952; MBA Harvard 1954; LLB Harvard 1957; DBA Harvard 1961. Taught at the Harvard Business School 1957–61; joined the faculty of the Amos Tuck School of Business, Dartmouth College, Hanover, New Hampshire 1961–92; retired as Laurence F. Whittemore Professor of Finance in 1992 and since has maintained a consulting practice specializing in utility business. Until he entered TCS as a boarder, he was a general catalyst for all sorts of juvenile activities, directed plays and edited and printed *The Monthly War Drum*. He maintained a serious interest in hand printing.

WILLIAMSON, Mary Frances (1933–), daughter of Marie and John, sister of Peter. Attended Oriole Park School 1937–41, Brown School 1941–46, then Bishop Strachan School 1946–51; Trinity College, University of Toronto, 1951–55; BA, BLS, MA (Fine Arts), MLS University of Toronto. She was Assistant in the Textile Dept., Museum of Fine Arts, Boston 1957–59; librarian in the Fine Arts Dept., Toronto Public Library 1960–65; librarian with the Education Centre, Toronto Board of Education 1965–69; Fine Arts Bibliographer, York University 1970–95; adjunct faculty, Graduate Department of Art History 1989–2008. Collector of Old Master Drawings; author of numerous works on art history, art libraries, and culinary history. An enthusiastic co-conspirator with Tom Sharp and Anne Innis* in various wartime family ventures, including the fair in aid of the British War Victims Fund reported in the *Toronto Telegram*. In 1953 she travelled to

England and stayed with Mary Tout* and watched the coronation procession with Tom. She is godmother to Tom and Margaret's elder daughter, Helen.

WILLIAMSON, Emily Gertrude (1876–1957), elder sister of John Williamson. Emily graduated from Queen's University in 1929 with a B.Comm., practised as an accountant, studied law at Osgoode Hall, and was called to the bar in 1935. On the side she dealt in antiques, and in buying, fixing up, and selling properties. Lived in a pre-Confederation house in Burlington, backing on to Lake Ontario, and near the Estaminet restaurant where the Williamson clan and the Sharp boys gathered for Christmas dinner in 1941. Marie and John had a summer holiday with Emily in her separate apartment, and the children came to visit and play on the beach. Peter stayed with Emily while earning money picking fruit on his uncles' farms. In 1942 Emily sent the children in Toronto a Valentine's cake decorated with gumdrops on the eve of sugar rationing. With the exception of Clara, John's sisters and brothers lived in Burlington: Sarah Eleanor Blanchard, née Williamson (1879–1947); David Franklin "Frank" (1880–1976), a farmer; William Edgar "Bill" (1883–1954), a farmer; Walker Murray (1888–1964), a salesman; Clara Ida Anderson, née Williamson (1895–1981).

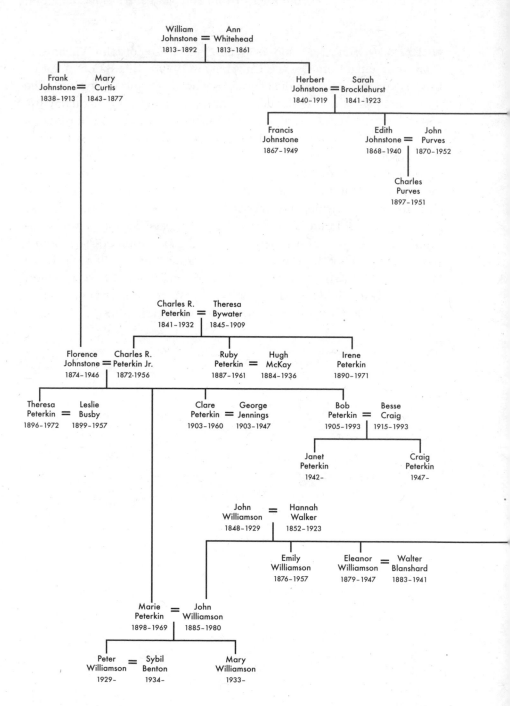

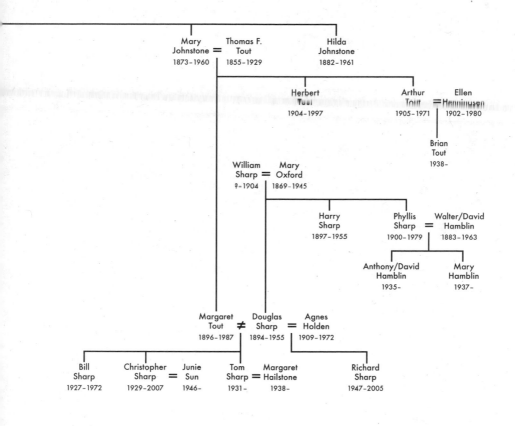

Mary Johnstone 1873–1960 = Thomas F. Tout 1855–1929   Hilda Johnstone 1882–1961

Herbert Tout 1904–1997   Arthur Tout 1905–1971 = Ellen Henningsen 1902–1980

Brian Tout 1938–

William Sharp ?–1904 = Mary Oxford 1869–1945

Harry Sharp 1897–1955   Phyllis Sharp 1900–1979 = Walter/David Hamblin 1883–1963

Anthony/David Hamblin 1935–   Mary Hamblin 1937–

Margaret Tout 1896–1987 ≠ Douglas Sharp 1894–1955 = Agnes Holden 1909–1972

Bill Sharp 1927–1972   Christopher Sharp 1929–2007 = Junie Sun 1946–   Tom Sharp 1931– = Margaret Hailstone 1938–   Richard Sharp 1947–2005

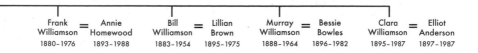

Frank Williamson 1880–1976 = Annie Homewood 1893–1988   Bill Williamson 1883–1954 = Lillian Brown 1895–1975   Murray Williamson 1888–1964 = Bessie Bowles 1896–1982   Clara Williamson 1895–1987 = Elliot Anderson 1897–1987

1940

"It will just be a little larger family"[1]

Dear Margaret

I do hope that by now you and the boys, or at least the boys, will be on the way to Canada, though it is apparently not easy to get transportation.... So you had already in mind the idea of moving out here. Of course as you know now, it is impossible to bring any money out, but we would be <u>very glad</u> indeed to have you come to us, and your mother too if she could be persuaded to come, though I do not expect she would want to leave Herbert and Arthur. Of course the journey is undoubtedly hazardous but several shiploads of women and children have already arrived.

Practically everyone here who is in a position to do so is willing to take in at least one child. A very dear friend of mine who does not live very far away would be glad to take Bill.[3] I think he must be 13 now, so he would be in secondary school—that is, proceeding toward matriculation. We call them High Schools or Collegiate Institutes and she lives only 5 minutes walk from the newest and best equipped one in the city—also it has on the whole much the nicest kind of children attending it as it is in a good residential district. In addition the headmaster is a very old friend of John's. Vivien (her name is Vivien Ratcliffe) has a lovely, quite large house with a big garden (that is, big for a city house) and a large skating rink at the back of the house. She has a boy of 15 and two girls 12 and 6. I would keep the other two myself, or if you came with them I would like you to stay on with us and one of the boys could go to my sister Clare[4]—probably Tom. I think it is Christopher who has not been strong—I have had information about

There seems little doubt that old
Abominable's sister is done for as 1   1 Belmont
it will you heard.   Sun 21st. 10·40 p.m.

Dear Chaps

When Phiz and I left you we went and
had a very good lunch with wine & all. Then about
4 o'clock - what a funny time to finish lunch! - we
went back & mingled with the crowd at the Pier
Head & picked up lots of bits of gossip such as
the name of your steamer etc etc. It was very
interesting. About 6.30 we went to telegraph home
& tried to send you a telegram too. The P.O people
were uncertain if it would be delivered. I wonder
if it was? The Liverpudlians are chatter-bugs (Bill
will have to explain what that means to Tom)
When we left your own train about 10 to 9 one of
the gangways had been drawn up. There was a
rumour you would lie some days in the river. We
were longing to go back next day to see. However
we gladly came home on the last train, arriving
at midnight. Next day we kept telling William
he didn't make enough noise for seven boys.
Jack & Gulu stayed at Aunt B's 3 days. Miss.
Brown says it was Ribbles' Stopher so as

them from time to time in your mother's letters but one does forget. Clare is
some distance from the nearest school but I should think Tom (he's 9 isn't
he) would not find it too far.... If the boys should be coming without you I
would be glad if you would let me know what diseases they have had and
what inoculations and vaccinations and things.

the train went by. I believe he had been put out
for some naughtiness! It was very horrible here
without you so Phyl & I went & had dinner in
Barrow with her brother who is in the army & we
called at the Childs on the way. Yesterday Saturday
I went a walk from Ambleside up Kilnshaw
Chimney with Miss Potter, Mr Porritt & Mr Daw.
Wasn't it nice of them to ask me to join them?
I liked Mr Daw very much. He asked for Bill's
address, but I daresay as he may be joining the
military police next week he won't have
time to write. There have been a number of
Glaciers on the road to Ambleside since our
Grasmere trip. Compere to road to Barrow but
more so. Mr Forrest wrote a very nice letter
about being sorry to lose B & C. The History job
is now advertised & I shall go in but I
don't expect to get it. Edie is said to be
leaving hospital shortly. Brian brought up my
Bible which Tom had had at school. Ian
hopes to see Mr Helme about Bill's work
next week. He had 3 tiny lettuces from C's garden
today & I putting 1/- in his money box. Tom's
flowers are lovely now. I will miss you such

Please do not worry about financial arrangements. We (and
Mrs. Ratcliffe) are fully prepared to maintain and clothe and look after
the boys just as though they were our own. If in the future there is any
means available of recompensing us that will be all right but meantime
it will just be a little larger family and the more children we can have out
of England the better we will be pleased. And I hope you will not decide
to stay in England yourself just because of the money question. I can
quite understand anyone hesitating to become dependent, even upon a

relative but we would really like you to come. After all, if you were here with us too, the responsibility of the boys, in case of illness or decisions to be made, would not be so great, not that we are not willing to accept those responsibilities but I just want to point out that there would be advantages to us in having you here. Possibly you could get a position of some sort later on. I don't know much about it, but certainly if one is right on the ground it is easier to obtain whatever is available. I should think with so many schools being brought out there would at least be need of teachers.

There is not much use my writing more until I know more of what you have been able to arrange.... Meanwhile I am "standing by" as the Provincial Lady says.[5]

Sincerely yours
Marie[6]

[2]   PARADISE LODGE, HALIBURTON, AUGUST 14

Dear Margaret

The boys have been with us ten days now and I should certainly have written you earlier. However I knew Theresa wrote you of their safe arrival and the boys have been writing since, and I thought I would have a second letter from you soon, as I did yesterday.[7]

We were delighted that the boys were able to leave as soon as they did—so many seem to be held up indefinitely—and <u>so</u> glad to have them with us. As far as can be seen there has not been a sign of homesickness which is remarkable, and they are adapting themselves splendidly to what must be an entirely strange way of life. They are all three so different we can scarcely believe they're brothers! I don't think you did Bill justice in your letter, or perhaps you had no way of knowing how he would respond to responsibility. He is simply splendid, thoughtful and helpful and so good with Christopher and Tom and spends hours playing with Tom and entertaining him in a constructive way. He is so anxious to fit in to our household and to see that the others do. When I got your letter yesterday I spoke to him about going to Vivien Ratcliffe and he is quite agreeable, though he asked if he could see the boys often, which of course he can. I really think it will be a little fairer to Bill not to be with them, as while he is with them, he takes so much responsibility. The Ratcliffes have a boy of 15 and I will be glad to have Bill able to take advantage of all possible new experiences. Vivien will be writing you—she had intended to do so earlier but I did not want to speak to Bill of the plan until I had your view.

Mary, Tom, Christopher, Peter, and Bill at Paradise Lodge, in cottage country north of Toronto, a week after the boys arrived in Canada

I am sure Christopher and Tom will get on all right with us. Tom is such a sweet child everyone loves him at sight. He constantly amazes me with his wisdom and reasoning power, he is such a childish looking child. All the people around here love to get in conversation with him, to hear him talk. Christopher is a fine boy too—not quite so easily managed as the others but no real difficulty. He is very like Peter in some ways, but has more fun in him than Peter and can give way more gracefully. I am sure we can manage the two very nicely. Bill is afraid that if they go to the same school they will be put in the same class which he thinks would be fatal to their friendship so I will have to see what can be done about that. John will see Jack McKellar, the headmaster of Lawrence Park Collegiate about Bill as soon as we get back to the city.

They have been introduced to life in the wilds of Canada with a vengeance. I had arranged for us to holiday here long before there was any thought of the boys coming and as all the little cottages are the same size there was no way of getting more accommodation so all of us had to fit in to what we had intended 4 to occupy. However since the weather has been nice (it was rather bad at the start) Bill and Peter have slept in the tent. C. & Tom are very anxious to sleep in the tent but I wanted to make sure of dry warm weather for C. to be out and it does get damp at night. We were trying this place as an experiment—we have tried all kinds of holidays, camping in tents, renting rough & ready cottages, renting fairly luxurious cottages, and staying at summer hotels and they all have their

Tom with his big fish

disadvantages and any place desirable for the children is usually not as much fun for us so we hate to spend a lot of money on it. So this year I looked for some place that would be good for the children and not cost as much and decided to try this. The boys have probably told you about it. There are a lot of cottages built along the lake with a central Lodge which supplies ice, water, linen etc. and collects garbage and sells supplies. The cottages are equipped for housekeeping but any meals we want may be had very reasonably at the Lodge dining room. So we get dinner there and prepare our own breakfast and supper. It is a very safe place, not rocky, the ground sandy so rain soaks in immediately and fairly well wooded. The lake is not a particularly attractive one in this country of lakes, having a muddy bottom but there is a bathing place which the Lodge keeps raked so it is sandy and clean a good way out and the slope is very gradual. In the other parts which are uncleared the muddy bottom discourages children from venturing too far out. It is sandy at the edge and several feet out, in front of the cottages and to-day the boys are constructing an elaborate canal and water way system along the edge.

There are lots of expeditions they could go on if it were not for the mosquitoes—they are usually over by this time of year but we have had so much rain this year that they are very bad still in the wooded places or high grass. Bill and Tom got badly bitten when they first came but we got that cleared up and now with more precautions they are getting on all right. Christopher has had a sliver or something in the ball of his foot and has had to soak it a good deal in a basin of warm salt water. I daresay I was too fussy about it but he has been a marvellous patient—has never complained or voiced the slightest objection to sitting with his basin while the others play. It is practically cleared up now. All the boys are so good at entertaining and amusing themselves, they make me quite ashamed of my own children....

We were so delighted when Tom caught his big fish—I have never seen any-one so pleased as he was—but so modest and he kept insisting that he had had help in pulling it in so it wasn't quite all his doing! Mary of course would have liked one of the boys to be a girl but she and Tom get on very well together and play together more all the time, with much fun and laughter.

Mrs. Bland put the boys on the University group list before they landed at Montreal so their passports, money, papers and luggage were looked after with the group.[8] When I went to Toronto to get the boys I had to go and sign various papers to get their luggage checks and passports. They were entitled to a complete physical examination through the University but I did not want to wait for that as it meant tests for diphtheria etc., for which you have to wait 0 or 0 days for a reaction and go back. However I think they will still give the examination after we go back and if so I will arrange for it—they seem in the best of health but it is a very good and thorough examination and they might as well have it.

The money which they brought with them Bill insisted I was to take towards their upkeep so I gave them each $2.00 and deposited the rest in my name in trust. I will keep it for pocket money and any extra expenses for them. They are amazingly careful with money. Christopher bought some crayons (Mary was very rude about being unwilling to lend hers) but aside from that they've bought nothing. I think the poor kids feel when what they have is gone they won't get any more!

AUGUST 17

I am ashamed to have had this unfinished so long! There is so much I could say that I keep thinking I can't possibly finish it! Poor Christopher has only to-day been able to run about with the others but his little infected spot is finally quite clean. He never once complained of having to sit still, he has drawn pictures, played games and amused himself for hours and even when he had to be hurt he never squealed. I am sorry he has had to miss a lot of the sunshine but he will have to make it up now. We get them to keep their shirts off a good deal of the time and they are all getting brown—each one turns a different shade, their complexions are so different. Tom's face is all golden pink like a peach. They are looking very well indeed and their appetites are splendid and a good example to my two.

We will be going back to Toronto about the 24th and Bill will be going to the Ratcliffes then or a day or two later. I do wish we could keep them all with us but we just have not the room. We have taken out the large double bed which Peter had in his room and are putting in two single beds

Peter, Tom, Bill, Mary, and Christopher at Paradise Lodge

for Christopher and Peter. Tom we are putting in a small room which John has always used as a dressing room. It has a cot in it and has a basin with running water. I am sure Bill will be happy at the Ratcliffes. They are a very happy sort of family, both Harry and Vivien have a very good sense of humour and their children are well brought up, very self reliant and get on well together. Vivien is one of my oldest and dearest friends and Harry was in my year at the University and I don't know any couple I would rather have a child of my own living with. Bill is very pleased that John Ratcliffe is a stamp collector. John is also an athlete and he and his father are sport enthusiasts (as spectators I mean) so Bill is bound to learn a lot about sports and games which will be good for him even though he doesn't particularly care about playing them.

The boys, that is Bill, Christopher and Peter, went to a corn roast which the Lodge gave last night. Bill and I decided that C. might stay up a bit late and go, as he has missed a lot of fun with his sore foot. I think they enjoyed it—it was the first time they had had corn on the cob and while Bill said he quite liked it C. was rather noncommittal. John said the corn was not particularly good, it is too early in the season. Bill is very eager to learn everything new and try everything new and compare things Canadian with things English. For a boy so young he is remarkably free from any prejudices of any kind and I have noticed in all his dealings with the others he has a highly developed sense of justice and fairness.

Theresa looked after the boys in Toronto for a couple of days until I went down for them and as their trunks did not arrive until after we had left again, she has been unpacking them while we are away. I don't know how you managed, in such a rush, to send them so well equipped. There were plenty of clothes in their suitcases to do them here, with a couple of pairs of shorts and shoes which Theresa sent up from their trunks. All they need here is cotton shorts and those coloured shirts. I had quite a stock of cotton things a friend had passed on to me which her boy had outgrown so altogether they are very well equipped, for their present life, and I am sure they will be for the city too, I have two friends, Vivien Ratcliffe and another, who each have 3 children and the three of us always keep clothes circulating as one child outgrows them. Your boys apparently are used to clothes passing down the family so I hope they won't mind entering our travelling wardrobe service. I don't mean we buy no new ones, but good things like overcoats and suits and things one is always loath to discard when they are outgrown but only slightly worn.

We have asked the boys to call us Uncle John and Aunt Marie—Cousin always seems an awkward title for a child and we want something more intimate than Mr. Mrs.

I am afraid this is a very jerky letter. It has been written in fits and starts. I will be writing again soon and often. It must have been dreadful for you to part with the boys. It is such a difficult decision to make. Please don't worry as to whether you did the right thing in sending them alone. I tried to tell you that we would be glad to have you if you came, but we are perfectly willing to assume the responsibility of them without you. After all we can only give them the same care and thought we do our own, in fact look on them as though they were our own. Anyway, the regulation you speak of, which permits a mother to escort her children, applies I believe only in cases where a child or children are under 5 years. I do hope you are successful in getting the teaching position. I am sure you must feel anxious to have your days filled with the boys gone.

I am sorry not to have answered your mother's long letter. As she is with you now perhaps this will do for both of you, and I send her my love. We are taking some pictures of the boys here and will send them when they are printed.

Affectionately
Marie[9]

Dear Margaret

I was talking this morning to Mrs. Bland—she has been away with the Wilkinsons and it was my first opportunity to talk to her.[10] ... She says Bill was simply splendid coming out, looking after the little boys, which is exactly what I found....

It seems a long time since we came home, we have been so busy. I arranged for the medical examination the University offered all children coming out, and took the boys to the hospital for it. They were given a tuberculin test (routine) and we went back two days later for a reading, which was positive in all three cases. That apparently means, not there is any trouble, but that they are the type which might possibly have trouble so they all had a chest x-ray—the routine procedure. They must have been satisfactory, as I have heard nothing further. They were all given a first dose of diphtheria toxoid and are to go for a 2nd and 3rd at 3 week intervals. The toxoid treatment gives practically certain immunity for years if not life. It is not compulsory here but is almost universal; it is done in the schools unless the parents object. My children were both done some years ago.

Bill was here yesterday afternoon after his first day in school. He was viewing school with a great deal of trepidation—no wonder, with the prospect of 1300 strange children!—but I don't think he found it too bad, and he found the Provost boy at the same school, though a form below, and living quite close.[11] His work being so good should make his adjustment easier. I took him last week to see Jack McKellar, the headmaster and he is trying him in the 3rd Form to start, but told Bill to come see him in a fortnight, when, if he found the work too difficult, he could go back to 2nd Form or if too easy, he could try his hand at 4th....[12]

The boys' reports came yesterday and <u>what</u> a report Bill's is! He is going to show it to Mr. McKellar when he goes to see him in a fortnight's time. He may have told you that Mrs. Ratcliffe is going to see if there is any possible means of getting him into U.T.S. (University School) but the headmaster is out of town at present.[13] There is not much hope, as in the higher forms the only new pupils taken are just to fill vacancies left by pupils leaving, which are not many. However, she is going to find out. U.T.S. does not open until Sept. 16 and if by any chance he should be able to get in, the fortnight at Lawrence Park will help to give him an idea of how 3rd Form suits his attainments.

I am quite thrilled at Christopher's and Tom's school prospects. Theresa is very fond of the boys and her husband (at present on voyages round about South America) is so excited about them being here and anxious to do something for them and she has arranged to finance them at St. Paul's School (where Peter has been going for 4 years) for a year anyway. The Public Schools are very good and the one near us (where Mary goes) is in a good district, with a very nice group of children but we did foresee difficulties for both boys (though naturally we did not tell them so!). Christopher as far as I can discover is very "uneven"—I have been trying him with Grade 4 spelling which is really too difficult for him, while in Arithmetic and some other subjects I imagine he could hold his own in Grade 6. So placing him in Public School under a very inelastic system (I suppose inevitable with large classes and so many schools) would be difficult. If he were placed too low we were afraid he would be disgusted and if too high, discouraged. I can understand how tragic it would be if Tom and he were in the same room. With Tom the difficulty would be quite different but just as real. He is so serious about his work, and interested and <u>so</u> anxious to do what is right and what is expected of him but in a large class I am afraid that very often he would not grasp general directions and instructions—either from the different expressions and phrasings used here or because with his tremendous power of concentration, he had his mind on something else—and then he would get <u>so</u> worried and muddled. I can't bear a child to suffer such anxiety just because he really <u>is</u> trying, and wants so hard to understand that he worries about it!

St. Paul's is a very small school—only about 54 though they hope to have a few more this year but their limit is 60 odd. The staff is excellent, and they are all teaching because they love it (they'd have to, at the salaries they get!) and they are so kind and understanding (a little <u>too</u> kind I sometimes think, to scamps like Peter who take advantage of them). There is Mr. Waddington, headmaster, Mr. Hass, quite young, whom the boys all adore, Mrs. Underhill an exceptionally good teacher who had a school for small children herself (mostly attended by children of the University Staff) until last year when she went to St. Paul's, and Mrs. Hodgson, who has the little boys and is young, pretty and vivacious and like a mother to them only much more fun than most mothers have time to be![14] There is also a handicraft teacher and workshop and if the boys are interested they can do a lot of work. Peter has done a lot of handicraft of all kinds—plaster casts, lino cuts, clay modeling, boat building, model villages, airports etc., leather work, and work work of various kinds. The physical instructor and music teacher come in part time. I have a prospectus I will send you—it is a year or two old but there are not many changes except that the prospect of building a new school has been shelved for lack of funds.

Mr. Waddington is a perfect dear—he was such a help to me when I had so much trouble with Peter a few years ago—bad temper, defiance and general disagreeableness. I took the boys to see him a few days ago—he just had a talk with them to try to get their friendship. He has promised to put them in different rooms. He didn't even need to be told it would be desirable, after talking to them. What we hope is that they will have a pleasant introduction to school life in Canada and with the individual attention which can be managed in such a small school they will be "evened up" so that if they go to the Public School next year they will be at the proper stage in all subjects for whatever grade they enter. St. Paul's follows the same curriculum as the Public Schools though their methods differ in some respects. Also, in a year's time they will have made their social adjustments and the larger group and consequent increases in regimentation (of a mild kind) would not be terrifying. The school does not open until Sept. 11 and Peter's (U.T.S.) Sept. 16. So after Mary went off to school (yesterday) I initiated lessons for Peter Tom and Christopher for an hour or two each morning and hope to continue until school opens. I give them all different work—one does arithmetic while I give another dictation, etc. I want the boys to do a little arithmetic in Canadian money and I have given them some of Peter's books on the early settlers in Ontario—that is one subject that is in the new curriculum and there are so many really interesting yet simple books. Peter needs brushing up as he always rusts frightfully during the holidays. I think they all rather enjoy the lessons though Tom is the only one young enough to admit it!

We took them to the Toronto Exhibition[15] last week and Clare and Theresa were to take them again one day but it poured so they went to the movies to a Walt Disney medley—Snow White and some shorts. They are all three going to Clare's for the day to-morrow so we will have to get lessons over early. They are so amusing when they get your letters—they can't decipher one word in ten until Bill arrives to interpret! Bill was here for the weekend—John took Peter up to his sister's in Burlington, so I was glad to have room for Bill from Sat. to Monday. It <u>was</u> nice to have him back. I think he may have found the Ratcliffes a little lonely. Vivien has been ill ever since he went there and of course Bill is not used to girls. However John, the 15 year old, arrived home Monday, which will make a great difference, and John Roberts (who lives along the street and whose parents are friends of ours and of the Ratcliffes) is very anxious to take Bill under his wing at school. I am glad he found the Provost boy, and another boy who came out on the Duchess of Bedford lives close to Bill—he was here for tea with the boys Sunday. Mr. Waddington, by the way, expects quite a few English boys, and Mary has a boy and girl in her room at school.

Before I forget—I promised Christopher to ask you if possible to keep the stamp from the last parcel he sent you—the canoe. He forgot to tell you. Tom sent your birthday present to-day, and C. a parcel of drawings, I don't know whether they are for your birthday. I wish you could have seen Tom doing that map. The three of them had been talking while we waited at the hospital and Bill warned them that they must send their presents to you by Sept. 20. Tom got so worried about choosing something so I suggested he make you something and Bill suggested the map, as Tom had helped him to make a highway map while in Haliburton. He started the minute he got home—I got him a highway book and he worked all afternoon and the next morning. I have never seen so young a child carry through anything he undertakes as Tom does. When he got the important highways marked I wanted him to stop but he never considered it! I got it ready to post and to-day he asked me if he hadn't better post it and mark it NOT TO BE OPENED UNTIL OCT 19 and I, knowing my memory to be no better than Tom's, thought it a good idea.

They are very well indeed—Christopher used to cough once or twice in the early morning but he has not coughed since we came home (almost 2 weeks) until this morning, when John heard a cough so we gave him a little baking soda in water before breakfast. Their appetites and dispositions are good. Tom seems very happy—he and Mary get on very well together and have very hilarious ping pong games. He spends hours in the sand pit while the others play there for a while and then leave to have a change to something more vigourous....

Much love to your mother—I hope she is not suffering too much with arthritis. I will be writing again soon....

[4]   118 HILLSDALE AVENUE WEST
          TORONTO, SEPTEMBER 18

Dear Margaret

I'm afraid I haven't time in this letter to do more than explain my writing at Tom's dictation, in case you were worried. His eyes have been rather sore— it began Saturday morning but was not too bad to prevent his expedition with Bill Saturday afternoon. Sunday he didn't feel like facing the light all day so Monday morning I took him to Dr Macrae one of our best eye specialists. He said it looked like what he called "Vernal catarrh," though there is not the discharge usually associated with that. It is something akin to hay fever (which is all too common here) but affects the eyes—is not serious, does not lead to anything serious, is not infectious, but very annoying. He gave me a prescription for eye drops which I have been using. I took him to school Monday afternoon but yesterday (Tuesday) by the time he finished breakfast they felt worse so he spent almost all day in his room (darkened). He came down about 4 and sat and talked to me until supper time and said they felt much better when he was talking. Poor little man—no wonder they felt worse while he had nothing to do but lie and think about them! I felt so sorry for him but aside from reading to him which I did as much as I had time for, there seemed nothing to amuse him which did not require the use of his eyes. This morning they felt better and he was about to go to school but it was such a sunny morning that the outdoors was too much for them. So he stayed home but got out his jigsaw puzzle of the map of the world and spent all morning on it and they seemed all right. So I took him to school this afternoon and asked Mrs. Hodgson, his teacher, to let me know if they were worse and I would come and get him. I telephoned Dr. Macrae who says they should be <u>much</u> better, at least by the end of the week. I got him dark glasses on the doctor's advice and he is wearing them. The eyes do not look badly inflamed at all—in fact it is really only his left eye that has the trouble at all. He has twice before complained of his eyes hurting—first the day we were at the Exhibition, when there was a lot of dust blowing about, and one of the two days they spent at Clare's, when they ran about for hours in the fields chasing butterflies. Otherwise they are in excellent health. I took them to the dentist's with my children before they went to school. He says Christopher has <u>almost</u> a cavity, which he would like to see at Christmas time and Tom's teeth are in good shape.

I think they are enjoying their school. Christopher is not very communicative (like my Peter) but Tom talks about it quite a lot. The taxi calls for them at our corner and brings them back and I have arranged for them to have their dinner at the home of one of the boys near the school. His parents find it difficult financially to keep him at the school and his mother makes a bit by taking half a dozen St. Paul's boys for dinner every day. It saves them having a cold lunch and having to have dinner at night, which wouldn't fit in very well with Tom's bedtime.

I had a little talk with Mrs. Underhill, Christopher's form teacher, yesterday. She says the boys in her form all seem good at imaginative things but not so good in the dull prosaic things like spelling and assured me many of them were poor spellers! Her husband is a professor at Toronto University. She told me that he was offered a post under your father, when he left Oxford but refused it because he didn't want to do Mediaeval History. They have five English boys at the school! I think there are 16 boys in Christopher's room and they take a personal interest in each one, and Mr. Waddington is like a father to them all.

Bill will have told you that Vivien was able to get him into U.T.S. in the form they opened for English boys. They are mostly boys from English University families who are staying with University people here so I think the standard should be high and the competition good.

Peter has started in U.T.S. and finds it a little overwhelming after the "home atmosphere" at St. Paul's—especially home work for the first time.

The children are all settling down well together and I do hope we shall have a good healthy winter.

This is very jerky and hurried—will try to write again soon.

Marie

[5]   118 HILLSDALE AVENUE WEST
       TORONTO, OCTOBER 9

Dear Margaret—Your letter of Sept 11 arrived Oct. 5 and that of Sept. 22 on Oct 7! Also those for the boys, and Christopher got several birthday letters yesterday—well timed! A parcel (evidently a book) arrived for him yesterday while he was at school so I hid it until to-morrow. I think all the letters you have sent to all of us have arrived safely. Bill rather hopes some have been lost so there will be hope of getting them later on marked "Saved from the Sea"!

Tom has had no pains since he arrived and I hope will not—he looks such a frail little thing but his health has been excellent and he is a very good colour. The only trouble he's had was with his eyes and they have given no trouble since.

Christopher had a very slight cold since we came back to the city but he has scarcely ever coughed. He seems well and husky.

About the underwear—I am sure Tom's will be warm enough. As a matter of fact Peter has never worn woollen underwear until last year when a friend passed on a supply just about the weight of Tom's, but I think that Peter is very warm-blooded—he scarcely needs any clothes. The other boys' is perhaps a little heavy but Christopher seems to like to be good and warm—I notice he is always the last to shed his sweater. We have the houses here pretty warm in winter and put heavy things on for outdoors. I am glad you didn't try to get more clothes for the boys because undoubtedly they would not be the same as boys wear here in winter. They wear breeches—that is, trousers cut like riding breeches, buttoning or lacing at the knee, and the woollen sock pulls up over the bottom of the leg, which comes several inches below the knee. Most boys' suits (except flannel ones for summer) are sold with one pair of shorts and one pair of these knickers. The boys are now wearing shorts and pullovers to school and in winter will wear breeches instead of the shorts. The separate heavy weight ones which we use with pullovers for school are cut quite like riding breeches—the ones of finer cloth with suits are narrower. (This all sounds rather silly I'm afraid.) For school in winter most boys wear warm outer jackets something like wind breakers but longer—coming about the seat of their trousers, with a belt. Peter always preferred something like that to an overcoat as he is very active and hates to be hampered. I have a very warm overcoat which Peter has outgrown after very little wear and I think would fit Tom. Tom seems to feel the cold more than the others. They wear woollen toques on their heads in winter—I have two in St. Paul's colours which Peter had. When they play outside in winter they usually wear heavy woollen "over-stockings" which go right over their shoes and pull right up over their thighs and on top they wear overshoes. Overshoes are the regular outdoor footwear all winter (made of heavy cloth with rubber soles, fastening with buckles.) ... I have quite a collection of winter clothing and a friend who has two boys who have just gone into boarding school is handing over a lot of things which her boys can't wear this winter as they have to have all navy blue there. I hope the boys will enjoy the winter and I do hope when it does get cold that we have snow along with it—it is much pleasanter and more fun for the children. Christopher is talking about saving up for skates already and I would like them all to learn to skate. Skates are quite inexpensive for the younger boys—they come all attached to the boots, the whole outfit at not more than $3 or $4 new and at St. Paul's the boys all turn in their outgrown ones each year and Peter got new (secondhand) ones each year there for about $1 or $1.50.

I am going through your letters as I write, trying to answer your questions. About the bed time and allowances—I am sorry I didn't mention them in an earlier letter—I am sorry you were worried, I didn't know C. had taken things so much to heart as to tell you. You see, when we are away in the summer we have made a practice of letting our children stay up later than at home. We are usually in a cottage or cabin where they can't be shut away from the household sounds and it is daylight so late, that we found they didn't sleep and there was so much calling for drinks, complaining of heat and so on that they really didn't get as much sleep as if they went later. Then we had them rest after dinner in the middle of the day—an hour or an hour and a half, not often sleeping but at least resting. So when your boys arrived Mary was going to bed about 8 and Peter about 9. Bill was very firm about Tom's bed time being 7 and C's 8 and the boys must have complained to him because he talked it over with me and we agreed to set 7.30 for Tom and Mary. This pleased Tom and Mary made no objections as Tom who is older was going at the same time. Bill felt that C. should stick to 8 and we felt we couldn't push Peter ahead a full hour, especially as he slept out in the tent with Bill. So Peter went at 8.30 so that he was well settled when Bill went at 9. Bill thought C. was quite satisfied and realized it was because of his illness that he had to have a little more rest. In fact C. on several occasions went to bed earlier than 8 at his own request. Since we came home Mary and Tom both go at 7 and C. and Peter at 8, and it is a source of never-ending wonder to us, how agreeably our children go to bed since yours came! There used to be endless arguments about what time so and so went to bed, and pleas "just to finish this or that" and the fact that they never succeeded never prevented them being tried every night! I don't know whether it's the fact that C. and T. never question bed time or whether it's because someone else is going at the same time—probably a combination of the two—that's made the change. At any rate it's a great relief. Mary and Tom take turns having their bath first and the one who has [a] bath first is allowed to read in bed until the second one is finished. C. and Peter take turns the same way and I usually find they are quite ready to start as soon as the other two have finished with the bathroom, not waiting for 8 o'clock. We have rearranged the boys—made Peter's room into a dormitory with 3 cots for them and made the little room where Tom slept (which is also John's dressing room) into a study for the boys with two tables, a bookcase and shelves for games, Peter's radio etc., and it seems to work very nicely. The first few nights it disturbed Tom having the others come in to go to bed but he soon got accustomed to it and usually is sound asleep.

The allowance question came up several times in Haliburton and each time I assured them that they would be given allowances when we got home again. Our children didn't get any all summer as it's hard for them to look after money at a cottage and there was nothing to spend it on. I made it up by giving them all spending money when they went to the Exhibition. I didn't want to go into details about amounts because of Bill. He was very serious and earnest about explaining to me how much they all got at home and to him the important point was that the difference between his and C's should be twice as much as the difference between C's and T's! I knew quite well what I intended doing, which was to give C. the same as Peter (15¢) and T. the same as Mary (10¢) but I didn't want to tell Bill that and upset him because I knew he would think 25¢ for him was beyond reason (I know he has found out since that it isn't, but he had no experience of Canadian values then). I was quite sure Vivien would be giving him that much but naturally I didn't want to promise it to him for her! So I let things go until we got back and Vivien and Bill made their arrangements and I think everyone is satisfied. I would not think of giving C. less than Peter. Money means very little to Peter and Mary yet—she puts it in her bank. C. and T. spend very little money, in fact I don't think Tom has bought anything but one ice cream cone and a birthday present for Christopher. His ambition is to have one of each Canadian coin and note so I thought it very decent of him to give 25¢ to the Red Cross appeal at school last week. C. gave 20¢— he made us laugh when Tom thought he should have given 25¢ too, C. said "I couldn't. I only had 20¢ that wasn't in notes and this thing is like the collection plate in Church, you can't get change." Tom worked out his scheme himself. He asked me to advance him the 25¢, and keep back his allowance for 5 weeks and then give him a 25¢ piece for his collection of coins. He has his Christmas expenditures very much on his mind. I have suggested that he make some presents at school in the handicraft class so he started an ash-tray for his father in the clay modelling class. They have just changed handicraft teachers and the new one has started them on lino-cuts so Tom is rather worried as to whether his ash tray will get finished. However I told him we could mount the lino cuts and I'm sure they would be very nice for Christmas. He and Mary have a system of "racing"—one I instituted with Mary some time ago. At bath time I get him upstairs, say "Go" and I go and turn on the taps and he starts undressing and if he's ready in the bathroom before the bath is ready he gets a cent. Needless to say neither he nor Mary have ever lost. They finally gave it up for fear as Mary said, that I wouldn't have any money left for food!

About the letters from home—yours don't seem to upset them at all as far as I can see. Tom had one from his father about 3 weeks ago in which he told him in a jocular way of having to leave his bath for an air raid. Tom came and read me that bit out of it and laughed heartily but I saw him wipe his eyes too and when he folded the letter he said—"well I know now that my daddy was safe at the 25th of August but I don't know about him now." That was just when the bad raids on London were starting and I saw him wiping his eyes a couple of times over the newspapers, so I just carefully hid the papers while he was home for several days. He didn't think to ask for them. Any time he worried we reassured him in every possible way and I think he got over that phase. He had another letter from his father yesterday and I wondered what effect it would have but he seemed quite cheered by it and brought it to me saying "This is quite interesting, perhaps you'd like to read it." It described air raids too, but mentioned that your house and your mother's were undamaged and in fact, that he had as yet seen no damage in London, spoke of the improved defenses and confidence of victory etc.[16] I think with the first news of the bad raids on London the child pictured the entire city in ruins, as well he might but I think he has been gradually reassured. Those are the only signs of anxiety he has given—he doesn't seem to feel that you are in danger and has shown no signs of homesickness. When people ask him the inevitable (how I wish they wouldn't!) "How do you like Canada?" he always answers, "All right, it's no different from England." So that is very satisfactory to me....

When he first came he burst into tears easily when disappointed in any way or frustrated by the other children but as he settled down you can see the change in him and his increasing self control and he scarcely ever sheds a tear now. I can see that changes of routine are upsetting to him, he likes to know exactly what he's expected to do and is very eager to do it and if he has an ordered life in a steady routine he is quite happy. When I go in to say goodnight and turn out his light he always has something to say to me that he has been thinking of in the few minutes he has been alone. Last night he had had a game of draughts (we call it checkers) with Mary after tea, so when I went in he said "I could tell a Canadian how to play draughts in 7 words." I said "What are they?" He said "It is just the same as checkers." One night during the period of hiding the newspapers he said "St. Paul's School reminds me of St. Paul's Cathedral and that reminds me of England and that reminds me that I never heard what happened to that bomb!" "Oh," I said "that bomb hasn't gone off and may never go off and they are piling sand bags on it and the longer it doesn't go off the longer they can pile on more and more sand bags till probably they'll have the sand bags higher than St. Paul's." So he went to sleep quite happy and was completely relieved when he heard next day that the bomb had been removed....

C. and Peter get on very well considering everything—quite as well as most pairs of brothers I've seen and are very good for one another—at least C. is good for Peter, it's so much easier to see reactions in one's own child. Anyway the longer their relationship lasts, the better it gets, which is a very good sign. They have plenty of arguments but no real storms for a long time and they have got on better since Bill is not with us which I think is natural. C. was inclined to be jealous of Peter—to start off with, at Haliburton, Peter is a very good swimmer and diver and does all those things and I have no doubt bragged about it (though not in my hearing). Then Peter has done very well at school and is one of those people who through no effort of their own are good spellers—he has a photographic mind, can glance over his lesson for half a minute and have no mistakes. I had a couple of talks with Peter about C. and pointed out the handicap he had had physically and the resulting handicap scholastically and I think it impressed Peter, who is quite sensible and kind when he lets himself be.[17] However he in turn is sometimes jealous of C. because he feels C. is treated better, being a guest. But as time goes on they are both beginning to realize that everyone is treated alike and as they are at different schools they are not in competition and I rather think Peter used to brag trying to keep up his end with Bill, as he is not used to being with bigger boys. I have put on a campaign for tidiness in their room and entirely against the advice of the School for Child Study I instituted fines for unmade beds and articles left on the floor. With remarkable results in two days! They only slipped up one day since, rather badly, 2¢ for P. and 3¢ for C. but I let them work those out by polishing their own shoes and also Tom's and Mary's! Tom thinks he is getting so tidy that he can soon be included in those liable to fines!—apparently one of the standards of being grown up!

About your worry over Bill and the problems of adolescence I don't know just what to say.[18] As he is shy and reticent, none of us feel we know him well enough to attempt anything which might result in a barrier of embarrassment being set up. However there is no hurry, I think as you that these things are better handled as they naturally come up and meanwhile we'll all get to know Bill better. The Overseas Children Committee of the Univ. sent me a letter yesterday offering the facilities for consultation at the Institute of Child Study and they might have some helpful suggestions—perhaps as to books he might read.

EVENING

Christopher's two cables came this afternoon—from you and his father—and caused great excitement among our children and all the neighbours' children.[19] Also another parcel came to-day. Bill is coming up from school to-morrow. I asked C. several days ago what he would like for supper and he found it difficult to choose so I suggested he make a list of all the things he specially liked and I would choose. His list included plum pudding, mince pie, sausages, turkey, ham, peas, chips, birthday cake and ice cream, so I hope sausages, peas, chips, birthday cake and ice cream will prove sufficient and we'll leave the plum pudding and mince pie till later! These parcels came book post and are stamped DUTY FREE so apparently they are safe things. I will try to find out from the customs what other things are not dutiable....

I hope you were able to wade through all of this—better try it in small doses. I'm glad you like the snaps—I shall certainly send that negative. Love to you and your mother.

Marie

Dear Margaret

... C. seems to feel Christmas obligations rather worrying him so I wondered if you could tell him what people he should send presents to in England. I suggested that he limit himself to you, his father and his two grandmothers (and a chocolate bar to his dog) and to any others he could send cards made from his own drawings or the lino cuts they are doing at school. However he says he has two cousins in the same house with one grandmother, who, in his opinion, would not appreciate his handiwork. That also brings up the question of the aunt, which in turn brings up other aunts. He is rather vague about his relatives. I will talk to Bill about it and you might tell him what you would suggest—if it's in time, all right and if not it doesn't matter as we'll work out something. I think C. enjoyed his birthday—I hope so. We had just a family party, with Bill here but it seemed quite a success. The books from his father and aunt arrived in time—yours has not come yet—and the two cables were very exciting.

He had <u>no mistakes</u> in spelling at school on Thursday! Mrs. Underhill, his form teacher, telephoned me Friday and had quite a long talk. She says there has been a tremendous change in him since he was put in 3A, he is so much happier, enters into the work and play—just as I have seen the change in him at home.[20] She says it would be a great pity not to have him in 3A as writing and spelling are his only handicaps, in everything else, general knowledge, and ability to grasp a subject he is just as good as any boy in the form. She says he is particularly good at spotting false reasoning and at elucidating difficulties of interpretation in Social Studies. His reading she finds is quite reasonably good—she thought at first he could not read at all well but thinks it was largely due to nervousness and fear of failure. Now that he feels more secure he can read quite well. She has been delighted and surprised at his progress in spelling—I told her how he was working at home. She says in the normal way the boys in that form should not have to do any work at home—they'd have a spelling period every day which is used to prepare the work for the one period a week when they have spelling dictation, but with C. having three lessons a week he has not that time in school for preparation. I do hope his enthusiasm will keep up. We keep encouraging him and I'm sure she does at school also....

Peter and C. have been helping with the housework this weekend as Mary Murphy has gone home for the weekend.[21] She is a very nice girl whom I've had for two years now. She is only 22, I don't like to give her much responsibility with the children but she is very cheerful, willing and loyal, and a fair cook. She looks after the kitchen and downstairs work and I have a laundress housemaid, a Norwegian woman, whom I've had for two years also, who comes every weekday morning from 9 to 12 and does the washing and upstairs work. Mary Murphy is one of a family of 12 (very nice people, we've been to their farm) and her little brother (5) had a most horrible accident last summer, had both legs cut off with the mower—it happened the day after your boys arrived which complicated things here! So I like to get her home for a weekend once in a while. She always leaves as much as possible prepared and the boys are good dish-dryers!—if not particularly enthusiastic ones!

I have always forgotten to mention Church. We are not particularly religious people but we started going to Church some years ago, after we had the children baptized and we both liked it and found it helpful, especially as we have an extremely good rector who preaches most practical and sincere sermons.[22] We felt that the children should be "exposed" to religion as part of their education but I have never thought much of Sunday Schools in so far as I have known them. Also they are an awful nuisance coming from 3 to 4 in the afternoon. So for every reason we decided to take the children to Church with us—I want them to be familiar with the Church service and the beautiful language of the prayer book. They have a Children's Service at our Church—before the sermon one of the curates goes out to the Parish Hall, all the children under 12 following him and they have their own short sermon, pictures etc. We soon found that the only way to have the children go without endless arguments was to make a weekly habit of it with no "backsliding" on our part if we expected none on theirs and so we have done so, and have been very faithful, except when we've all gone to the country for the day or something of that sort. We had really just got Peter and Mary to the point where they accepted regular Church attendance as part of the weekly routine, and I knew if your boys were not included in the now "taken for granted" Church attendance the arguments would start all over again, so we take the whole string every Sunday. I don't think they mind—in fact Tom quite enjoys it and C. makes no objections. Tom was quite disappointed the Sunday he stayed home when his eyes were bad. C. had one Sunday at home when he had a slight cold and I think he found it rather dull. There isn't much for them to do in the city on a Sunday morning. We try to take them on some sort of outing every Sunday afternoon—somewhere in the country if it's fine, and if it's raining there is always the Museum, which they find very interesting.[23] I hope all this lengthy explanation is satisfactory to you. As I said, the boys have made no objection, it's just the regular Sunday morning occupation of the whole family and as such is taken for granted. I want our children to be free to make their own decisions about religion when they get older but in order to make a decision I feel they have to have some experience of Church and religious training, to judge by. I have never tried to give them any religious training or instruction at home, I'm not sure enough what I believe myself!

I will try to get the boys to write their letters in the morning before we go, and send them in this one. They are well and cheery.

P.S. The letters are not ready so we will send them later.

[7]   118 HILLSDALE AVENUE WEST
       TORONTO, OCTOBER 29

Dear Margaret

Your letter of Oct. 2 arrived about a week ago. By the way, I telephoned the Customs here to find out what you could send over duty free. They say that clothing can be sent the boys and almost anything else up to the value of $5.00. The man said if you were sending Christmas presents and wanted to pack them in one box, if you wrapped the parcel for each boy separately with a declaration or invoice on it, they could then be sent in one outer package, and the parcels could amount to $5 for each one. Christopher's knife arrived last week—what a beauty! It was held in the Customs—John sent a messenger for it—but they did not charge any duty. C. set to work immediately and carved a totem pole.

At present they are all violently engaged in making Hallowe'en decorations. Hallowe'en is quite an event here—the children all put on false faces and old clothes or costumes of various kinds and go from door to door along the street beginning at dusk, carrying bags or baskets and everyone in the houses "shells out" as it is called—puts candy, nuts or apples in the baskets. It is a sort of contest to see who can collect the most. They usually go around in groups, and stick mostly to the houses of people they know. Some of the groups we ask in and some of them provide entertainment—a song or dance. John and I went away for the weekend—left Saturday aft. and came back Sun. evening—Clare and George came and stayed here to look after the household. When we returned Peter and C. had arranged "spider webs" on the front windows—string criss-crossed and strips of paper woven around and around and a paper spider in the middle. They are all making witches and cats of paper to hang about and I am getting the pumpkins to-day to make Jack-o-Lanterns— we cut a face in the side of the pumpkin and put a candle inside. To-morrow they are all out of school early (Wednesday) so I will take them to get false

1940   53 faces (masks) and with those and an old cap of John's each and a handkerchief around their necks I think they will do very well.

They are all very well, thank goodness. The weather has been good—quite cool with frost at night but bright and sunny. The boys are still wearing shorts but I think it's about time to get their knees covered. I have not heard Christopher cough once for weeks. The diphtheria toxoid had no bad effect on any of them. The third and last dose (it is a strong one) gave them a sore arm for a day but that was all and it's all over now. C. has lost 3 teeth since he came but the others are coming in. The William book, much looked for, came the other day.[24] I'm afraid the boys didn't get their letters written on Sunday as I was away—I must get them at them to-day. C. is not doing badly with his spelling—he works away at it, sometimes not very enthusiastically!—it is not easy for him as Peter does very little homework and is always full of ideas of projects for them to do, from leaf forts in the garden to caterpillar boxes in the cellar and scenery for a play in the play room. I see that he has the time to spend on the spelling but sometimes it's hard for him to keep his mind on it!

They both seem happy at school. Mr. Hass, the maths. teacher is giving Tom some more advanced arithmetic, when he has a spare period now and then. He gives him so many pages in the book and Tom can do it as fast as he likes in his spare time at school, or at home, and when he has it finished, Mr. Hass takes it up with him when he has the time. Mrs. Underhill, C's form teacher, took the form home to lunch at her house one day and then to the Museum and Tom was included....

Bill's schoolwork has been very satisfactorily arranged—I don't see how it could be better. Mrs. Ratcliffe and the school have spared no effort to get him placed in classes where the work suits his ability.—I daresay Bill and Mrs. R. have both told you of it. He will get Pass Matric. in some subjects next June and go on to Honours in those next year while completing Pass in the others. Everything depends on his own work now, he can get ahead just as fast as he is able. I rather think that the Matric. here covers more advanced work, at least in the sciences, than the English School Certificate. I had all the curricula sent to you—I hope you can make head or tail of all those separate pamphlets! I had to ask them to send the whole thing but there is a great deal—agricultural science, shop work etc. which is entirely irrelevant. I have a St. Paul's prospectus which I will send you too and will see if I can get a University calendar to send along. It will help to give you an idea of the sort of work they do here.

The children get on very well together. They all argue a lot and squabble at times but that is to be expected. I think C. is happier than he was at first. He very seldom loses his temper now. Mary considers Tom her private property—when Tom arrives home and Mary says in sugar-coated tones "Here's Tom, cute little Tom, here's darling little Tom" he doesn't know whether to be pleased or insulted! They have great difficulty with your letters—they start off picking out a word here and there but usually give up by the end of the paragraph. I am always glad to read them but don't like to appear to be prying so I usually wait for them to ask me. If you could possibly manage to print them, even if they were short, so they could read them themselves, I think they would enjoy them more.

They are all taking cod liver oil. My children have always taken the plain cod liver oil from Oct. to April and liked it. I gathered from what T. and C. said that they didn't like it so I hesitated about starting it because I knew if they objected it would only be a day or two till mine wouldn't like it either! So I got the concentrated kind—10 drops equals 3 teaspoons of the plain. They get their 8 or 10 drops after tea every day and are quite eager for it—especially as a little chocolate drop follows each dose!

They both have good appetites and Tom is improving in his food habits. At first there were very few things he would eat—we have so many vegetables and salads in the summer. We try to pay as little attention as possible to his expressions of dislike and he seems to feel he <u>ought</u> to eat what is given him. They have fruit juice for breakfast, then porridge with a couple of spoons of wheat germ on top. We always use honey on the porridge and recently I have been getting glucose in syrup form and mixing it half and half with the honey. Then toast and either applesauce, stewed fruit or jam, and a glass of milk. Tom usually has at least 3 slices of toast. At dinner, which they have at Mrs. Chalmers', except Sat. & Sun., they have meat, potatoes, a vegetable and usually a milk pudding or something of that sort, and milk to drink. They have tea about 5.30—soup or eggs or baked beans (which Tom loves) or macaroni (which he doesn't) or something like that, and bread and butter or sandwiches, a milk pudding or fruit or jelly and more milk to drink. I am so glad they have good appetites—I must weigh them soon. I do hope they have gained. I think Tom has certainly grown and his cheeks are pink—they are all looking extremely well, even Bill has a <u>very</u> good colour. I got them both shoes two weeks ago—they had outgrown all they had and also got them rubbers which I don't think met with their approval—they say they don't wear them in England but we all do here. As Tom says, it doesn't rain here as often as in England, but when it does, it rains more! They still haven't quite mastered the technique for easy rubber-donning but they are learning!

We try to take them somewhere on Saturday and Sunday afternoons—there is a very nice "wild" park not far away with open space where they can play football and wooded hills to run in, a stream and a sand bank.[25]

It is only 10 minutes drive away and is much nicer for them to play in than the cramped space about the house. Tom is very keen about soccer—they are starting it at school next week when the Rugby season ends. It seems the only thing he really likes is to go out and play with the others around the house. He likes to play marbles, parcheesi, checkers, croquinole,[26] ping pong etc., with anyone who will play—usually Mary, but is at a loss if he has to amuse himself, except for reading which he doesn't like to keep at for long at a time. I think he had been so much with Bill, who has directed his recreations that he has not developed initiative of his own. So I am trying to encourage him to find things he would like to do himself.

I know there are a lot of things I would like to tell you but I must get this letter off and they will have to wait for the next. If I don't mention the war in my letters it's not that it isn't a constant weight on our hearts and minds, but what's the use? We all feel the same way. None of your letters, by the way, have been censored except the Air Mail one.

[8]   118 HILLSDALE AVENUE WEST
       TORONTO, OCTOBER 31

Dear Margaret

Your letter of Oct. 10 came yesterday—you had just heard of Tom's eyes. As I have written since, they cleared up in less than a week and he has had no trouble with them since. He wore the dark glasses until they were better and then left them off. What I am afraid of is the winter, if we have snow and bright sunshine—we find that the hardest light on the eyes. However there is no use borrowing trouble—it may not affect him and anyway we may not have snow—some winters there is very little. Tom will be very much disappointed if this is one of those winters—he is looking eagerly for snow.

I wrote just the other day but I think I forgot to tell you that Christopher is going to the Art School at the Art Gallery on Saturday mornings.[27] There has been a very active children's Art School in connection with the Ontario College of Art, at the Art Gallery (what a lot of "art" I have) for some years, under the direction of Arthur Lismer. The children of the members of the Art Gallery have been eligible and on Saturday mornings they have classes for all children, all over the city, who are recommended by their schools as having talent and interest. Mr. Waddington gave Christopher a recommendation so I took him down the opening Saturday and again last Saturday. I was rather busy those days so I drove him but next Sat. I hope to take him, and go back for him, by bus, and if he becomes familiar with the bus he can manage the trip himself later on. He seems to have enjoyed it so far and I hope his interest will continue. They work from 9–11.30 in age groups, from 6 to 14, so he is with the 11 year olds. They come from all ranks of society and all nationalities and do all original work with great stress on imagination and free expression. The first day they painted—the subject given them was "any dream they had ever had." The second day they were shown a movie on town planning and then did clay modelling. C. has also made a very good relief map of Ireland in his spare time at school. He drew the map on cardboard and covered the surface with the mixture they use (salt, flour & water I think), moulding it to the proper contours. It was very good.

Tom managed to get one print off his lino cut yesterday and brought it home. His lines were so fine that they have had trouble printing it. It is very good indeed so we decided he had better go over the cut, widening and deepening the lines so it will print better and we will mount them for him to send for Christmas. Bill was here last night so we discussed Christmas—I think I wrote and asked you about it but we have it settled now. Tom was so worried I wanted his mind relieved and Bill's idea was the same as mine—that it wasn't worth while sending small gifts all that way to his uncles & aunts etc. and that Canadian Artists' Christmas cards or ones of his own make would be more suitable and less trouble to send.

Clare and Theresa took the four children to the circus last week, which they enjoyed very much. They have not been to many indoor amusements of that kind—they have seen two movies and I would like them to see "Convoy" when it gets around to the suburban theatres (neighbourhood theatres we call them). Also there is a new film "The Royal Canadian Mounted Police" which I think the boys would like to see. We never take Mary to movies, her sympathies or imagination or something are too strong—I took her once and she was quite ill and even little children's stage plays, such as she sees occasionally, upset her if there is any injustice, or rudeness or "crossness" as she calls it. I didn't dare take her even to see "Snow White," and it seems impossible to find a film that is <u>all</u> "sweetness and light."

Christopher started Latin this week. I am a little doubtful as to the wisdom of it but don't want to appear interfering so I will wait a few weeks before approaching Mr. W. Also I don't want to appear ungrateful as Mr. W. is himself giving French and Latin to all the English boys in the school from 3rd form up just as a "free will offering" because he thinks they would most of them be getting them at their schools at home, and so they won't be at a disadvantage when they return.

I know C. wouldn't be having Latin at home yet. I wouldn't object at all to him starting it if it weren't that he has the two extra spelling courses on his hands and (I think) extra Social Studies work, and I don't want him to feel he has so much that he gets discouraged. I am trying to persuade him that the Latin is the least important (in his case) and should be given last place in his home work but I think because it's new he finds it interesting so I'm afraid of the spelling suffering! However they may very well not intend to do anything very strenuous in Latin, or stress it very much and his teachers should be able to tell sooner than I whether his work is suffering from too many subjects. So I think I will say nothing for a few weeks and see how things go and how C. takes it. If he goes to the Public School next year of course he won't have either the French or Latin for at least two more years, but of course Mr. W. is hoping to keep him at St. Paul's!

I sent you a University Calendar yesterday but then discovered that it didn't contain the Matriculation Curriculum which they are sending me separately and which I will send you. It will also have particulars of Matric. Scholarships available which might be of interest later. It seems a long way off and Bill, fortunately, is convinced that the war will be over before there is any question of university for him. I hope he is right, but anyway these might interest you and give you an idea of the sort of thing his courses are aiming at. That mass of pamphlets the Dept. of Education sent you may be confusing in their Grade classification. They are gradually rearranging the school curriculum according to Grades (1–8 in the Public or Elementary Schools, and 9–13 in the Secondary or High Schools) but in the actual high schools the classes are called by the old terms (Form I, II, III, IV, & V) so Grade 9 = Form I, etc. Bill's work, I think, is all distributed between Forms III & IV (Grades 11 & 12). Pass Matric. is taken part in III and part in IV and Honour Matric. in Form V.

The boys got your letters yesterday (of Oct. 10). They are so excited about Hallowe'en to-night. We have Jack-o-Lanterns in the windows and they can all think of nothing else.

[9]   118 HILLSDALE AVENUE WEST
       TORONTO, NOVEMBER 5

Dear Margaret

The boys are late with their letters this week. Sunday was a lovely day so John took the five of them (Bill, C., Tom, Peter and Mary) to Burlington for the afternoon and they had a little fun by the lake.

I am enclosing this note, as I saw all the boys' teachers this afternoon at a meeting of the Mothers Guild of the school. The staff came to tea following the meeting, so I had a chance to talk briefly to them all. I think they feel that Tom should be moved up as he is so far ahead of the boys in his room (Mrs. Hodgson says he is not doing the work of the class in anything but the sand table and projects, every other subject he works at independently). So I told her and Mr. W. to use their own judgment and do whatever seemed best for the child. They are afraid of him getting restless, and dissatisfied—he does not seem so yet,—only once in a while he expresses surprise at not having "gone up" yet. It would gratify him very much to be moved on, I'm sure and I think they are both "settled in" pretty well now, and Christopher well established in 3A so that it should not be a problem to have Tom in 3B, even though it is in the same room.

Mrs. Underhill is pleased with C.'s progress. She says his spelling is improving with ups and downs (I always know when it will be "down"—those are the days after the evenings he hasn't studied it) and he is doing very well generally. She has given the class two tests in Social Studies, in the first test his paper was the best in the class for knowledge of the subject though he wrote only about 1/4 or 1/5 as much on each question as the others did. Of course I think writing does not come easily to him—both the actual mechanics of writing and the expressing of his ideas. I wish he would read more, but I don't like to urge him to, as he has very little free time and I feel he should use that as he pleases. This term they don't get home until about 5.15, have tea at 5.30 and start for bed at 8, and he has his spelling and some other home work to do in between. He is working now on a relief map of Central America—he did one of Ireland last week as a spare time project and is doing this one as a school assignment. I found him a map, tracing paper, etc, last night and he got the outline done but in all the atlases we have I could not find a physical map that he could get his topography from. I went to the Boys and Girls House at the Library this morning but the girls there couldn't find anything.[28]

To-night I suddenly thought of the Encyclopaedia, and found one there so he was able to finish it and now has decided to do another, of Mexico.

They started soccer this week. Mr. McCatty says Tom plays quite vigourously and as though he enjoys it—though he will never be a football star! I am glad he is getting some fun out of games.

I haven't time to write more now. The boys should hear from you within a day or two. The last letters were those of Oct. 10.

[10]   118 HILLSDALE AVENUE WEST
         TORONTO, NOVEMBER 11

Dear Margaret

This is a school holiday here—why, I don't know.[29] It is raining steadily so there is no outside play but the holiday is rather a convenience, as I am taking Tom and C. to do their Christmas shopping this afternoon. They are anxious to get things off at once and it is as well to be safe. They made Christmas cards with their lino cuts yesterday.

Theresa's husband, Leslie, is home on a holiday, just back from the Canary Islands. They were here for the day yesterday and Tom was most interested in the various places Leslie has been since the war started.

They are very well and cheery. Tom is much more light hearted than he used to be and not so timid. Christopher unfortunately had his finger banged in the school gate—right on the nail, which I am afraid will eventually come off. The skin was not broken at all and it did not hurt long. It must have been very painful to start but he was very good about it—he never complains about hurts. Bill came down Saturday morning and took Tom for a walk while C. was at the Art Gallery. In the afternoon John took them all (Bill too) to Sherwood Park and Sunnybrook Park (not far away) to run in the woods. Bill is looking so well—his face has filled out and he has a good colour. They all are looking well and in excellent spirits.

I will stick this in with the boys' letters—it must be two weeks since we had any English letters here (yours of Oct. 10)—I forgot to ask Bill if he had later ones.

[11]   118 HILLSDALE AVENUE WEST
       TORONTO, NOVEMBER 17

Dear Margaret

Your letter to the boys dated Oct. 28 and your mother's—to me and to Tom—of the same date, arrived on the 12th (also one to Tom from his father, from Wales). These were the first we had since yours dated Oct. 10—to the boys, to me and to Theresa—so there must have been one lot lost, I think. As far as I can discover those are the only ones we've not got, which is really rather remarkable. I hope you have had all ours—the boys have written every week. I have written two long letters since they have been at school, and several short ones.

Tom probably told you in his letter that he has been moved up to the next form, which is [like] a higher 2A, in the same room with Christopher. He is naturally very happy about it.

We have had some colder weather with a little snowfall—only about an inch but they were very excited. They all went out to shovel it right after breakfast—which was as well from their point of view, as by noon it was all melted. John took them to the golf club yesterday—they thought there might be enough snow for the sleds but they had an afternoon's walking instead.[30] This afternoon he took them down to the lake shore at the east end of the city.

I took them all yesterday (Bill too) to see the annual Santa Claus parade which Eatons hold every year. It goes through the city, the third Saturday in November, with bands, floats and clowns and Santa Claus in his sleigh (mounted on a platform) bringing up the rear, and ends up at Eatons store where Santa takes up his post in Eatons toyland, and remains until Christmas—rather to the exasperation of parents, as the small children, under the urge of modern advertising, all insist on going to see him to tell what they want for Christmas and his invariable reply is "you'll get it" or something to that effect. However ours are rather past that stage now.

John was in New York most of last week at a meeting of the Home Office Life Underwriters, of which he was elected president. He is working very hard as usual.

The children are very well. Christopher seems to be getting on very well at school—the finger he squashed is about to lose its nail, but is otherwise not damaged. I am keeping a glove finger over it until the nail comes off, so it will not be caught and pulled. Mrs. Underhill had the boys in his class to supper at her house on Friday evening and they apparently had a rousing time. She is going to have the younger ones some day soon—that will include Tom as he is in her room now.

We got the Christmas parcels off the middle of the week and also a birthday card for their grandmother and they got their Christmas cards ready to post to-day. Christopher wants to send cards to his godparents but "America" for one and "England" for the others seem to be his closest approximation to their addresses. However we may send them to you for forwarding. I was so glad to have your mother's nice letter and will answer it very soon.

[12]   118 HILLSDALE AVENUE WEST
       TORONTO, NOVEMBER 25

Dear Margaret

Your nice long letter of Oct. 29 or 31, I'm not sure, arrived Saturday (23rd).... I have passed your letter on to Vivien to read—she thinks one of hers to you written about Oct. 1 must have been lost—she also wrote two or three days after Bill went to her, and has been writing more frequently the past few weeks—she rather suspects Bill was not including in his letters a lot of things which mothers like to hear, so thought she'd better undertake some of that! I think Bill is quite happy there and I don't know any place that would be better for him. They are very sane people and very understanding and above all have a "live and let live" attitude to everyone and everything and would never dream of trying to alter any of Bill's ideas or interests to theirs. (They may get a little quiet amusement "on the side" out of some of the things that Bill takes so seriously but Bill will never know it.) By the way, I wouldn't take too seriously any pronouncements on things Canadian which Bill may make to you. He is a bit inclined to form firm opinions based on limited experience and superficial observations—which is quite to be expected at his age. He is so amazingly intelligent that it is hard to believe he is only 13 and naturally can't be expected to grasp quickly underlying principles of cause and effect which give rise over long periods of time to differences in habits customs and points of view. You don't need to worry about sports. They are not compulsory at U.T.S.—in fact not even "pushed" and the Ratcliffes saw at once that Bill wasn't interested in games and would not think of even suggesting that he play them. He is anxious to skate and they will see that he has every opportunity. Meantime Vivien feels he is getting the necessary exercise in his long walks tracking streetcars to their lairs—he knows a great deal more about our transportation system than we do! We are all very proud of Bill and so are the Ratcliffes. He is fitting in well and is looking simply blooming and has visibly grown a lot![31]

Christopher and Tom likewise are blooming. C's finger nail finally came off last evening and revealed the new one growing in. I have kept a white cotton glove finger over it continually and will do so a while longer. They have not lost a day of school except the two or three days of Tom's bad eyes. They all four went to Clare's for the day on Saturday. C. and Peter in their tremendous zeal to earn money tackled a trench she wanted dug across the back of the garden and got her quite worried with the tireless energy they put into it. However they seem none the worse for it and are gloating over their earnings. Tom and Mary of course had to be provided with remunerative labour too so they dug around the garden and were suitably rewarded.

Tom has been tackling an oral composition with very commendable industry and great intelligence, the past week. It is now ready for triumphal (I hope) delivery to-morrow. He decided to speak on the history of sailing ships as Peter has a most attractive book on the subject, well illustrated. I was awfully pleased at how willingly C. offered to help him—he traced off the pictures of the ships they selected as typical of various stages of development. (Peter the "old stager" has tipped them off to the old St. Paul's custom of having plenty of illustrations for an oral composition, so that the passing of them out to the audience consumes a good part of the 10 minutes required.)

C. has just finished a map of the Medit. showing the missionary journeys of St. Paul—in the back of a Bible and so minute that even with a reading glass they dazzle you so I found him a couple of good books on the subject at the library. Peter has just completed a model of the "Craven Heifer" as his project on life in the early days of Toronto.[32] After a diligent study of the subject he decided that the outstanding feature of life in early Toronto (York at that time) was its taverns (I dare say he's right) so he made the model from an illustration in a book, out of a soap flake carton and it's a really creditable piece of work when finished and painted. So you see our house is a hive of industry—and my own education is benefiting enormously! Mary has been letting herself go on writing poetry (?), drawing Christmas cards (and caricatures of the other children), knitting, practicing the piano, and, out of desire not to be left out of the "home work," writing out her spelling lessons for the next three weeks. She is also ransacking all the old magazines for pictures of "helpers" (firemen, policemen, postmen etc.) and now has her assortment complete except for a plumber—apparently he's the "forgotten man" of the advertisements. It's getting serious now as if she's among the first 6 to get her "helpers' book" complete she gets a much coveted "star." Sometimes modern education seems to be planned to ensure that mothers won't be idle! However it's all most interesting.

The Christmas lists you sent the boys were most helpful. A good many they had already sent cards to, and they got them off yesterday to all the others on the lists—in England. I do hope none of the Christmas parcels they sent are lost. None of your letters seem to have been lost except those I mentioned in my last letter—about three weeks ago there was a gap between Oct. 10 and Oct. 28.

We have had mild weather up to now with a cold day here and there but last night was quite cold and there is a sprinkling of snow this morning. I think the boys are quite warm—I got them both toques, which all the boys here wear. They are of wool, knit, like this— ⌂
just like a section of stocking but shaped to the top of the head, with a little tassel on top. They cover their ears and are very cosy. I have got them wool gloves and Clare is knitting all four another pair and another friend is knitting them each mitts. I have got them cow hide or muleskin mitts too which is what the boys wear for playing in winter. I had a warm plaid windbreaker which Peter has outgrown so Tom is wearing it to school as his own is rather light. A friend has sent me two beautiful overcoats

which look like new (outgrown) and Peter has outgrown one, so if the winter turns out severe and C's and T's not heavy enough, we should be well provided for.

I will not write more now but will try to write your mother in a few days. I think perhaps it's safer to write at short intervals—I hate to have a long effort sunk! About the skates—I'm glad you didn't send them as we can easily fix them up.

I am sending a few copies of Saturday Night—our best weekly, just thought they might interest you.

[13]   118 HILLSDALE AVENUE WEST
       TORONTO, DECEMBER 15

Dear Margaret

Just a note and I'll try to write more fully next time. About the clothing—I understood from the customs that any amount of clothing could be sent, but the boys certainly don't need any—they brought such quantities! The only things they lacked were things that they need here but don't in England, so you couldn't get them. Shoes of course they outgrow faster than clothes but I think they have to be bought on the spot. When they need shirts and underwear perhaps you could send them as you can't get such beautiful wool and flannel here except at very fancy prices, but I'm sure they have enough to do for years! The only other thing that it might be possible to send would be the heavy knee-high socks, but those they have will certainly not need to be replaced before next autumn at the very earliest....

John took them all to the Golf Club yesterday afternoon with their sleds and toboggan and skis. Tom and C. both tried Mary's skis—her ski harness is one that will go over overshoes while Peter's is meant for ski boots with grooved heels. They were both much intrigued and to-day when John and Leslie took them out again (Theresa and Leslie were here for the day) and Mary had to stay at home as she has a slight cold, they took her skis and had turns at them.

I am enclosing a Christmas card which I have a guilty feeling I should have sent weeks ago. I know Mary made it expressly for "Tom's mother" and why it wasn't sent when Peter's was I don't know unless she changed her mind and had me send a different one. Anyway I ran across this one to-day so I am sending it just in case.

Bill came down to-day and went to Church with us. The boys got out the first issue of their paper yesterday—they have made Tom circulation manager which means he's to sell the copies for whatever he can get, on a commission![33]

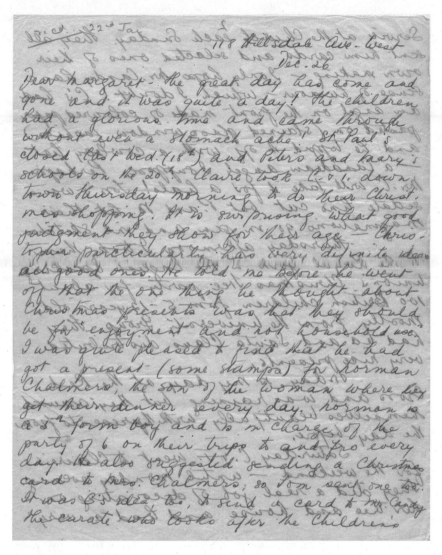

Christmas 1940: "The great day has come and gone"

---

[14] 118 HILLSDALE AVENUE WEST
TORONTO, DECEMBER 26

Dear Margaret

The great day has come and gone and it was quite a day! The children had a glorious time and came through without even a stomach ache! St. Paul's closed last Wed. (18th) and Peter's and Mary's schools on the 20th. Clare took C. & T. down town Thursday morning to do their Christmas shopping. It is surprising what good judgment they show for their age—Christopher particularly has very definite ideas all good ones. He told me before he went off that the one thing he thought about Christmas presents was that they should be for "enjoyment and not household use." I was quite pleased to find that he has got a present (some stamps) for Norman Chalmers, the son of the woman where they get their dinner every day. Norman is a 5th form boy and is in charge of the party of 6 on their trips to and fro every day. He also suggested sending a Christmas card to Mrs. Chalmers, so Tom sent one too. It was C's idea, too, to send a card to Mr. Candy the curate who looks after the Children's Service at the Church each Sunday. They all sent him cards and selected ones of their own making—I only hope Mr. Candy has a sense of humour—which I doubt! C's had an angel on the front made of coloured paper pasted on (stained glass window fashion) and he topped it off with a cowboy hat—a Canadian angel I suppose. Perhaps Mr. C. will take it for a halo! Tom's was a sedate lino cut but P. and M. let their imaginations go in pen and ink sketches.

Thursday afternoon I took them to the Royal York to the English Speaking Union's Christmas Tree party for about 100 British children from 5–12 years old, mostly from the University group. They had teas and Santa Claus distributed very nice presents.

To-day is my day at the Red Cross and was raining but they amused themselves beautifully with the presents from the day before.[34]

Saturday C. & T. went to Clare's for the weekend—until Monday evening. They did a real job of decoration on her tree and house and had a very good time though the weather was bad. John went up to his sister's in Burlington for the weekend and took Peter with him so Mary and I got our Christmas preparations done. We decorated the downstairs with hemlock and pine (holly is very scarce this year as imports from U.S. are forbidden) and Sunday night when John came home he set up the tree. The children decorated it and it is very pretty—at the end of the living room. John thought he might be able to take a picture of the children in front of it but it has been too dark and rainy.

They all hung their stockings at the fireplace in the living room—the 3 boys optimistically hung their hockey stockings which come up well above the thigh and are wide in proportion! However, they were filled to the top—I had got small books, toys, games, notebooks, scratch pads, balloons, pencils, paint brushes, dominoes, cards, balls and odds and ends and a big soap Scottie looking over the top of each. I had got sleds for C. & T. but the last time they were out at the Golf Club they tried Mary's skis and were so enthusiastic that I thought sleds might be an anti climax. So I got skis and harness for C. and had quite a time deciding what to do about Tom. Two years ago we got Peter skis with "beginner's harness" made of leather which can be worn with overshoes (so you don't need special ski boots) and holds the foot only loosely on the skis so in case of falls it's easier on the ankles. He did very well so last year we got him new ones, 6" longer, with the real harness and passed his on to Mary. She used them last winter and got on well so we had promised that she should have the real harness and ski boots this winter. I intended to have the new harness put on the same skis but found that to put on the leather "beginner's harness" they had had to put a slot through the skis which would weaken them for screwing on the other harness.

I had intended to get new skis for Tom and have the leather harness put on them but after going over all the complications I finally got new skis for Mary with the real harness and gave Tom a sled and am turning over the old skis with leather harness to Tom. I worried over it a good deal—I did not want him to feel like a step child but it did seem the only sensible way because I think the leather harness is the only safe kind for him to start on and if I had it on new skis it would mean the same bother next year as with Mary's this year. He didn't seem disappointed—I told him that if he got on all right I would see that Santa Claus got him new ones next year. Mother gave both C. & T. ski poles so I think that quite set him up! Christopher had told me that he asked Santa Claus at Eatons for skis—Tom said he asked for "games and things." If the weather stays as it is there won't be any skiing anyway. It was nearly 60° on Christmas—the snow is nearly all gone, just dirty ice, and to-day has been raining and misty. What weather for the holidays! I don't imagine Tom will ski much anyway, but C. is quite keen and I wanted him to have the same sort of equipment as Peter. I hope you're not frightened when I talk of skis—Bill's idea of skiing seemed to be the movie news reel type—enormous mountain sides with jumps! They start very modestly here—on the level, with little gentle 3 foot undulations—that's about as much as I have achieved myself! Peter has got on well and can do some decent hills—say 50 feet high—he could probably do higher ones if I let him! Neither C. nor P. seem inclined to take any risks so I don't think they'll attempt any more than the possible, and one or both of us is always there to watch.

· I must go back and explain about Santa Claus. Mary's faith was waning last year but for some reason she came out strong for Santa Claus when Christmas was in the offing. Tom with his insistence on accuracy tried to put her straight, but C. and Peter just for devilment sided with Mary and insisted that of course there was a Santa Claus. After many arguments and threats from the others to tell Santa Claus of his disloyalty, poor Tom began to doubt his own common sense and finally consented to believe "a bit," and since then they have all cheerfully talked of Santa Claus—it really sounds a little silly!—and what they're going to ask him for next year—Mary's going to ask for snow! Of course Peter is wise enough—he's never renounced Santa Claus because he figures it would be unprofitable—when you can get presents from parents <u>and</u> Santa Claus, why throw some of them away?

I got them all books and various other things and tried to give all four an equal amount. Quite a few of my friends and nearly all my relations sent presents for the boys (some lovely ones)—every one here is anxious that the British children should have a happy Christmas. Ruby McKay, Irene Peterkin, Theresa & Leslie and some others gave them money, so C. will be able to buy his own skates (when there is ice) and Tom fortunately can wear the ones Peter had last year so he won't need to buy new ones.[35] I was quite willing and ready to buy them skates but they so often mentioned saving for them and I think often children think more of the things they buy themselves. Peter got money for Christmas too so he can buy his own new ones.

We let them up at 7.30 on Christmas. They came down and went through their stockings, had breakfast and then attacked the main objective, under the Christmas tree. Bill arrived about 10 and John took them all to Church. I was <u>rather</u> busy as I had let Mary Murphy go home for two days—she is one of a family of 12 and Christmas is the only time they all get home and she counts on it very much. And nowadays one does have to treat maids <u>very very</u> well or else! Anyway I felt I wanted her to go—her favourite brother, 4 years old, has had both legs cut off recently and I would have been filled with remorse, which would be worse than doing the work myself! The woman who comes in the mornings of course didn't come on Christmas so I was all alone but I think everyone had a good time. Ruby McKay came down and had dinner with us, at 1 o'clock. Bill went back to the Ratcliffes' by 4, for their present-opening and dinner, and the rest of us went down to mother's for an hour. When we came back the children all had a boiled egg and ice-cream and the little ones tumbled into bed. C. & P. spent an hour in the cellar play room assembling a wooden gun out of a kit someone had given C. All the parts come in a box so that with a certain amount of cutting on the soft wood, and glueing, etc. a model can be made. They brought it up triumphantly and went off to bed. Peter is now trying to make a set of hanging shelves to display their models—he has made a ship and has another ship started. By the way, I found three walnut shells, each fitted with 3 square sails (tooth pick masts) on the basin's edge to-night. They were very sweet—C. & P. had made and sailed them (they were Columbus's fleet).

John took C. & P. to the movies to-night to see "North West Mounted Police"—they'll probably be firing guns in their sleep! We had dinner early so they could get to the first showing and got home before 9.30.

I am going to take them all to the dentist during the holidays, and have their teeth looked over. He thought C. would have a cavity by Christmas.

DECEMBER 27

The English mail has been rather disappointing. A tremendous mail arrived in Halifax the 23rd or 24th which they hoped to distribute by Christmas but it is coming in slowly. Your parcel to Mary arrived Christmas afternoon and your letter to me (Dec. 2) and your mother's cards to Peter and Mary came this morning. Thank you so much for the subscription to Punch. We used to take it years ago but the past few years we have not often seen it and we always enjoy it very much....

1941

**"This war guest situation is something
entirely unheard of before"[1]**

[1]   118 HILLSDALE AVENUE WEST
      TORONTO, JANUARY 10

Dear Margaret

This is my first letter since Dec. 28 or 29—spare time has been at a premium. I think I shall start (with this letter) numbering our letters to you, whether from me or the boys, and I will keep a record of the dates when the letters bearing each new number are posted. It will simplify discovery of whether any are lost. I will put the number at the top of the letter with the date and also on the back of the envelope—now let's hope I don't forget!...

The holidays were simply horrible—rain and slush and dirt, most of the time. I took all 4 of them to the Museum one afternoon to see a very good film "Dark Rapture" of an expedition into the Belgian Congo and other parts of Africa, and they spent the rest of the afternoon looking at the exhibits. I let Peter and Christopher go one day to see "The Thief of Baghdad" too. One evening from 7–8 I took them to a friend's house to play with her new puppy and have ginger ale and cookies. We had some walks to the library for books and various other mild forays for the disguised purpose of getting fresh air and exercise. On New Year's Eve John took them all to the Golf Club thinking they could have a walk but the discovery of a stretch of icy snow (somehow overlooked by the thaw) in a valley sent them into such enthusiasms that he drove them home to collect their skis and they went back for an hour's skiing. It was their first venture (except for a slight venture on Mary's skis when they went sleigh riding) and they were most enthusiastic. On the Saturday (Jan 4) there was another very light snowfall so Sunday afternoon we went skiing. The boys do very well on their skis—it

71

Christopher, William Paterson (the boy next door), Tom, Mary, and Peter on the skating rink near Clare's house

was good snow for beginners—just covering the ground with the grass sticking up through so it was slow going and their skis didn't run away with them. C. went off across country a bit with Peter but Tom, Mary and I stayed together, on some gentle slopes and Tom got on very well. He had only one or two tumbles and he never stopped talking from start to finish of the afternoon he was so excited. There was a little more snow yesterday so I hope we shall get out again this weekend. The weather has hovered just above freezing by day and under freezing by night for several days but to-day is down under 30°. I would be glad if it would stay about there.

Peter and Mary went back to school on Jan. 6 so Clare took T. & C. to stay with her for the two days (6th and 7th) until their school opened on the 8th. They took their skates with them still unused, and she discovered quite a good pond in a farmer's orchard near her. They apparently spent most of their two days on it and got a good start with their skating. Wednesday afternoon they got out of school early so I took all 4 of them to the pond for an hour or two.

JANUARY 14

It seems a struggle to get this letter finished. We had more snow on Friday night (10th) so Sat. and Sun. afternoons I took the children skiing for about 2½ hrs. each day. They all had a beautiful time and the boys are doing very well. It was not cold—just under freezing—in fact Saturday, when the sun was shining, we all got quite hot. John came with us Sunday and took a few pictures. I hope they will be some good, but Christopher will look a little

JUST A LARGER FAMILY

queer as the zipper on his windbreaker broke just as we were starting out so I had him put on two sweaters and a belt around the windbreaker to keep it slightly in place, though open down the front. It gives a very jaunty bolero effect. I am getting a new zipper on it but was rather at a loss as to what he should wear to school meantime. However I have had him wear Peter's ski jacket so he is all right. Peter wears an overcoat to school and keeps a heavy turtle-neck sweater there for hockey. They have the rink in use at St. Paul's. The boys skated last week and started their hockey league games this week. Tom played yesterday—I must go up some day and watch. I'm sure it's fun.

This has been one of our jumpy winters with the thermometer doing leaps and drops like an elevator. Yesterday got very cold and this morning it is down to zero. Tom looked absolutely stuffed starting out to school. He wears a windbreaker which was Peter's, and I had him put his overcoat on top—I don't know that he really needed it but I do want him warm. The taxi calls right at the door for them but they are usually out waiting for it for 5 or 10 min. C. keeps active, chopping ice or doing something but Tom just stands, which is a cold business. They have to have their windbreakers as well as the overcoats, for their skating at school as they can't very well skate in overcoats.

Norman Chalmers, where the boys have been going for their dinner, took whooping cough at the beginning of the holidays, so his mother of course let me know before school re-opened. As the boys have had wh. cough I thought it would be all right for them to go particularly as he is in bed and they would not even see him but I asked my doctor and he advised me not to take any chance whatever, especially as Peter & M. have not had it. So I have let them go to a restaurant close to the school where several of the boys go (I think they enjoyed it) and I sometimes bring them home in the car for dinner and take them back.[2] I think by next week I can surely let them go back to Mrs. C's.

Tom is getting better all the time about his food—he eats spinach like a lamb—also spaghetti (if it hasn't cheese) and stewed tomatoes. Salads are the only things he seems to have to work at. I gave him a little booklet to read "What to eat to be healthy" and he was fascinated with lists of various kinds of foods and what they contained and what they did for you. I don't know whether he will translate it into practical action or not! Raw fruit and vegetable are really the only necessary things that he balks at. My children love celery and raw carrot cut in strips and I always have them on the supper table but T. & C. won't eat them voluntarily. I am starting to put a dish of sliced raw apple on as well and I think surely Tom will grow to like that.

I seem to get my letters so full of physical information I don't have room for anything else!—but I do want to keep them well—as they have been so far. They seem very happy and take to new activities enthusiastically. When we were skiing on Sunday Tom began going off to the side every time he went down the little slope. I suggested to him that perhaps he was not getting his skis quite straight when he started and he said "Yes, I think that's it—you see I feel very lively to-day and I think I'm so lively that I start off too quickly at the top before I have my skis quite in the right position."

John took their reports to the office during the holidays and had them photographed and I posted copies to you the other day. Tom said very cheerfully when he brought his home that it was "completely rotten" but I think the reason he dropped a bit in December was that he had been moved into the higher form. He never complains of easy work anymore. I got him to do some reading in the holidays to help him with his Social Studies work. Neither of them is very fond of reading but both are getting to like it better and will now start in without it being suggested. C. has got some interesting books—for Christmas and from the library—and seems to quite enjoy them. Now that they have started hockey they will play their games in the early afternoon (as during the football season) with school from 2.30 or 3 to 4 or 4.30 so they don't get home until 5. Peter & C. are getting out the January issue of their newspaper, the "Monthly War Drum"—news is conspicuously absent from its pages which are jokes and comics!

Peter gets a report only once a term and his Christmas one gave him quite a set-back—in spelling, which has always been a good subject and an easy one—he only got 60%! His teacher put a very pointed note on the report on the advantages of careful daily preparation—which Peter has always scorned. I think it has given him quite a shock and will do him good—he gets at his homework now without urging and it is a help to C. when Peter does his homework too. They get it done right after their supper and then have some time for their various enterprises. They cleared one shelf in the study bookcase for a display of their craft work—two ship models of P's and two gun models of C's, Columbus's fleet, made of walnut shells, some animals of plasticine, relief maps, etc., all labelled carefully.

Bill has not been down for 10 days or so—he is so busy with his skating which he apparently is enjoying intensely. You have of course heard how well he has done at school. We are all very pleased—he should have a good chance of winning a scholarship which would indeed be a triumph. He is very happy and looks so well![3]

I am enclosing the boys' Sunday letters. C's disappeared after he wrote it and I did not find it until this morning—in the waste basket! It would be a pity to lose what takes so much effort to achieve! They seem to find letter writing a great chore—I have not got them to write to their father yet but must insist on it to-night. The Sunday after Christmas when I suggested they write to you, Tom said, as always "What can I tell her about?" "Oh Tom," I said "surely you can think of something to say this week, just after Christmas. What do you think she would like to hear?" "Well" he said "I suppose I can tell her what presents I got." "Yes" I said "and what kind of a day you had on Christmas." "Oh yes" he said "but I can't remember—did it rain on Christmas?"—literal-minded Tom!—we did laugh!

They both have oral compositions in the offing. Tom chose his subject long ago—the Universe—no less! However he has now decided to confine it to the Solar System!

I notice you asked me for Clare's address—I rather think I put it in my last letter but this is it any way

Mrs. G.L. Jennings, 82 Park Lane, Glengrove P.O., Ontario.

Also your mother asked for Mary's birthday—it is June 14 so she and Tom will have to celebrate together.

John and I went to Clare's for dinner Saturday evening—it was the first time all of us (3 sisters and one brother) with our husbands and wives (I should say "wife") had been together and all 8 of us had a jolly time.[4] It was also the first time John and I have gone out to dinner since we have had 4 children (except once when Clare & George came over and saw them to bed) but Mary Murphy assured me they got on beautifully.

I had a letter from Mrs. Beamish[5]—she sent Tom a lovely set of Meccano for Christmas, which arrived in duplicate, so scenting an error I wrote her about it. As I thought Eatons' had made a mistake (as they so often do). She has apparently had the flu but I hope has had no further setbacks and will be able to settle into life in Canada comfortably. She said she would like to have Tom for a visit in the summer if they are able to get a place with a little more room. I would like him to go for a little while—I do hope the boys will be able to see more of Canada than just Toronto and its environs while they are here. I do wish we could afford to take them all right across to the Pacific!

I hope things are still peaceful in Ulverston at least.[6] One can't help believing that a storm of some kind is about to break soon.

[2]   118 HILLSDALE AVENUE WEST
       TORONTO, JANUARY 19

Dear Margaret

The thermometer has taken another dip—it was cold last Monday—nearly zero, then it melted for 4 days and is now freezing again—about 15°. It's a very unsatisfactory method of conducting a winter but it seems to be the way it's done the last few years. John took the boys skiing this afternoon. Yesterday it poured rain all day so we took them all (Bill was here for the day) to the Museum and left them there for an hour or two.

C. has been doing quite a bit of reading lately—is now on the book which his father sent for Christmas and apparently finds it absorbing. He was telling me parts of it while he dried the dishes for me to-night. Tom has another oral composition which he's beginning to worry about already (Feb. 23)—I hope it won't bother him as much as the last. He is taking the Solar System and I have got him a few books to consult. C. has one on Tuesday but he is not worrying. He is going to speak on Ulverston so no one can correct him! and he assures me he doesn't need to prepare anything.

We have had a very great shock in the family this past week. Leslie, who had resigned from the Imperial Oil so he could have a much needed rest, decided he had rested enough and went to apply for an engineer's post in the Navy. In the course of his medical exam they were disappointed with his chest X-ray and a check-up with another physician showed he has an active T.B.—apparently has had it for years but has such good recuperative powers that every time it's become active it's healed again without his even knowing it. He has no cough, no temperature, no symptoms at all. He went to the hospital last night for a day or two, for careful examination and will then go to the sanatorium at Hamilton for treatment. It is a terrific blow for Theresa, and for all of us, but everything points towards his being quite recovered inside a year. Theresa herself will have to be carefully watched for several years but it is rather unlikely that she would be infected when he has had no cough—however one cannot be too careful.

It is rather a calamity financially, too, as of course Leslie's income will stop, while expenses will increase and they will have to fall back on their small capital (Leslie is also the partial support of his mother, in Australia). Theresa is rather worried because they will not be able to continue paying the boys' school fees after the end of the present term (ends at Easter). I have assured her that that need be the least of her worries. I have appreciated their being at St. Paul's with all the extra attention and help, and the sports which they haven't room for in our little garden but they both seem to be keeping up pretty well with their work and I don't see that it need be a great disappointment to anyone (except St. Paul's) if we put them in the Public School (where Mary goes) after Easter. We had intended them to go there next year anyway and it will be a short term, in good weather and they should get nicely acclimated before the holidays. They have 11 English children at that school (Oriole Park) now and have made them very happy.

This is all 3 months off yet of course and I do not intend to mention it to the boys until just at the time. There is no use giving them a long time in which to worry about a new school. If it comes suddenly it may appear more like an adventure.

I have not much time to write now—this has been a very busy weekend (and a busy week too). The boys have not heard from you for two weeks at least—I think the last time 2 letters arrived together, one written about Dec. 14 and one about Dec. 20—one of them was from Carlisle. I suppose another bunch will come together.

I am going to enclose 2 tea bags—a lot of my friends always do in letters to England if the letters not full weight. Each one makes 2 cups. We use them all the time—they simplify the steeping and the washing of the tea pot!

The boys are still in good health and Bill looks wonderful.

[3]   118 HILLSDALE AVENUE WEST
TORONTO, JANUARY 25

Dear Margaret

We had a surprise visit from Mrs. Beamish yesterday, to our great delight. She is simply charming and I was so glad she was able to be here even for a short time and see the boys. I am sure she will be writing you immediately and I know how much it will mean to hear about them from someone who has known them before.[7] She telephoned yesterday morning when I was at the Red Cross but luckily I came home early and she was able to get me just in time for me to go to lunch with her at the hotel, where I arranged to have her come up later in the afternoon when the boys were home from school, and stay for dinner. Fortunately Bill happened to come in on his way home from school, so he did his homework here and stayed for dinner with her. She seems such a sincere, sound, and warmhearted person, I am sure she would make a wonderful friend. I could see how fond she is of Tom—and so interested in them all. She is very anxious to have Tom visit her in the summer if it can be arranged and I know he would enjoy it....

I don't know whether I ever mentioned that Tom had a letter in December from Miss Kenyon,[8] enclosing notes and cards from some of the boys and asking him to write a letter which she could read to the class. I got him to start the letter in the holidays and he has written two installments since—he finds it tedious to write much at a time, but he wants to write a full account. So if you should see Miss Kenyon you can tell her the letter is under way.

Things seem to be going quite smoothly at school so far as I hear.... The boys have been playing hockey with great gusto! I thought Tom might not care for it—it's pretty strenuous with lots of bumps, but he loves it. We had not seen them skate since their first start but they brought their skates home last night and John took all four of them skating this afternoon. He says they are getting on well—C. goes over on his ankles in spite of his supports—John thinks his boots are a little loose so Monday morning I will get good thick insoles for him and have them ready for his hockey after lunch....

Bill seems fairly bursting with health and happiness. He is exactly the same height I am now—we measured yesterday. He is so keen about hockey—not only watching, but playing. I'm afraid Tom is becoming very Americanized—he was talking about games the other day and said "I wonder what cricket will be like. I'm rotten at it. I don't like it much either, if you're not batting or bowling you just have to stand—it's very dull!"

I am so thankful that the boys are well it seems a miracle for four children to go this far through the winter without illness. I had Mary home most of this week but there was very little wrong. She had no cold, no temp., was feeling tip-top, but had a hearty cough about once a day and I thought she might be working up to whooping cough. But nothing developed so I sent her back to school. We do try to take good care of them—lots of vitamins in their food, lots of milk and I always have them change any damp clothes as soon as they come in. We watch their bedrooms too and when we go to bed we always go in and pull up their extra cover and adjust the window and the radiator according to the temp. and the way the wind blows, so they'll be comfortable and their room not too cold to dress in the morning. We have just got two electric humidifiers, one downstairs and one up—one trouble with our warm houses is that they're so dry. These things moisten the air—we put in about 8 or 9 gals of water a day between them—and they do make breathing more comfortable.

The first copy of Punch arrived yesterday—we are going to enjoy having it very much.

P.S. I forgot to tell you I had a nice letter from Mrs. Burns.[9] They sent the boys each $2 at Christmas and I wrote her when the boys wrote their thanks, in order to explain who I was. I gather from her letter that she and her husband are English—she apparently expects that the boys have told me about them, but the boys are in complete ignorance except that Dr. Burns is C's godfather, which they seem to think a very shrewd piece of business on C's part. I thought Bill might know, but he is equally vague, except that he says "his parents stayed with the Burns's every time they came to America" which has a very impressive sound but I can't help feeling is slightly misleading! Perhaps he means his grandparents? Anyway it really doesn't matter much. They are in Washington directing research work, he for the 20th Century Fund of N.Y. and she for a Gov't. Dept. They have a year's leave from Columbia. She gave me as a safe address c/o Central Hanover Bank and Trust Co. Lexington Ave. at 43rd St. New York City ...

Tom has just discovered there is to be a census of Canada taken this year and feels quite important at the idea of being included.

[4]   118 HILLSDALE AVENUE WEST
      TORONTO, JANUARY 29

Dear Margaret

The English posts get wilder and wilder. On Jan. 27 the boys had two letters from you, one written Dec. 16 from Manchester and one Jan. 1 from Ulverston, one to each from your mother dated Jan. 2, one each from their other grandmother dated Jan. 8, a card and letter to each from Elsie dated Dec. 10[10]—oh yes! another from you written on the train from Manchester to Preston on Dec. 22—also cards from John Gerrard[11] and diaries from Mrs. Redford[12] and a letter to C. from his father written Jan. 12, and one from you to me from the school written Jan. 12. So unscramble that if you can! However I think it's simply amazing that they all got here at all! I don't think anything coming this way has been lost (that is, addressed to us). A large parcel has just arrived for the boys from the Army & Navy stores, apparently from your mother. There will be great excitement!

We were tremendously interested in your new appointment and I can well imagine with what sinkings of the heart you were waiting for term to begin.[13] But I am sure you will be a great success—you are certainly accustomed to a crowd of boys and I am sure you get on well with them and that must be half the battle in teaching. Then I'm sure also that you know the work well so it will just be a matter of becoming accustomed to the teaching routine. At any rate it must be a relief to feel you have an absorbing job on hand which will take all your time, energy and thought. I can understand how lost you must feel without the boys and I'm sure there are depressed moments when you wonder why you ever let them go. I can imagine you will be glad to have your mind completely occupied with new work and experiences.

The parcel from your mother to the boys has been a most tremendous success. Mary has been very disgruntled because Tom would not admit her into the secrets of his conjuring tricks but poor Tom had to have someone he could mystify with them—Peter & C. were so superior about their complete knowledge of how they were all done—but none the less they were delighted to take part in them. However Tom is breaking down and I notice he let Mary do one with her dad as an audience, to-day. C. has been sharing the pastels with Peter and they have produced a set of landscapes—they'll probably want to hang them.

Tom finally got his letter to Miss Kenyon done—I am rather unhappy about it—when he started he had quite an ambitious plan, it was to cover his voyage out and last summer in the north and his school. He did it in sections when I reminded him, and, as I was afraid, after completing quite a long description of the voyage, he wearied and I had to get him to reopen the letter even to put in anything at all about his present life, and then it was only a few words. And I'm sure that is what Miss K. and the boys would like to hear about! However I don't like to interfere any more than I've already done but I am trying to find some post cards or greeting cards with decent Canadian scenes on them that I can get for him to send to the boys who wrote or sent him cards at Christmas. They are hard to find but I believe there are some published.

The boys had letters to-day from their Auntie Phyl[14] with bits of anti-aircraft shell and bomb fragments which excited them all very much....

John is taking the children to the Golf Club this afternoon. The skiing was not good yesterday—the snow has got a little soft—so they are going to sleigh-ride, but they are taking their skis to wear for a little while while Ruby McKay takes moving pictures of them. She makes a hobby of moving pictures and has very good films of various countries. It's rather nice and bright to-day so she wants to get some snow pictures.

Theresa's husband is still in the hospital waiting until they can take him into the sanatorium at Hamilton. It is two weeks now and they think it will be another week before they have a vacancy. I wish he could get into the San. right away—it would be less trying than this hanging in suspension as it were—also a lot less expensive. Theresa goes to the hospital every day after lunch and stays until about 9 P.M. and it is pretty tiring for her. We don't have nursing homes here, you know—each hospital has a huge building of private rooms, as well as their blocks of public and semipublic wards. Leslie has a nice room on the 8th floor of a new building—it faces south and he can see all the planes of "Little Norway"—our Norwegian "village" on the waterfront where the Norwegian Air Force is doing their training, having been given our city airport for the duration.

"Punch" is arriving regularly and we are enjoying it. Did I tell you how amused we were at Bill?—when I told him you were going to send Punch, he said "Oh good! that will be two magazines for me to read when I come down here" (He always reads "Life" here as Vivien doesn't take it.) I said I always enjoyed Punch, that there were always some good things in it and Bill said "Of course, there's one page you won't understand—that's the political one. You have to be familiar with the English political situation to understand that!"

The boys have written to your mother and I will enclose a note with theirs. She must miss you very much but I am sure she makes the best of it as she does everything, and I suppose she is happier in Ulverston—and safer—than most places. Wishing you success and happiness in the new school.

[5]   118 HILLSDALE AVENUE WEST
       TORONTO, FEBRUARY 10

Dear Margaret

Your letter to the boys came Feb. 8, Saturday—written from the school (Jan. 10 I think it was just after you arrived there). There were cards enclosed from a former nurse. I do hope you are finding the school and the work pleasant.

We are all thriving, life goes along smoothly. John and I drove Leslie and Theresa to the sanatorium at Hamilton on Saturday afternoon and left him there. It is an enormous place, pavilions and pavilions on the brow of the mountain (what we call the "mountains"—it is the Niagara escarpment which carries all the way around the side of Lake Ontario). It was a stormy day, with a howling wind blowing snow about so the landscape was bleak but is beautiful in good weather. The San. itself seems a very nice place with excellent equipment. He is quite resigned to life there, whatever it proves to be like and I think will make a quick recovery. Clare had the children up there for the afternoon and they had a marvellous time building a snow fort.[15]

Sunday Vivien had asked the three boys up for tea to celebrate Bill's birthday so I had thought we would just occupy the early afternoon with a drive down to the lake front—Tom had remarked that he hadn't seen the lake with ice on it. However, Clare thought the snow fort was such a good effort that we wanted to take some snaps of them with it, so we came back

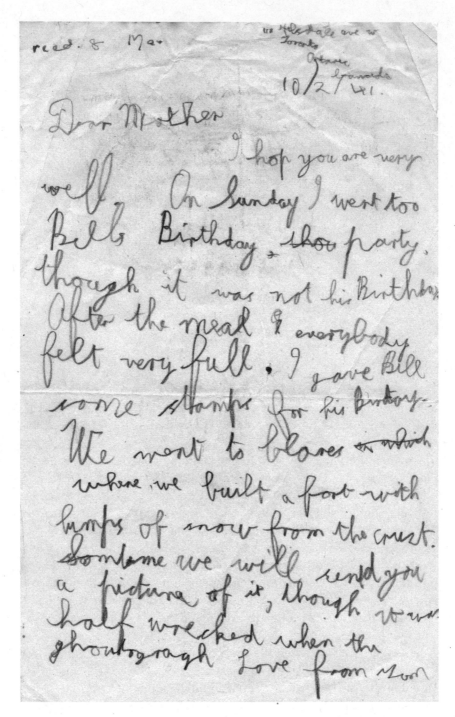

recd. 8 Mar.

113 Hillsdale ave w
Toronto
Ontario
Canada
10/2/41.

Dear Mother

I hop you are very well. On Sunday I went too Bill's Birthday ~~show~~ party, though it was not his Birthday. After the meal & everybody felt very full. I gave Bill some stamps ~~for his birthday~~.

We went to Clare's ~~in which~~ where we built a fort with lumps of snow from the crust. ~~Somtime~~ Some we will send you a picture of it, though ~~it was~~ half wrecked when the ghoutogragh Love from Tom

Tom's letter to his mother about Bill's birthday and the snow fort at Clare's

Christopher, Peter, Tom, and Mary on the remains of their snow fort

from Church, had dinner, got their clothes changed and John took them up for an hour, got the pictures, they demolished the fort (as much fun as building it) came back, got dressed again and went to Bill's. So they had a busy day. Then John took Mary and the little boy next door skating and brought him back for tea with Mary so everyone was happy.[16]

Vivien told me an amusing story of Tom at tea last night. She gave them ginger ale and grape juice mixed, to drink, but asked if anyone would prefer milk and after Tom had emptied his glass she asked him if he would like more and he accepted. Bill, looking as though he didn't believe his ears said "Remember Tom, this is the first time you've had that drink, are you sure you want more?" and Tom with great dignity said simply "I've changed, Bill." He has, indeed—he eats practically everything now, without a word—even mixed salads of shredded cabbage, lettuce, raw carrots etc., and takes great pride in his "change." I try not to give him quite as big helpings of vegetables as the others and to alternate things which he has schooled himself to eat with things he really likes. He is getting much more self reliant too about the small details of life—hangs up and folds his clothes—if he finds his pyjamas have been removed to the wash, gets out clean ones from his drawer and can change his things himself, when he comes in from the snow, getting out dry ones. In the morning he, C. and Peter get up as soon as they're called—(John goes in and turns on their light and shuts the windows)—dress, make their beds, wash and come down to breakfast, go to the toilet and get ready for school with out any promptings (except, like all boys, they once in a while need a reminder not to forget to wash!). Peter has to leave for school right after breakfast but the others have time to read the paper but they watch the clock themselves and get their things on when it's time and are always ready outside before Mr. Hass calls for them. I think they do very well. Tom always used to ask me if I thought he should get ready but I have got him to work it out for himself. Their outdoor clothes for school and play are always hung in the furnace room in the basement—we have hangers and bars and spring clothespins suspended for toques, mitts and overstockings, so they always know where their things are and it is so warm there that wet clothes and overshoes dry over night. When they come in they go straight down and hang everything up.

They got their January reports—C's is very good—Tom took a slump in Art and a slight drop in English. We had expected to go to the school tomorrow evening to the monthly lecture but I rather think my sister-in-law is coming to town so I'm afraid we won't get there. I am sorry as I would like to inquire about Tom's report. "Art" includes writing, drawing and handicrafts so I don't know where the trouble is. Tom says if it's writing, it's all right because he has discovered a new method of writing which improves his work "tremendously" but if it's handicraft he's afraid he can't do much about it! I did see Mrs. Underhill last week and had a talk with her and she seemed satisfied with their work and is awfully pleased with the way C. has adjusted—he seems so happy and contented. He apparently was more miserable the first month or so than she ever told me and certainly C. gave no inkling of it at home. After the form got out that paper we sent you (St. Paul's Bits and Pieces) they held an election for an editorial staff for the next issue. C. was elected editor in-chief. (Mrs. U. had appointed him the first time because she thought the holding of a post of importance would be good for him.) The class called "Speech!" and C. responded. Mrs. U. was so struck with the speech that she memorized it and is going to write it out for me to send you. She is very much interested in C. She showed me a map he had made of Jacques Cartier's voyages which is excellent. When he brings it home I am going to get him to send it to you. She says Tom is getting along very well, too. They play hockey on the school rink 3 or 4 times a week and enjoy it very much.

Bill has not been down for some time—he had a cold over the last weekend and is pretty busy through the week. He seems very happy and is fitting in well at the Ratcliffes. They are such a happy, harmonious family, it is a lovely place for him....

No more just now—we are thinking of you all in England these anxious days—I wish the next 3 months were over.

Dear Margaret

The boys have probably told you in their letters (enclosed) that C. has German measles! However he has not been ill or even inconvenienced by it except for having to stay in bed. It is too bad, but with four children in the house I suppose we can't expect them all to come through a whole winter unscathed as there is a real epidemic of it in Toronto—though not so much among children as young adults. It is a pity it had to be Christopher that took it—I am wondering whether he caught it at the Art Gallery, there is such a motley crowd of children there. We have never had any kind of contagious disease in the house before but apparently if we have to have one, this is the easiest to cope with. C. is quarantined for a week but there is no quarantine for the other children—they go to school as usual. On Wednesday evening I noticed he sneezed several times and next morning blew his nose vigorously and seemed just a little sniffly. So as he was getting ready for school I thought it might be well to take his temperature. As I put the thermometer in his mouth I noticed a little rash on his forehead so I put him back to bed and called the doctor. He came about noon and by that time the rash was out, red and bumpy, all over his face, and the glands behind his ears (right on the skull, not in the neck) swollen (the distinguishing feature of German measles). There is no treatment other than staying in bed so we moved his bed into the study and he has been reading, building with Tinker Toy, playing with Chinese checkers, drawing, keeping up his spelling, doing a little arithmetic and reading up on Champlain from some books I've given him. He amuses himself very well but it is rather boring, though he has the little radio beside him. The inspector from the Health Dept. called Saturday for all the information for Govt. statistics. He gave him a slip to re-admit him to school on Feb. 19, which is really 6 days, but tells me that if anyone has caught the disease from him it may take up to 21 days from the 19th to develop. However he says it's unusual for the other children in a house to take it and I hope the others won't. I have not kept the study door closed as it would make it lonely for him but the others don't go inside. There is a wash basin in the room (it was John's dressing room) so he only has to use the bathtub and toilet and I wash them with Lysol after he uses them. It's really too bad Peter didn't catch it too—he is consumed with envy over C's fortunate (?) lot—not having to go to school. The rash was very light on all his body except his face—you could scarcely see it—and that on his face subsided to just a flush after the first two days. It is all gone now—and the swollen glands too. I am going to telephone the doctor this afternoon to see when he can get up. He has a little hard cough—not frequent—he tells me he has often had worse coughs at home and gone to school—but I don't want to take any chances with him. Friday & Sat. evenings his temp. was up to 99° but yesterday it didn't go above normal even in the evening.

I have also had Mary in bed ever since last Tuesday, with a cold in the head which is not at all a bad one but doesn't seem to get any better. The doctor thinks I should have her tonsils out in the spring but I am not convinced. She has had too many colds (3) this winter for such a healthy child but they've none of them been in her throat and all been slight. So we have had quite a hospital—also Mary Murphy's mother has brought a little brother (who had his legs cut off last summer) to town to see about getting artificial legs for him so I have been trying to let her have as much time off as I can. Incidentally neither Mary M. nor Mrs. Casson (who comes in in the mornings) have had German measles so I hope none develops there!

Mrs. Chalmers (where the boys go for dinner) wanted time to consult her doctor when I asked her if she was afraid to have Tom come on Friday— her boy who had wh. cough is still at home and I knew she would not want to take the slightest chance with his health. So I gave Tom money on Friday and he went to the nearby restaurant and had, he told me, steak, potatoes, peas, milk and a jelly dessert. I think he was quite pleased with his independence. Tom simply hangs on the weather reports these days he is so afraid the snow and ice will not last. We had some very sunny days last week and the sun is so strong now that even with the therm. in the 20's a lot of melting goes on. Then we had one day of rain after which it froze again, so there was ice but no snow. To-day it is snowing so Tom will be delighted. He loves skating & skiing and hates to think of them being over. He will indeed be lost during the time of the spring "break-up"—it takes quite a while for the ice to melt and then for the resulting mud to dry up, and in that stretch there's not much to do outdoors except walk and even that not pleasant except on pavements.

John was in New York for a day last week. It seems quite an adventure to get to New York now, what with passports and finger prints and visas and no one being allowed to have American money unless you can convince the Govt. that it is absolutely essential for you to go to the U.S. However it undoubtedly is essential to conserve exchange. We are trying to use as little imported goods as possible using our own Canadian canned and quick-frozen vegetables instead of California ones, etc.

The parcel of clothing arrived the other day—the things will all be useful. Also two books came for the boys from Mrs. Tylecote.[17] Your letter from the school (Jan. 23) came Tuesday, also a letter for Tom from his father. I will send either enclosed or separately the snaps we have taken of the children. I wish my lessons in how to put on a toque had taken effect before these were taken, as they have since. It was so hard to get the boys (Peter is as bad) not to put the toque too far forward on their heads—then, if they pull it down far enough to cover their ears it almost covers their eyes as well. The trick is to set it on further back so it can be pulled over the ears but still leave the forehead uncovered. Anyway you can see they are enjoying life.

Tom brought home the oil painting he has been working on in handicraft and thinks he would like to send it to you. So I will parcel it up and post it. I think it is extremely good, especially as Tom didn't seem to have much interest in drawing. C's is finished but still at school. It would be as well to send them separately in case something is lost.

I hope the new school is working out well. It must be very hard at first—particularly with the boys ill. I am glad you find the papers of interest—I will keep on sending them....[18]

[7]   118 HILLSDALE AVENUE WEST
         TORONTO, FEBRUARY 22

Dear Margaret

All the family are now "in health" again and no more have caught the measles—as yet! Christopher was up for part of Wednesday and all of Thursday and was able to reunite with the family Thursday evening. His temp. was normal every day up to the evening when it would sometimes go to 99° and he had a cough though not frequent. However by yesterday (Friday) he scarcely coughed and had no temp. in the evening. I would have let him out a bit yesterday had it been sunny but, though not cold, it was raw and windy.

This morning I did not let him go to the Art Gallery but I did not want him out in the damp snow (Mary has been home with a cold in the head and only got back to school Thursday so I was watching her too) so as soon as I could get away in the morning I took them all out and we went to High Park (a very large natural park in the west end) and saw the big toboggan slides there (they are kept up by the city—ice tracks with snow piled at the sides and they go right down and across Grenadier Pond). They were simply entranced (Peter & Mary had never been there either) and as they were wishing they had their toboggan, a lad who was waiting for a friend to join him offered to let them go down on his. As we got them settled on with manifold instructions, Tom got a little panicky and decided not to go so the other three had a most thrilling slide. The lad who owned the toboggan felt a little sorry for Tom (he realized the boys were English) so when the others came up he took T. and C. down for a slide with him. It was a marvellous experience for them all. We drove through High Park down to the lakefront—Tom has been commenting for weeks on the fact that he has never seen the waterside in winter time. All along the boulevard there is ice, mostly broken, from the shore to the breakwater and thousands of gulls make their home there. Also every one in Toronto is interested in the hundreds of wild ducks which have spent the winter in one particular spot, a sort of bay at the end of the break water, instead of going south as most ducks do. People feed them constantly, which helps, of course, to keep them there. We drove along the shore back to the city and along the harbour front, looking at the ships bedded in ice in their slips for the winter, among them the Norwegian ships on which so many of the fliers now training in Toronto came over. We came along to where the ice boats are kept, which people use in the bay, and got out and walked down the frozen slip to the end of the docks, to see them. Tom was rather nervous and had to be assured there was no danger. I think he expected the ice (several feet thick) to crack open and swallow him at any moment. However I showed him that the DANGER signs were all placed well out beyond the ends of the docks so he did not feel afraid, just agreeably daring. This afternoon I had intended to take them to a hockey game but the military ski-jumping competition was on, not far from us so John took them there and they found it very exciting. The competitors were mostly Norwegians.

This has been rather a busy week with children in bed, and Mary Murphy was ill all day Friday and (of course it always happens) Mrs. Casson who comes in the mornings was ill Thursday and Friday. However every one seems to be recovered now. We have not seen Bill for some time—we thought it foolish for him to take any risks with the German measles. He has a cold in the head to-day but if he is well enough to be out tomorrow I am going to try to get C. & T. up to skate with him for a while. Tom has been dying to skate with Bill for some time so "he can see how Bill skates and Bill can see how he skates," but I expect Bill, older-brotherishly, has been quite content to get his information from questions and answers.

Theresa's husband has got comfortably settled in the Mountain Sanatorium at Hamilton—it is about 45 miles away. She gets over about twice a week. She does not have a car but if there is no one to drive her conveniently the bus service is very good. He has resigned himself quite cheerfully to being a good patient and I hope will not be there long.

Father has not been well for some days and now has pleurisy but it seems a light attack—just a small area. He has a marvellous constitution so I don't think it will be in the least serious.

All the rest of us are in excellent health but the grown ups are rather weary of this long winter—it started so much earlier than usual. I do hope we shall have an early spring....

[8]   118 HILLSDALE AVENUE WEST
      TORONTO, FEBRUARY 27

Dear Margaret

These are the snaps at last.... To-day the Senior and Junior Hockey teams went to play Appleby School (a boy's boarding school at Oakville, about 25 miles from Toronto) and Tom said wistfully last night that Mr. Waddington said if they could get enough cars the whole 3rd form could go along. So of course I volunteered to drive a car full. Six cars went so the 2rd form came too. It was a beautiful sunny day though cold—we have had from 7 to 18 all week—and they all enjoyed it. We left at 1.30 and got back about 6. The school grounds go down to the lake so I took C. and T. and two other English boys down to the shore to see the cliffs of ice, like a row of small ice-bergs jammed side by side all along the beach, about 20' high. They were all much impressed....

[9]   THE GENERAL BROCK, NIAGARA FALLS, ONT.
      MARCH 2

Dear Margaret

John and I have stolen off for a day's change and quiet, leaving Clare and George in charge at home. There are so few places to go for a winter week end but this is a very wee hotel—overlooking the falls—which I had never seen in winter before!

None of the other children have taken the measles so far. I hardly think they will, though there is still a week to go. Christopher was at school all week and seemed quite well except in the evenings after supper at home-work time when he seemed tired and restless and complained of headache. I did not know whether he was tired or whether he was bothered by having missed some work, or both. Friday he coughed a bit so Saturday I had him stay in bed all day to have a good rest—and also it gave him a chance to read up the history he had missed, which I found it difficult to get him to do while he was up!... He has had no temperature—I find it rather hard to read Christopher—Tom is so transparent but C. has so many depths! I try to skate over the surface as much as possible and avoid issues on anything that is not really important because he does dislike doing anything he doesn't want to! ... The doctor says his tonsils are enlarged but I imagine that has been the case for some time. We try very hard to get him to breathe through his nose—he has a habit of mouth breathing but his nose does not seem to be blocked at all—I sometimes go in when he is asleep to see, and he is always breathing through his nose then.

Tom is blooming—he has a high colour and his face is round. He gave his oral composition on the planets very successfully and gave a short talk on llamas the other day. He can't bear to think of the winter going—he simply loves it—I never expected him to like the winter but he loves the skating and skiing and the snow and doesn't seem to mind the cold a bit. And he does luxuriate like a kitten in the warmth of the house (we keep it 70°–72°) and especially the bathroom!

They all felt very badly used when they found we were going to Niagara Falls without them but we intend to bring them over when the weather is better—perhaps in the Easter holidays. We have had no letters from you for over two weeks. I hope the school post is working out but it must be very hard at the start. If you are pressed for time, I would suggest that you needn't write very long letters to the boys. They love to get your letters and open them eagerly but I have decided, from watching them, that it's the fact of getting a letter from you with a loving message that counts—not the contents of the letter. I found my own children were the same when they were at camp last year—they would have liked a letter every day but after me racking my brains for bits of news I thought would interest them, they didn't really care about that part at all. So if you are busy, as you must be, don't worry if you can just write a few lines.

We are leaving here about 4 to drive back. We may go around by Hamilton to see Leslie and will drop in at John's sister's in Burlington which is on the way. I will put the boys' letters in with this when I get home.

MARCH 3

The boys apparently had a marvellous weekend—they consider it a real picnic when I go away and Clare is in charge! Christopher seems full of beans again—I am working with him on a map to show Champlain's voyages—I do wish Champlain had confined himself to shorter trips!

Dear Margaret

I have taken the liberty of looking at the boys' letters because I thought they wrote rather longer ones than usual and some of the references might be rather obscure by originalities of spelling and writing. I think the maps are lovely and C's "missionary" work I thought very amusing. Tom and Bill were playing chess, Peter was busy and Mary professed a desire to learn so C. spent a half hour or more of concentrated patient instruction. Mary was very interested but I forgot to find out how she had progressed....

We have had lots of sun lately so though the temp. has been below freezing, there is a lot of melting every day where the sun hits and I am afraid the skating is nearly done. There has been no skiing for some weeks unless one goes quite far north. I have been wanting the boys to see some hockey of a little better calibre than what they have at school among themselves so on Saturday afternoon I took them all to Varsity Arena to see some of the Junior Toronto Hockey League games. John had to go to a funeral so we drove down to Canada Life at 1 o'clock to get him. I took them up to his office on the 11th floor and then we went up into the tower (17th floor) and climbed up the stairs to the roof of the tower where you get quite a good view of the city and across the bay. Then we went up to the Arena and John went on with the car and I brought them home in the bus.

C. went back to the Art Gallery on Saturday. He hates missing it and it seemed too bad to keep him home just on the off chance that he might catch something. (Bill thinks Canadians are very scared of germs!)

Bill came down and went to Church with us yesterday and came home with us for dinner. John has been pressed into duty as an occasional sidesman and made his first appearance yesterday—evidently impressing the children greatly. I think we make such an impressive showing with our large brood filing into a pew every Sunday that the wardens felt John ought to be recognized in some manner! That's what I say to tease him, anyway....

C's parcel of printing things arrived much to his and Peter's delight. They still work on their paper but have not yet succeeded in selling Bill a copy, so they rely on all the adult relatives who are willing to encourage juvenile industry. I think they have $1.00 in their treasury now.

They still intend to produce their play which they work at in violent spasms whenever the mood seizes them. They got as far as frequent rehearsals last week but there is a lull again. They have scenery, lights, etc. ready and I have promised a curtain when the production is actually coming off.

I have been very busy the last two weeks as Mrs. Casson who comes in the mornings from 9–12 and does the washing, ironing and upstairs work, has been ill so I have had to do it myself and it has kept me going all day. There is no sign of her coming back yet so I managed to get the former maid of a friend (now married) to take it over temporarily. The maid situation gets more and more difficult and I expect it will keep on at least as long as the war lasts, and will be much worse when the munition works now building get into production.

I think I had better send this letter to Ulverston as I believe you said you would be back there for the month of April. Doesn't the time whiz past!

[11] 118 HILLSDALE AVENUE WEST
         TORONTO, MARCH 16

Dear Margaret

... By the time you get this I expect you will be home for the Easter holiday and I am sure you will need it. I do hope you are not wearing yourself out and that you were able to pick up after your bad cold. It must be a very great strain to plunge into teaching when you're not used to it. You mention in your letter my telling you of Tom's anxiety over his oral composition. You know he has got over his fussing over things like that wonderfully. His last oral composition on "The Planets" he prepared with a lot of pains but, aside from getting me to hear him practise delivering it once, he did not talk about it at all, and did not seem at all excited or nervous about it. He is growing much more philosophical about small difficulties and changes in routine. Of course he still likes exact and minute instructions down to the last detail if they are possible to give him but I have tried to encourage him to think out his own solutions when necessary and he is very proud when he manages things alone.

Mary doesn't often tease him anymore, and the boys not as much. The situation was a little difficult because when I discovered them teasing him I scolded them (as they deserved) but then I found that when it happened, Tom, though he never complained directly to me, would keep up a constant "Please stop" or "Please give it to me" (or whatever it was) with his voice, full of tears, rising higher and higher, to reach my ears if I were not in the room, or with his eyes constantly sliding in my direction if I were, waiting for me to come to his assistance. So, while I continued to come to his assistance, I would stop whatever was going on and then got Tom aside and explain to him a much more effective line of conduct he could have followed, to try to show him that he could do something about it himself. Two or three times when he & C. were in the basement taking off their outdoor things C., as soon as he saw that Tom would be ready before him would start saying "I'm not going to turn the light out Tom, you'll have to." (The light is at the top of the stairs and "last man up" is supposed to turn it out.) "I don't really need the light down here and you'll have to turn it out, I'm not going to even if I'm the last up." And Tom would begin a shrill expostulation and argument, to which C., in his stolid way, would simply keep on retorting "I'm not going to turn it out." Tom would finally reach the top of the stairs in tears with his voice going ninety to the dozen imploring C. to recognize the fact that the last person up should turn the light out. When I saw this happen I went to their room, where they'd both arrived by that time, Tom crying and still arguing. I ignored C. but just asked Tom who was supposed to turn the light out. Of course he said the last one up. "Well" I said "were you the last one up?" "No" said Tom and began a flood of explanation. "Well then" I said "you had nothing to do with the light and had no need to listen to any one who talked to you about the light. Unless you're the last up you haven't the slightest responsibility for the light so you didn't need to say a word—just walk up the stairs." Before I had finished C. had quietly slipped out and gone down and turned out the light (which Tom noticed) and either C. hasn't tried it on again or it hasn't worked.

Peter doesn't tease him as much as criticise what he does. Tom had some homework assigned with a week to do it in, so the first night he did part of it and brought it down to me to hear it (it was memorising). Then he said he wouldn't do any more that day. Peter heard him, and as he still had homework to do and therefore not liking anyone else to be free, began to give him a lecture on a high moral tone on the necessity of doing your homework at once, etc. I stopped it by telling Peter to get up and at his own homework and when Tom went to follow him upstairs I called him back and said "Now remember Tom if Peter talks about your homework, it is none of his business. Pay no attention to him." I listened from the bottom of the stairs. Sure enough when Tom got up, Peter asked "Well, are you going to finish your homework, Tom?" and Tom said with an air of finality "I don't talk to you about your homework Peter so you needn't talk about mine" and that was that! He is learning to stand on his own feet a bit (and that's all that's needed to stop most of the teasing) and seems very happy. He gets better and better about food all the time and has a splendid appetite. He eats spaghetti and even cheese soufflé— in fact he eats everything he's given and very rarely even shows that he doesn't like it much. In fact he really has grown to like some of the things he didn't use to.

I seem to have taken up a lot of space with Tom but I'm sure you like to hear these things. I'll have to skip C. pretty well, but he seems quite happy and is showing more and more desire to be co-operative. They are both in good health....

Dear Margaret

This is really a continuation of No. 11. I wanted to tell you of a rather strange coincidence. We have some very dear friends, Dr. and Mrs. Cruikshank. After John and I came home from England in 1923 we lived in a flat above them in a converted house (I had known her slightly before) for a year. That was the year I was so ill for so long and although she was far from well herself they were so good to us that we have been very good friends ever since and see them almost once a week, visit them at their camp up north and at their "farm" about 15 miles from Toronto where they have about 30 acres of woods and rolling hills. They have just a weekend cabin on it which they use in the summer and for skiing in winter. We took the boys out there one Sunday last autumn. Well, to continue, Dr. C. (Tal) has a brother Doug who, after the last war, married an English girl and I have just discovered she was a friend of yours—Frances Billington....[19]

We are having what I hope is the last fling of a long winter.... I am looking forward to being done with windbreakers overshoes and overstockings and toques and mitts. By this time of year they are getting shabby and worn and short in the sleeve etc. but we make them do as long as they're needed. I don't think I ever gave you the really authentic ruling about sending clothing, but the Customs Office man read me their letter of instructions which says that any amount of clothing may be sent duty free from relatives or friends in England to children evacuated to Canada or the U. S. for the duration. However as far as I can foresee, the boys will not need anything for a year....

Weren't you simply thrilled to hear of Bill's success with his algebra? We were all delighted. He seems to be doing well in all subjects. John telephoned Mr. Waddington to tell him about the boys' leaving at Easter and he asked him to do and say nothing about it at present, while he spoke to the teachers (and I expect the board). He said that he personally would be willing to keep the boys on the extra term without fees in view of various things we have done for the school in the past when they've been in difficulties. John, I know, is rather loath to keep them on under those conditions but I think if they offer it he will accept. They had a deficit, several years running, at the school which we helped to make up, and when they launched the fund for a new school two years ago we gave donations and turned back most of the money saved in fees by a scholarship Peter won, as a donation from him. So I don't see why we shouldn't accept. However we shall just wait and see—no matter what turns up, we don't intend to mention it to the boys until necessary.

C. and Peter each have a bowl with 3 gold fish, on their dresser. Peter bought a most enormous snail to put in his and a week later it produced 2 babies much to everyone's wonder and surprise. To-day C. missed one of his goldfish. I felt his suspicions definitely rested on me, though I can imagine nothing on earth I would be less likely to pilfer. However Peter went "on the trail" complete with finger prints of all the family who would give them and found the fish—it had wriggled inside a large empty shell which was on the bottom of the bowl, and must have got stuck because they still haven't been able to extract it—it's so far in they can just touch its tail. Great excitement!

[13]   118 HILLSDALE AVENUE WEST
          TORONTO, MARCH 23

Dear Margaret

Spring seems to have really come to-day. I do hope it stays. John took the children down by the lake shore this afternoon (where a lot of wild ducks winter every year) and to see the animals in High Park....

There was great excitement this morning after Church when C. announced he had been made a warden of the children's congregation. (I rather think Peter was a little jealous.) I was very pleased for C., because I think he felt it quite an honour, as it is. They have had a little trouble with the behaviour of the children (not our children—the whole 150) during their service and I think one reason for appointing C. was to swing our four over on the side of law and order—rather shrewd. We haven't been able to find out much about the warden's duties—all four have different ideas so I guess I'll have to ask the curate. He is supposed to attend all meetings which will take a little managing as they're at 4 P.M. However he says the office only lasts a month and so there may not be many meetings.

The boys have got small presents for their father, as Bill warned them of his approaching birthday. They don't know the date but we will get them off soon.

I am enclosing three copies of snow snapshots for your mother. They are duplicates of those I sent you and I thought she might like to have them for her own. I want to write her as soon as I get time.

Do get a good holiday before going back to the school. All the children are thriving—I was looking at Tom's blue serge suit on him to-day—the sleeves are away up above his wrists (they can be let down though) and the coat will scarcely button around his waist! (but the buttons can be moved)

P.S. After writing my last letter, a friend told me she had heard an announcement on the radio to the affect that parents in England could send a child clothing to the value of $45.

[14] 118 HILLSDALE AVENUE WEST
TORONTO, MARCH 31

Dear Margaret

We feel that spring has really started, and the mud has arrived. The pavement and roads are dry and clear but if you step off them! We have had a lot of sunshine, bringing the frost out of the ground—to-day for the first time it was melting in the shade as well. I took the three boys to the shoe store after school and put them in the X-ray and fortunately their shoes are still big enough. I hate to have to get black shoes this time of year. They don't wear them much longer and then by September they are too small. When the mud dries up they wear soft leather shoes with heavy rubber soles (except for dress wear). I got them each a pair to-day and will put them away for a few weeks—it will save me rounding them all up to take them down again.

The boys are getting their exam results which seem highly satisfactory. I looked at their letters to see if they told you. I improved on C's spelling (of his letter) sufficiently to make it understandable. He is anxiously awaiting his spelling mark—wants to know the worst. They seem to be both doing very well in everything else.

They are all four very well and very ruddy. There is not much to do at this season and I have difficulty getting the boys outdoors. Mary can never have enough time outdoors. She skips rope and plays marbles and has to be dragged in (metaphorically) but the three boys like to come in as soon as they get home from school (quite early now) and have to be chased out! I made them walk home from the shoe store (about 1 mile) which was not popular but I thought it was good for them. I am not looking forward to the Easter holiday—I was so glad to hear that holidays weighed on you—I had always pictured you as calm and unperturbed by confusion! However

Easter is pretty late this year so it may be dry and springlike. The robins are back in force now—our tulips are up several inches. I have had forsythia bloom in the house for a long time by cutting the branches and putting them in water in a sunny window. I don't think you have forsythia—it is a shrub with a yellow flower somewhat like jasmine—the bloom comes before the leaf....

Peter and C. are full of projects as usual. They have been writing poems on "topical subjects" and printing them and Saturday afternoon they cleaned the playroom (you couldn't step inside it)—moved everything out and scrubbed the shelves and floor. They took their gold fish down and arranged lights behind the bowls. Then they discovered that when the lights were off the gold fish were left in half dark so they heaved them up to their bedroom again. Peter has an enormous snail in his bowl which he bought for 10¢. It has had twins twice now and he has sold one pair to C. and one to Tom for 5¢ a pair so he feels that any further progeny will be pure profit! He is very anxious to buy a second hand aquarium and is watching the Articles for Sale columns though as he is flat broke at present it won't help him much to see one advertised.

We are beginning to think of the summer but have made no plans as yet. It is always a problem to know what to do and where to go so that John and I can have a bit of a holiday as well as the children. It is almost impossible to get a maid to go to a summer cottage which complicates things!

Isn't the war news comforting this past week (Jugo Slavia and the naval battle in the Medit., in case it's so long ago when you get this letter you've forgotten—but I don't suppose you have the feeble kind of mind I have!). We _were_ due for a break!—and now the U.S. are seizing the Axis ships and I'm sure they'll hand them over to Britain.

I have not got up to see Leslie but Theresa says he is getting on very well. We dropped in there yesterday, it was her birthday and the children had all bought her little gifts.

[15] 118 HILLSDALE AVENUE WEST
TORONTO, APRIL 7

Dear Margaret

We have not heard from you for 2 or 3 weeks (I will look up the date before posting this if I remember—the letter is in the boys' room and they are in bed), but I think Bill has had letters since so I hope none are lost (your letter was dated Mar. 2). We are having spring at last. Yesterday (Sunday) after an all day rain Saturday, it became warm and sunny and continued to-day. Our crocuses on the south side of the house are in bloom, though there is still a sizeable ridge of ice across the north side, and lots of mud.

The boys' school closes Wednesday for Easter. We have been very undecided as to what to do about them after Easter—in fact John has gone up to talk to Mr. W. to-night but before he went we decided to put them in Oriole Park School with Mary. I think, from what Mr. W. said earlier, that he would be willing to waive their fees for the term but there would still be taxi fare, sports, transportation, books, handicraft supplies, etc., which would probably amount to about $25. We would very much like, if we can afford it, to send all four children to camp for a month (or at least 2 weeks) of the summer. I think it would be a good experience for the boys, they would have a lot of fun and would learn to swim etc. much faster than with us. Bert Green, the director of Camp Woapak, where Peter went last year, came to see John and very nobly offered to take the two boys for the price of one, so we feel it would be worth more, both to the boys and ourselves, to save the extra expense on the school term if it will enable us to send them to camp. I have said nothing to the boys about changing school as yet—of course they know they are to leave St. Paul's at the end of this year.

Christopher is very anxious to write the entrance exam to U.T.S. and I felt that in fairness to him I had to promise he could, as Peter goes there. However I don't think he can make it as the exam is just in five subjects arithmetic, spelling, writing, reading, and English, three of them being his worst subjects. (I don't think U.T.S. is the right school for C. really—they drive them pretty hard.) Tom is already quite interested in Oriole Park School and asks Mary about the teacher he is likely to have, and so on. Oddly enough, I think the change would upset him much less than C. I have been surprised how much easier than I expected him to, Tom has made adjustments to school and changed circumstances—much more easily than C. They say the same thing at St. Paul's. C. apparently had a long period of stress getting adjusted there but Tom, after a few days' intense excitement, settled right in. He seems to be enclosed in a sort of insulation or cocoon—a little world of his own—and so many things you think will distress him simply pass by without his even noticing them. Easter is so late this year that the term will be short and it may give them a chance to settle into the new school so they will not suffer apprehensions about it all the summer holidays. Also the public school summer holiday starts two weeks later than St. Paul's, which is no small help when you're trying to get the family clothes etc. ready for summer holidays.

I got out all the spring clothes last week and Clare came over for two days and helped me with the mending, letting down, etc. Tom's grey flannel shorts which he wore last year won't meet around his waist by 2 inches!

However Peter has a good outgrown pair which will do him nicely. I will not have to buy anything, as far as I can see, except a light cravenette windbreaker for C....

I have not said anything to the boys about going to camp and won't until it's all settled. I heard them discussing the summer—the 3 boys—and C. said he would like to go to camp. I think Tom thought it completely out of his orbit. He said "I don't think I'll go to camp. I think I'll spend the summer either in Ohio or at Mrs. Beamish's!" Dear Tom, he has such sublime confidence that he'll be looked after! I don't know whether Bill told you that his godfather in Ohio mentioned, in a letter at Christmas, the possibility of all 3 boys visiting them in Ohio this summer.[20]—I expect Bill had told Tom. Also Mrs B., when she was here, said she would very much like to have Tom come to them for a visit this summer if she has enough room, which she hasn't in her present house. Of course we don't know how these things will all work out and will have to wait a while to see. I would like them to be able to see and do as much as possible while they are here. If they go to camp for one month we may take a cottage for the other month, while John has his holiday.

C's art classes are over for the year. I think he has enjoyed them though he says very little about them. I know he hated to miss any of them.... C. feels quite important over his office as warden of the children's service at Church—I am so glad, it's good for him to feel important. He wears an arm band and takes up the collection. They have had services every Monday during Lent for the children. The children have only been to one—they wanted to go, so I took them. The curate apparently took them into the Church and each Monday explained something to them—one day the clergy's vestments, the day they went the altar, altar cloths, reredos, etc., and another day the Church furnishings. I thought it was quite interesting and a good idea but I didn't urge them to go, in fact I forgot it every Monday myself except the once when Mary persuaded them all to go—out of curiosity I think. She _does_ hate to miss anything. She is like something on springs or a mosquito (but a good buxom mosquito) never still a minute and always full of a dozen things she wants to do, tell you, show you or explain. She was home two days with a slight cold some time ago and when I put her to bed I simply could not get away—every time I tried to shut the door she had something she _had_ to tell me. I said to John "That child has been with me eleven hours to-day and hasn't _yet_ said all she has to say!" She is very bright and happy, and has almost given up teasing Tom, of whom she is very fond.

These are such anxious days with this dreadful new offensive under way and so little reliable news as yet. It seems too much to hope that the drives into Jugo Slavia and Greece can be stopped before they become disastrous.

I hope this will be legible. I am under the dryer at the hairdresser's and thought I might make use of the time to write this addition—I don't seem to have had time since Monday night when I wrote the first part. John had a long talk with Mr. Waddington and he was loath to let the boys leave, of course. He is rather disappointed in the progress C. has made in spelling and writing though his other work is very satisfactory and as good as that of any boy in the class. He is afraid that if we put C. in the public school now they might place him in Grade 4 (or even Grade 3) on the basis of his spelling and writing and that would be disastrous. He says Mrs. Underhill has worked untiringly with C. and they would very much like to have him this last term to continue their efforts with him. Tom, he thinks, would fit in quite well in Grade 4 anywhere, average in everything—he has been doing Grade 5 arithmetic as well. He says Tom adjusted quickly to the school but C. was a long time settling in, but has improved in that way tremendously. They have not had an outburst of tears from Christopher for several months. I remember Mrs. U. told me about the last one—it was just after he returned from being at home with measles and he got behind in his spelling dictation and "blew up." I think the root of the whole trouble is his consciousness of being so inferior in those subjects. He tries to conceal and ignore it but in school he can't. He doesn't seem to have enough self-control and discipline to take himself in hand and apply himself steadily so he just explodes with despair and frustration. He did seem to be working diligently the first few months but since then, though he has prepared (?) his lesson (he has usually to be reminded to do it) and we dictate it to him (every night), his heart and mind were not on it. Tom, on the other hand, has the consciousness of his own ability being equal to the other boys (and greater in some subjects) and he really enjoys school work.

In all respects except school C. has adjusted more quickly than Tom—he is more observant and he does like to act, look, dress and talk like everyone else his age, while it doesn't bother Tom in the least to be individual. So I really think that our conclusions (given above) are at least close to the truth.

Well, to go back to Mr. W. He was willing to waive fees for the term ($50 each) and cut down the other charges (amounting to $15 each) to just the $8 each for taxi fare. John felt he should not accept so much (the school is in such financial straits) so he suggested taking Tom out and leaving C. (paying the $15 for him) and Mr. W. was quite favourable. He thinks that Tom, after a few days' natural excitement and anxiety as to "what it will be like," will find himself quite up to the work and will settle in. Also it should have a good effect on C. if we explain to him that we are giving him special consideration so that he may have two more months of the special atten-tion he is getting to fit him for Grade 7 next year. The classes in the public school are pretty large and if he goes in at this stage, unless he strikes a very exceptional teacher, he is not likely to meet with the patience with, and at-tention to his poor subjects, that he would have entering with a whole new class in September. And we will hope that by September he will have made a good stride forward. When he really applies himself he can do so much better! Mr. W. sent home with John a copy book (I didn't think they existed any more) and an exercise book with samples and suggestions as to how he should go about practising writing. We are going to make an effort to keep him at it for a certain time each day in the holidays as a start and keep it up as much as possible right on and through the summer. He must surely realize how great his handicap is and I have tried to show him that only he can overcome it, and not by any shortcuts, but just by honest work. It is rather discouraging—if we have to come to saying "You must do this" I feel progress will be negligible—he is so resentful of compulsion.

They both look so well—I am ashamed not to have had them weighed before this. We haven't scales and when we're out, with all their winter clothes it would be hard to get a true weight. However they have discarded coats now and are back into shorts and sweaters. They are wearing those green tweed trousers—they are the heaviest so I started them off in them. The belts are let out to their utmost and even so are pretty snug though when they get the heavy underwear off it will make a difference. They both have quite a paunch if you can believe it! They have good appetites espe-cially Tom—he eats more than any of the others—that is, he eats far more bread and butter and pudding and the other things about the same. I am so glad his appetite is so good—he would not have "come round" so well to a varied diet if he hadn't been hungry at meal times.

They each had a composition to write last week on a scientist or a scien-tific discovery. We helped Tom with his material but he wasn't at all fussed and bothered about it and turned out a very creditable essay. I didn't even know C. had one to do—he did it all himself and Mrs. U. considered it very good indeed. They have taken them to the Children's Public Library from school every two weeks—I take them some times too and it is within walk-ing distance so they can spend some time there in the holidays if they like.[21] Some of the books in the Reading Room fascinated C. and I think he would like some time at them. He has been doing quite a lot of reading.

The weather has been simply perfect for days and if it holds John and I are thinking of taking the children to Niagara Falls on Easter Monday. We are saying nothing about it because if it's bad weather there's no use going.

Tom, Peter, Christopher, and Mary in front of Niagara Falls on Easter Monday, 1941

I do wish we could take Bill too but I'm afraid 7 would make too close quarters to avoid squabbles on a long trip. It is about 90 miles to the Falls.

Bill came in yesterday from school—looking better than I expected after his sore throat—how fortunate that it didn't interfere with his exams. And how well he has done! We are delighted and he is walking on air.

I can't write more now. I hope I have conveyed what I feel on the school question and that it will work out all right.

[16] 118 HILLSDALE AVENUE WEST
TORONTO, APRIL 16

Dear Margaret

This will be brief—there is not much time for letters in holidays.... On Good Friday [the children] cleaned the leaves off the garden in front and a section in the back. Saturday they spent at Clare's and C. & P. made a little cold frame which they brought home and planted on Sunday. They got quite a bit of garden dug up—I suppose it is to take the plants from the cold frame if, as and when. Monday we went to Niagara Falls. They all had a very good time and saw everything possible. Tom was very much exercised because some roads are closed—the one that goes close to the power plant and the part of the river drive where the new bridge is being built. He was convinced that he was missing the best views of the falls because of it. We had mid-day dinner at the General Brock where the dining room overlooks both falls and had a splendid view from our table—and between courses the children could stand in the window and take in the details. We met the Ratcliffe menage just going up to dinner when we came down. We stopped at John's sister's in Burlington on the way back and the children had such a good time playing on the beach she insisted on us all staying for a pot-luck supper. We left Peter with her over-night—he came home by himself (feeling very important) by bus and street car, Tues. evening. Tuesday morning I took Mary up to Clare's to stay overnight (poor Mary has been saying she <u>would</u> like to visit someone if anyone ever asked her) so I had Bill come down to spend the day Tuesday—it gave the 3 boys a chance for a whole day together by themselves....

[17] 118 HILLSDALE AVENUE WEST
TORONTO APRIL 20

Dear Margaret

... The holidays are nearly over and the weather has on the whole been unbelievably good. I cannot remember an Easter holiday like it—very warm and almost always sunny. This past week there have been scattered showers but no steady rain. The children started to clean up the garden on Friday and continued yesterday and have their own plots staked out and prepared for seed. We went and got the seed yesterday and I let them choose whatever they wanted—only standing firm against celery and tomato seed! P. & C. want potatoes but in our postage stamp garden I'm afraid that's too ambitious. Tom is the only one that wants flowers—he is all against adding to the amount of vegetables already in this world and likely to encumber his dinner plate at any time! C. & P. already have lettuce and carrots sprouting in their cold frame which they planted a week ago.

I hope my letter of April 9 arrived safely. It was a long one in which I went all over the school situation and our problems and explained what we had decided. However now, all of a sudden, things are altered—much for the better. To begin at the beginning, we have very good neighbours next us, John and Edna Rowland, who were married and bought the house next us when we bought ours, 15 years ago. They have no children and he is a lawyer and she has her own business, an expensive dress-making shop....

John happened to see John R. outside last evening and stopped to apologize for the noise the children had made playing outside on Friday when they didn't know Edna was ill in bed. In the conversation John told John R. that we were sending Tom to Oriole Park School after Easter and explained the whole story, including our hopes for sending all four to camp.

John R. was distressed at the idea of the boys being separated, particularly as it seemed that Tom was being penalized for C's failure to do his work well—of course that is the aspect that has worried me, too. He said in effect "Edna and I are interested in the English children out here, we feel it is a very worth while endeavour and wish that more could come. All winter as we've watched you with these two we've felt more and more like slackers. Because it's impossible for us to take a child or children in our home there is all the more reason why we should do something in a financial way towards looking after the needs of some of these children. I don't want these children to be separated at school and I would like them to go to camp and I want to pay for this last term for Tom, and send him to camp as well. And don't look on this as an offer to "help you out." I feel that I have as great a responsibility towards English children as you have and have simply been evading mine so far."

There was no time then for further talk, so at the first opportunity, which was this afternoon, we went to talk it over with them, and have it all settled. He wants to send the one boy to camp for four weeks and, as I told you in a previous letter, Bert Green, the camp director has offered to take the two boys for one boy's fee. We feel that if John R. did that, that we can send Tom to St. Paul's for the term, paying the $15 for taxi fare and incidentals, just as we intended to do for C. Mr. Waddington will be delighted to have them both and it really is a great relief to me. I feel that Tom would settle in to the other school quickly but he was bound to feel upset at the news and a bit overwhelmed starting in all alone, and I do agonize over children's feelings. So I am awfully happy over it.

I do hope you won't look askance on all this, as charity. This war guest situation is something entirely unheard of before—I mean the fact of no money being allowed out of England—and therefore has to be met in an unusual way. We ourselves are accepting it as he has offered it—as an easing of his obligation, not as incurring one ourselves. Of course that's not to say that we don't think it extremely kind and thoughtful of him, we appreciate it, you've no idea how much—it makes it possible for us to do just what we want to do.

There is another complication to the whole business. John and I have been feeling all winter (in fact we have felt long before your boys came) that if it were at all possible we would like to get into a bigger house, where the children could each have a separate bedroom and we could have another bathroom and a sitting room for the children as well as (if possible) a ping pong room. We have had the 3 boys in Peter's (good sized) bedroom, as a sort of dormitory, with John's dressing room turned into a study for them. Since spring has come, we put Tom's bed into that room and a little desk for him and C. & P. have the big table in their bedroom, with the games, books etc. divided between the two rooms. Then there is a play room in the basement where the boys have their printing press etc. We have two bathrooms but one opens off the maid's room on the third floor so we can only use it on her day out! It does seem ridiculous that she has a whole bathroom to herself while the six of us share one! We had a basin installed a few years ago in John's dressing room which he uses to shave but I do feel that with the strenuous life he has down town he should have more privacy and peace at home. However the larger house has just been a dream in the back of our minds for a long time (nearly 2 years) but quite unexpectedly, as these things happen, a purchaser for our house has turned up—John's assistant actuary, who lives in a rented house just down the street with his wife and 2 year old daughter. John just happened to mention to him that we would like a larger house and he immediately became interested in buying ours and, in fact, I felt that they decided on it so quickly they might repent later so I insisted on their coming over to be shown all the defects! They want the house from Sept 1 so we will have to start looking for something—in fact we have been looking a bit. The sale is not absolutely settled yet but I think it is pretty sure.

Well, with the possibility of this move in our minds all the time, we were all the more loath to change Tom's school, as if we move it will probably be into a different school district, which will make a new change necessary at the beginning of the school year in September.[22] And it was not until two days ago that there was any assurance that we could sell our house (and of course as I said it is not quite sure yet) without all the business of listing it with an agent—which I don't think we would have done, both because of the inconvenience and bother of having people shown through, and because of the Rowlands. As I said, they have been ideal neighbours for fifteen years and having a mutual drive to our garages makes it rather important to the tenants of one, who is in the other house. We have already felt it would be unfair to them not to be very particular to whom we sold the house. And now it did seem ironical that they should offer to solve the school problem partly involved by the moving, just when we had to break the news to them that we are probably leaving! However, of course they fully appreciate our necessity and we have the satisfaction of knowing that the Grays will be just as good neighbours as we are—better, in that they have only one small child who won't attract all the children in the block to play noisy games as ours do—and did long before yours came!

I do hope this letter isn't lost in the Atlantic, so I won't have to make all these explanations again! Also I hope you haven't been worrying since I told you I was changing Tom's school. Fortunately we had said nothing to the children about it, so he has had no worry over it. We were going to wait until to-day to tell him (the public schools open to-morrow and St. Paul's the next day, Tuesday). I will send you the prospectus of Camp Woapak, where we hope to send the three boys. We think summer camps are splendid places for them. They get excellent supervision and learn a great deal and have heaps of fun. I do hope both boys will learn to swim....

[18] 118 HILLSDALE AVENUE WEST
TORONTO, APRIL 25

Dear Margaret

I hope my last letter (Apr. 20) arrived safely. It was a long one, telling you of our decision to keep both boys at St. Paul's for the rest of this year. I hope you did not worry over my previous letter, when we intended to keep C. on and take Tom out. Also I told you that Mr. Rowland, our neighbour, wanted to send one boy to camp for four weeks this summer, and as the camp had offered to take one boy without charge if we sent the two, that will take care of both and we will send Peter and Mary too, so they will all be away for nearly a month. We are delighted at being able to arrange this.

I also told you that we have sold our house and are looking for something bigger where we can spread out a bit and not be so on top of one another. We have looked at quite a few houses but will not decide quickly as we have this house until Sept. 1. There are lots of houses available but all have some defects of plan, size or lot or location so it is a case of balancing advantages. If we don't find what we want we can always rent for a year or two.

I am dreadfully disquieted at present—my doctor insists that I go into the hospital next week for a slight operation. I have had a little lump under my arm for several years which is nothing at all—some sort of little tumour but apparently it is connected with the muscle and my own doctor and a surgeon he called in think it should not be allowed to go on for fear of complications later. I would much prefer to wait until summer when the children are away—when it's gone this long I don't see why a few months more should matter but unfortunately the doctor spoke to John about it (I didn't intend to tell him what they had said) so I guess I am for it. I do hope everything will go all right at home while I am away—they say I should just be 4 or 5 days in hospital.

T. and C. started cricket at school to-day. Tom came home and said "One good thing and one bad thing happened to me to-day. The good thing was that we played cricket and I made more runs than any one else on my team. The bad thing was that my finger got caught in the door and it hurts here, is hot there, and is a bit sore in this place." Fortunately the 'good thing' was apparently good enough to outbalance the 'bad thing' because he has not mentioned the finger again. It was a little red around the nail but I don't think there is any damage done.

The boys had a letter from you yesterday written March 30, enclosing a newspaper cutting. Also the four Dr. Dolittle books arrived for C. the other day.[23] He was much surprised at their arrival and, I think, a little taken aback, and seemed rather at a loss as to why they'd come and rather disappointed when he found what they were. I suggested that he must have asked for them and he finally recollected that "when I was sick I think perhaps I did." It is too bad you went to the trouble and risk of sending them—we have one of them and all the others the children get constantly from the library. I must watch his letters—I think perhaps he often asks for something to be sent—it pops into his head that it would be nice to have at the moment. I know he asked you to send him bricks and we have quantities of bricks here—not just the same kind as he asked for but several varieties—which he never thinks of using.[24] If he asked for the D. books when he was sick, it was probably because they were brought to his mind by having 2 or 3 of them from the library at the time!

C. did very well with his writing during the holidays and Mr. W. was pleased with his book which he took back half filled. However since school started he has slacked off and has not touched it. I think the night he has no homework or very little he should copy spelling for 15 minutes or so—it would help both spelling and writing—but he does not seem to see any need to work at spelling except the night before his spelling lesson. His attitude is "I shan't do it unless they make me" and how he resents (silently but none the less unmistakably) being "made"! So we do not "make" him. I try to point out every once in a while the great desirability of making the most of his opportunities this year and getting off to a good start next, but the rest I am leaving to him.

They all got their gardens prepared last weekend and we got the seed but Saturday it rained and Sunday it turned much colder. However they have got the seeds planted now and it is getting warmer every day and the sun is shining steadily. It is a very early spring (if it stays like this). They manage to play cricket in our tiny garden. Peter's bat has been broken and repaired so it is a good one for a small space as you can't hit far with it!

Punch for Mar. 26 arrived on April 20, the Mar. 19 number arrived on April 21 and the April 2 number to-day (25th) so the mails are pretty mixed up.

SUNDAY, APRIL 27

I am going into the hospital to-morrow evening, with the operation Tuesday morning and should be home again for the weekend.

Bill's school report is simply marvellous as you have no doubt heard from him and Vivien. I wish Peter's were better. He is still not quite adjusted to harder work and more personal responsibility for it (all part of U.T.S.). Also I must confess the cultural subjects do pull down his average—music, art etc. are not his strong points! He did very well in maths, spelling, French and English expression—rather a mixed bag!

I suppose you will be going back to school soon. I do hope you had a good holiday. I am sure you needed it. It must have been a great strain starting in to teach.

[19] 118 HILLSDALE AVENUE WEST
        TORONTO, MAY 5

Dear Margaret

Your letter of April 6 from Ulverston arrived May 1, when I was in the hospital but John brought it to me. I went in last Monday evening and Dr. Shenstone operated Tuesday morning.[25] They had the little growth analyzed and it was not malignant so there should be no further trouble. I left the hospital Friday but instead of going home, Ruby McKay asked me to come to her for a few days' more rest and I very gladly accepted. I am going home this evening. I feel very much better though I can't use my arm (the left fortunately) until the incision heals up as it is right across the armpit. The doctor expects to take out the stitches in a day or two so it should not be a long process. It is most annoying but apparently everything has gone on well at home. John is a tower of strength—he has taken over the children—of course he has always shared in their care—completely. He brought them all in to see me yesterday afternoon for a few minutes on their way to Sherwood Park—a natural bit of woods and stream quite close. He says they had a lovely afternoon playing ball and digging in the sand. Clare had them all up for the day on Saturday.

I am enclosing a letter from Mrs. Burns which arrived last week.[26] We are simply delighted with her offer—I do think it is so good of them. It should be a simply perfect summer for the boys and settles so many problems for us about the summer. I told you in my last letter (or the one before) how we had been able to arrange for all four to go to camp for a month and we were very happy about that but of course this is so much better both for them and for us. For one thing we had all felt that Bill should be with the boys for the other month of the summer or part of it and it will be good to have them able to spend the whole summer all together and in what sounds like an ideal place. Also I am glad they are going to be able to see something of the United States—one thing we constantly regret is that we can't afford to show them a lot of Canada and the U.S. while they're here. Of course no matter how much money we had we couldn't take them to the U.S.—or go ourselves as we can't take money in to the U.S. or buy U.S. funds except in case of necessity, when one can get a permit from the Foreign Exchange Board. For instance when John has to go to New York on business, he gets a permit allowing him to buy enough U.S. funds to cover his expenses. I don't think we shall have any difficulty about the boys crossing the border. We will get visas on their passports and a permit for them should be no difficulty as they won't have to take money. (They each have the $2 U.S. which the Burns sent them at Christmas as a little pocket money.) I sent just a note to Mrs. Burns, of appreciation and thanks, and promised to write more fully when I feel better.

John tells me the boys wrote their letters to you last night—I suppose they told you what pillars of the Church they have become. It gives John and me a lot of amusement though naturally we treat it as a serious matter—as they do—I should perhaps say "important" rather than "serious." I really feel we'll have to get this new house of ours near the Church if they're all going to become involved in executive positions!

We have looked at quite a few houses but of course have had to halt househunting temporarily. John leans a bit towards renting something that will give us all the accommodations we need and be close to school (the important things for the immediate future) even if it's not just located where we would like to be permanently. Houses the size we want are very plentiful at quite low sale prices but he thinks in another year there may be many more on the market with the income tax taking such huge jumps every budget day. Any way we have lots of time to think about a house. We will send Peter and Mary to camp for a month and probably Peter will go to his uncle in Burlington for a while (on the fruit farm) so we should be able to concentrate on the moving and still get a holiday ourselves.

I must have mentioned that the doctor suspected C's tonsils but don't think I ever <u>thought</u> of having them out. I wouldn't dream of taking anything of that nature upon myself unless it was a case of life and death and anyway I feel as you do about tonsils. I think doctors are too apt to take them out just "on the chance" it will do some good. Mary is in the same situation, and I am holding out against it as long as I can.

Tom mentions his eyes only very occasionally and seems able to stand a lot of sun. I intended to take him to Dr. Macrae to whom I took him last

September, for a real eye examination, in June, but I think I'll ask the Dr. whether it would be better to wait until September. If it <u>should</u> happen that he needs glasses the holidays would be a bad time to start wearing them, as well as the time when they're least necessary. So I'll see what he thinks.

We are having our first rain in weeks—in fact it rained only two days all April!—and then not steadily. This has been an unbelievably early spring. Yesterday was "Blossom Sunday" in the Niagara Peninsula, when the peach and cherry blossoms are at their best. Usually it is the middle of May and last year had to be postponed to the 24th or 25th! We have had constant sunshine and some very warm weather and the trees have come into almost full leaf in 5 days.

I will put the boys' letters with this to-night when I get home.

P.S. The boys' frogs' eggs are hatching out.

EVENING

I am home now and thought you would like to know that I was welcomed with a bouquet of white carnations accompanied by this (printed on the printing press in coloured inks).

> Welcome Home!
> Welcome home once more;
> The hospital is a bore
> For, the anesthetic of an operation
> Isn't as sweet as a carnation
> Welcome home once more!
> From Peter, Christopher, Mary and Tom.

It was their own idea, and Peter's composition, and quite warmed my heart! They had scratched up the money for the flowers among them and C. and P. had shopped anxiously in the face of high prices and they were pleased and triumphant.

[20] 118 HILLSDALE AVENUE WEST
TORONTO, MAY 9

Dear Margaret

I seem to do my writing to you in the hospital, but this time Peter is the sufferer and I the attendant. I came home Monday evening, and early Tuesday evening while I was getting Mary and Tom to bed Peter was walking on the top of the low fence in the garden, lost his balance and fell, feet first, into a bush, a dead branch of which scratched the back of his leg from knee to thigh, piercing the skin only in one small place. John and I examined it and there seemed to be a lump, which made us think that a bit of the branch might have been broken off under the skin. John took him straight to the doctor, who thought the lump was swollen tissue so we had it bandaged up but Wed. aft. his temp. went to 101° so the doctor started giving him dagenan. By Thurs. (yesterday) the wound was a little inflamed and his temp. went up again so he had a surgeon in last evening who thought that, though the wound looked very superficial, we had better bring him down and have it opened in case there was a sliver there. So down we came this morning and they found he had almost the whole bush in his leg! They had to make a very deep cut about 4 in. long and found 3 big slivers nearly an inch long, imbedded very deeply, one right in the muscle, and of course, infected. So we are indeed lucky that we had it done, as it would have made heaps of trouble. He has been pretty sick from the anaesthetic (well he knows now it isn't "sweet as a carnation") and I have been sitting with him all day. Dr. Shenstone says he will have to stay 4 days, probably. The wound of course is kept open and they wash it off and change the dressing every two hours, to keep it moist, but that doesn't seem to hurt at all. He is pretty fed up with the nausea, and the hypodermics, blood tests, etc. that they keep disturbing him for. John and I were to go at 1.30 to look at a couple of houses but I did not want to leave Peter as by that time he was just conscious enough to want me by him. So John went alone. This has certainly put me back on my feet smartly! No use trying to play the invalid. I had my stitches out Wednesday and the incision has been more comfortable since. I still have a bit of gauze on it and wash it with alcohol once a day as it is not really healed yet.

Clare is taking Mary home with her for the weekend, this evening. A friend of mine, Jo Robinson, has asked C. & T. over to-morrow, to play with a little English boy who goes to St. Paul's and who is staying at present near Jo, as his foster parent is ill.[27] She will call for them in the morning and after their dinner John will collect them and take them to the meeting-place from which they go on a walk to hunt fossils, arranged by the school. They are to take sandwiches and have a picnic supper, so that should give them a satisfactory day, and me a free one, for Peter.

Troubles always come in bunches—Mary Murphy has given notice and is leaving the end of the month. I think she is a heartless wretch but I didn't even argue with her. She has nothing against the place or us (I should hope not after all the care we've taken of her in trouble and illness) but she just wants a change of work after 6 years of housework! She is going to a summer hotel as a waitress and had to go June 1 in order to get the job. I don't think I'll try to get anyone permanent until September. If I can get a temporary in June, I expect C. & T. will go to the Burns about the 14th, and we hope to get Mary & P. off to camp about the 29th so I think I can manage through the summer with daily help—John and I can have a lot of meals out in July and I expect we'll be away part of August (how much depends on when we move). And I can have Mary's room to get the trunks out in and get a lot of the packing done bit by bit.

MAY 13

Sorry I didn't finish sooner....

The boys had a marvellous day yesterday (Monday). The senior cricket team was leaving at 9.15 A.M. to play Lakefield School and at the last minute there was an extra car so Mr. Waddington let all the English boys in the 3rd Form go along, for a treat. In all the time they've been here, I've never seen them so thrilled as when they came home last night—at almost 10 P.M.! Even C. was enthusiastic! Lakefield is 100 miles from here, north east, up in one of the summer resort districts, on a lake. It is a small boarding school with a very nice atmosphere. The boys had been taken out in boats on the lake, and shown over the school and had a perfect day.

They are both trying hard to make the second cricket team, which is to play Upper Canada on Thursday. I am busy getting some long "whites" ready for them "in case." The ones Peter had last year just fit Tom and I am shortening one of two pairs which a friend passed on to me, for C.

A letter came from you on the 12th, written April 20 also one to the boys, who received one each from their father too. I do hope you got some rest in your holiday—it seems too bad to come home from school worn out and have to plunge into the trials of housekeeping—complicated by the vagaries of paying guests! I do hope you are not worrying about the boys' clothes. I'm sure there isn't anything they are going to need that you can send them. They have ample shirts and things and shoes I think it would be a waste of money for you to buy. They have to be fitted. Everything they have is holding out well. They have heaps of summer things that will be suitable, I'm sure, for the farm. I certainly do appreciate your position and problems and the last thing I want to do is add to your worries. And please don't skimp yourself in trying to save to repay us. It is not at all necessary—I know you feel you want to do it but we're not counting on it or expecting it and we would feel very guilty if you overtax yourself trying to earn more money for that purpose.

I am asleep over my pen and can scarcely see what I've written. Will try to write again soon.

Dear Margaret

The Williamsons are now recuperating. Peter got along very well indeed. Once his leg was opened the infection cleared up quickly and we brought him home Wednesday evening, just before John left for New York. He is still in bed but can hobble to the bathroom and hitched himself downstairs for a little while yesterday.... I am feeling much better—the incision is all healed and except for a rather "achy" shoulder—they took out a piece of muscle—am all right, though rather tired.

The boys are visiting. Jo Robinson, a very dear friend of mine and Vivien's, insisted on taking them to her house when Peter came home from the hospital, in order to relieve me while I had to give him a lot of attention, and to keep things quieter for Peter. I was not very keen about it at the time—it seemed to be rather pushing them about—but she was so insistent that I gave in. They seem to be getting on very well and she is full of praise for their good behaviour.... The Robinsons have a large garden which runs down the ravine, at the foot of which Jack keeps chickens and rabbits so C. should enjoy that. C. made the second cricket team—I was so pleased. Tom was very much disappointed at not making the team but of course he is pretty young. They played Upper Canada on Thursday so I packed up the long whites, cricket shirt and sweater for C. with his things and he proudly wore them to school, Jo tells me, and enjoyed the game thoroughly in spite of St. Paul's losing.

John came back from New York this morning after seeing Mr. and Mrs. Burns there—he waited over an extra night in order to connect with them. The boys should have a marvellous summer with them and they are looking forward to it eagerly. Bill is so excited at the prospect. St. Paul's closes June 17 so we are going to try to get them down right after that. We will probably drive them down to some place on the border at the eastern end of Ontario (Cornwall or Gananoque or somewhere where there's a ferry or bridge) and Mr. and Mrs. Burns will meet us there to take them on. I can't go into the U.S. as I have no passport and anyway I don't know whether we could get permits to leave the country for that purpose. We will try to go far enough on our side to allow the Burns to make their return trip in one day. We are sending the boys' passports to Ottawa—Bill's has to be renewed as it expires July 1941.

I'm afraid this will have to be all for now. I don't know whether the boys will think of writing you to-day but I expect I'll get them home in a day or two anyway. I saw them at Church—they seem to be enjoying their visit but I think they miss Peter and Mary (as P. & M. do the boys). The Robinson children are Joan 16, Jack 14 and Meredith, not yet 6.

[**22**] 118 HILLSDALE AVENUE WEST
TORONTO, MAY 25

Dear Margaret

The house seems quite empty without the boys and Mary and Peter miss them very much. They are very insistent that the boys should be brought back but Jo Robinson refuses to give them up! Peter's leg is practically finished healing and I expect to get him back to school tomorrow so I had intended to bring the boys home to-day but as Mary Murphy is leaving on Thursday (May 29) and I can't get anyone to take her place, Jo insists that my family be kept to a minimum and threatened to cable you for confirmation if I objected! Her firm intention was to keep them until the end of school (June 17) just before they leave for the Burns' but I have compromised with her for June 6, so as to have them back for a while before they go away.

June 2–6, the semi-annual meetings of the Home Office Life Underwriters Assoc. (of which John was made president last autumn) are being held here at the Royal York Hotel. John has been working on the plans and arrangements all year and as he expected a lot of his friends would bring their wives and there is to be a cocktail party one day and a dinner another, he had hoped that he and I could spend those days right at the hotel where I would be "on tap" to take any of the visiting wives to lunch or shop or so on (the hotel is providing him, as president, with a suite of rooms anyway). I do want to give him what help I can because this organization means a lot to him—he was one of the "fathers" of it—and he is anxious to have the convention a success. Besides we are all trying hard to encourage all the Americans possible to travel in Canada—both to promote good-will and to help balance the exchange. Clare has promised, maid or no maid, to come and stay here for those days and, to simplify things, I think I will accept Jo's hospitality to the children until that's over.

The boys are enjoying being with her—they accept changes like that so well—and Jo and Robbie, and Joan (the 16 year old) are all so interested in them. They have a very large garden which is on different levels right down into a ravine, with a good-sized shallow pool and fountain mid-way down where they can sail boats so they have much more scope for play than here. Meredith (the 5-year old—almost 6) is devoted to both of them, and Paul Carr the little English boy who goes to St. Paul's, lives just a few doors away, so they are quite happy and contented. Yesterday was May 24 (always called simply "The 24th" here and one of the most widely observed Canadian holidays—Queen Victoria's birthday, which we celebrate as Empire Day) and I brought the boys over here for dinner at noon and then John and I took the four, and Bill, out to the Honey-Pot, the Cruikshanks' farm about 15 miles northeast of Toronto. They had a beautiful afternoon grubbing around the woods and stream and a picnic supper, after which we all went to the Robinsons' for fireworks, pooling ours, the Robinsons', Tom's and C's (which they have been weeding, and doing odd jobs for Jo for the last week to buy) and those of various other children round about and had a most satisfactory display of rockets and Roman candles (incidentally these are to be the last fireworks until after the war) followed by cocoa and a most thrillingly late bedtime—after 10!

It was most satisfying to see how pleased all four were to be together again—C's face simply burst into a wide grin when he saw Peter, and they all had a lovely time. We saw the boys at Church this morning—Joan brought them—Christopher carried the Cross again and Peter and Tom wore their warden's and sidesman's arm bands. Tom met me after Church in a great state because he has been detained to practise carrying the flag (for next Sunday) next Friday at 4.45 and he explained it was a "most difficult situation" as school is not out until 4.30. However I assured him that it could most certainly be arranged. I can see that we simply <u>have</u> to get our new house near the Church if all this activity on the part of the children continues and all signs point that way—Tom and Mary are very anxious to get into the children's choir in September which will entail choir practice too.

The boys apparently forgot all about writing to you last Sunday and Jo didn't think of it but I expect she'll get them at it this week. We have got their passports validated for the U.S. and Bill's is at Ottawa being renewed. We are going to get their new pictures taken tomorrow (necessary for U.S. visas) and then they will have to go to the U.S. consul to be finger printed—such a lot of fuss for 3 small boys to go visiting! I suppose when that's settled we have to get a permit from the Foreign Exchange Board and then formalities should be over. I wrote Mrs. Burns the other day giving her a lot of information she had asked for about the boys' routine, activities, food, tastes in books and so on....

I hope this letter in understandable—I have been interrupted at least 50 times during it, and I will try to see that the boys send theirs off. My love to your mother. I had hoped Ulverston was sufficiently secluded to be neglected by enemy air activity but I suppose Barrow attracts it. There was a letter from you for the boys on May 20—I sent it on to Jo's, so don't know its date. C. has had 2 Lilliputs from his father this week.

Dear Margaret

There has not been a letter from you since I last wrote, a week ago. I can well imagine you have no time for writing. I do hope you are not working too hard—teaching and marking papers and managing the house from a distance seem just too much.

The boys are still at Jo Robinson's and seem to be enjoying it very much, though I think Christopher misses Peter. Jack has a lot of new little chicks and Tom spends hours watching them and scaring away the crows which he is sure are going to snatch them up. He and Meredith try to keep counting the chicks to see that they are all there but you can imagine counting about 20 chicks and they get a different number each time, to their intense consternation. I thought C. would have been interested in the pigeons the chickens and dog but he doesn't seem to be—I think he likes his <u>own</u> animals.

We are getting their papers in order for the U.S.—all the passports are back from Ottawa validated for the U.S. I went down to the U.S. consul today to see about visas and had to write post haste to Mr. Burns for a letter stating he was willing and able to support them for the summer! We also need a letter of reference from some one here, which is simple enough, and then we can make an appointment to take them down for finger-prints, upon which the visas are granted.... The boys are simply thrilled at the prospect, especially Bill. Mrs. Burns asked me about sleeping arrangements, as she has one double and one single room for the boys. I left it to Bill to decide and he consulted the boys and they decided that Bill and C. should share a room. I was rather pleased because I think C. feels that Bill passes over him for Tom so often, so that when Bill does single out C. for a favour, C. is quite likely to refuse, none too graciously, because, I think, he feels Bill is doing it from a sense of duty. I am glad the three of them will have this summer together, without other children.

I am going to insist on the boys coming back the end of this week, though it has been a great help having the family reduced during our strenuous past weeks. Mary Murphy left last Thursday but I am getting on with the woman who comes in the morning and a former maid of Jo's whom we all call on in difficulties—she comes 3 days a week, from 9 a.m. until after dinner. Then I call on Clare in an emergency or for evenings.

We have not yet decided on a house but still have lots of time. There are plenty to be had though most of them have some drawback.

P.S. I have been going over the boys' summer clothes and what a stock!—having inherited so much from Bill (and various outgrowns from friends) I don't think they will need one single thing to go away—not even a pair of socks....

[24] 118 HILLSDALE AVENUE WEST
TORONTO, JUNE 15

Dear Margaret

I am afraid I have not written since June 2—I am so sorry but I have simply not had a minute. I will write a real letter by the end of the week but I know you look for news....

Vivien and I will drive the boys to Cornwall (250 miles) on the St. Lawrence and stay there overnight and the Burns will meet us there next day—it is about 260 miles from their end.

Tom is still at Jo Robinson's. Christopher came home Wednesday but Jo insisted on keeping Tom. He had 2 or 3 small boils—starting about 10 days ago and then one very large one on his upper arm started about a week ago. Jo and I took him to the doctor on Tuesday—it had just opened—just to relieve our minds but he said there was no need to worry. It has cleared up completely. She kept him home from school two or three days (exams were over and it didn't matter) but I took him to the Field Day, though he didn't go in any races. They both looked very smart in long white ducks and Tom in Peter's St. Paul's blazer and C. in his brown one. C. did quite well for his team in the races.

I am taking all 3 boys to the U.S. Consul to-morrow afternoon and I hope the visas will be handed over....

I forgot to say the reason Jo is keeping Tom on after his boils are over is that my "daily help" has left me now! So all I have is a girl 3 days a week from 9–7! It's a scramble but we manage. Clare is coming to stay while I go to Cornwall.

[25] 118 HILLSDALE AVENUE WEST
TORONTO, JUNE 22

Dear Margaret

Such a lot has happened this week! We have bought a new house and got the boys off to New Hampshire.... We set out at 2 and arrived in Cornwall about 10.30. The drive was not at all bad though the temperature was over 90° and the boys stood it very well and were cheerful and not too tired when we bundled them into bed in a lovely airy room beside the St. Lawrence, with 3 beds and a tiled bathroom adjoining with (to Tom's great delight) a shower bath. Mr. B. had arrived in Cornwall much earlier and had gone to bed but I talked to him on the telephone and I'm sure he was greatly relieved to know we were actually there. We all had breakfast together at 8 A.M. and we left them at the entrance to the bridge to the U.S.A.[28] All the boys were very excited over their summer holiday, though Tom was just a little overcome at leaving me when it came to the point. I am sure in a few minutes he would be perfectly restored and they were all looking forward to a perfectly grand summer, which I'm sure they'll have....

Of course you've been told how well Bill did at school. We are all delighted. He should have a chance of a scholarship for next year. The Ratcliffes are <u>very</u> pleased. Vivien is a little worried about John's results this year. He is trying to take the exams now and they seem to have "got him down" more than any other year. However I think he'll come out all right. He has a very good brain. His father ... is considered one of the best brains in financial matters in Toronto, and he was one of the committee which handled the Canadian Victory Loan, which overreached by 200,000,000 its objective $600,000,000 on Saturday. The campaign lasted 3 weeks— one thing the boys looked for in every little town on the way to Cornwall was the huge "thermometer" in front of the Town Hall or Post Office which recorded the town's progress towards its objective. Every one was extremely pleased each time we saw one with the top blown off—which was almost always the case.

We got our house on Friday. Please don't worry about your boys being the cause of our move. We have always intended to have a larger house before the children got much bigger. We have only one sitting room here and though there are 2 bathrooms, one adjoins the maid's room, so she lives in splendour while all the rest of us wait in a queue! A year ago we decided to look for a larger house for which we could exchange our present one as part payment but that is always rather difficult and while we were looking at what was available, the collapse of France came, it looked as though England were to be invaded, and we rather lost heart about the whole thing—there seemed so many things more important than our own comfort and we hesitated to take on any greater financial burdens than we already had.

However, the market in the kind of house we want is very dull at present, and prices pretty low—with the income tax more than double last year's, and next year's to be double that again, people whose houses have got too big for their grown-up families want to get rid of them. So we thought we might just as well make the change now when we really need the room and especially as we had a very good opportunity to sell our own without agent's commission or any trouble and fuss. We have got a house in exactly the district we wanted—about ¾ mile south of where we are now. It is convenient to a street car, to the Church (for our workers!) and close to Brown School—the public school considered to have as nice a group of children as any in the city.... We take possession Aug. 1 so with all my family away in July I hope to get curtains &c. arranged for and all the other things planned and we can have the work done early in August. I would like to move about Aug. 15, so as to be settled before the children start school.... The address will be 90 Dunvegan Rd. (It is close to Upper Canada, and also to Bishop Strachan's, the girls school where we hope to send Mary later on.) It has a much larger garden than here and lovely trees and the house itself is comfortable—it looks like a house for a family, though at present it is utterly lacking in charm.

Mary goes to camp Friday, the last day of school (I have got her excused for that day). They all go by train in a private car—the camp is about 150 miles away on L. Ontario near the Bay of Quinte, behind Amherst Island. She will stay four weeks and Clare will take her up there for a while in August if the help situation is still bad. Peter is at his aunt's in Burlington— John took him out yesterday but he insists on coming back Wednesday to go to the "recital" at which Mary is performing on the piano. (I shudder to think of it, but will probably shudder still more when it actually comes off!) He goes to camp on Saturday and I think we'll let him stay 6 weeks this year. Then if things are busy here he can always go to Burlington for a while....

I do hate to think of you working so hard and I don't see how you can stand such a strain. Please don't do it in order to repay us after the war, because we don't expect it. Just living in England must be a terrific strain and it does seem that you are taking on far too many responsibilities for your health to stand. I hope you got Vivien's letter which she told me she wrote, asking you to forget about clothes for Bill as she has everything planned for the autumn and would much rather you didn't try to do anything about it. As far as C. & T. go they don't need anything at all except a few Canadian winter things, and some of those have already been promised by friends with growing boys.

I have written Mrs. B. about C's cough but I do trust his good health will continue. Marob, I understand is quite high (about 2000 feet) which should be good for chests. And I have a feeling it may be good for Tom's eyes too, if, as Dr. Macrae thinks, his trouble is something akin to hay fever.

Last summer, when we were in Haliburton which is fairly high (though not nearly 2000 ft.) he used to play in the sand all day with the sun shining on the water and it did not affect him in the slightest—in fact I knew nothing about his trouble with his eyes until after we got back to the city. Then in the winter I was afraid the sun on the snow would be bad for him but nothing happened. He has occasionally complained of them through the winter and spring but only once have I had to use the drops which the doctor gave me....

Please give your mother our love. I have been meaning to write to her, but I expect she reads my letters to you, so hope she will forgive me.

P.S. Theresa's husband is going on well—is allowed out of bed a little. I haven't been to see him at all since he went but hope to soon. Bob's wife is expecting a baby in November so there will be another Peterkin after all![29]

P.P.S.—I forgot to mention the report on Bill's tonsils, which disturbed Vivien very much. I felt she was quite right in deciding not to take the step of having them removed without consulting you, much as we dislike to worry you. I am not in favour of the indiscriminate removal of tonsils but Dr. Smith is one of our leading pediatricians, who leans to conservatism and his opinion was that in view of their diseased condition, and the presence of a lot of adenoidal tissue, they should be taken out at once. However, as I say, she felt she should have your opinion and besides Bill would have been terribly disappointed if his trip to N.H. had to be postponed. If you think it wise, it can be done as soon as he gets back as they will be coming at least 10 days before his school opens.

[26] 118 HILLSDALE AVENUE WEST
TORONTO, JULY 10

Dear Margaret

By the time you get this I suppose you will be starting your holiday—and I do hope it <u>will</u> be a holiday—and also that you consider everything <u>very</u> carefully before taking on the school again in the autumn. Don't you think you are trying to do too much? If you are doing it in order to put by money to repay us, we would <u>much</u> rather you wouldn't. I can't believe that you are not overtaxing your strength and nerves.

John and I are having a most peaceful month—that is, peaceful in the lack of children—but we are as busy as can be over the new house. We don't take possession until Aug. 1 but we want to be ready to start work the <u>minute</u> the other people move out, in order to have all the alteration finished in time for us to get settled in before the boys come back. The owners are very kind about letting us come in any time and bring all the workmen for consultations. I think it will be very comfortable when we get finished. We can't afford of course to do all we'd like, but we are putting in a ground floor washroom, modernising the kitchen a bit with new sink and cupboards, putting electric wall outlets in all the rooms and a lot of new lights and switches, replacing some old bathroom pieces and redecorating almost all the house. The children will be able to each have a bedroom. That will eliminate a lot of minor friction—though I think Peter & C. will be a little disappointed at not sharing a room. There is a good third floor, very airy, with high ceilings and lots of windows and we are going to insulate the roof and put in a new furnace (with an automatic stoker) so it should be warm in winter. There are 3 rooms and bathroom there—we are going to put Peter, Tom, and the maid (if we get one!) up there. Then on the second floor there will be our bedroom, C's and Mary's and a fairly small room about 11 ft. square with a heated sunroom adjoining which will be decorated (both rooms) in a nice sunny yellow and turned over to the children for their sitting rooms. Peter's room is very large—14 × 20 in the main part with big dormers in addition at each end, so about half of it can be used for his printing press and other equipment which he and C. find so engrossing. They will all four have a desk or table in their bedrooms to do their home work and writing in quiet and privacy. We are putting Tom rather than C. on the top floor with Peter for two reasons—there won't be so much mischief hatched on the 3rd floor!—and we thought it better to have each bathroom shared by two who go to bed at a different hour, so there can be no arguments as to "whose turn it is to have first bath to-night."

Off our bedroom is an open balcony overlooking the garden, beneath which is a verandah opening off the dining room. There is no breakfast room but there is a corner between the kitchen and pantry where we can put a table for the children to have their tea—in fact as long as the weather's nice they can have it out on the verandah. The living and dining rooms are very pleasant and there is also a little sitting room (10 × 11) on the ground floor. The halls are roomy and the ceilings quite high and I think we shall have a feeling of space which is lacking in a house as compact as our present one. The basement is a good one with high ceilings. There is one room with lots of space for the ping pong table and also room to get in a work bench for the boys later. The garden is quite good with two good trees and lots of shrubs—about 175 ft. deep. There are also nice trees in front—in fact it is one of the best shaded streets in the city. We feel very happy about it—I think we got it at a tremendous bargain and it will make us a very comfortable home for the rest of our lives and in <u>exactly</u> the spot of Toronto we want to be.

Mary and Peter seem to be enjoying themselves—they write quite newsy letters about their doings—Mary's are very amusing. They have gone to camp for 4 weeks but if they want to stay 2 extra weeks I'd be glad to have them do so to give me even more free time. I think Peter will want to stay but if Mary wants to come home, Clare will take her up there for a couple of weeks. John is starting his holiday on July 18 and we will go to see both children that weekend and then find some quiet place to spend a week or so. We are having a lot of fun planning for the house and though it keeps me busy it's a real holiday for me—to be busy at something interesting while relieved of my usual duties and responsibilities.

I am enclosing the letter I had from Mr. Burns after they arrived at Marob. I had a letter from Mrs. Burns—a very comforting one—a week later, from which I quote "the boys seem to have settled down amazingly well and for me the most interesting thing is how well they hit it off with my husband—and how much he is enjoying them. He has always been nervous about having children and appeared to be quite scared about the prospect........anyway the 4 appear to be inseparable and the house fairly buzzes with projects and schemes and after supper they all play games (many of which involve spelling and were selected by Arthur for the purpose). They certainly are no trouble so far—we've had one wet day but it didn't seem to matter. I am feeling very happy about it.... We are finding it very interesting to discover resemblances to M. and D. in the boys. C. is exactly like his father physically but Bill is in some ways more like him personally. Tom doesn't seem to be very much like either. We like all 3 of them <u>very</u> much"....

I sent you the boys' reports which arrived a few days ago. I think they have got on very well. They and Mary will go to Brown School next year (where Ann Wilkinson goes).[30] I have registered them—the head master seems a very nice person. He is putting Tom in Grade V and C. in grade VII. I explained C's difficulty with spelling but he said he would not put him lower on account of that. He felt that when a child has had a bad start in spelling there was not a great deal one could do about it except extend all the help possible as he went along and he felt C. would probably do Grade VII spelling just as well as he would Grade VI, which is exactly my feeling about it....

I hope you got my last letter, asking you please not to worry about clothes for the boys—Vivien joins me in assuring you that we don't want you to send a thing or even think about it. As far as C. & T. go they have simply heaps of everything and Vivien says Bill is amply provided for....

Anyway, with clothes rationing I'm sure it would be quite impossible for you to get anything, but rationing or not, please put it right out of your mind. Clothes rationing must make just one more spot of gloom in life—how you all keep your spirits up under the depressing circumstances I don't know. May it not be for long!

[27] WAUPOOS, ONT., JULY 28

Dear Margaret

John and I are just finishing a most restful week here staying at a farmhouse and leading the simple life. We have a bedroom, sitting room and large screened verandah under the willow trees at the lake's edge and go up to the farmhouse for our meals. We are on Lake Ontario, in Prince Edward County, which is an island connected with the main land by a causeway at one end and a ferry at the other, and is a most peaceful backwater, where you feel far away from the world in general....

I have had no letter from the boys since the one from C. which I sent you but Vivien had a long letter from Mrs. B. just before we left (about 2 weeks ago, I think it came) and they seem to be getting along very well indeed.... The boys and Mr. B. apparently got on like a house afire right from the start and she says they look on him as their idea of just what a man ought to be. It's going to be hard on John and Harry when they come back! She says they have good appetites are happy and busy and <u>very</u> fit.

[28] 90 DUNVEGAN ROAD
      TORONTO, AUGUST 31

Dear Margaret

The boys arrived home Friday blooming in health and spirit. I think Bill has grown 2 inches. He is 5'8" in his socks—we measured him this afternoon. They have had the most marvellous holiday—Mrs. B. said they all left in tears. If she and her husband are able to go to Marob next summer they want to have them again.

I am too tired to write a letter. We finally got moved on Tuesday (26th). It was our last possible day but the house here was still full of painters, paper hangers, carpenters & electricians to say nothing of linoleum layers, carpet layers, telephone men, etc., who followed them. However we can see order emerging from chaos and I think it's going to be very comfortable when we get finished. Meantime it's been, and still is, hard work. I think the boys are pleased with their rooms. I start them to school on Tuesday. Will try to write properly soon.

Dear Margaret

We are all settling in to the new house and new school. The boys seem to have taken very well to the change of school. C. says this school is more like his school in Ulverston. He is working very diligently and methodically—I think the greatest difficulty is not knowing the boys but he is very philosophical about that and is resigned to its taking time to make friends. Tom seems quite happy and contented. I think they are both thrilled about having rooms of their own, especially C. Mary likes the school much better than her other, which is a help. Fortunately, two girls who were in her class at her old school, have also moved into this district, and are in her class now. Peter started school yesterday.

I have been working pretty hard trying to get things straight but I expect I'll be working even harder as the maid is leaving Monday and there are simply no domestics to be had. Every employment agency simply laughs at me and the clerks show the stacks of cards of employers waiting for the first applicant. They won't even take my name at the agencies!—and don't even trouble to ask what wages I will pay. My only hope is to broadcast through all my friends in the hope that something will turn up. I have a very good woman who comes from 9–12 daily and I suppose we'll just have to get along as best we can. The woman I have now, who is leaving Monday, has only been here a month but has been a great help. She is about 60 and has varicose veins and simply can't stand it.

So if you get very sketchy letters from me from now on you'll know why. I wish I could write more fully about the boys, as I used to do, but maybe I'll get a chance for a long letter soon.

The summer seems to have done C. a great deal of good. He is more "natural" and not so tied up in knots (except that he was pretty strung up last week but that was anxiety over the new school—he was so afraid he wouldn't know the customs of the school and would do the wrong thing. However I managed to foresee any difficulties in that way and consulted his teacher the first day about them, so he got on very well). I have put him in charge of the other two on the walk to school and back and think that is curing him of one bad habit he had which used to worry us—of crossing the road on red lights or in the centre of a block. I do hope you had a good holiday and things go well with you.

[30]   90 DUNVEGAN ROAD
      TORONTO, SEPTEMBER 20

Dear Margaret

Your long letter arrived during the past week, also, the air mail letter to the boys and two post cards. Punch has been arriving regularly and we enjoy it.

You will be relieved to know that I took Tom to Dr. Macrae, the oculist, and he found his eyes quite all right. I told him your man had been afraid he might become short sighted and he said he would say Tom was just on the verge between normal and short sight but as long as he had no trouble with his sight there was no reason for glasses. I was very relieved as the thought of glasses bothered me. They are such a nuisance to a child— particularly to a forgetful child—and also Tom's eyelashes are so long, I'm sure they'd rub against the glasses! Dr. Macrae advises me to speak to his teacher, asking her to keep an eye on him for any sign of difficulty with his sight, and I will do so. He is sitting in the 2nd seat from the front which should help.

I don't think you need to worry about Tom. He is definitely improved in self-reliance and independence, and has almost entirely lost his habit of constant apprehensiveness and worrying over trifles. I remember you told me he needed constant calming and reassuring and that was true at first. I can't say how long it lasted, but when the discussion arose about changing school last Easter and we more or less "examined" Tom's attitude and temperament we realized he no longer worried about things. He never talks about the war now, except perhaps a word or two of discussion of the headlines—in fact he scarcely looks at the newspapers. When he started the new school this month he was excited, but quite pleasurably so, at the strangeness and newness but he seems to have had not a single worry or anything to puzzle or perplex him. You mention Mrs. B. and some of your English friends looking at him as "needing protection." I don't quite agree—he craves protection, rather than needs it. He can stand on his feet quite well but he has an intense and, I think, subconscious, dislike for taking any responsibility. It is a very curious attitude and shows in so many different ways. It accounts for a lot of his docility and his willing obedience—he wants to be told exactly what to do and not have to think it out for himself. He doesn't use his powers of observation much and has practically no curiosity so the worst feature of his dependance is that it's hard to make him understand general principles so, though he will follow instructions, and if they're given often enough, will make them a habit, he very often hasn't the slightest idea <u>why</u> the instructions are given, and isn't enough interested to listen when it's explained. However all these things are improving gradually.

I told Mrs. B[urns] that she was seeing Tom at his worst in respect to his lack of self reliance, because of his being with Bill. I expect in his uprootal from home he came to depend on Bill completely on the voyage out and when they were first here and we have always noticed that when Bill was at our house, even for part of a day, Tom seemed to lose the independence he had acquired in the interim and would become a shadow of Bill—this would last sometimes several days. Bill always has treated him with a sort of indulgent patronage and would "poor Thomas" him, with an affectionate laugh, when he was forgetful or absent-minded, or didn't reason things out, and I think he felt these things gave him Bill's attention and he subconsciously used them, as a bid for that attention. With us, the response is not quite the same—we try to explain to him, kindly and patiently, but as firmly as possible, that at his age a boy is <u>expected</u> to remember certain things and take certain responsibility.

The first few months he was here, when I would take away his soiled clothes at night and lay out clean ones, if I ever forgot to lay out one article, I would find him sitting on his bed crying because "there aren't any socks"—or pyjamas or what not, but <u>now</u> he would simply dig in his drawer and get what was missing. That is just an example which comes to mind, but the change is the same in all kinds of things. He was told at school to get a certain kind of atlas which I tried in a lot of book stores to find, without success. I asked him to find out where it could be got and the very next day he brought home the information that Woolworth's (of all places!) carried it—so yesterday on our way home from the dentist's I stopped in front of Woolworths and giving him the money, told him he could go in and get it. A year ago he would have had a dozen questions to ask before he would have gone but yesterday he ran right in, and though they hadn't it, still I think he felt quite a thrill of independence in having carried out the business alone.

Speaking of Woolworth's reminds me of Mary's birthday present which she sent with the boys'. I took her out to buy a present for her daddy, whose birthday was Sept. 9 and she said she would like to get one for "Tom's mother" too (she never calls you anything else). Mary doesn't think a birthday present is quite legal unless it's bought at Woolworth's and she insists on <u>no</u> supervision of her purchases so I busied myself with buying curtain rings while she went off with her quarter and returned simply bubbling

with delight. She apparently had been undecided between a necklet of cel-
luloid letters spelling "There'll always be an England" in red, white and
blue and the pin but I assured her that the maple leaf was very suitable
as a present from Canada. John and I had a lot of amusement over it but
poor John was caught next morning when she gave him <u>his</u> present which
was a maple leaf pin attached by a gold (?) chain to a Union Jack pin and
he had to wear it to the office or else break her heart. So he nobly pinned it
on with great pride and as a matter of fact, I think quite enjoyed showing
it to everyone in the office. At least you are spared having to <u>wear</u> yours!...

I took the four to the dentist for a look over yesterday and T. & C. are
all right. I think it's rather ironical that Tom, who eats as little as possible
of all the things supposedly good for the teeth, should have such almost
perfect ones! Peter has his first cavity now—Mary's teeth were perfect until
last winter when she had one filling and now has to have two or three. I'm
afraid she is <u>not</u> faithful with the cleaning.

That reminds me, of Tom again—he is immensely improved in his eating. He <u>never</u> mentions not liking anything any more—once in a long while
he asks, after working away slowly at his plate "Do I have to eat all of this?"
but that's all and in fact he quite likes lots of things he didn't use to. Mary
has a fluctuating appetite and on one of her "off" days the boys finished
their dinner while she was still at her meat and vegetables. She had let her
stewed tomatoes get quite cold and was complaining to my unresponsive
ear that she didn't like them anyway. Tom was just leaving the table and he
stopped beside Mary and I heard him say in a low voice "<u>I</u> don't like them
either but I <u>ate</u> them."

We are having beautiful autumn weather—yesterday after the dentist's,
we went down in the Don Valley to look for milk weed as Peter is supposed
to get a monarch butterfly caterpillar which grows on milkweed. We found
milkweed but in a surprisingly healthy and uninfested state so we gave up
and went to the Zoo, it being close by. To-day I was pretty weary so John
took them to High Park for a run and a game of ball. We are all trying to
use as little gasoline as possible so we won't be taking many jaunts. We expect rationing by Oct. 1. We really don't use the car a great deal and it will
just mean inconvenience, no hardship, to us.

SEPTEMBER 22

Tom came home from school in the greatest excitement at noon. He has
been moved into another room, a combination Grade 5 and Grade 6 and
says he is to finish up Grade 5 work in 3 months and will then be in Grade
6, and will go on next year to Grade 7. I know, since they lengthened the
course to 8 years that they have these combination classes at 2 or 3 places
in the course, to enable brighter children to get through more quickly. I

was very pleased—the only drawback is that I'm afraid C. is not taking it any too well. He has badgered and teased Tom ever since, but I hope it's only temporary. Of course, Tom was not exactly tactful in his boasting! I will have a word with C. to-night. After all he is still one grade ahead, and is less than 2 years older than Tom, aside from all the school he missed. But jealousy is sometimes unreasonable....

My own job is pretty strenuous at present. There does not seem a domestic to be had in all of Toronto. It apparently was the wrong time to move to a bigger house!—in spite of which I'm glad we're here. I have my nice Mrs. Fairfoul in the morning from 9 to 12 and Violet, who is always my stand-by in time of need, is coming 3 days a week. She won't want to come many weeks, though, so I am "leaving no stone unturned" as the politicians say but none of the stones seem to have a cook general under them. Violet comes at 9 and stays until after dinner, so I have breakfast to get every morning. However I can manage alright if it doesn't last too long—and if it lasts long I expect I'll just have to manage that, too! The most annoying part of it is that I have to pay Violet more for the 3 days a week ($8.25 week) than I paid Mary Murphy for 7 full days a week!—of course she only has 3 days meals too but that doesn't amount to very much—I would like to feel that all my hard work was saving me more. Of course she's a better maid than Mary M. and in a full time job would rate at least $10 a month higher wages.

You will have read my letter to your mother in which I went into C's improved disposition. It is really remarkable and I do hope Tom's success at school will not give it a setback. I don't think I told you that Mrs. Burns wrote, when the boys were leaving Marob and said that she and her husband would like to help with financing C's education. They are very fond of him and certainly must have used just the right handling with him to "bring him out" so—he is not nearly so moody and is much more at ease and sure of himself and easier to get along with. I wrote thanking her and expressing our appreciation of their offer but explained that we couldn't accept anything from them, in honesty, as his education is now costing us absolutely nothing. Even books, pencils, writing books, everything is supplied in the Public Schools—art materials and handicraft materials too. We feel we are at last getting a return for our school taxes (about ⅓ of our property taxes go for schools) which we have paid for years! (Our taxes on this house are $450 a year so that means about $150 a year for schools but it would be the same if we had no children going to school at all.) ...

I must get to bed now. I suppose you are back at the school by now. The news is pretty discouraging (Kiev has just fallen) but what's the use talking about it?

Dear Margaret

I haven't time for much of a letter this time. We are all well—the boys in excellent health and spirits. C. has developed a most gratifyingly enormous appetite (particularly gratifying the 4 days a week I'm doing the cooking)— invariably asks for a second helping at dinner and eats the complete second plateful—of meat, potatoes and vegetable with apparently as much enjoyment as the first. He has two full glasses of milk for dinner and for tea and one for breakfast. Tom has a very good appetite too though his second helpings are usually puddings. He eats a bigger breakfast than any of the others—they all have fruit juice, a good big dish of porridge with honey and wheat germ on it, apple sauce or stewed fruit and toast—and Tom usually eats twice as much toast as the bigger boys—he and Mary usually have a contest to see who can eat the most. He has never had a pain in his stomach since he came (touch wood!).

They put on a play on Sunday evening which was a riotous success and enjoyed by performers and audience (John & I).

I wrote a note to Tom's teacher explaining about his eyes and asking her to seat him at the front and watch him for any signs of short sightedness. I said nothing to Tom—you know how suggestible he is—as a matter of fact the doctor realized that too, and all he told Tom was that his eyes were perfectly all right. Tom told me to-day that the teacher had put him in the front seat but apparently he didn't connect it with his sight at all—for which I'm glad.

Your letter (birthday, air mail) to C. arrived yesterday and the parcel to-day. I put the parcel away to keep for his birthday, and I have the one his father sent early in the summer, put away too. A letter arrived for Tom from his father to-day.

I am besieged with interruptions so this will have to do for now. I hope school is going well and you are finding the second year at it not so trying.

Dear Margaret

... The September reports came home with great excitement. They are supposed to be issued only every 2 months but the teachers felt that the parents might like to have some idea of the children's progress in the first month so they sent home reports with grades (A, B, C) in only Effort and Conduct, and in some cases a comment by the teacher. Tom had A in both Effort and Conduct and the teacher had written "A splendid worker, quiet and ambitious"—Tom was thrilled! C. had A in Effort and Conduct also and no remarks, so I think they have done very well indeed. They seem quite happy at school and tell me that they are making friends to the extent of having boys to play with at recess. I would like them to make some nice friends at school and would be glad to have them bring boys home but I think it is best for them to go slowly, as they are doing.

As soon as Tom was put in the Combination Grade (5 and 6) he said "Now I'll be able to try for U.T.S. next year." It has worried me a little because I suppose he takes it for granted that's the thing to do, and I dare say he could pass the exam but I am very doubtful about it being the right school for Tom. I don't mean academically—I think he could do the work all right, though they do crowd them a bit—but psychologically. As I told you in my last letter, he is gaining self reliance, but they are so "on their own" at U.T.S.—a little too much I think. I believe in it as far as school work is concerned, but the little tackers just entering, and pretty overawed by the size of the school, might, I think, have more explanation of the customs and activities of the school—even the geography of its departments and their workings. I think Peter is very self reliant for his age but he came home in tears the first day—all wrought up because he didn't know whether they were really supposed to come home or not. Tom has emerged from his worrying habits so well and become so calm and philosophical about things that I would hate to have him all stirred up again. Also it would mean another plunge into strangers, just when he's had a year at Brown to get well acquainted. Then too, I think the effect on C. would not be good. He seems to have accepted Tom's promotion (after the first day or two) without any heartburnings and I think he is getting on satisfactorily himself. His class had a test in Social Studies on Friday afternoon when he was away so the teacher is letting him try it after school to-morrow.

I might say that Tom has not mentioned U.T.S. since that first day so he may not think of it again, and I won't borrow trouble....

We brought the boys' goldfish back from their "summer holiday" in Eleanor's outdoor pond and they have grown to at least double their former size.[31] So we now have Peter's aquarium with two guppies (one pair died) and two bowls, each holding two over-size gold fish. C. is now toying with the idea of buying a zebra fish or two but feels he must investigate their habits first to find out whether they need stagnant water, like guppies or fresh, like gold fish. Peter has a book from the library which they are studying....

Dear Margaret

I'm afraid I'm late writing and the children's letters have waited for mine to be ready. C's birthday was most successful. Bill came in from school, and Ian Fraser whom the boys knew at St. Paul's and whom they have visited. Also William Paterson, 8 years old, who was our neighbour on Hillsdale came, and he stayed and played with Mary while the boys went to the early showing at the movies. Mary doesn't go to movies yet but I knew she would be terribly disappointed if left at home alone but she and William had a beautiful time. They went up to Peter's room, drew the curtains, turned out the lights and listened to the radio in the dark and thought it a great thrill....

Tom is in a high state of excitement at present. They needed boys for the choir at Church and Tom was very anxious to get in if he could. So yesterday I took him over to the choir master who had taken him into his class of small boys whom he's training for the choir. Tom can scarcely believe it's he! He <u>loves</u> to sing and really gets very little opportunity as we're not a musical family. He has a sweet little voice but lacks practice. He will get a good deal of music and singing in the Public School but of course is just starting that. I think he will try hard, and is practising the breathing exercises which Mr. Langlois gave him yesterday. I think the choir is excellent training musically and Tom will get a lot of enjoyment using his voice, both in Church, and later in life, having had this training. I hope it will not be too long until he actually is in the choir. It will be one of the great days of his life (he says) when he walks in the processional! (Don't take this to mean that he's come all over religious—it's the singing, and the importance of it, that impress him.)

C. has bought himself 2 zebra fish—little half inch striped things, and is boarding them, after much haggling, in Peter's aquarium (with the guppies). I think the board was finally settled at 1¢ a week, with P. providing food one week and C. the next.

We had a glorious weekend of warm, fresh, clear weather with blue skies and sunshine. Monday was Thanksgiving Day, our last holiday of the year. John took the children to a nearby woodland park for an hour or two on Sunday but otherwise we did not leave home at all. The children spent all the time in the garden, playing with the dead leaves, building forts and barricades and all manner of things.

I wrote to C's principal, asking him if possible to include C. in Brown School's quota to the art classes at the Art Gallery. I have a letter from him and he has very kindly done so—although his quota is only 7 for the school, which must have about 1000 pupils! However, this year C. will have to be tested this Saturday to determine his qualifications for the classes. I hope he will be accepted. I think he enjoyed the classes last year.

I have had to write this in such a rush. I do hope it is legible (and intelligible). Things have been pretty hectic lately—Monday being a holiday Violet didn't come. I've surprised myself with what good meals I can turn out, but it keeps me busy from early morning to dead of night! However, Mary Murphy is returning to us to-morrow night—I hope in a chastened mood. She telephoned me and asked if I'd like her back. She says her conscience has never been at rest since she left, she feels she left me "in a dirty spot" (her words) and I had always been good to her. I think her repentance is in part due to finding waitressing and factory work (both of which she's tried) have longer and more inconvenient hours than housework. She's at present on the 4.30 P.M.–2 A.M. shift in a munitions plant, so I am none too optimistic as to how it's going to work out when she comes back. But I had no choice as positively no other candidates presented themselves. It will at least be something not to have to start with a stranger....

[34] 90 DUNVEGAN ROAD
TORONTO, OCTOBER 19

Dear Margaret

... I am in a desperate hurry but I just had to get a line off to you at once. Your letter of Sept. 20 enclosing Mrs. Burns' of July 30 arrived yesterday. I am awfully sorry she ever wrote it to you—as you say, I'm sure a mother would not have done so. However, if she erred in judgment in dealing with you, she did not in dealing with Bill and was so extremely successful that the situation is entirely changed and there is nothing for you to worry about. The change in Bill's whole attitude is simply remarkable and was apparent immediately on his return. He shows great strength of character in recognizing his weaknesses and making a determined and successful effort to overcome them, and seems so much happier over it. I will write fully as soon as I have time, though I'm sure she will have written since that letter, and Vivien, to whom I showed it and your letter, is writing you to-day. I wish you had been spared all the worry you've had over it, for even if the problem were not solved (as it is) it would have been fatal for you to have tried to do anything about it. Nothing could have been worse than to let him think he was being talked over or complained of to you.

As for Tom I think I covered him fully in a previous letter. Mrs. B's description of him sounds exactly like the Tom of a year ago, the first month or so he was here but he is not a bit like that now. The shift to another strange place and consequent dependence on Bill must have set him back. He is to go with his whole class to the Museum to-morrow. When I asked "What day did you say you go to the Museum?" He said "Monday. We are all to meet at the car stop at 9 o'clock instead of going into school. But I haven't even an <u>idea</u> where the car stop is!"—in the airiest least concerned tone imaginable !! What do you think of that?

[35] 90 DUNVEGAN ROAD
       TORONTO, OCTOBER 28

Dear Margaret

Vivien has written you a long and, I hope reassuring letter about Bill (which I have read) and has found it a most difficult business. In the first place, it is hard to cover things satisfactorily in letters and to convey the impression one intends—one longs for the chance of a good hour's talk. In the second place, Bill has changed so completely that it seems rather cruel to drag up his failures of last year. However, after your letter came with Mrs. Burns' enclosed, we realized that we would have to make an attempt to explain the situation or you would never feel satisfied about Bill, nor would you have much faith in any future reports from V. or myself. We both feel very deeply how frightful it is for you to have him, for an indefinite time, so far away and under the care of competent strangers whose ideas and general outlook you can judge only by letters.

I do want to assure you (as I have already done) that of all the people I know there is no family [the Ratcliffes] with whom I would rather have my own son live under similar circumstances and I was delighted when they offered, without my asking it, to give a home to Bill.[32] They are not merely <u>kind</u> people, but intelligently kind and the atmosphere of their home is one of friendliness and understanding and, above all, fairness, where every member has his or her individual life and interests uninterfered with but all are united by affection and mutual respect. Their children are above average in self-reliance and co-operativeness. So there was no attempt made to cast Bill "in a Ratcliffe mold" and their concern over Bill's vagaries was not actuated nearly so much by the resulting inconvenience to themselves as by their genuine interest in Bill's development as a happy well-adjusted member of society. They were fully aware of, and sympathetic of, the difficulties Bill was facing, starting a new life in a strange country and living with strangers and therefore made due allowance for the lack of tact and even rudeness to themselves and their friends which he at first displayed.

Bill fitted very quickly into the household in so far as enjoying and sharing all its benefits and privileges (and having no hesitation in demanding what he thought his just and equal share) but he utterly failed to assume any share of the joint responsibility necessary to keep any such household going. By this I don't mean only the giving of actual physical assistance in the tasks of the household, but also the acceptance of minor inconveniences and postponements, due to occasional small emergencies or breaks in routine common to all households, or to the greater immediate urgency of someone else's interests. Bill, as a newcomer, was naturally shielded from these as much as possible but it was soon apparent that he considered his interests inviolate and that any scheme of his, however trivial, was the most important activity in the house.

In this, and in fact in all, his manifestations of selfishness, one great difficulty was the fact that Bill has been treated here almost as an adult. Perhaps this was a mistake, but he seemed to expect it, and though only 13, he was mentally so advanced that there was no other way for strangers to treat him. Tom has the same self-centredness as Bill but it is so much simpler to handle in a small child, who quite expects correction and guidance. I could keep constantly pointing out to Tom when other people's rights were being infringed on—when, to give an instance he would lay out a game of patience on the floor right in the playroom doorway and then complain loudly when the other children walked over his cards, going in and out. I could also keep explaining to him that, while I welcomed and was interested in his stories of the daily happenings at school, it was scarcely thoughtful of him to interrupt my conversation with a caller or to burst into my room while I was dressing, to tell me them. Tom is very honest and fair and by constantly having his eyes opened in this way he has come to have far more consideration and thought for others than he did, and to look beyond himself much more.

I think all children are born selfish, and it takes years for them to learn that thought for others pays dividends in happiness and improved relationships. Christopher's selfishness, like Peter's, is of this natural variety and I think, being the same age, they have arrived at about the same stage in its subjugation. But Bill and Tom seem to have a different kind, springing from complete absorption in self and utter lack of interest in any person or thing or activity which doesn't directly affect them or appeal to them. They both have a strong sense of fairness but this "unawareness" of, and lack of interest in, other people and their rights and feelings, together with very slender use of their powers of observation, keeps them from even knowing that they <u>are</u> being selfish. In Tom's case I don't think it is at all serious. He is young and has a so much humbler opinion of himself than Bill, is so anxious to do the right thing and accepts so willingly an adult's opinion of what is the right thing that, as I said, I have made good progress in turning his mind "out."

Also, Tom is standing on his own feet so much better. He is much more purposeful in all his actions and is never at a loss for "something to do." I imagine, from what I've learned about him, that when he came here the upheaval in his life set him back a good way from the state of self-reliance to which you had brought him—apparently the change to the Burns had the same effect. When he came back here in Sept., there was a slight set-back but only for a short time. Incidentally, we were much amused by the reference in Mrs. B's letter to the fact that "we no longer hear 'I don't like this' or 'I can't eat that'"—we hadn't heard it in our house for at least 6 months—and also "they are growing accustomed to lettuce and greenstuffs"—which they had been eating here every day for a year! It just goes to show how a child will "try it on" at every new opportunity!

To return to Bill—what you say about his laziness is quite correct—that he was lazy only about the things he didn't like doing and he is a good walker. Walking was at first his only physical activity and Vivien encouraged it and he was a bit ostentatious about his long solitary walks and quite evidently scornful of the "lazy Canadians" who didn't do likewise, overlooking the fact that the lazy Canadians were quite probably at home raking leaves, tidying the garage, shovelling snow, taking down screens or putting up storm windows or doing other useful and necessary jobs. I can well understand that at first all these duties would not seem to have any relation to him, some of them being unnecessary in England and others, due to the more plentiful supply of labour, not performed by the family. But one would expect a person of honest outlook, when he saw that these were the responsibilities of the family, to feel that as he shared all the treats, outings and privileges of the house, he should also share the duties, and that if he shirked his share it would have to be done by some other member of the family who might not like doing it any better than he did.

This seems to sound as though we spent all our days at hard labour but actually, aside from the snow shovelling, which depends on "acts of God" and is therefore unpredictable, the activities I mean are seasonal ones and occupy only a very occasional Saturday. It also sounds tremendously smug, as though all Canadians were models of industry which is of course absurd—that is the difficulty of trying to explain such things by letter. Anyway it was not the actual help on Bill's part that concerned Vivien but the effect on his future life and happiness of his lack of thought for others and lack of co-operation in a common enterprise. She had a talk with him at the New Year and with his usual honesty he agreed with her principles but continued to fail in putting them into practice whenever they interfered with his own convenience.

It was the same attitude, and the same fear of its consequences, that concerned Mrs. B. as soon as she got to know Bill (though naturally we had not mentioned it to her) and when she wrote Vivien and me, commenting on it, we immediately entered into correspondence with her, not in a spirit of criticism, of Bill, but with the aim of mutual assistance towards helping Bill. She had one or two long talks with him and she was able to put things much more forcibly to him and speak more strongly, than Vivien, because, as she said, if he should resent it (which he didn't at all) it would be better that it should come from someone whom he was just visiting for a short time. Also, her words had infinitely more weight with Bill because of her being a friend of yours and of his father's and of her having a common background with you—an English upbringing and a life of intellectual activity.

I think it was probably a surprise to Bill to find her standards exactly the same as the Ratcliffes'—whom, with ourselves, he had (more or less unconsciously) patronized as being business people and outside his own intellectual world. Mrs. B. must have convinced him of the necessity of re-shaping his whole outlook, for the change in him was apparent as soon as he returned, and has been noticed not only by his immediate circle, the R's and ourselves, but by people who see him infrequently and for short periods. He can take time now to be pleasant and agreeable, even at a chance meeting and to show thoughtfulness in little things. As V. told you in her letter, we give Mrs. B. full credit for all this. Nevertheless John and I feel that the Ratcliffes laid the groundwork through all this past year, by their daily presentation of family life as a joint enterprise, operating successfully only by the co-operation of every member, and kept balanced by the "give and take" of the members. Mrs. B. opened Bill's eyes to the desirability of putting in his 5 cents worth of "give" as well as "take."

Your fears as to his having felt a failure in human relationships and retired into his shell are, I think, quite groundless. As Vivien said in her letter, he was never conscious of the concern which he aroused or the difficulties he presented. Aside from the one friendly talk which I mentioned, and one John had with him about the same time, he was not criticised, and his shortcomings were pointed out to him only very rarely, on very glaring occasions. Nor was there any diminution of the kindness and consideration accorded him. His personal relationships with the Ratcliffe family improved steadily through the year through increasing knowledge of, and trust in, them. When we left the boys at Cornwall with Mr. B., Vivien was quite touched when Bill said "I have two homes to write to now." So I think your first judgment, as to why he wrote the sort of letters he did, was the right one—he was living in the moment, absorbed in the things that interested him, and he has always seemed quite happy and contented and secure in his place as a member of the R. household.

Now, however, his happiness seems of a keener and more positive kind, due to the fact that he feels an active and not passive partner in the family, and takes pride in the fact. A good part of Thanksgiving weekend was given over to preparing the garden for winter and Bill entered into the job willingly and thoroughly enjoyed both the open air exercise with pleasant companionship and the glow of satisfaction from the accomplishment of a piece of work well done. (This sounds most revolting, like a paragraph out of the Fairchild Family or whatever was the name of that awful family of prigs we used to read about in our youth, and cordially detested—but I'm sure you understand what I'm driving at.)[33]

Also when Viv. returned home one Sunday after being out to tea, he met her at the door, simply beaming, and announced with pride that he had spent the entire afternoon sorting, tidying and arranging all his books and papers in his new desk (which with its many pigeon holes seems to please him very much). It is in this matter of looking after his personal belongings and his clothes that he will need most supervision and reminders. He has never quite accepted as just the explanation that he should hang up his clothes properly when he takes them off and take decent ordinary care of them. He apparently feels he has a "mind above such trivial things." I have known other young people who felt the same way, but if they were quite honest they would realize that it is not the loftiness of their minds, but laziness and selfishness which impels them to neglect tiresome and boring small duties if they feel that someone else (who finds them just as tiresome and boring) will do them, if they're neglected long enough. However, V. has been so encouraged by Bill's ability to change his ways in other matters that I know she intends to persevere in this.

A short time after Bill's return from N.H., Harry thought V. should comment on his improved attitude to Bill, and commend and encourage him, but V. hesitated, lest Bill should suspect that he had been a subject of discussion between them and the Burns. Bill himself solved the problem by opening the subject himself. The night before school opened, being a sort of anniversary, he asked if she thought he had developed and broadened during the year. That gave her the opportunity of letting him know how they appreciated his improvement and he went back (of his own accord) and made a resumé of the year, explaining how so many of his ideas had changed. He admitted that for some time he had been very secretive about all his affairs (a fact she had noticed and rather resented, but never mentioned) and said that when, last year, she asked anything about his school work or personal activities (or just the usual rather meaningless "Well, Bill, what have you been doing to-day?") he thought she was curious!!!—but now he realized that she had just been showing interest!! Also he said some of his early judgments had been proved false by fuller knowledge. He showed great understanding and power of self-analysis, and it was a heartwarming talk for Vivien.

I really think I have come to the end of this horrible letter. I have hated writing it—it all sounds so smug, as though the R's and we were two families of complete paragons without a single failing amongst us. Naturally we don't tell you about the difficulties we have with our own children. I can truthfully say that since Tom is standing on his own feet and C. so much less moody and better tempered, your two cause <u>much</u> less difficulty than my own two.

We all regret very much that you have had all this worry and such a long wait for reassurance. Vivien forgot to mention it in her letter, but we are both most anxious that you should give Bill <u>no</u> hint of any of this. Everything is now on an even keel and even if it weren't, it could only cause strained feelings for you to try to help at such a distance.

I will send the boys' letters and my usual "newsletter" under separate cover, as I know you pass them on around the family. I do hope this will be one of the occasional letters that sometimes get a quick passage, and that it and Vivien's will help to set your mind at rest. We will tell you quite honestly of Bill's progress.

[36]   90 DUNVEGAN ROAD
       TORONTO, OCTOBER 29

Dear Margaret

I've held the boys' letters up again—they wrote them two days ago. Everyone is thriving—the boys are carving pumpkins into Jack O'Lanterns for Friday night which is Halloween.

Tom went to choir practise this afternoon and came home with the thrilling news that he is to be in the choir on Sunday morning, though he is just to sing the hymns. Apparently not <u>quite</u> anthem material yet! He came home at noon quite excited over a school choir to be selected from three of the classes from volunteers who were to assemble at the school at 1.10 (afternoon school starts at 1.30). He was eager to try for it, so set off early and tells me this afternoon that he is to attend practises 3 days a week at the same time. With all these days of continuous song he should be practically a Caruso by the end of the year. He simply loves it!

C. did not get accepted for the Art Classes. I was very sorry, and had a talk with him and offered to start him on a series of classes for children at the Women's Art Assn. given by Dorothy Stevens & Kathleen Ward on Sat. mornings. He seemed reluctant to enter what would be small classes (12 or 13) of probably fairly talented children. So I offered to join the Art Gallery (we have not been members for a few years, since we started cutting down on luxuries) which would entitle him to attend the children's classes there on Friday afternoon. I left it entirely to him but tried to make him understand that I would be very glad to give him the opportunity of classes if he wanted them but would by no means try to force him into them if he didn't. It is always very difficult to find out what C. <u>does</u> want to do. However he decided against it. I think he would have liked the regular Sat. classes which he tried for but I don't think he's frightfully disappointed & certainly the outlet is really not necessary for him now.

The children all got to the circus last week. Tom went with Bill—Harry had bought 3 tickets for Sat. aft. so Bill took Tom and Judy.[34] C. & Peter went Friday afternoon & Mary Murphy took Mary. The Brown School children were allowed to leave at 2.15 on Friday for the circus. It was apparently a very good circus and was "enjoyed by all." The children gave a play on Sat. eve. and on Sunday Bill came for the day and went to Church with us. After dinner we took them all to the Art Gallery to see an extremely interesting exhibit on the Growth of Toronto which is on this month. It is very well arranged and includes some lovely old water colours & coloured engravings which have been loaned for the exhibit. After tea Bill and Tom put on a magic show—mind reading which was not a howling success as Tom had not enough time to learn the code!—but we enjoyed it anyway....

I went to Hamilton with Theresa this afternoon to see Leslie. He is improving steadily—is to have another X-ray next week and is also having tests made. I do hope they let him out soon....

Did I ever tell you St. Paul's School had closed? Mr. Waddington resigned—he is in the R.C.A.F. doing ... training work so there was no use trying to keep the school on. It does seem a pity—he was a wonder with boys and the school was doing very good work.

I must get on to bed now. I hope all goes well with you. The boys are busy with plans for their English Christmas presents which we hope to post the end of the week.

Dear Margaret

All continues to go well. Mary Murphy seems quite happy, likes the house, and seems more like she used to be before the onslaught of her discontent, slackness and sullenness which plagued me for months before she left last May. The children are well and happy.

Friday was Hallowe'en and in the afternoon all children (at Brown School) who wished to were permitted to wear costumes to school and most of the afternoon was taken up in parading from class to class. They were warned to wear <u>home-made</u> costumes and save any money which might be used for costumes, to buy war savings stamps. Mary had an old costume (old lady) of Peter's which she had been counting for weeks on wearing but the boys showed no desire to "dress up" until noon on Friday, when C. asked me if I thought he might dress up as a tramp. On this Tom, of course, thought he'd do the same—poor Tom is not strong in initiative. I persuaded C. that there would be no harm, as Tom is in a different room, so we dug out various old garments. C. combined his with great resourcefulness and added a black eye (with crayon) for good measure and they all went off in high spirits and had a jolly afternoon. I had got 2 large pumpkins and turned them over, 1 to P. and 1 to C. to carve into Jack O'Lanterns so we had those on either side the front steps. We did not think there would be much Hallowe'en "shelling out" on our street as, being an older district, there are practically no children about. So John took the children to our old street and visited a neighbour for ½ an hour while the children "did" their old friends' houses. Then John took them to the houses of several of our friends who live not far from us—all people without children, who gave them most sumptuous kinds of candies. So the evening was most satisfactory for me as well as them—instead of a 6 qt. basket full of the cheapest candy they had a smaller (but <u>very</u> ample) amount of very good candy!...

Dear Margaret

We had our first hint of winter this morning. Snow fell for nearly an hour, but melted as fast as it fell, and now the sun is coming out....

Tom made his first appearance in the choir at evening service yesterday. Jo Robinson had Bill, C. & Tom over for dinner and tea yesterday (which they apparently enjoyed very much) and dropped Tom at the Church afterwards.

To-morrow, being Armistice Day, the schools are closed, which seems a ridiculous idea. Brown School is to have a Remembrance service this afternoon in Timothy Eaton Memorial Church, close by. It seems to me it would be much more suitable to have them go to school to-morrow and have the service then, instead of having a holiday, so that Nov. 11 loses all its significance. However, that's how it is. Tom is singing in the school choir at the service this afternoon. He has been scuttling off to school 20 minutes early every second afternoon for two weeks, to practise.

All 4 children spent the day at Clare's on Saturday.

NOVEMBER 11

I did not get this finished yesterday. I took the three boys down town this morning and we met Bill at a Honey Dew restaurant at 11.30 where I gave them "hot dogs" and "Honey Dew" and we all went to see "Target for To-night" which is extremely well done and very thrilling....[35]

I don't know whether I've ever told you that both the boys are reading a great deal now. When they first came C. scarcely ever looked at a book and Tom would read for very short and widely spaced periods. But they have gradually come to it more and more as we have tried to ply them with attractive books. Now they both read in almost every spare moment and after they wake in the morning if it's not time to get up and C. even slips into his room to read if he has a few minutes in the morning or at noon, before time to leave for school. I take them to the library and let them choose their own books. Tom said to me last week in rather a surprised tone—"I find that now-a-days every book seems to me to be a good book. Each one I read I think is the best I've ever read." Last year the only books that seemed to interest him were very childish ones but now he is getting his teeth into some worth while ones. C. & Peter read and re-read the Ransomes, but sandwich in a good many others.[36]

A parcel came for C. & Tom this morning with nothing on it to say it was a Christmas present. I suspected it might be but did not like to withhold the parcel in case it wasn't, so I had them open it and it was their Christmas presents from their father—photographs in leather frames. They were both very pleased with them—I asked whether they would like to keep them out or wrap them up again until Christmas but they were all for keeping them out, which seems to me most sensible—they may as well keep on enjoying them.

Christmas seems to be fairly leaping at us. I'm afraid it won't be a lavish one this year but we'll try to make it jolly.

Mr. Churchill has rather cheered us up this week by his evident confidence in the face of the gloomy picture in Russia, and the Americans seem to be waking up to the need of action as well as words.

[39] 90 DUNVEGAN ROAD
TORONTO, NOVEMBER 16

Dear Margaret

... We were overjoyed to have the Beamishes in town for the day Thursday. Unfortunately John spent the week in New York so he did not see them but it was good to see Mrs. Beamish again and to meet her husband who is just as charming as she is, which is saying a great deal.[37] Vivien was particularly delighted to have them at her house—she has felt from the beginning, and especially since your worry over Bill, how trying it is for you to have him living with people whom you don't know at all and whom you can only hear of through letters—hers and mine—and you really don't know <u>me</u> very much better! It was like an answer to prayer that Mrs. B., whom you know so well, should be able to see a bit of their home life and see Bill in his present environment and I know Mrs. B. was delighted with both. I hope she will be able to <u>see</u> you after she gets to England but even her <u>letters</u> are bound to mean more to you than ours.

I met Mrs. B. at the hotel Thursday morning and took her to do a bit of shopping and brought her up here for lunch which the boys and Mary had with us. I had sent notes to the boys' teachers in the morning asking for an extra hour at noon (they have 12 to 1.30) so they had the extra hour alone with her after Mary went back to school. She noticed a great change in C. from last year—so much more relaxed and at ease and less self-conscious—and also that Tom seemed to stand on his own feet better. It was Mary Murphy's afternoon out so Theresa came up about 2.30 to keep house for me. At 2.30 I took Mrs. B to Vivien's, and I had to go to Brown School to their Open House (more of that later). Vivien had hoped to have the B's for dinner but Mr. B. (who was busy with meetings all day) expected to have to entertain business people at dinner. However he telephoned here just before we left for Vivien's and said his party had fallen through except for one man, so would I dine with them. I was at the school until 5 and then drove down to the hotel to pick up Mr. B. and took him to the Ratcliffes, where we all had a drink and spent an hour or two, by which time they had persuaded Vivien and Harry to dine with them too. (Harry had not been feeling well, so had not gone to the office, which was too bad for him but rather nice as giving him more time with the B's, as he doesn't get home from the office until 6.30 or 6.45 normally.) So we all had dinner together at the Royal York and sat and talked until 11—we could have talked with them hours more, we all liked them so! It was <u>such</u> a satisfying day!

They seem to have made simply ideal arrangements for their children when they go back. I hope we shall be able to do something for Andrew while he is at T.C.S.—it is only about 80 miles from Toronto.

The Open House at the school is a function held once a year, when each teacher is in his or her room after school hours and all parents are invited to come and talk over their children's work and progress and, if they wish, look over the children's work books, which are in or on their desks. I felt I should not miss the chance of talking to Tom's & C's teachers—I had met Mary's at a tea the Home & School Club had some time ago. I was glad I went because I was able to have a good chat with both of them. Miss Blair, Tom's teacher, is a stout, jolly "comfortable" sort of person. As I expected, she has no problems with Tom, nor does he seem to have any. He is well-behaved and gives no trouble, as you would expect, can do the work without difficulty and expresses himself very well when answering questions. She mentioned Tom's habit, when he is talking, of taking an audible breath, like a gasp, at every pause, and said with a laugh "I find it rather attractive. I suppose some teachers would try to get him to overcome it, but to me it seems something peculiarly Tom's that no one else has, and I rather like it." So she apparently is no "standardiser." She had noticed a slight tendency towards helplessness in minor, mechanical things—such as extracting a rusted nib from a pen, etc., but those things she treats with a joke and he has never failed to master such little difficulties of that kind, as have arisen. Altogether one can see that she is very fond of Tom, and he seems very happy with her. She has put him in a front seat, as I asked her to do, and he never makes a mistake in copying from the black board or a book, nor has he shown any other signs of short sight or difficulty with his eyes. At home, too, he has not mentioned his eyes for months and months. I think I told you he has been reading a great deal more, but his sight seems perfectly normal and he does not rub his eyes with the palms of his hands as he used to do almost habitually when he first came. He has just finished "Siegfried" and "Castaway Island" and has started "Men Against the Sea." C. is reading Jules Verne.

As I expected, C. is the one who has given concern at school. He has two teachers—Miss Orok and Mr McEachern. They are really High School teachers (Brown School includes the First Form of High School) but this year there are only enough pupils for one High School class, instead of two, but more elementary pupils than before, so these two teachers carry on the two classes by alternating. I did not get an opportunity of talking to Mr. McE. but as he is leaving soon it was not so important. Miss Orok was quite encouraging about C's work and his ability—except his writing which is the worst she's ever seen!—if he keeps on working as well as he is, and maintains his present rate of improvement she thinks he is sure to pass, which is more, she says, than she can say for the rest of the class, the average of ability in that particular class being very low this year.

Her concern was for the child's own nervousness and his personal adjustment in view of his handicaps. The first week or two she had him he was in an obvious state of inner torment. His nervousness made it almost impossible for him to answer a question orally (and when he stood up to try he was trembling all over) and his writing was made even worse by his nervousness, which increased his lack of muscular co-ordination. The frustration caused by this inability to express himself naturally increased the nervousness, making a vicious circle. She is a most understanding sort of person and her only feeling was sympathy for the child, so she set to work to build up his self-confidence and help him to relax. She never asks him a question unless it's one that none of the others can answer and she can see by his expression that he <u>can</u>—and of course that's always a help to the ego. She says she would never think of asking him to give an oral composition for instance—it would be agony for him and do him no good at all. She thought at first she would simply have to put him back to Grade 6, but after 10 days or 2 weeks he began to improve and has continued to do so ever since—gradually settling in and getting more and more at ease. She particularly mentioned his nice smile which was beginning to be shown once in a while, and said even in the midst of his frustration he had given no signs of bad temper but seemed to have a rather sweet disposition. Also there had never been any tears, which were so frequent during the first months of last year's school, so apparently the adjustment, though painful, was much easier than last year's.

It is too bad he had the second change of school, but can't be helped and the worst is over now. I told Miss Orok of my conversations with C. about school and of his talking of "standing about alone at recess." She said she had watched from the window and noticed that that was what happens so one day she talked to the class about making strangers welcome and how to treat them, and watching from the window again, saw that he was included in the games from then on. She says he has become quite friendly with 2 boys, both very nice and desirable as friends. I would like to get hold of them and encourage the friendship. One is McAllister whom he mentioned to me some time ago, but I've just not had time to look him up. The other, Miss Orok told me, is Duncan Graham and I <u>almost</u> met his mother that afternoon but she'd <u>just</u> gone. I am telling you all this—I hope it won't worry you unnecessarily, but it is the background for whatever C. achieves in school while here. He undoubtedly has some big gaps in his foundation work but Miss O. agrees with Mrs. U. that he has a good brain and very good reasoning power. He is apparently very good at maths. Now that he is settling into the work better I think his next report should be better, as naturally this one covers all the early part when his work was far from satisfactory. (His last maths test he got 100%.)

He got his report Thursday afternoon (the day I was at the school and out with the B's) and Theresa told me the other three children were very outspoken in their criticisms and <u>very</u> lofty in their own smugness over their A's—children are so horribly cruel! I think poor C. expected me to be very critical, but I got hold of him alone next morning before school and tried to make him see that I was not at all disappointed. I explained to him that I had talked to Miss O. and she understood that the new school had made things hard and upsetting for him so he had not been able to do himself justice, that she knew he had good work and a good brain in him and that as he grew more at home in the class it would "come out" more easily, and if he kept working hard, especially at writing, [this] next report would be better. I gave him a hug and told him <u>not</u> to worry about it. John came home yesterday and he talked to him in much the same way. We are going to try to get him to practise writing 10 or 15 minutes every evening, as we did last spring. It is an awful nuisance but it did have results while he was doing it. He uses ink at school, too, which he's not used to, and Miss O. says his work book is a mass of blots and scrawls and quite disgraceful. So we'll have to get him to do his practising with ink. Of course I've always felt that St. Paul's gave ridiculously rosy reports and so have other parents. You will notice C. has A for effort both months, which is good. He asked Miss O. if he could keep the report a day or two to have it photographed but she wanted them all in Friday (they were so late being issued). So she asked him to copy the grades for you this time, and I think C. said she would give him an extra copy next time.

I hope I've made it clear to you that Miss O. feels he is steadily <u>improving</u> in every way so there is no need to worry about him. But he will certainly need to be shoved a bit in his writing.

Tom, for the first time since he came to Canada, had one of his stomach pains on Friday evening. I had forgotten all about them until Thursday, when discussing Tom's health with Mrs. B., I remembered your writing about them and remembered that he had never had one. It came on about tea time so he went to bed (had to miss choir practice) with a hot water bottle and I gave him a box of medicine. When it was time for C. to go to bed I put him in Tom's bed and brought Tom down to C's room so he'd be near me, gave him another dose, and he went off to sleep and slept all night and was perfectly all right in the morning. However, being Saturday and a rainy day I kept him in bed all morning to have a good rest. I am not letting him go to Evening Service to-night. He has choir practice Mon. & Fri. night (Mon. imperative, Fri. optional) and Evening Service is optional. I think 2 late nights a week are the absolute limit and the practices are really more worth while, at the present stage, than the Service, so I'll have him skip Evening Service this winter, and sometimes Fri. eve. practice, too. He & C. both need a lot of sleep....

I suggested to C. a month or so ago that he might start making some Christmas cards but he said he had used up all his ideas last year and had no new ones so the matter rested and then these arrived (a dozen for each of them) as a present from the University Overseas Children's Committee. They were not exactly my idea of an attractive Christmas card, but one can't look a gift horse in the mouth in these days of financial stringency, nor would I want to appear to the boys to be critical of something kindly meant so I handed them over to them without comment except to suggest to C. that they would be prettier and gayer if he coloured them. He started at them but only coloured 3 or 4—he was sure the child on the cover was a girl, which rather dulled his interest. (Personally, if that rather adenoidal, not to say, imbecile person is intended to typify an English evacuee, I could scarcely expect him to be enthusiastic!) Anyway he and Tom finally got a bunch designated and signed so I am sending them off, and trust their recipients will not regard them as the height of Canadian artistic effort!...

The weather is a bit colder now but far from wintry. In fact John picked a few last flowers in the garden yesterday when he and the children were raking up the last of the leaves. I helped them do the front lawn last week and they got the back garden finished yesterday. Peter and C. take turns (2 weeks each) at looking after the coal for the furnace. We installed one of those marvellous Iron Fireman furnaces, which feeds itself from a hopper. The boys keep the hopper full of coal from the bin. They do it every day so they won't forget, and as the hopper holds about 3 days supply, they don't need to put much in each time. It gives them a little job to be responsible for, which is good for them, and also relieves John of it.

This will be quite a budget, with the reports and exam papers. All your letters are opened by censor now—I expect ours are too.

[40] 90 DUNVEGAN ROAD
TORONTO, DECEMBER 1

Dear Margaret

Your letter of Oct. 23 and one to the boys and Mary (Oct. 26) both arrived Nov. 29.... You can't imagine how thrilled Mary was with your letter. She wouldn't let me read it but worried it out herself, with me telling her the words she couldn't make out and then she read it over and over, to her daddy when he came home and to anyone who came to see her. When she came to the part about you wearing her pin to the party she said "It's a good thing I didn't get the necklace," so her mind is finally at rest over her choice! ...

C. came home last Monday noon and asked if he <u>had</u> to eat his dinner as he had a stomach ache. I said certainly not but I didn't want him to go back to school without it, so suggested that he get into my bed with a hot water bottle. He did, and the ache gradually faded. Next morning he felt quite all right but I kept him home till noon to be quite sure. When he left for school in the afternoon I gave him a note addressed to Miss Orok and he said "Didn't I tell you our class has been changed around and we have Mr. Pugh for teacher now?" Of course he hadn't mentioned it to me, but that gave me an inkling about the stomach ache. I think it was largely nerves, knowing C.—though he <u>does</u> get constipated at times—I try to check up but it's hard to get anything out of him. I am sorry about the change of teachers. Miss Orok seemed so understanding—I hope Mr. Pugh is too. I am going to try to see him some time soon for a chat about C. C. brought home a notice to-day that he is to have a physical examination Wed. afternoon—all pupils in the Public Schools are given one annually. They like the parents to be present, to talk to the doctor, so I will try to go down for it and I may be able to see Mr. P. at the same time. He is the teacher C. had the first 2 weeks of school—then there was a shift and his class had Miss O. and Mr. McEachern. Now Mr. McE. has left so there's been a reshift. It does seem too bad it has to happen to the one most easily disturbed emotionally. I have been having him practise writing every evening from the copy book—he can do quite well when he tries, but has a distressing tendency (common to all children) to consider his writing <u>exercises</u> as something quite apart from all the other writing he does, and having no relation to it.

However he tells me that Mr. P. says his writing is much improved since he had him early in the term. I forgot to say that the doctor came in to see Mary, the morning C. was home and he had a "poke" at his stomach but could find nothing wrong.[38] I kept a close eye on him all week and he did seem a bit white and quiet for a few days, though his appetite was good and he said he was quite well. By the end of the week he seemed as happy as ever so I'm sure it was mostly nervous tension and after a few days he adjusts himself....

DECEMBER 2

... I have been considering getting Tom skis for Christmas—last year he used the little 5' beginner's skis, which Peter & Mary had had and the other 3 children all had 5'6" ones with proper harness. I think he would be quite happy with the small ones again if the others would let him—they didn't make remarks about them last year but I'm sure they would a second winter (you know the line—"little baby skis"). Tom's range of interests is not very wide and skiing is one thing he loves. I will have to get after them right away as they are very scarce this year—the govt. has taken over the output of a good many factories for the ski troops and the metal for the harness is scarce (aluminum I think).

Tom came home from choir practice last night simply in a dither. Mr. Langlois had given them each 50¢—evidently a monthly hand-out of pocket money to the choir boys, which I'd known nothing of. I suppose it's given if they are faithful at choir practice. Tom could scarcely believe it!

We had a letter yesterday from the Univ. Overseas Children's Committee about the health and accident insurance on the boys. The underwriter lost so heavily on last year's policy that they would not renew it on similar terms. So the benefits have been reduced—it still looks after illness or accidents that cost over $10—and up to $300 but allows hospital expenses only up to $3.50 day and 75% of nursing care and there are limitations on doctors' and surgeons' bills. However, the committee is still paying the premium and it is a great help to know that if anything serious arose it would be looked after—at least to a large extent. For minor things—necessitating perhaps one doctor's call, our doctor doesn't charge for the boys, nor does our dentist for the small amount of work and regular examination he does.

I asked Mrs. Beamish to try to explain to you how we felt about the money question. It would be foolish to deny that having the boys has meant material and financial sacrifice, especially with taxes leaping every year (our income tax is now about 35% but there are all sorts of indirect taxes, such as a 10% sales tax on all goods) and we would naturally not refuse some reimbursement after the war if you find it possible and the government allows it. But we most emphatically do not want you to feel oppressed by a load of debt or obligation or to undertake more work than your health and nerves will stand in order to earn more. Whatever we do is done gladly and is not influenced in the slightest by whether or not there will be repayment. Perhaps it's silly of me to go over all this again, when I spoke of it before and you told me how you felt about the school (I can quite see that you may be happier with your time and thoughts completely engrossed) but I know you are a superconscientious person and wanted to reassure you again. (I might say Vivien feels as I do about all this.)

I expect Vivien has told you that Bill has started in having his teeth straightened. The plate apparently broke during the summer and couldn't be fixed, and it really did not seem to have made any improvement in the year he's been here. It was through her own dentist that she got this marvellous offer to have the work done just for the cost of materials. You see there is an arrangement here whereby the last year students at the Dental College (it's either a 4 or 5 year course, I can't remember which) at the University, do dental work for any overseas children. Vivien had been pondering this but just didn't quite like the idea, but her dentist persuaded her at least to go with him to the College to enquire about it and much to her and her dentist's surprise, the member of the staff who supervises all straightening work, offered to do it himself, and he has been very good about arranging Bill's appointments after school hours, though he is a very busy man. I have not seen Bill for some time (as naturally he hasn't come to the house since the chicken pox) except for a few moments at U.T.S. the other night, but I believe the work is getting under way.

I do hope you get a good holiday at Christmas. The boys will have 2 weeks Dec 19 to Jan 5. I love this mild weather but still I would like to have some snow and ice by then, for the children's sake.

[41] 90 DUNVEGAN ROAD
      TORONTO, DECEMBER 8

Dear Margaret

Christopher has been the second victim of chicken pox, but the worst is over now. He came down Thursday evening and I thought it was going to be a light attack, as his temp. was only 99° but Friday his temp went up, the spots came out in force and multiplied daily. He had two bad nights,

Friday & Saturday with the spots torturing him, but last night they eased off and he had a good night and to-day they have not bothered him at all. Each time his temp. went up I managed to bring it down with quarts of fruit juices and ginger ale, combined with aspirin, which brought on copious sweating. The spots I tried to soothe by sponging him with baking soda and warm water and then anointing them all with calamine lotion—the poor child looked like an African native in war paint—or, by the time his face got covered with spots—like a circus clown—we would put on moustache and whiskers to finish things off. I don't need to tell you that I have given him constant attention and have done everything I possibly could to make him as comfortable as he could be under the circumstances. I was so sorry for him, and particularly as he is such darned good stuff—never once whined or complained. He is amazingly philosophical—just made up his mind that he was for it, that it would be very uncomfortable, but that it wouldn't last forever. Mary was dressed to-day for the first time—to-day and yesterday she has spent most of the day in C's room and it helped take his mind off his troubles. They have worked at the mats they're making, read to one another and told one another stories.

DECEMBER 9

I didn't get far with this yesterday, what with lack of time and the distraction of all the alarming events in the East. It does seem that the Americans were caught badly off their guard in their "impregnable" bases. It is rather amusing to hear the American radio commentators pontificating that if Russia desires to show herself a true friend she will immediately declare war on Japan and attack Manchukuo to divert Japanese strengths! But amusement aside it is all too serious. Perhaps it's just as well to have manifold domestic problems such as children and chicken pox to occupy one's mind when one can't do anything.

C. is much better again to-day, and I hope the spots will soon begin to fade. We have some very soft sloppy snow so I let Mary outside to play in it. I don't think she has been infectious for several days but I didn't let her with the others until to-day. Her spots lasted much longer than they normally do. C. is dying to have M. get back to school because he is timing his recovery by hers and is desperately afraid he won't be up and about by Christmas. He does seem to have such bad luck—he was just starting his exams—had only had 2 of them and was confident that he could improve very much on his last report. Of course they will mark him on his daily work but the shift of the teachers won't help that either. He was really distressed at missing the exams.

John's two sisters in Burlington have invited the whole Williamson connection (20–25) to Christmas dinner at an inn in Burlington, and I have accepted for as many of us as are still on our feet when Christmas comes. Mary & C. should be all right but Peter and Tom have a danger stretch about Dec. 21 when they'll come down if they caught it from C. The incubation period is 17 days. If any are ill, John can take the others and I'll stay to look after the patient or patients. I do hope we can all go. I have to let Mary Murphy go home for Christmas so it makes a heavy day if I have the dinner to do myself as well as everything else.

Tom is having his exams and has done very well so far. His writing seems very poor to me—rather getting worse than improving. Perhaps it's because he's started using ink, but it looks to me more like carelessness—so many crossed out words and some letters 3 times the size of others. I made him rewrite the letter I enclose, the first draft was really very bad (perhaps I shouldn't say I <u>made</u> him—what I did was ask him whether that was really the best he could do, and didn't he think he ought to do his best for his mother).

I hope to send Mary back to school in a day or two. She has been doing lessons with me all the time she was home—arithmetic, spelling, writing and reading aloud—so I don't think she'll be far behind. I am going to start C. in a day or two. I already have given him several books with sections on early Ontario settlements to read, to keep up a bit in his Social Studies but I don't want to start him on any real work until he feels better. I am asking his teacher about work for him. He will not get back to school of course until after the Christmas holidays. When the doctor came to see him, last Friday, he said his tonsils were pretty bad and showed me the glands under the end of his jaw, swollen quite noticeably to the touch, which he says are caused by the tonsils—possibly just because of the chicken pox. However, I would not <u>consider</u> having his tonsils out unless it became absolutely <u>imperative</u> and I'm sure it's not that now. His voice is undeniably very adenoidal and I can't decide whether its always been so or has become so (or more so) recently.

Tom brought home a long document from school—he is very vague but I gather the children have all been "gone over" (or at least, certain ones referred by their teachers have been) by a speech specialist. Tom's trouble is that he pronounces "the" more like "v," using his lower lip against his upper teeth instead of his tongue against his upper teeth. The sheet suggested 10 minutes practice a day and gave words and sentences to use. However I must confess that I am completely disregarding it. If he's been talking that way for 10 years I'm sure I can't change him now.

By the way, re C., I forgot to tell you he had his medical exam at the school, though really it is such a perfunctory and superficial one that a defect would have to be pretty glaring to be spotted. The doctor examined his throat (he said he would class his tonsils as "midway") sounded his lungs and heart, gave him a sight test (normal) weighed and measured him, without shoes—56 ¾" and 77 ¾ lbs. He said he was in very good shape but advised him to scrub his teeth better as they are pretty brown—suggested that I have the dentist clean them. As a matter of fact the dentist did so last spring and intended to do it again when I took the boys in Sept. but there had been a mistake made in his appointments and he hadn't time so I will try to get it done in the Christmas holidays.

Mary Murphy went to see the doctor to-day about a small cyst in her eyelid which has not been responding well to a month's treatment so she is to have it removed next week. It never rains but it pours! However, it shouldn't incapacitate her for long.

The Germans being halted short of Moscow is very heartening—could anyone have possibly predicted it!—and the southern campaign is even more encouragingly disastrous. Also the news is better from Libya. But we are all very uneasy as to how the grave situation in the East is being met. No news being let out except of actual Japanese attacks. However, by the time you get this we'll know all about what is happening....

Must be off now and get Mary and Tom in—they are shovelling the snow—about 1 inch.

P.S. I saw C's teacher the day of his medical exam. He says C. is getting on very well—work is good except his writing (which he thinks shows great improvement) and spelling (a lot of which he thinks due to carelessness, such as "the" for "they" etc., and also he does not get many mistakes in actual spelling lessons but misspells much simpler words in ordinary writing). Says C. seems well-adapted and happy.

[42]   90 DUNVEGAN ROAD
       TORONTO, DECEMBER 15

Dear Margaret

There have been no letters from you since the last I told you of, one to the boys & Mary written Oct. 26 and one to me written Oct. 23. They arrived Nov. 2 (3?). I have wondered whether mails were being lost more frequently this autumn—I think they have only had, Tom, 2, and C., 3, letters from you since Sept. 1.

I intended writing several days ago as I know you are anxious to hear about C. and his chickenpox, but time has not permitted—after all a few days here or there doesn't make much difference in a letter's arrival in these days of bewildering posts. You may well get this one before my last one, which told you of the chickenpox. C. is very much better—in fact he has been feeling perfectly well and with no temp. for almost a week. He has a heavy crop of vicious spots but they are clearing up much more quickly than Mary's did. I have had him doing lessons every day for about a week and Mr. Pugh sent home the arithmetic, geography, composition and grammar, and social studies exams so those kept him busy all day Friday and Sat. morning. I took the papers back to-day. Mr. P. says he is sorry he cannot use the marks on C's report but they will give C an idea of how he is getting on. I was so disappointed about his missing the exams—and he was too—it seems almost unnatural in a 12 year old, but he was so anxious to prove to himself and every one else that he could do much better than his last report. However we'll have to hope for better luck in the New Year. I also went to the handicraft room to-day and got the letter rack which C. had partly finished and was making to send to Mr. & Mrs. Burns for Christmas. I got him some sandpaper and he spent most of the afternoon rubbing it down. It is in 3 pieces but John will help him put it together and I will get some stain for him and I think he can get it done in time to send it to them....

We had snow on Saturday, to the children's great excitement. Tom & M. went out in the garden at 1 o'clock and played until 5 building a snow man with much inefficiency and merriment. I bundled C. up in eiderdowns in a nest made of two arm chairs in the sunroom overlooking the garden so he could take at least a vicarious part in the fun. When they came in for their tea Mary said "Poor Christopher, I've been out all afternoon," so after tea she went in to his room, pulled up a chair and settled herself and said "I'll sit with you now—I'll sit with you always except when I'm at school."

If Tom or Peter or both take it, it will probably be about Dec. 21—I do hope they don't—I've had plenty of chicken-pox!—and I'd like all the meals downstairs and the beds empty for a while. I haven't been able to do much about Christmas but haven't much to do anyway—we are not having any presents among grownups this year (as last) not even between John and me, and with the invitation to Burlington for Christmas Day I don't have to think about the dinner. There are no nuts and very few dried fruits to be had, and no cheese. I have not bought oranges for nearly a year—I don't think we should use American exchange for anything we can do without and by using canned grapefruit juice (from Trinidad) and quantities of Canadian tomato juice (it has the same properties as orange juice but more dilute so that one needs 3 times the quantity) I feel we do not need oranges. Some tangerines are coming in now so I think I'll have to relax enough to have those for Christmas. Nothing else is scarce (though fruit & vegetables are very expensive and meat sky-high) and of course there are all the sweets in the world and as much confectionery of every kind as ever there was. We have been asked to cut down bacon and pork 50% but we scarcely ever had pork anyway. I don't think it's good for children. We have a large roast of beef once a week (about 8 lbs.) and use it up cold, with mince one day, have fish one day and liver one day, as a rule—occasionally sausage or minced beef patties or a meat loaf, once in a while a roast of mutton. The children each have a quart of milk a day—three or four glasses to drink, and the rest on their porridge, in cream soups and a milk pudding every day (it never fails to amaze me how all 4 of them love rice pudding and tapioca and cornstarch puddings).

I seem to be wandering all over the map—I think I was talking about Christmas. I have got practically everything for the children now. I got Tom new skis and harness. I thought he should have proper ones, like the others, and he has Peter's ski boots which P. has outgrown, so he can use the harness. (I gave C. & Peter ski boots for their birthdays—real men's ones.) For C. I have got a set called "Magnetic Facts and Fun"—a box with a magnet and various different-shaped pieces of magnetized steel, with all sorts of things—a little bottle of shot, a bottle of iron filings, a piece of wool and equipment and instructions for doing all sorts of tricks with them. I think a boy would enjoy it. For Peter I have a telegraph set (boy scout model) and C. can use it. I found Mary difficult this year—she never cared for dolls and is beyond them now, and I couldn't spend much, so I've got her one of those old-fashioned samplers to work in cross-stitch (I think she should be learning to sew) and a box of chunks of coloured rubber sponge, to be cut up and stuck together to make figures or pictures or what you like. Then I have a book or two each for them. I got Tom a comparative world atlas, which I think will interest him and of course a lot of small stuff for their stockings. I hope there are enough ornaments for the tree. We usually get a few new ones each year but they all came from Japan so they're "out" this year.

Did I ever tell you that Besse, my brother Bob's wife, had a daughter born the end of October (Janet Elizabeth). She is coming along very well and they are full of joy and pride in her. Bill and Tom have combined in a Christmas present to Mr. & Mrs. Burns—a book about clocks (apparently a hobby of Mr. B's) which Bill knew he would like to have. It was fairly expensive for their resources if given only to Mr. Burns so I persuaded Bill to send it to both of them. He felt that might be hard on Mrs. B. (it being his hobby), but as Viv was going to have to help out with money if a separate one went to Mrs. B, I assured him that when it was so exactly what her husband wanted, she wouldn't mind....

[43]   90 DUNVEGAN ROAD
         TORONTO, DECEMBER 21

Dear Margaret

The house is practically a hospital, with myself as staff and Christopher as assistant. C. lost his last scab to-day—he has been up for several days, but not out yet. Peter burst into spots Thursday eve. and Tom Friday morning. They both are attaining their peak production to-day—at least I hope so! Tom is pretty full of self pity and likes to go into the complete history of each spot, but on the whole is bearing up better than I expected. They have neither of them felt at all sick, have eaten every meal—their temps., like the others, wavered up and down but never very high, and are only 100° to-day—were normal yesterday. I expect to-night and to-morrow will be pretty uncomfortable but I do hope by then the worst will be over. C. has been a great help. He makes and takes up drinks of fruit juice—or ginger ale—3 times in the morning and 3 times in the afternoon. He carries up meals and brings down the trays and does everything he can to help.

Mary unfortunately has developed a cold in the head.... I have John in bed to-day too, with a beautiful boil on the back of his neck which I am keeping hot compresses on. I do hope it will finish itself to-day—it's hard to look after it when he's at the office....

Mary Murphy is going home Wednesday evening to stay until Friday at least. I was hoping we could all go to Burlington so I wouldn't have to do anything about a Christmas dinner here, but of course Tom and Peter will still be in bed—though feeling quite well by then, I expect. Ruby McKay has offered to come here and stay with the patients so I can go with John, Mary & C. I will see how things go on, and may accept her offer.

Mother has been in bed with a cold for nearly a week. It is not bad, but it weakens her, with her asthmatic chest. Theresa could not leave her to go to the Red Cross warehouse, where we work Fridays, so I simply had to go chicken-pox or no (I had begged off the two former Fridays). Fortunately we got through by noon and C. had taken charge very ably while I was away....

I must be off now to change John's dressing and dab calamine lotion on the boys. I do hope you get a good holiday at Christmas and that we get some good news from the East to start the new year.

Dear Margaret

Christmas is over, and a very successful one in spite of everything. Tom and Peter were well enough to come down to get their presents from the tree and to come down later for their dinner. However, I have kept them in bed since—they are easier to keep track of there and I know they are warm. The spots are giving them no more trouble but we anoint them with vaseline at night to keep the scabs soft so they won't rub off before their time.

I got them all at writing their thank-you letters to-day and the activity is terrific, with pens and pencils flying and myself constantly called on to straighten them out on what came from whom. They are getting on with it pretty well. As a matter of fact, the top floor has been popping and cracking with activity for days, chicken pox or not. Besides the Christmas preparations, the parcelling and labelling and sending out for the few things Tom & P. had not bought when they went to bed, Peter had set his heart on getting out a Christmas number of the "War Drum" (enclosed). John had got a typewriter for a month, so they'd have it over the holidays and Peter did not want to waste his opportunities and there was a steady flow of written notices from his bed—peremptory notices to contributors of the press dead line, solicitations of potential advertisers, salesmen and prospective buyers etc. We would not let him up to use the typewriter so he pressed Mary into doing one or two copies and the poor child (who had never typed before) fairly sweated and wept over it in her effort to avoid mistakes and do it "just like Peter." We finally let him have the typewriter on his bed and he worked so steadily all day and evening on Dec. 24 that he couldn't sleep all night with what he called grandly "rheumatic fever"—really a stiff and aching leg from having it bent under him all day. However, he achieved 4 or 5 copies and after paying contributors made a clear 7¢ profit on the issue so all was well.

They hung their stockings on their door knobs, and by 7 A.M. I knew they were all awake so I went round and closed windows and let them have their stockings. Then we all had breakfast and gathered around the tree, in the dining room and what excitement! We have a very pretty, thick little tree, about 6 ft. tall and with a lot of little cones on it (C. & Mary decorated the tree the day before Christmas). They were all <u>highly</u> delighted with everything and very much surprised at the number of presents (I suppose I had warned them this might be a slim Christmas). Mary said "My! People must like us to give us so many presents!" Tom and C. thought it even better than last year....

Mary Murphy went home Christmas eve at 5 P.M.—was supposed to get back last night (Dec. 26) but missed (?) her train and had to drive 18 miles to Orillia to get one at 4 A.M. to-day, which was two hours late so she arrived about 9 this morning, not having had a wink of sleep. So I'm a little weary myself and am looking forward to the end of the holidays. I think Tom and P. should be ready for the first day of school (Jan. 5) or very soon after. The weather is simply foul—raw east wind but not freezing, no snow, but sometimes rain. The only good thing about it is that it reconciles P. & T. to spending the holidays mostly in bed. It was colder yesterday and a tiny bit of snow fell so I sent Mary & C. out to play when things seemed to be getting a bit hectic in the sick rooms (about 3 P.M.) but to-day is slop again. I sent them over to the shops (3 blocks away) to get groceries etc. and John walked them to the library this afternoon just to get them outside for some air and exercise.

On Christmas Day after they got their presents Peter & Tom returned to bed with their loot and Peter set up his telegraph set I'd given him (two instruments worked by batteries with 50 ft. of wire) between their rooms and they spent a most blissful day sending messages back and forth, dipping into their books and both (much, I think to their own surprise) found it a <u>very</u> pleasant way to spend Christmas. I must say I regarded them enviously myself! John took C. & Mary off soon after 10—they went to mother's to deliver presents and see her, and then to Church. I got their place tidy & breakfast cleared off and made up a picnic lunch—sandwiches, celery, raisins etc. in little individual packages and when they came home the children took them and glasses of milk up to Peter's room and all ate their lunch there—a great saving of dishes! Ruby and Irene arrived about 2.30 and John, Mary, C. and I left at 3 for Burlington. We went to Emily's where all the family gathered (except for one brother, his wife and son who couldn't come, and of course Peter & Tom) and walked over to the Estaminet a very busy highway restaurant where we had an excellent dinner.[39] Mary & C. sat side by side, behaved beautifully and had a most marvellous time. (There were 18 of us altogether.) ...

C. has been most helpful since the boys were sick. I should have <u>had</u> to move them down to the second floor (and that's a nuisance—they always think of millions of things left behind) if he hadn't saved me so many trips by taking drinks and trays up and down and taking up messages for me. Mary has been useful too—she can't carry trays but can manage a glass of milk in each hand and as C. can't manage milk <u>on</u> the tray it's a joint effort at meal time. Mary runs a lot of errands for the boys and altogether it's been much better having them up there. For one thing, all 4 are usually up there since holidays started and it <u>is</u> more restful to have them almost, at least, out of earshot with all the Christmas and War Drum excitement on!...

Our Christmas of course—I mean everyone's—was saddened by the news of the fall of Hong Kong and the serious situation in Malaya and the Phillippines. These are tremendous days and the U.S.A. have had a terrific awakening. The disasters in the East have at least affected almost unbeliev-able unification of feeling in that country. Who can say but that in the end, it will have been worth it? I do hope Churchill's visit will have real tangible results in unity of plan and action, and not a lot of high-minded but (to me I must admit) rather meaningless words like the Atlantic Charter. He has certainly been tumultuously acclaimed in the U.S. and I have never in my life heard such a speech as he made yesterday in the Senate. I do hope you heard it. When I went up to Tom's room the other morning I told him Mr. C. and Lord B. were in Washington.[40] Tom looked at me, completely startled and said "Who's in charge of England?" So I answered him his mummy and daddy could look after England <u>very</u> well in Mr. C's absence....

1942

"I think [Bill] was rather bewildered by the Canadianisation of his small brothers"[1]

[1]   90 DUNVEGAN ROAD
         TORONTO, JANUARY 4

Dear Margaret

Everyone is up and out again except Tom. His chicken pox is all right but he has a cold so I have kept him in bed. How he got a cold in bed I don't know, though it may be the development of the slight throat disturbance he had for a week before he took chicken pox.... He seems perfectly happy to stay in bed till Doomsday—reads continuously from morning till night—lucky they got lots of books for Christmas, though Peter still has lots Tom hasn't read. I have had Friar's Balsam boiling in his room since the start. He has had no temp. whatever at any time with the cold—except 99° one evening when the Fr. Balsam had brought the room up to about 80° and he had had mustard on his chest all day—it's a wonder he wasn't 102°!

I am very much disgusted over this cold—Tom has never had so much as a sniffle before, since he came here. So many people from England tell me that they go through the first winter in Canada in fine style, not feeling or suffering from the cold but by the second winter their blood is thinned so that they fall victim to it. I don't know whether it's the drier climate or the heated houses or the hot summers here that makes our blood thinner than that of English people—or what it is. Anyway I do hope this isn't the fore-runner of more colds. Vivien tells me that Bill, who wore his trench coat to school almost all last winter (finding an overcoat much too warm, though it was a much colder winter than this has been to date) has been wearing an overcoat for 2 months now, and has also donned his woollen underwear which last year he scorned and never put on once. So apparently he feels the cold more.

... I was rather anxious about Christopher going back to school to-day, but at noon he reported everything as having gone well. Last evening he asked me if he hadn't better gargle as he was so hoarse and seemed quite surprised that I hadn't noticed his hoarseness—not to say indignant! I looked at his throat, which showed no redness, but encouraged the gargling anyway, though my heart rather sank. Long experience with boys warned me that it was a sign he was <u>not</u> looking forward to going to school. However he said nothing about it this morning—he apparently hadn't been able to think up a sore throat. Once the actual plunge of returning was over I'm sure he'd be glad to be back. But after being away slightly over a month (counting holidays) I could readily understand how he felt. We kept his work up pretty well until the holidays started and I don't think he should find himself at a disadvantage. They are all 3 in rather a dither over their reports—Mary has promised to bring Tom's as soon as it's available.

Peter kept himself busy as soon as he could be up, with the Monthly War Drum.... I think I told you John got a typewriter for a month and he wanted to make the best possible use of it, so got out the Jan. number. He typed 12 copies in all—3 times, making 4 copies each time—quite a lengthy job with one finger! He was quite disgusted at the lack of co-operation the others showed but he'll have to learn that as long as he insists on "bossing" his projects so completely, he can't count on other people being as enthusiastic workers at them as he is! It really doesn't bother him much—he'd sooner do it all himself and have it done the way he wants it. The others threw themselves heartily into the Dec. issue but were a little tired of it by the time that one was over. However, in most things he and C. work together very well....

I have been consulting the doctor about the advisability of having the children vaccinated (or whatever they call it) against scarlet fever. He feels that the serum is still experimental—in so far as (1) they don't know for how long it immunizes and (2) there are about 5 different strains of scarlet and it's difficult to immunize against all of them. There are a great many cases in Toronto (though not enough to designate as an epidemic) (so many soldiers in barracks always start these waves of communicable disease in a community) and I would <u>hate</u> to have to go through <u>that</u>! I think what we'll do—the most that my conservative doctor would recommend—is have all 4 given the "Dick" test[2] to determine whether they are susceptible and see how that comes out and then decide what to do.

The boys each had $1 sent them for Christmas from Mrs. Anthony.[3] She sent the money to Bill and I had C. phone Bill for her address so they could write her. (C. has now $10 and T. almost $7.) The address is Dept. of Statistics, Dominion Gov't, Ottawa, so she must have a post there.

The boys each had letters to-day from the Burns. I think they were awfully pleased with the letter rack C. made for them—and also with the book Bill and T. sent. The boys seem to look on their stay in New Hampshire as an interlude of pure heaven. I do hope they can go again this summer but I imagine it is very doubtful whether either of the Burns will be able to leave their important and responsible work in Washington.

I am sending Tom's exam. papers, which he wants you to see....

Our A.R.P.[4] organization which has been going on in a rather desultory way for a year or two, is being speeded up and systematised. Our local warden left a card for us to fill in names and ages of occupants of house, etc. I believe they are making all preparations and arrangements for the evacuation of Toronto children to the surrounding country in case of air raids. I suppose I don't know much about it but it seems to me that, while raids are <u>possible</u>, they would be "token" raids—one or two planes would unload incendiaries, then land and give themselves up. It could be very serious—most Toronto houses, though built of brick, have shingle roofs—but I don't think any amount of preparation could have much effect against it—except AA guns,[5] firewatchers with sand & water, etc, which are certainly not being considered on the <u>very</u> "off" chance of a raid. I think if the Germans (or Japs) sent planes over Ontario they would be far more likely (and more well advised) to aim at power plants and such like vital spots.

I do hope that I can tell you in my next letter that Tom is back at school. However there is nothing to cause the slightest anxiety. As a matter of fact, he has still not been in bed as long as Mary was with just the chicken pox. His spots (and P's) cleared much faster than the other two.

No time for more now. I do hope all letters are arriving now. The autumn seems to be the time for sinkings.

[2]   90 DUNVEGAN ROAD
      TORONTO, JANUARY 11

Dear Margaret

The boys have had a letter from you this week (Nov. 30) also one each from their father and a Christmas card and letter from Elsie. I don't know whether I told you they each had a letter from your mother a week or two ago.... I know they never mention receipt of mail to you so I try to keep track of it to let you know. Tom usually shows me anything he gets but C. always takes his off to his room and if I ask "Who was your letter from?" I'm afraid he thinks it's curiosity on my part. Sometimes I feel rather badly about your letters to him—I know he can't read them and yet I don't want to appear to pry. I usually say "If you can't make it out, bring it to me and I'll read it"—sometimes he does & sometimes not. So if I don't report all letters and cards I'm sorry. I try to get them to answer letters but it's pretty hard. A Christmas cable from Mrs. Tylecote (?) arrived this week. A lot of the Christmas cables from England to Canada took 3 weeks which is annoying a great many people.

I let Tom up yesterday afternoon—his cough seemed practically gone. We celebrated all the beds being empty (for the first time in two months) by all having dinner together at 6 yesterday (Saturday)—dining on a 15 lb. turkey which John's brother Murray got from Saskatchewan....

AFTERNOON

This week has been pretty busy. The material which I ordered Oct. 30 for draperies for the living room (and had given up as unobtainable) arrived, so Clare and Ruby McKay came down and spent 2 days making them. They have the curtains for the two open door ways—to the hall and to the dining room—almost finished, so we were able to put them up and then decide what to do about the windows (which have been curtainless) and I got more material while it's to be had and next week they will make them for me. It was like the days last September when Theresa, Clare and Ruby came several days and made and altered all the other curtains (there are about 65 windows in the house)—when I had no maid and we all had picnic meals in the garden with George coming in for dinner. But this time there were no meals in the garden!—we picnicked on one end of the dining room table—extended to its full length to accommodate the sewing machine and the curtains spread out for cutting.

We are really beginning to feel the war in other ways than taxes and labour shortage. All manufactured articles are becoming very hard to obtain—all sorts of simple little things one has always taken for granted. Of course you have had this situation for a long time now. Our expansion tank for the heating system sprang a leak last week (a tank in the highest part of the house which acts as a "safety valve" for the water in the radiators when it expands from growing hotter, and also acts as a reservoir to keep the radiators filled when any of the water evaporates) and we are having to wait some time to replace it. Even the tiniest bit of metal cannot be used for anything without an order from the metal controller. The ridiculous part of the situation is that I think the tank was ready yesterday but couldn't be installed because plumbers (like all building trades) are not allowed to work on Saturdays. This is by a law which the labour unions got passed in pre-war days and is still effective on all work except actual war jobs!

We are having all sorts of blackout instructions and demonstrations of "refuge rooms" with complete equipment—stirrup pumps and bomb shovels are still not available but are promised soon. However, I must say I can't get alarmed over the prospect of being bombed—I don't mean that being bombed wouldn't alarm me—far from it, but I just can't believe it probable. And if we are bombed I think it's far more likely to be in daylight than at night. I believe surprise blackouts are to begin next month—we have had two well publicized ones before.

C. discovered during last week that Mr. Pugh had apparently given out the reports before the holidays. He may not intend to give C. one as he missed the exams but I advised C. to ask him anyway, in case he'd forgotten him, but C. has "forgotten" every day. I think it's shyness, really, so I am not saying any more about it. There is a Home and School Club meeting to-morrow evening and I may see Mr. Pugh there if I go, but I think I shall have to keep off my feet as much as possible for a bit—I developed a bad leg this past week. Eighteen years ago I had an abscess of the bone removed just below my knee and have never felt it or scarcely thought of it since and why it should start to hurt now I don't know—it's most provoking. When the scar healed, it grew to the bone, and now it seems as though every time I move my leg it pulls on that adhesion. The doctor who attended me at that time (and to whom I'm sure I owe my life) is now Medical Director at the Canada Life and sent word to me by John to come see him but it has not been very convenient to do so yet.[6] If it continues I'll have to see him, but in the meantime I can't take the children out skiing which is rather hard on John. Last year we took turns, Sat. and Sun. afternoons. However, he is very good about it and has taken them all out skiing this afternoon. The temperature has gone up to 25° and the sun is bright after quite a heavy, though short, snowfall at noon. I thought it would not hurt Tom and I'd like him to have some fun. I thought they could walk over to Upper Canada themselves and take their skis but distant fields (or hills) look greener (or whiter) and John thought if he took them to the golf club in the car, Tom could take refuge in its warmth occasionally if he needed to.

I do hope we've had all our illness for the winter and it would be nice if the temperature would settle around 25° for a bit, so the children could have some fun—a little more snow would add to the fun. Of course the lack of snow has made the driving much better though we scarcely use the car at all anyway.... We are very lucky here, being so conveniently placed for transportation, school, Church, etc. Very few of our grocers deliver any more—or I should say, there are very few independent grocery shops left—for the past 15 years or so the grocery (and meat) business has passed into the hands of the large chain stores which operate on a self-serve, cash and carry basis (they have baskets and little pram affairs to put them on and you help yourself from the shelves and push your load up to the checker who puts the things in bags and a boy carries them to your car). The few independent grocers left charge much higher prices—I suppose they have to, and the "mass" system does seem wrong but we've nearly all come to use it to protect our own purses. I am wondering how lack of cars and gasoline will affect all this. We are only 3 blocks from the shopping district of Forest Hill Village (a suburb of Toronto which reaches almost to our house) and I can send the children over with the wagon for everything we need (or go with them).

I suspect Tom will get his report when he goes back to school. Mary got hers the first day of school—quite a good one. I'm sure Tom's will be very good. He did quite a lot of arithmetic while at home last week and while he scarcely had a mistake in the mechanical arithmetic (multiplication and division) he had a great many in the problems. It's the same old difficulty of his not using his reasoning powers. When one sees the intelligent reasoning he uses in following the various campaigns of the war, and a few other things that really interest him intensely, one realizes that it is certainly not <u>lack</u> of brains, but that same instinctive disinclination to reason things out for himself that makes him ask for instructions in every detail of practical life. I must hasten to say that he has come a <u>long</u> way in overcoming this and I am constantly working on it. When I marked the problems I simply marked the wrong ones with X and did not tell him what was wrong. Usually one reading was enough to tell him where he had slipped.

I think his dreaminess and absent-mindedness are connected with this same trait, but whether they are the <u>cause</u> of his lack of concentration on anything that doesn't interest him intensely or the <u>result</u> of it I don't know. His stay in bed, when he's been alone a lot, and which entailed a break in his usual routine, has rather intensified his abstraction and lessened his concentration on the matter in hand but when he gets back to school and normal life that will right itself....

[3]   90 DUNVEGAN ROAD
       TORONTO, JANUARY 18

Dear Margaret

My joy at getting all the beds empty proved premature as I am occupying one myself at present—though recuperating fast. I think I mentioned in my last letter that I was having a bit of trouble with my leg, just below the knee, where I had an abscess of the bone removed 18 years ago. It got worse and worse so on Monday I saw the doctor, had some Xrays and saw the surgeon who had done the operation—he has now become such a famous bone surgeon I was almost afraid to go to his office.[7] He said it was a flare-up of the old infection which had lain dormant all these years—it seems extraordinary and no one knows how it happens—possibly a run down condition invites it. Anyway he peremptorily ordered me into the hospital Tuesday evening to have it opened Wed. morning.

It turned out to be very superficial—nothing like as serious as he had feared it might. The bone was not affected at all—just a pocket of infection right in the old scar, which he easily cleaned out and stitched up, with a little packing for drainage. I stayed in hospital until Friday but then got my own doctor to get the surgeon's permission to come home. It seemed such a waste of money to lie there when I could lie in bed at home. The bandage was not even removed until this afternoon when my doctor came and had a look at it and he will be back in a few days to take out the stitches. It feels perfectly splendid—no pain and I can hobble on it enough to get to the bath room myself. I have been taking one of these marvellous new "sulfa" drugs which fights staphylococcic infection. They are unbelievably efficacious but have a rather depressing and "limp-making" effect. But aside from that I feel quite all right and Mary Murphy is very anxious to do everything possible. I think she is trying to make up for the past—in fact the day I told her I was to go to hospital she said she has been going to suggest that now the children were all well again, I should go away for a couple of weeks.

My troubles were rather complicated by our heating.... Our expansion tank sprang a leak and the stupid plumber who put the new one in did a real job on us—by blowing out not only the new tank but one section of the boiler in the furnace. However we were not long enough without heat to be uncomfortable and are getting on with 2 of the 3 sections of the boiler while the plumbers comb the country for a section to replace ours. Anything metal is getting as scarce as the proverbial hens' teeth....

I am enclosing Tom's marks from his report for Nov. & Dec. I think they are very good. The children teased him about his E for music. Apparently the exam consisted largely of identifying music—operas, symphonies etc., from records, after hearing them several times. So I don't think it is anything very serious. It was an excellent report. I guess C. is not getting one this time. I hope you received their Nov. 1 ones.

P.S. MONDAY, JANUARY 19

Tom is off to choir practice to-night.

Mary and C. went to the library after school and C. brought home a present for me of half a dozen iced cakes—it was a great surprise—he brought 4, no less, up on a plate with my dessert at dinner, and urged me to eat them all. However I assured him I would enjoy them much more if I shared them with him and the other children. Peter had also brought me a present—a bottle of bath oil. I was much touched by their thoughtfulness.

[4] 90 DUNVEGAN ROAD
       TORONTO, JANUARY 25

Dear Margaret

... The children are all well and I am recuperating fast. I came home from the hospital a week ago Friday and though I've not been dressed yet and spend most of the time in bed, I can get around a bit to see that things are going on all right, and the last few nights I have gone down for dinner, putting my foot up on a stool, and have lain on the sofa downstairs the rest of the evening. The doctor came Thursday and took out the stitches and packing and the incision is healing up very nicely.

The boys had letters from you yesterday—Tom got me to read his to him—it was written Jan. 1. I am afraid C. could make out very little of his but he doesn't seem to want me to read them—whether from pride that forbids his confessing that he can't read them, or from fear that I am "prying" I don't know, but I avoid appearing to press my assistance on him. They had each a letter from their father yesterday, and also one joint one. They were postmarked Dec. 20, Dec. 26, Dec. 27. They also had a joint one from your mother. There was apparently a heavy English mail yesterday, after none for some time. The last the boys had had were letters from you, written Nov. 30 and one each from their grandmother (Tout) which came several weeks ago.

Bill was here yesterday for the first time since the chicken-pox attacked us. He came early in the afternoon and stayed for supper with the boys. They all had a beautiful time playing detective games—or so I gathered from my bedroom.

From what I could overhear I was particularly interested in, and pleased with, C's attitude. Whenever Bill started to throw his weight about as he does when with the boys, in order to impress C. and Peter with his superiority and position of authority (of course it doesn't impress them—just infuriates them but naturally he doesn't realize that) C. went no further than to repeat in an exasperated tone "Oh! come on Bill! be a sport and give us the clue" (or whatever the trouble was). A little over a year ago, under the same circumstances, he would have gone into a blind rage.... He says nothing about his school work but seems quite happy and to like school so I imagine everything is all right. He has been working very steadily all week copying out his entire Social Studies note-book—I only knew what he was doing from Peter and took it for granted that he was doing it of his own accord because he was not satisfied with the appearance of the one he had. However, Peter tells me that the teacher told him to do it as the old one would not pass muster for neatness and legibility.

Tom is getting on very well—I was talking to his teacher, Miss Blair, the other evening—she telephoned me about the arrangements for the Toronto Symphony Orchestra's children's concert next week. She says he is very ambitious and not satisfied with anything but his best (I only wish he had this attitude towards household duties, personal tidiness, etc,) and I can tell she is fond of him, as well. The T. S. O. give about 6 children's concerts a year, in the afternoon and all public school pupils from grade 4 and up can buy tickets at their schools, for 25¢. A bus is chartered for each school, which takes the children to Massey Hall and returns them to their schools (for another 25¢). I wondered that Tom and C. had never mentioned them, as there was one in Nov. and one in Dec., but always forgot to ask them whether they'd been announced. However some of the boys in Tom's room apparently told him about the Dec. one (which is a Christmas concert and always heaps of fun) and he thought he'd like to go to the January one. Owing to the shortage of man-power (and of buses too I expect) they are not going to be able to have buses this time and the children will have to use street cars to get home. I was rather worried about Tom as he has no idea of getting about by himself and C's not interested in going to the concert so I wrote a note to Miss B. asking her advice. She tells me a teacher will take all the children to Massey Hall in the street car and she is delegating a very dependable boy who lives near us and is used to using street cars alone, to shepherd Tom home, so I'm sure he'll be all right.

He has so entirely lost his old anxieties and apprehensions that I forgot he ever had them. I think his physical and nervous systems have both improved very much and that this is the cause. He is growing a great deal and looking more and more like Bill all the time. He has been working on an oral composition. They drew subjects out of a hat and he drew "An Adventure with a Boat." I purposely offered no suggestions and was interested in the unflurried and competent way he went about it. He decided to use the book "Men Against the Sea" which he recently read—the story of Captain Bligh and his 19 men's 4000 mile trip across the Pacific in the 23-foot long boat of the Bounty, after the mutineers seized the ship. He got the book from the library again and settled down to condense it into not more than 10 minutes' speech. He brought it in finished a few minutes ago and read it to me and I think he has done it <u>very</u> well indeed. He has not the slightest trepidation at the thought of giving it, possibly to-morrow. (They are to draw lots to-morrow for the order in which they speak their pieces.) He is going to memorise it as much as he can after supper.

John and Peter set the ping pong table up in the basement to-day. I had intended to wait until I could get the big room properly cleared and the floor painted, but goodness knows when that will be now, so we thought it might as well be up "as is" and they can at least have some fun with it. I expect I shall be pretty much laid up for some time yet. It is very annoying, with so much to be done, and yet there is something very pleasant about having the rest.

The news from the East is still pretty sickening though the communiqués the last two days would indicate that aircraft reinforcements must have arrived. And the Dutch navy and air force is certainly proving a tremendous asset. Some bits of the report on the investigation at Pearl Harbor were given in the news last night. It sounds pretty bad but none of us are in a position to cast stones after the Malayan disasters. One would think that Crete was a sufficiently expensive lesson to be taken seriously, and profited from. I can understand the growing concern in England over the preparations to defend the airports there in the event of an invasion. Our Canadian Government is in for a bad time over the Hong Kong fiasco—not only because of the affair itself but because of the doubt it implies as to the truth of the ministers' repeated statements that so far voluntary enlistment has been sufficient for overseas requirements.

We have all (each household) been issued large cards of Air Raid Warning Instructions and are to start surprise blackouts next month. I'm afraid I've done nothing yet about blackout so if the first surprise one is lengthy we'll just have to sit in the dark.

I do hope you had a good holiday at Christmas. It must be lovely for your mother to have you home for a bit.

P.S. Sugar rationing is to start to-morrow, but will be no hardship as the ration (¾ lb. week) is more than we now use, I think, and we are promised plenty for jam etc. at preserving time. No other food is rationed—by the way, that reminds me—I did not carry out long my original intention of enclosing tea bags in my letters—the letters got so bulky and full of enclosures they wouldn't stand the extra. I was relieved to learn, on mentioning this to Vivien some time ago, that she has been providing Bill for some time with stocks of tea bags and asked him to enclose them in his letters to you.

Dear Margaret

I am numbering this letter 5, as apparently I forgot to put a number on last week's letter, which should have been 4. The boys had letters yesterday from their "little" Granny and C. had one from his father, postmarked Altrincham, Jan. 11.[8] They are getting their picture papers regularly and seem to enjoy them very much. Also we are enjoying Punch. There were 3 numbers came this week—naturally mails are erratic but it is marvellous how little is lost. (Vivien told me Hilda[9] called Bill yesterday by knocking on his door and saying "Time to get up Bill! Half of England has written to you!") ...

　　Mary and Tom went to the Symphony Concert on Friday. I thought I had everything arranged for Tom for the concert but my efforts proved vain as the boy who had been detailed to look after Tom coming home found out on Thursday that he could not go. After several tries at arrangements which wouldn't work, I arranged to buy Teddy's ticket and let Mary go with Tom, and John took the car down town with him and drove around to Massey Hall at 5.30 to pick them up. They both enjoyed it very much. Sir Ernest MacMillan (the conductor) explains the music and instruments to them and they are each provided with paper on which they answer questions he gives them at the end of the concert (mostly, I think on interpretation of music)—these are handed in at the door and prizes are later awarded for the best answers.

　　Bill was here yesterday afternoon for an hour or two—he seems bigger each time I see him—not only taller but broader and he holds himself so much better that his chest has filled out....

　　Gasoline rationing is to start April 1—about 300 gal. a year for "nonessential" cars such as ours—it is not to be allotted in equal amounts each month, the year's amount divided into quarters, but more will be allotted for July, Aug. and Sept. than for the other quarters. You can't "carry over" any unused coupons from one quarter to the next. The quantity may be reduced at any time if supplies run short. The ration will allow us about 5000 miles a year—last year we drove about 7000 miles. So we cannot feel that it is much of a sacrifice—in fact if we have to do without a car altogether it will be, of course, an inconvenience, but no real hardship. Of course eventually that's what it will come to, as no new tires are allowed to be sold except for cars and trucks for essential services—none are available for private cars. It is going to be a bit hard on some people who live on the outskirts of the city, with children to get to school, etc. So many of our habits, customs, and ways of life have been developed and predicated on the practically universal ownership of cars that doing without them creates more problems than in communities where cars are simply luxuries which can be eliminated without altering any of the essentials of life. However that's not to say we can't all do without them and be very thankful if we have no worse hardships.

Brown School is having one of its regular collections of newspapers, bottle tops and silver foil and C. is working on newspapers.[10] He asked for my scales and weighs his papers and keeps them in a carton in the basement. He is aiming at a contribution of 50 lbs. but that's a lot of newspapers! I think he has about 15 lbs. so far.

C. T., and Mary have just taken the sleds and toboggan over to Upper Canada to see if there is enough snow for sledding. Peter has a little sniffle so is spending the day in his room—I expect it will be gone by to-morrow.

[6]   90 DUNVEGAN ROAD
TORONTO, FEBRUARY 8

Dear Margaret

Winter has come at last, and with a vengeance. After almost 24 hours snowing, with the temperature hovering around freezing, it dropped to zero during last night, with a howling north west wind, and even the brilliant sunshine to-day has not brought it much above 10°. We thought the keen wind would make it too bitingly cold for John to take the children off skiing this afternoon (anyway the driveway is well drifted and the driving very bad and the car much better left in the garage). So they have taken sleds, and loaded their skis on the toboggan and gone over to Upper Canada College grounds, well wrapped up and their faces anointed with oil against frost bite. It is only two blocks away so they can come back anytime if they're cold.

My leg is coming on very well—in fact I was brought to my feet with a bound by Mary waking me at 7.35 Tuesday morning and discovering that Mary Murphy had not returned from her previous evening out and the little matter of breakfast preparation had urgently to be dealt with!—followed by the other meals and the rest of the housework for two days. I am convinced that fate or providence or whoever guards our "immortal souls" has firmly determined that any lurking inclinations towards laziness which I may harbour must never be permitted to develop! The silly girl had not realized that the inflamed eyes and dull ache in the forehead which she'd had for 3 or 4 days were from sinus infection and went out Monday evening to a friend's house and the long walk back against the icy wind in zero weather gave her a terrific sinus attack. She got back late Wed. evening and is improving, thank heaven! but has to visit her doctor every second day.

I went out for the first time yesterday—took the children to the shoe shop as the state of their growing feet has been worrying me.[11] However the three boys still have some room in their shoes and Mary was the only one who needed new ones. They all had to have new overshoes—we have been very lucky this winter, have had to buy very few new clothes of any kind so far. I am getting C. a new pair of breeches to finish out the winter and got Peter a new pair like his school suit (they wear suits to U.T.S. but the others wear pullovers and breeches) and by darning the sleeves and edges of his jacket about once a week am struggling to eke out his school suit until spring. I expect Peter will be in High School next Sept. when it's customary to get into long trousers, so my Scotch soul recoils in horror at the thought of buying new clothes now! I got Peter and Tom each a new warm "bush" coat for school and play at the start of the winter and a friend gave me one, of the same kind but of very superior material and make—much better than I could afford to buy, and just like new—and by having the tailor shorten the sleeves it fits C. perfectly.

The school dentist examined the teeth in Tom's, C's, and Mary's classes last week and Tom and C. were both given cards saying they needed attention. The usual Christmas holiday visit to the dentist was prevented this year by chicken pox so I was afraid there would be some work necessary. Mary was all right, so I made an appointment for the 3 boys for yesterday (Sat.) afternoon—Peter needs a look-over frequently—his teeth are almost perfect but he knocked a chip off a front one just after it grew in and the dentist likes to see it every few months. They went down by themselves by street-car—Peter knows his way all about the city by street-car and I am glad to have C. and T. get some experience in getting themselves about. C. has to go back for a second visit, but Tom apparently had very little wrong.

The children did their shopping for Bill's approaching birthday yesterday. Peter got him chocolate, Mary a little clip file for papers and C. and Tom quite let themselves go in the stamp line and when I met them after buying Mary's shoes, they were simply beaming over having purchased, C., 60¢ worth and Tom, 40¢ worth of stamps to give Bill—I am struck so often with how much more generous (out of smaller funds) they are to him than he to them. I do hope he likes the stamps.

I have ordered notepaper for Bill with his name and address. I imagine that will be as useful a gift as anything as he must use a great deal.... ·

Dear Margaret

The boys had a letter from you a few days ago—Tom had me read his to him—it was written on the train on your way back to school. How nice that you had a holiday in London!... Vivien tells me she had a letter yesterday from your mother.... It is remarkable how little is lost but I think we must be prepared for a great many sinkings in the spring. The war news is so ghastly I won't mention it—but I'm afraid it's going to get worse before it's better.

Both boys are very well and we have had lots of snow for a week. Bill came down yesterday afternoon and John, Bill, Tom and Mary went skating. Peter stayed home to shovel some snow around the garage and also (this was his <u>own</u> idea) he cleaned the windows, washed the woodwork and vacuumed the floor of the sun-room play-room, in preparation for a ceremony in the evening when he presented the trophies for the croquinole tournament—which he has had the children playing off all week. Mary was winner and Tom runner-up. The trophies were cups made of thimbles (Peter made them). The base is a spool (I think you call them "reels"—the wooden thing on which sewing cotton is wound) with the ridge at one end cut off. Into this end he screwed a big screw, part way down and on top of it cemented the thimble, upside down. On either side of the thimble he stuck tiny safety pins, for handles. He painted the spool black and pasted a shield-shaped bit of paper inscribed with the winner's name, on it. They were really quite ingenious—not his own idea but he did them very well. Before the presentation C. did a "comic" act—got up and read jokes and couldn't find his joke book and in his search removed two pairs of pants and four sweaters. I provided drinks and as a crowning touch produced the Valentine cake which John's sister Emily had sent to the children as a Valentine[12]—I told them it would be the last iced cake for the duration so they'd better make the most of it—the ban has just gone on. Peter had put up his stage curtaining and brought down his radio for incidental music. He does love to "organize" things....

Peter got Bill to enter the croquinole tournament which he did very agreeably—Peter felt that with two prizes and only 3 contestants it would be rather flat for the loser so got Bill in as a fourth. I could see that Bill was doing his best to be agreeable—Bill had dinner with John and me and asked me before he went home if I thought his behaviour had been right and proper and I commended him warmly. I had talked to him one time (before the chicken pox kept him away from us for so long) about trying to use his influence while at our house for unity and co-operation rather than to divide the ranks by aligning himself always with Tom. I felt after I had talked to him that he wanted to do what was right but was rather bewildered as to just what was expected of him, so I was awfully pleased at the effort he made yesterday with such pleasant results.

Vivien and I are still rather disturbed at having had no reply to our letters to you about the one from Mrs. Burns. About Dec. 20 I had yours of Nov. 23, when you had just received my short letter, which I sent off immediately to reassure you, as we were picturing your anxious state of mind. (Vivien's first thought was to cable, but we decided that by that time you must surely have had more letters from Mrs. Burns.) Then when Vivien had your Christmas cable we took it that the "encouraging letters" you mentioned were the long ones we had written, but when we heard nothing more we wondered whether the "encouraging letters" were the ones about Bill's tonsils. We have been simply sick about the possibility of those letters being sunk as they were such horrible labour to write and we could _never_ do them over, and also we would hate to think that the helpless state of worry into which Mrs. Burns's letter must have plunged you was not relieved as soon as possible. I am so glad you were able to see Mrs. Beamish, as you said in Tom's letter you had. Both the Ratcliffes and I thought them both simply charming and we do hope to meet them again some day. I hope to be able to do something about seeing Andrew while he is at T.C.S. in Port Hope. Vivien and I had vaguely thought we might drive down in the spring and take the boys, some Sunday, but gasoline rationing may not permit. I might be able to get him up for a weekend, when I get on my feet a bit better.

Vivien is also hoping to hear from you in reply to her letter about Bill's future and his choice of a university course. Of course he will not be ready for the university until the summer of '43 but, with letters taking so long, and the possibility of their loss, we think it should be discussed and the possibilities canvassed on both sides of the Atlantic. We and the Ratcliffes would very much hesitate to make a decision in such an important matter— especially as in the first place Bill is pretty vague as to just what he wants to do when he grows up—except for the general subject "Transportation" and in the second place, his work will probably be in England (surely the war won't last more than 5 years!) and his preparation should be planned with that in view. I hope you will let Vivien know what your ideas are.

The boys are having exams now and will get reports the end of the month. I'm sure you must notice a great improvement in C's writing—I think it has been getting better ever since September, when John undertook to help him with it every evening. Our concern over his writing and spelling may have seemed to you excessive but as I have tried to explain before, we were anxious for him to acquire these skills not just for their own sake, but to overcome the sense of frustration and inferiority which, when he first came to us, was impeding his efforts at school and ruining his disposition—making him into a definitely anti-social individual. It was apparent from the teachers' remarks on the report from his Ulverston school that the situation there was the same. "Could do much better if it were not for the handicap of poor reading and writing" appeared over and over. It was as though the poor child were trying to run before he could walk or do higher maths before learning simple arithmetic, and, given a nature like C's, the result was utter hopeless frustration. One great difficulty was that instead of admitting his lack of fundamentals he bent all his efforts towards the hopeless task of trying to conceal them—I would find that the pages of history or the spelling lessons which he assured me he had learned, contained many words of whose meaning and pronunciation he had not the faintest idea! His reading improved very rapidly at St. Paul's as soon as his initial nervousness and acute self-consciousness wore off a bit—and the natural desire to read for his own amusement spurred him on. The writing and spelling, being more in the nature of drudgery, have taken longer, but his teachers last year took infinite time and patience with him (I'm so glad he had that year at St. Paul's, where the small classes and greater freedom of action allowed him so much individual attention) and John and I have done our best to give him every help and encouragement. On the whole we feel that his and our efforts have been rewarded—he seems to have got to the point where he can stand on his own feet and hold his own in his class if he puts his mind to it.

I had no intention of launching into such a dissertation on C.—much of which I'm sure I've already covered in other letters (but I have no way of knowing how many of my letters during the past 3 months have been lost) but I do not want you to assume because I stress them so, that we have a disproportionate idea of the importance of writing and spelling as accomplishments in themselves—of course a glance at one of my own letters should dispel that idea! I do find it difficult to express my exact ideas in letters—one of the benefits I am hoping to obtain from entertaining war guests is a much-to-be-desired increase in my powers of literary expression—from so much practice!

I hear that starting next year, they are going to eliminate the Junior School at U.T.S., so that settles the problem of whether or not to let Tom try to enter. They have been considering this move for years—I don't just know why, but I suppose it's to allow for a larger Senior School which I suppose they feel is more worth while.

I must stop now, to hear Mr. Churchill's speech. I don't envy him the task of composing and delivering it, with things in the mess they are!

[8]   90 DUNVEGAN ROAD
      TORONTO, FEBRUARY 22

Dear Margaret

The boys asked me to enclose these papers. They have had exams all week. Tom has had a cold in his head, but no temp., so I let him keep at school as I knew he would hate to miss the exams. Mary (who also has a cold) and he are staying in to-day to see if they can get cleared up for to-morrow.

I have been rather concerned at not having got them to the doctor's to have the "Dick" test for scarlet fever susceptibility, which I intended to do as soon as the ch[icken] pox was over—but of course I was ill myself and couldn't.[13] So I decided it might be some time before I could get out of the house, and got John to take the 4 of them to Dr. Stock yesterday for the test.[14] He injected a minute quantity of sc[arlet] fev[er] toxin in the arm and came this afternoon to make the reading, which has to be taken between 22 and 24 hrs. after the injection. They all show a very slightly positive reaction—Tom's the strongest, so I think to be on the safe side I'll have them all given toxoid. I don't think Dr. Stock thinks it's really a necessity, especially as the very slight reaction indicates that, if they took scarlet fever it would be lightly, but I have a very worrying nature and will have much more peace of mind if it's done, particularly every Monday morning when the report of new cases is published in the papers. There is by no means an epidemic in Toronto, and none so far in Brown School, but one never knows when there might be. They get 4 doses of toxoid (at weekly intervals) and there is little or no reaction from them....

I think C. feels he's doing pretty well in his exams. He had a Social Studies exam Friday (not the test enclosed) and got 70 out of 75, the highest mark in the class. He is to have reading to-morrow and has chosen the passage from "Three Men in a Boat" about the packing for the camping trip. He read it to me yesterday and I got him to read it to all of us to-day and he should do pretty well if he doesn't get nervous.[15] I think the spelling (Tuesday) is the one that's worrying him. He has been doing fairly well in his daily spelling but that's because he works at the words each night and memorises them—but in two days time forgets them! So it's pretty hard to mug up 20 or 25 lessons at once!

Peter has set up a Post Office and Telegraph Office in the playroom, and sends and delivers messages and letters for the others. He has two telegraph instruments with 40 feet of wire and has learned the Morse code—C. is mastering it too, and they do the operating and receiving.

The news continues sickening and sometimes it seems as if Canadians (some of them) are doing their best to tear one another apart and save the Germans & Japs the trouble! It's all very revolting but I think often <u>sounds</u> much worse than it <u>is</u>. Sometimes the less support spokesmen have the more vocal they are.

I do hope things are going well with you. I suppose your Easter holiday will start soon after you receive this, but I'll send the next to the school— one never knows how long they'll take.

[9]   90 DUNVEGAN ROAD
      TORONTO, MARCH 1

Dear Margaret

I had a lovely long letter from your mother this week (posted Jan. 30) and Tom and C. had one each from their father (Jan. 18 and Feb. 1). Tom gave me his from his father, to read, thinking it might interest me and I was surprised to learn that he is now in Manchester. Tom said he and C. had known this from previous letters but I suppose they had not thought of telling me—I wrote to him Feb. 15 and sent the letter to the London address but I expect it would be forwarded to Manchester. Vivien had a letter from you this week (of Jan. 20) and we were glad to know for certain that you got our letters last autumn.... The children had their first "shot" of scarlet fever toxoid yesterday morning and seemed quite surprised that it didn't hurt at all. They had a snowball fight yesterday afternoon, when C. and Peter besieged Tom & Mary in the remains of the snow fort—when the fort was captured the garrison refused to surrender and had to be rolled out by force and they all got very wet and had a hilarious time. Bill arrived in time to witness part of it and I think was rather bewildered by the Canadianisation of his small brothers. Then they all came in and changed their clothes and played inside—Bill stayed and had supper with them....

Dear Margaret

I am enclosing copies of the boys' reports.... We are very pleased indeed with C's report, and I think C. is—as he should be....

Theresa is in great excitement as Leslie is to be allowed to come home from the San.—she is taking his clothes up to him to-day and will probably go up for him in a day or two, as soon as all the proper doctors have signed all the proper papers. (Sanitorium care for T.B. is compulsory in Ontario, so to come home you have to have a government release.) She doesn't know how much he will be up when he gets home—I wish they could be in a house, with some garden to get out into, instead of mother's flat—but there's no use worrying about it—it isn't outdoor weather yet any way, though to-day is very springlike—warm and sunny with the dirty snow shrinking rapidly and rivers running down the streets and sidewalks.

We are just now being given the news of the cold and snow in England this winter.

Vivien is spending this weekend in Ottawa with Harry. She has been trying to have a weekend there ever since Christmas and I am so glad she managed it at last. The Victory Loan seems assured of a substantial over-subscription, which is very gratifying. We were afraid that the widespread dissatisfaction with the government and its halfhearted prosecution of the war measures might endanger the success of the loan but thank Heaven, common sense seems to have triumphed over prejudice and politics....

The war news is so ghastly—it is all pretty depressing, and much as we long for spring, for our own sakes, it is sure to be the signal for further onslaughts in the west and on the Atlantic.

I will send this to Ulverston—it hardly seems possible, but I expect it will be Easter holidays when it arrives.

Dear Margaret

... We are all well, though my leg still worries me a little. It seemed perfectly well last week so I have been using it more and it has begun to ache again so I am trying to keep off it as much as possible.

John and I went to "Parents" night at Brown School on Monday, and got very good accounts of all the children from their teachers. They have all got exceptionally nice teachers—and so discerning and understanding—I don't know how they can have such personal knowledge of and interest in each child with such large classes. I told you in my last letter what a good report C. had—we are delighted with his work—he had an average of 75% and was among the first 6 in his class—I'm not sure how large the class is but I think 40–45. Mr. Pugh thinks he has done splendidly and that his writing has improved enormously. I was rather surprised at his only getting D in art—I've also noticed that he does practically no drawing at home any more. However, I think I discovered the reason on Monday night. The best projects done in the class were on display—also the best posters advertising the Victory Loan, and it is evident that there are 5 or 6 pupils in C's room who are exceptionally talented—he had told me this before but I had no idea of how good they were until I saw their work. I remember your telling me in a letter that C. had been discouraged in his drawing some years ago by the same thing. So I have made no comment on it and I think he will come back to it eventually. If his interest in drawing is really deep it's bound to revive. C's project (mining in Ontario) was one of those on display. In each room the children had made placards with their names in large letters and affixed them to their desks. Their desks were tidied out and their work books, folders of art work, etc., laid out, each in a brown paper cover (they make the covers and decorate them either with drawings or designs cut from coloured paper). In the manual training room all the work "under way" was displayed. C's class are making lamp bases of wood, in the shape of rabbits, which they will paint, and wire for lamps.

Bertie Wilkinson was the speaker of the evening and Edith of course was there. They <u>are such</u> nice people—we are very fond of them and sorry we don't see more of them, we're all so busy. There were some other University people there we knew, from the history dept. and we were much interested in getting news of our new neighbours who are to move in next door in April with <u>four</u> children—this staid and rather elderly street is due to be well livened up this spring! They are Prof. and Mrs. Innis (head of the dept. of Political Economy)—by the way, in one of the bundles of "Saturday Nights" I recently sent you there is an article by Mrs. I. "Mary Quayle Innis," on the page they call "The Other Page"—I think it was entitled "Morning's at Nine"—it sounds as though she and her family would be very pleasant neighbours. Two of the children are older than ours but there is a boy 11 and, what pleases me most, a girl of 9.[16] I do so hope that she and Mary will get on well—it rather worries me that Mary has no little girls to play with. Of course I think living with boys is awfully good for her but there are no little girls around here at all and the one girl that she brings home from school some times I do not like much, I'm sorry to say. I think Mary is a perfect tom boy (of course there's no harm in that within bounds)—she makes Tom seem very gentle and "ladylike" in comparison—she is eternally active, as though on springs, but she practises the piano half an hour a day pretty faithfully and is good in her school work (has more stars for arithmetic on the black board than anyone else in her class) and is almost always in good spirits and enjoys herself all the time. She only got a B for conduct this time which did not surprise me but Miss Dunlop tells me she considers Mary one of the quieter members of the class (of 47)! Miss Blair, Tom's teacher is very much pleased with Tom and very fond of him. She says he is a most conscientious worker, anxious to do his best and to please and to be praised—and of course a model of quietness and good behaviour.

I don't think the children could be any happier in any school. C. seems to have made quite a few friends and to have fitted in very well. I rather wondered about Tom but C. says he has made some friends—in his own quiet way. I'm afraid most of the boys find him a bit priggish. With the first breath of spring all the children have gone mad on marbles and as Tom doesn't play marbles he is perhaps a little left out, but Tom never goes into things because other children do (the "mob mind" doesn't seem to affect him) and apparently would rather be an onlooker than bother playing marbles if playing marbles doesn't appeal to him. I believe it's best to let them all go their own ways as long as they are contented.

Theresa brought Leslie home from the San. on Wednesday—he is so thrilled to be back and I'm sure will be a very sensible and patient convalescent. He has gained 26 lbs. and finds the extra weight most uncomfortable, but as he gradually increases his exercise periods, he will no doubt lose some of it....

[12] 90 DUNVEGAN ROAD
TORONTO, MARCH 21

Dear Margaret

Yesterday I had such a sweet letter (dated Feb. 20) from your mother, enclosing a snowdrop from the garden. Today a letter came for C. from his father (postmark Feb. 22) and one from you to the boys, enclosing one for me (Feb. 15). This is the first I've had from you for more than 3 months—the boys' last was about 5 weeks ago, and dated Jan. 15. It is nice of you to be so sympathetic about my leg—I have had such good health for years that it is annoying to have so many breakdowns just when my responsibilities are so great. I am really quite right again as long as I can keep my leg up a good deal—I ventured to the big stores to do 1½ hrs. shopping on Thursday and had to make up by resting most of Friday.

I am really afraid that you have been quite unnecessarily upset over how the news about Gypsy's puppies would upset C. I really don't think he'd turn a hair. You know he's been away nearly 2 years now and children's memories are pretty short and I don't think Gypsy means a great deal to him any more. I suggested at Christmas that he might send her chocolate (he did last year) but he didn't seem at all so inclined or even interested. From his first arrival here we were always mystified by the family tradition of C's devotion to animals because he has never once shown any sign of it. I concluded that his attachment to his animals had been partly the result of his illness and being on his own with nothing to do for so long. I gather, since you feel you must tell him of the puppies' death, that you had in a previous letter told him of their birth—or the expectation of it, but he has never mentioned it. In fact, to be perfectly frank, I very much doubt whether he has read any of the letters he had from you this winter (there have been about one a month, I think). He stopped getting me to read them to him and I'm certain he can't decipher your writing himself. I never like to appear prying so I say "If you can't read your letter, I'll read it to you" and later I always ask "Could you read your letter?" Sometimes he hesitates a long time and says "Yes"—other times he says "I haven't read it yet, but I can." I don't know whether he doesn't like to admit that he can't read your writing or not. The one that came this morning (with Tom's and mine) is lying on his desk and I know he hasn't even unfolded it yet. All this bothers me very much. I think if you would print his letters it would encourage him to read them. I think perhaps he doesn't even bother to try when he knows he can't succeed and I suppose he feels it's babyish to have me read them. Tom undertook to read to-day's himself and managed alright except that he had to come in half a dozen times while I was dressing whenever he came to a particularly difficult word. It would have been easier to read him the whole letter because it's hard to decipher a word without the context but I was glad to encourage him in this bit of independence....

I'm afraid I'm due for a domestic upheaval before long—Mary Murphy tells me that her family may insist on her going home to the farm to help her mother. I have not told anyone, even John—there's no use worrying him until it's necessary—and am just trying to bury my head in the sand until I <u>have</u> to take it out! I think it will be hopeless to try to get any one to replace her so I'll just try to manage myself (by sending out the washing so Mrs. Fairfoul can help me in the house in the mornings) and hope for the miracle of hearing of some one through friends. Mary is far from being entirely satisfactory and I always feel that she hasn't (in spite of being with us nearly 4 years) the slightest personal interest in any of us, or cares two cents whether we live or die, but when I think of her leaving it sends cold chills down my back.

John took the 3 boys to the Maple Leaf Gardens this afternoon to see U.T.S. play hockey against Stratford. These play-offs are particularly exciting this year because (1) John Ratcliffe plays defense on the U.T.S. team (2) it is the first year U.T.S. has got into the play-offs. They won the Toronto Prep. School Championship which put them into the play-offs for the Ontario Hockey Assn. Junior B Group. This group is up to age 20 and of course the U.T.S. team averages about 17 years so they didn't expect to get far, but they beat Guelph 2 games out of 3 and then Oshawa in home and home games and that brought them against the Stratford team—always a good one—which all season had never lost a game and never scored less than 10 goals. There were to be 2 games (home and home) with total goals to count. You can imagine the excitement in the Ratcliffe household (spilling over into ours) when the day of the game at Stratford (Thursday eve.) came with John in bed with chills and fever and what seemed to be the flu! Vivien and Harry could not find it in their hearts to refuse to let him play, so instead of his driving up with the team Thursday afternoon, Harry took him up by train intending, if he was not well after the game, to keep him overnight at a Stratford Hotel. They simply astounded the Stratford team by leading them for a whole period and <u>almost</u> winning (Stratford won by one goal, 4–3). John so far recovered that he and Harry drove back with the team arriving at 2 A.M. Friday. The return game was this afternoon and U.T.S. won 7–6, so they are now tied with 10 goals each and there will have to be a deciding game. Poor Vivien—she is so keen on hockey and so proud of John's playing a good game, but what with agonizing over John's health, and the results of the games, and special meals at odd hours, she's going to feel by the end of the season as though she'd played the whole series herself!...

MARCH 22

... One day this week C. asked me when he came home from school, if he could go to Yonge St. to a store. I said "Yes indeed," of course having no idea what he intended to buy, and he returned to present me with 4 mutation tulips—a red, white, yellow and red. I was really touched. We had quite a discussion on the best place to put them and finally decided they would brighten up the hall if we put them on the table there. Mary was as excited over them as C. and insisted on their being right where anyone coming in the front door would see them first thing. It does warm my heart when he does such thoughtful things, and I appreciate it <u>very</u> much. I bought a new hat last week and as it was my first for 2 years I went a little hay-wire and got a bright scarlet. Peter was simply horrified at the idea of my wearing "a thing like that" (what he really meant was that I was <u>much</u> too old to wear it!) but the first time C. saw it on me his face lit up, he simply <u>beamed</u> and said "Oh! you have a new hat! My! I <u>like</u> it! It brightens you up!" It was most encouraging to the old girl!...

MARCH 24

I had to keep this open to put in the boys' letters which they wrote last evening. They had a marvellous day Sunday. Robbie and Jo[17] took them down to the harbour and the lake front and Robbie showed them all over the big sand boat belonging to his company (he is G.M. of the Standard Paving Co.) and they seemed to be entranced. (I notice neither of them mentioned either the hockey game or the visit to the Robinsons in their letters—funny kids, things seem just to evaporate from their minds.) When they came home C. simply burst in at me, saying "Gee! I had a <u>swell</u> time!" (you'll note the Canadianisms!) "and I <u>remembered</u> to say thank you!"

The blow has fallen—Mary announced yesterday she will have to go. I have told her she simply <u>has</u> to stay until after the Easter holidays and she agrees. It is very worrying—I'm not afraid of the work at all—it's just this gnawing fear that my health will give. However, something may turn up.

It's now Tuesday afternoon—your letters came Sat. morning and C's is still on his desk, unfolded. So it looks as though it doesn't really matter much whether the news of Gypsy's puppies would upset him or not! I asked him Saturday night if he could read the letter all right and he said "Yes," so I felt there was nothing more for me to do.

P.S. It was announced about 2 weeks ago that a ship with mail en route to Canada was lost—it did not say when.

[13] 90 DUNVEGAN ROAD
TORONTO, MARCH 29

Dear Margaret

About March 21 I had a letter from your mother (dated Feb. 20). C. had one from his father and the boys had letters from you (Feb. 15) with a note enclosed to me. I have wondered whether there mustn't have been a letter to me lost, as that was the first I'd had from you since the one dated Nov. 23.

On Wednesday Christopher had a slight accident which gave me rather a fright. He had taken a bundle of magazines over to the drug store where they keep a receptacle for reading matter for the troops and was riding the wagon home along the sidewalk (they put one knee on the wagon and push with the other foot). Our street slopes and he was coasting down it when the wagon hit a bump and he was thrown off and lit on his left hand, on the fingers, bent at the second joint. He showed it to me—it showed no marks and the skin was not broken but it was painful, so I telephoned the doctor, who said to apply cold water and see how it was by morning. So he kept it in a basin of cold water most of the time until bed time. In the morning it was a bit puffed and hurt more so I took him to the doctor at 9 o'clock and he looked at it through the fluroscope to examine the bones, which were all perfect. He said to change the treatment to warm water. I kept him home the rest of the morning but since then he has gone to school with his hand in a sling.... He wants to do all the active things that Peter does but his muscular co-ordination and sense of balance are not very good so he is bound to come to grief sometimes and I could not bear to discourage him or point out his limitations to him. All I can do is try to see that neither of them attempts anything really dangerous. When he came in to show me his hand and tell me how it happened he said "I was riding the wagon too fast down the sidewalk" so I gathered from that, that he realized his mistake and will just trust his common sense to keep him from repeating it, without any advice from me.

Aside from this they are all very well. We had 3 days of perfect warm spring weather this week—they have cleared up a stretch of the border in the garden and measured out a space 6' × 6' each for their own gardens and there is great discussion as to what they shall plant. I am trying to steer them away from the perennial favourites—radishes and carrots, which are the cheapest things to buy in the market—and at the same time to keep them from swinging right over to squash, marrows and cabbages which scarcely fit into 6 square feet. However, all I give are general suggestions and they can plant anything they like, it might be fun for them to try something new....

Every Saturday for weeks the weather has been horrible and yesterday was no exception—there was slushy snow all afternoon. However Peter had a relief map of Burma to do and Christopher collaborated on it (they use a ½ & ½ mixture of flour and salt, moistened with water and with care can make very creditable maps. After they dry they paint the surface the desired colours.) ...

They are all marble-mad at school—Tom stood aloof for a long time—I think he'd forgotten the large collection of marbles he had from last year.

When I reminded him and hunted them out he started too. I was glad to have him interested in something he could enter into with the other children at school—I don't think he joins in much in the more vigorous "running-about" games. C. says their teacher is trying to discourage too much marble playing and encourage some more active recreation at recess (what you call break) to give them more exercise, so he took a ball to school and they play handball and a modified and simplified cricket. (C. says he can manage with one hand so I feel his bad hand is at least not bad enough to make him feel out-of-sorts. The four of them played a simplified baseball in the garden yesterday morning and I watched them for a little while—C. was batting with one hand!) Mary and all the little girls have started the rope-skipping season. It's fun but she does wear herself out!...

Mary is getting quite interested in her piano work (incidentally she is giving Tom lessons!). She takes her lessons at school—each public school has a music teacher attached who comes at 3.30 and teaches piano in small group classes of 4 or 5. They have two ½ hr. lessons a week (at $5.00 for a term of 20 lessons) and it's an excellent way for them to get started at piano—much more interesting than the usual solitary lessons. Mary and another little girl are learning a duet to play at the recital in June, so in default of Ruth (she comes here about once a week to practise with Mary) I deputize for her on the bass. It's a long time since I played the piano (more than just to let the kids sing) but Mary is <u>delighted</u> with our spirited rendering of the "Arrival of the Brownies" or whatever it is! Half way through she will burst out "<u>Isn't</u> this fun?"

Tom is very faithful to his choir practice and seems to enjoy it very much. He still doesn't go to Evening Service on Sunday. I think Monday and Friday evening practices make enough late nights for him—he gets home about 9....

[14] 90 DUNVEGAN ROAD
TORONTO, EASTER SUNDAY [APRIL 5]

Dear Margaret

Tom had a letter from his father during the past week. Two weeks ago (March 21) the boys had letters from you, enclosing a note for me, and also C. got one that day from his father. They had letters from your mother too, and I had one from her dated Feb. 20 (not answered yet, alas.) ...

C. and Tom have ordered (through me) a parcel of 2 lbs. of maple cream (this is maple sugar beaten in some way as it thickens so that it's creamy instead of sugary), for their father's birthday, to be sent by Mr. Fred Austin, a maple sugar producer of Springhill, Nova Scotia. It will probably not arrive till sometime after the birthday (the boys aren't sure of the date but think it is in late April) and C. is working on a birthday card to send in the meantime. I don't know when it will be finished—he completely forgets it except when I remind him, when he does a little more work on it. So I thought I had better announce the forthcoming arrival of the parcel, in case it arrives before the card! In this part of Ontario the sugaring-off is early but I don't know how the season is in Nova Scotia. Vivien has ordered a similar parcel of maple cream to be sent to you, as a present from her, and I have ordered one to be sent to your mother. I did not give Mr. Austin the senders' names to enclose as I thought there might be mistakes which would only confuse the recipients. I hope all 3 boxes arrive in good condition.

This is a glorious warm sunny day, the fourth in a row. Schools closed Thursday afternoon. Good Friday morning we all went to Church and the children worked with John all afternoon raking leaves and tidying beds etc. They worked again all Saturday morning so faithfully and enthusiastically that they had everything in pretty good shape as far as they were able, by noon, so we sent the 3 boys off to see Kipling's "Jungle Book", which has just appeared in the movies.... I took [Mary] and a little friend to the Zoo, where the polar bear outdid himself in entertaining the crowds, making a very successful afternoon. I had boiled 8 eggs hard, so after their supper last night they took 2 each and went off with their paints and decorated them, each to suit himself. Then we shredded a lot of cellophane (the wrapping of a lampshade which I'd saved) and made a glittering nest of it in the centre of the dining room table, with the eggs in it. It is very pretty there to-day, and if it's a decent day to-morrow we are going to Burlington and can take the hard boiled eggs as part of the picnic and to combine use with beauty!...

I drove Leslie and Theresa one day to see his doctor (who has his office close to our house) so they walked up here afterwards and had tea with me. It was the first time he had been away from home—except for short walks—since he came back from the San. He is getting on splendidly but is so anxious to get to work again—which, as the dr. pointed out is ridiculous when he's been out of bed only 3 weeks, after 13 months on his back. However one can understand his feelings, particularly in war time, but he will have to resign himself to "building up" for some months.

Gasoline rationing started on Wednesday last (April 1). The unit at present is 5 gals. and the no. of units we get will give us about 5000 miles a year but of course the unit may be reduced any time (and no doubt will).

Peter, Tom, Marie, Mary, and Christopher skiing at York Downs Golf Club

All manufactures and sales are being very closely regulated and controlled and almost everything is becoming hard to get. However I don't think any of us are going to suffer any real hardships unless things get much worse. Housekeeping is bound to become more difficult but we have really been spoiled in the past in a great many ways....

I hope you are getting good weather and having a good rest from what must be pretty trying and tiring work.

[15] 90 DUNVEGAN ROAD
TORONTO, APRIL 11

Dear Margaret

I am enclosing some pictures—the skiing ones taken in Feb., the others Good Friday and Easter Day. I think the one of the 3 Sharps is particularly good [see illustration, page 189]—I will send prints to your mother and another at another date to you and then send you the film. I should hate the film to be lost, at least without your having some prints. Easter weekend was beautifully springlike but the following Friday (yesterday) we had a very heavy snowfall—it is melting but not very warm. I have been hauling out winter things I'd stored away, cursing heartily the while!...

Vivien read me, over the telephone, a letter Bill received to-day from you and which you asked him to pass on to Viv. as it concerned his school course

Tom, Peter, Mary, and Christopher ready for cricket in the back yard, Good Friday 1942

and choice of subjects. I feel, as Viv. and as you do, that he is well advised to cover as many subjects as he can handle, to be prepared for whatever line of university and future work he chooses, whether here or in England. I'm sure that is what Bill intends to do and as he seems to romp through all subjects almost equally successfully, he doesn't seem to find a full time-table any strain. As for his university course, there are undoubtedly all the complications you mention. At present Bill seems to lean slightly towards engineering. Viv. thinks this is rather due to Dr. Lewis' telling him that the Engineering Physics course (the stiffest engineering course) is a <u>very</u> difficult one—a stiff course always appeals to Bill's ambition. We are all confident that <u>whatever</u> course he elects he will do well in—it's a question of what will give him the best preparation for what he wants to do after graduation. I imagine the engineering field in England is quite different from that in Canada—here a great majority of the graduates are engaged in developing natural resources and extending communication lines to new territories—coping with all the forces of nature. We usually think of the engineer as having a bit of the frontiersman in him, which Bill hasn't. But in England I suppose the engineer's field is more within the already existing framework of community life. I should think, myself, that one of the Arts courses—Maths and Physics, or any of the Arts Science courses would open up opportunities for research work—the more purely scholastic or intellectual pursuits which would seem to suit Bill's temperament, character and disposition better than technical or administrative work. However, this is just my own guess work and I would not offer any advice whatever. We think Bill has a very accurate knowledge of his own abilities and is quite capable of making his own decisions with advice from you and his father and guidance from Dr. Lewis.

I don't remember whether or not I sent you, along with the University Arts Calendar, the calendar of Matric. curriculum and scholarships, so I am sending one now and marking sections of particular interest. You will notice that there are <u>very</u> few scholarships available at Honour Matric. for the Faculty of Applied Science and Engineering—in fact there are only 2 for which Bill would be eligible, the Emerson Wickett and the U.T.S. Engineering (p. 28). They are each of the value of $250 (which I <u>think</u> is the amount of one year's fees in Engineering—you can check this in the Calendar of the Faculty of Engineering which Bill is going to send you). I believe there are a few scholarships in subsequent years—the Calendar will give that information too—but not many. On the other hand there are masses of scholarships in Arts, some general proficiency of as high value as $850 and $900 and a great many of a value of $625—$125 cash plus an allowance of $125 a year on fees for the whole 4 year course, provided the student gets 1st class honours each year. (The fees in the Faculty of Arts are $150 year.)

You mentioned that you had understood (in the past) Toronto to have a good reputation in Maths. and Physics and that is still the case. A good many of our physicists have won recognition and we've had many brilliant mathematicians. I am enclosing a clipping reporting the winning of the Mathematical Prize for America by the Toronto team—they are all students in the Maths & Physics course—two of them, Preston and Lyons, have worked for John the last two summers in the Canada Life Mathematical Dept. The newspaper might have explained that the reason the Toronto team has won only 3 out of 5 contests is that no University is allowed to compete the year after they have won first place, so Toronto has competed only 3 times.

Vivien had a letter from you some time ago (written in January) in which you mentioned the possibility of being able to send money and asked her what she thought of it, and in the letter to Bill mentioned above, you refer to the delay there may be in getting a permit. You may have written to me about it too but if so, the letter has been lost, so I may as well tell you how I feel about it. We have always been rather pleased than otherwise that you were not allowed to pay for the children's support while they are with us. Even though it entails a financial sacrifice, it puts them on the same

Tom, Bill, and Christopher on Easter Sunday 1942

footing in every way as our own and any outlay we can make we can divide among the four. John has claimed exemption for them in his income tax returns both last April and this, though we don't know whether it will be allowed or not—the approval (or disapproval) notices for last year's returns won't be sent out until May or June of this year. Technically, the Govt. allows exemption (but only to the amount payable on an income of $5000 year) for British evacuees brought out under the government scheme but this scheme comprised so few children (as the evacuation was cut short by the sinking of the Benares)[18] that we felt they would allow it on children brought out by such well-authenticated organizations as the University Overseas Children's Committee. However, that remains to be seen. We understand the amount which is to be allowed is £3 [per] month for each child. That sum, not being sufficient to cover the child's upkeep, would not embarrass us in any way, and would therefore be most welcome, to use for extras. For instance, we intend to make a great effort to send them to camp this summer—of course we would not send any of them if we could not manage it (or something equally attractive) for all 4, and if, as you say, the remittance is retroactive to Jan. 1, that amount would go a long way towards providing for C. and T's camp or keeping them there for a longer period than we could afford from our own resources.

APRIL 13

... To go back to your letter to Bill—I've not had a chance to talk to him about it but I noticed that you discussed at length a choice between taking Latin and Problems. Bill must have brought up this question and I'd like to talk to him about it. Of course it's many years since I wrote Matric. (1915) and U.T.S. may have a different method with scholarship students from my old school—U.T.S. makes such a business of going after scholarships that they may give the boys extra training. But, when I wrote, the "Problems" was simply an extra mathematics paper which everyone trying for a scholarship in maths had to write, in addition to Algebra, Geometry and Trig.

Another thing I think you may not understand as it may differ from the system in England, is the method of awarding the scholarships. As I said above, they are awarded on the marks at the ordinary Honours Matric. exams. (with the one addition of the Problems paper). As you'll see in the calendar, there are various scholarships awarded in various subjects or groups of subjects. The candidate does not apply for any particular scholarship or for a scholarship in any particular subject. Provided he writes the full complement of matric. subjects—I think that is nine—to prevent one boy getting an advantage by specializing in one or two subjects he is given the most valuable scholarship to which his marks on any subject or group of subjects entitle him. Some particularly brilliant students, who write a wide range of subjects, in which they are equally good, naturally rank for a good many scholarships. and are awarded the most valuable one, the others being awarded to those next in line according to their standing.

When I wrote, I did Maths., Mods. (English French German) and History and Latin. In those days there were very few scholarships compared with to-day and the only valuable ones were the Edward Blakes. I ranked 2nd in Maths and 2nd in Mods. The winners in those 2 subjects each got the First Edward Blake in their respective subject but with those two out of the way I ranked highest in a combination of Maths & Mods and therefore I got the First Edward Blake in Maths & Mods.[19] (I think that particular Edward Blake has been discontinued—I believe that some of the older scholarships, provided by endowments had to be revamped some years ago when University fees went up and interest rates down.) I hope all this is not too rambling—and also hope it is still accurate as I've been out of touch with these things for a long time. But I think the system is basically the same.

APRIL 14

I find I should have postponed discussing the "Problems problem"—Bill came in yesterday afternoon, after I'd written all the above, and tells me that Problems has a definite place in the timetable of the "scholarship form" and conflicts with Latin. So many more boys from U.T.S. sit for scholarships than from any other school that I suppose they do more there in the way of preparation. He is apparently quite determined to drop the Latin which seems to me a pity—he thinks if by some miracle the war should end in time for him to try for Oxford or Cambridge, he could get it up himself. Vivien thinks he should make a great effort to keep it up next year and write it—apparently it is a very easy subject for him—but when he makes his mind up it is hard to change it....

APRIL 15

Mary Murphy left on Monday so I am managing as best I can. My legs get very weary by noon but then I rest for an hour or two and get through the day very well. We are all having dinner together at night—it is much easier than getting two dinners a day. Peter takes his lunch to school and the other 3 and I have lunch together. At dinner the children change the plates and Peter and C. clear the table and wash up one night—the next night I wash and Mary and Tom dry. They don't mind at all, and I find there are lots of little jobs they can do to save me steps and stairs. Peter makes his own lunch before he goes to bed. We have dinner at 6—John's office is now operating from 8.30–4.30 (the hours of all businesses are being "staggered" to relieve the transportation congestion which is terrific since gasoline rationing). Of course the 4.30 is more in theory than practice but he's usually home well before 6. Mary and Tom still start off for their baths at 7 and have their lights out about 7.45 or a little later (Tom of course has 2 late nights for choir practice). The others are supposed to start soon after 8 and have lights out at 8.45 though it's difficult to stick to it exactly. Peter really doesn't need that much sleep but C. is the one that keeps me worried—he seems to get very tired and I know he wouldn't like to go earlier than Peter. When he had supper at 5.30 he used to go at his home work immediately after so he was through that in lots of time, but now that the weather is nice he plays outside until dinner and then sometimes the homework isn't finished at 8.15 when he should get in his bath. He is <u>very</u> well—don't you think he looks it?—but he has started to jerk his head and twist his face and screw up his eyes—it goes on almost incessantly, even when he's playing. I thought of taking him to the doctor but I'm sure the only thing he would advise is "more rest." We had that sort of trouble with Peter when he was 5 or 6 but it gradually disappeared. I told Jo R. about it and she watched him while he was with her and said it scarcely ever happened but it certainly started the minute he got back. It is awfully nerve-racking to have going on all the time and I'm going to start a real campaign of early to bed and get his light out at 8.30. If necessary I'll have him do some of his home work before dinner. The last few days he's been making friends with Hugh and I didn't like to interfere. There always seems to be something!

That last statement is certainly true! Vivien just telephoned to tell me Bill has the mumps! I am dreadfully concerned about her as well as Bill—you know she's had a dreadful cough for 2 or 3 weeks and finally went to the doctor last Friday night. He told her she had a slight bronchial pneumonia and had better get to bed and take it seriously. He thought she should have a nurse to look after her but Viv assured him that her children were old enough and capable enough to look after her very well. She assures me she can manage to look after Bill all right but it <u>is</u> distressing to have the extra strain. John and Nancy have both had mumps but Judy hasn't and neither has Hilda (the maid) or her husband (who lives in the house) and they are panic stricken! I don't know how <u>we'll</u> fare—Bill was here most of Monday afternoon, just when he'd be at his worst for spreading it. I know Tom's had it but none of the other 3 have, <u>nor have I</u>! However there is no use crossing bridges before you get to them so we won't worry—I believe it's a rather long incubation period. If anyone here gets it I'll just have to get a nurse (if there are any available)....

I must get to bed now. Will keep you informed on the mumps.

[16] 90 DUNVEGAN ROAD
TORONTO, APRIL 27

Dear Margaret

... No mumps have appeared yet. Bill is quite recovered—the doctor says he can go back to school to-morrow though I think Viv. intends to keep him home another day just in case. He had the most painless and satisfactory case of mumps one could possibly hope for. If mine get them I hope they do the same, but Oh! I hope they don't get them! It's just all I can manage to get through the days' work with them all up and giving a hand. They have been doing very well with the dishes and dusting and table setting—I gave them each an extra 15¢ with their allowances yesterday—I hope that keeps them at it (they're apt to weary in well-doing after the first week or so)....

The children have their gardens planted—how or with what I really don't know. I let them buy their seeds yesterday but I don't really have enough spare time for more than a quick look around the garden once a day. However I think they like better to do things on their own anyway.

T. & C. are having exams. I'm afraid C. may not do so well this time—he has been slipping in his homework lately. I notice since the weather has been good, and outdoors more attractive he spends very little time on it. However the only thing to do is to let him find out for himself that you have to work to "get there." He may surprise me and do better than I expect. He says so little it's hard to judge how he's getting on until the report arrives.

Will have to get to bed now—morning comes early! We have breakfast in good time—I get up at 7.15 and have things ready the night before, and the children usually help with the washing up before they go to school. Peter & C. have a grand time the nights they do the dinner dishes—fill the tumblers with soapsuds and pretend it's beer, play tunes on the tin trays, and so on.

[17] 90 DUNVEGAN ROAD
TORONTO, MAY 3

Dear Margaret

C. had a letter from his father postmarked April 5. It arrived April 20, which seems very quick. Also, when cleaning out Tom's trouser pockets I found a letter from you dated March 15. It must have come on Saturday (April 19), as that is the only day that I don't take in the mail myself. Tom and Mary "do" the downstairs for me on Saturday so I suppose they got the letters when they arrived and Tom didn't think to tell me about it. I'm glad I found it or it would never have been acknowledged. I have not had an answer from you to any of my letters since the one of Oct. 30—I do hope most of them, at any rate, have arrived, especially the one with the boys' marks and some exam papers, sent the end of Feb.

I sent some of Tom's April papers last week and am enclosing the rest. He is to get his report to-morrow but knows he has an average of 80% and stands 4th in his class. He is very disappointed—says he tried so hard to be first this time. I have assured him that he is doing splendidly and has no reason whatever to be discouraged—that everyone is delighted with his attainments. But poor Tom does love to be the "best" and Peter was first in his class at Easter again and Mary is first this time too. This is the first time Mary's class has been given standing—she had an average of 92%—I was simply astounded—we were quite prepared when Mary started school for her to prove not very brainy—she has such a good disposition that I wasn't worried about it at all (I think a child, especially a girl, has a much happier life if she has a happy nature, gets on well with people, and has a lot of fun, and maintains just a good average in school work). So we were much surprised (and of course very pleased) at her success....

I think we are safely over the mumps menace—thank Heaven! It is 20 days to-day and the incubation period is supposed to be 18. Bill was here yesterday and is looking very well. How fortunate it was that he had such a light dose! Peter was not well on Friday and spent the day surrounded by maps, Globe, encyclopaedias etc., devising a "quiz program" to be held yesterday afternoon. He asked the two children from next door in and they had it at 4 o'clock, when Tom got back from Church (the choir was singing at a very large wedding—Tom was thrilled with the experience and also with the 50¢ he was paid. He is simply blissful that the choir, which he went into as a pleasure and privilege is turning out remunerative as well—he got his month's money Friday night and this time it was 90¢!—he says they are paid according to performance and his aim for this month is a dollar)....

We have not been able to make any summer plans yet. I hope we can manage something that will give everyone concerned the best kind of holiday possible.

I hope the maple cream arrived safely to you, Mr. Sharp, and your mother—also I do hope the pictures which I sent (2 lots) have arrived. I will send another one or two in this letter and send the film next week.

Dear Margaret

Your cheque for £18 ($79.71) arrived May 8. It is very welcome, as it will be a great help in providing the boys' summer holiday. Thank you very much.

C. got his report on Friday.... As you will see it is an <u>excellent</u> report except for the spelling—I'm sure if that had been better he'd have been top, or almost, of the class. As it is he wasn't given standing—I think only those with honours (75 or more) are ranked. We have pointed out to him that the B in effort is due to his falling down in spelling—relaxing the effort which was so evident he was making in the former months. It has surely shown him what he <u>can</u> do when he tries and <u>can't</u> do without trying. So we are leaving it at that and will see whether he feels the effort is worth while. I do hope he does—there are only 6 or 7 weeks of school left and I <u>would</u> like him to have a good report at the end of June. He has improved in his writing [from] 26 to 30 [out of 50] though more pains would help that still further—and also in his reading. For the reading exam the end of Feb. they could choose their own passage and he chose the incident from "Three men in a Boat"—"Packing" which is in their readers. He practised it over and over on me and got 38 in the exam. This month another teacher (not Mr. Pugh) examined them in reading so C. took the same passage!—I think he knows it by heart now! He says he thinks good marks in reading depend a lot on how much 'spression you put into it, and "Packing" is a thing you can put lots of 'spression into. We've tried to give him all the praise that was due him for his fine marks in Comp. Lit., Maths. and Soc. Studies. Your letter commending him on his last report came yesterday, just when he had showed me his report and it just followed exactly the same line of encouragement which we try to take with him so I hope that will have some effect too.

By the way, these 2 letters of yours which came this past week I was determined he should not leave unread, as the previous ones were, so I just "happened" to walk past his room as soon as he got them, stopped at the door and said "Shall I read your mother's letter to you? I read Tom's to him—it was rather long so it was hard for him to make it all out." And he handed it to me, explaining rather elaborately that he knew he <u>could</u> make it all out but it took so long to make out each word that he sometimes missed the meaning. I think it was a better way than when I used to ask "Could you read your mother's letter?" He didn't like to say "no" and admit failure.

I am sure he is certain to pass into Grade 8—I'm sure they wouldn't let his spelling keep him back—of course I've never had any doubt of his passing.

I am so glad to think you had a good holiday at Easter—I suppose after that you have a deluge of your matric. papers. It must be a terrific grind....

About Bill and his work, I hope soon after you wrote you received my letter of about April 15 in which I went into that subject, and you'll notice that I also thought M. & P. would be the natural course for him. That was John's course, but for some reason he seems prejudiced against it and inclined to the Engineering Physics course at S.P.S.[20] However, as you say, that's all some time ahead. At present, as far as his school course goes, the only difficulty seems to be about Latin. Vivien is very anxious for him to keep it up but he is very much against it. I think he should too, especially as it's easy for him and he does well in it. I don't think there would be any reason for an English boy being barred from a Univ. scholarship. I'm sure David Bland is to try for one this year. I remember when I wrote, the girl who took top place, ahead of me, in French & German, was a German girl with a French mother. As a matter of fact at the time she won the scholarship (1915) her father was interned as a dangerous alien! All the Honour courses, I think you'll find, are 4 year courses. The only 3 year course is the Pass Course—it used to be 4 years and could be entered with Junior Matric. but now you have to have Honour Matric. to enter university, and the Honour Matric. covers the old first year of the Pass Course. Of course the Pass Course is out of the question for Bill....

I think Vivien has already written to you about Bill's prospective summer. We are simply thrilled at the opportunity it gives him of seeing something of Northern Ontario. It should be a most interesting and enjoyable experience and the people do sound so nice—I don't know them at all but have heard Vivien speak of them quite often.[21]

We are still rather vague about summer plans. I happened to see Mrs. Mudge (of the Overseas Children's Committee at the University) some time ago and we were discussing summer camps and she asked me not to make any plans for a fortnight or so as the Committee was seeing what they could do about getting a reduction in rates at the Y.M.C.A. camp (which is a very good one) and some others, for war guests. They expected that some organizations and clubs in the city might raise money to give to some boys' camps to apply on the fees of English boys, and she urged me if any such help was available, not to hesitate to accept it as it simply represents the desire of a lot of people to help with the financing of war guests, when they're not able to undertake the full care of one. I have not had any report from her as yet but if it is possible I would like very much to send the boys to camp for the full 8 week period. I would like them to have that typically Canadian experience while they're here and they would get so much more out of it if they stay the whole period. I expect Peter will go back to Woapak for 4 weeks but if it's at all possible I'd much rather not have C. & Tom go to the same camp with Peter. Peter is pretty good at swimming, diving, paddling etc. and I'm afraid if Peter were at hand to witness his efforts, C. (who hates to be shown up at a disadvantage) would not even try to learn these things. Anyway I think it would do them all good to be separated for a time and they'd enjoy being together in the autumn all the more. Of course all this is just what I'd like—I'll have to see what I can do.

We are getting on very well without Mary Murphy—I find I can run the house all right if I don't do anything else. Of course I haven't much chance to do anything else as I can't be out when the children are home. The bit of going out I have to do (shopping etc) I manage by going directly after lunch, when the children leave for school (at 1 o'clock) and if I want to, I can give them their lunch to take to school (they love that) but I don't often do it, in fact I've only done it once but it's nice to feel I have it in reserve, as it were. They are really awfully good about helping. The boys help with the breakfast dishes each morning (Peter has to leave early and Mary does her practising tho she sometimes finishes her whole half hour's practising before breakfast—such an early riser!) and the 3 help with the lunch dishes or sometimes do them themselves if I have something else I have to do, like getting dressed to go out so I can leave when they do. (Peter gets home soon after 3 so I like to get out early as I can, if I'm going.)

Just for fun I am enclosing the "domestic help wanted" from the evening paper—these same ads are in night after night, so you can imagine how little chance one has of getting a maid in a house with 4 children. However as long as I have Mrs. Fairfoul and the children keep well I am quite surprised at how well I can manage—and Mary, at least, keeps telling me how much better I cook than Mary Murphy!

I had Peter home one day, rather "off colour" and much to my surprise, Tom was ill last Monday—sick at his stomach—he had never been so before since he came here and I don't think it can ever have happened to him before, because he didn't seem to have the slightest idea what to expect—with disastrous results!! I thought after the first spasm or two he would recognize the symptoms but each seizure seemed to take him completely unaware! It started at 4.30 A.M. but by noon he was able to start sipping ginger ale and sit up and read, and by evening he was ready for some supper, and made a quick recovery with no after-effects which is more than I can say for myself as I've spent all my spare moments this week washing bedding and pyjamas!

He had no temp. at any time and I sent him back to school Tuesday afternoon. I think it was the result of a rather over-stimulating weekend (he sang in the choir at an enormous wedding Sat. afternoon and I didn't realize till later how frightfully it excited him—then right after the wedding Peter had the "quiz," a treasure hunt and sports program, then he stayed up late because Bill was here and on Sunday afternoon John took them all to the Island and got them their supper there to give me an "afternoon off" to rest)—with the final straw of whole-kernel canned corn for midday dinner on Sunday which he had swallowed whole—it came up in the same condition next morning! We have tried, ever since he came to us, to get Tom to chew his food and when he thinks of it and is constantly reminded, he does, but it never seems to have become a habit, and whenever his mind is on something else, or he's excited, he gulps his food unchewed. He informed me solemnly that "this will be a lesson to me!" However I'm afraid the lesson was forgotten again by next day.

Oh dear me! what a lot of space and time I've taken describing a not important incident—but I noticed Tom mentioned it in his letter so thought I'd better give more detail. I also had Mary home for a day this week with a swollen gland on her neck—something I've never had to cope with before and am rather afraid of, as I believe if not treated with respect they sometimes become chronic. It appeared Friday morning and though it was gone by noon I kept her in bed till Saturday noon—out of harm's way, because Mary is the kind of child that, if you let out of bed, is quite likely to be out skipping or down the street on roller skates as soon as your back is turned. We sent C. & Peter down to see Blackstone the Magician on Saturday—they were thrilled!

These odd days in bed (of the children's) have shown me how demoralizing to my housekeeping it would be to have a real illness so I am doing my best to keep them all well. With the good weather we're having that should not be hard.

Our spring is at least 2 weeks in advance of normal. We find we have 4 huge lilacs of different purple varieties and an enormous white one. They are so old and tall one needs a step ladder to cut even the lowest blooms! Tom takes a great interest in the garden and it interests me how he, usually so unobservant, spots every new flower that appears. He thoroughly enjoys the constant surprises that meet us (none of us being good enough gardeners to recognize a great many of the plants until they bloom).

The children have planted seeds which are coming up erratically, as children's gardens do. John put up the wren houses which C. & Tom made at St. Paul's and there are wrens about but as yet none have chosen the houses for homes. We have at least one pair of cardinals about, some orioles and a lot of other birds which we didn't have at Hillsdale (it was a new section with few big trees).

MAY 11

To-day is my birthday and C. & Tom have given me a most beautiful box of chocolates—a big heartshaped box covered with pink silk—I was really very touched. Mary gave me an egg-timer—her mind runs to practical things. I think she's going to be matter-of-fact and down-to-earth like her mother. Peter gave me a bottle of bath oil. Clare and George are coming in to have dinner with the children and put them to bed so John and I can go out to dinner and a movie....

I must get this off now—Vivien had a letter from Mrs. Anthony, who expects to be in Toronto about May 23 so we hope to have her see the boys while here.

[**19**] 90 DUNVEGAN ROAD
TORONTO, MAY 18

Dear Margaret

I had a letter from your mother to-day (April 23) and C. one from his father (April 25). I hope my last letter (18) is safe—it contained the film of the 3 boys. In it I told you I had your letter of April 19 and the boys had letters of April 19 and April 9 (the latter arrived a week earlier than the former). Tom had one from his father of April 13....

The new neighbours are a great success. The boy Hugh (11) is rather quiet and a little odd but very nice. C. was determined to overcome his shyness and did and he plays a good deal with C. & Tom—I'm glad, it helps to get Tom outdoors—he's rather inclined to stay in unless "pushed" out. The little girl of 9 (Anne) is the great acquisition as she and Mary are good friends and I _am_ so glad for Mary to have a girl to play with—and such a nice little girl. Mary and Anne brought half a dozen little girls home from school to-day and had a guessing contest (they had prepared puzzle pictures yesterday) in the garden and some games. I had been asked in advance for some sandwiches, which I passed out the window in due course and they apparently all had a very hilarious time. I try to encourage them all to bring their friends home—C. does sometimes....

P.S. In my last letter I also told you I had received the cheque, for which many thanks. I have opened an account with it and put it in and am adding what I save by doing without a maid (about $50 a month) to help with the summer expenses.

Dear Margaret

I put off writing this week until after Mrs. Anthony's visit. She was so rushed during her 2 days here that she had very little time to spare but she got to Vivien's for lunch yesterday and came here to dinner to-night. The boys were rather shy with her—surprising with Tom who is usually quite talkative with adults. I think he had forgotten her completely except as a name. We did enjoy meeting her and thought her charming and I am so glad she got a chance to have at least a peep at the boys so she can tell you of it....[22]

I have Mary in bed again to-day worse luck—the same gland that was swollen a few weeks ago is kicking up a little again. It seems all right now but I think I'll keep her in again to-morrow. I hate having a child in bed—it does complicate things.

We have had no English mail since I wrote last week.

C. had some tests this week and brought the papers home Friday to be signed by me and returned. He produced them last night and confessed he had been "kind of" putting off showing them to me. The grammar paper and the maths were excellent but the social studies very careless and sloppy in the answers (Queen Victoria instead of Elizabeth etc.). The spelling paper was pretty bad too. I tried to "steam" him up to putting more interest and thought into his work for these last few weeks and I do hope he will. He can do exceptionally well if he will make the effort. I think he is perhaps rather tired—the jerking of his head and blinking still persist, though I am getting him to bed with lights out by 8.30. He plays so hard (like Mary) that he wears himself out physically and nervously. It might not be a bad idea to keep him in bed for a day too but I'm rather afraid he would resent it.

They are all so helpful in the house it warms one's heart. To-day when M. was in bed, C. & Tom washed up after lunch without my asking or suggesting it. To-night dinner was rather late as Mrs. Anthony had to come just when she was able, so when we finished I suggested we should postpone coffee and Tom might take her up to show her their rooms (so she could have a little while alone with them). Then I turned back to the dining room where I found Peter busy with the dishes. "Don't you touch them" he said "I'll attend to these." And he did—washed up the whole lot, though when the boys & Mrs. A. came down, C. slipped out to the kitchen and helped him finish up. The knowing that they want to be of assistance is just as much help as the actual work they do!

90 DUNVEGAN ROAD
TORONTO, MAY 31

Dear Margaret

... We are arranging to send Tom and C. to camp on June 29, to the "Pioneer Camp". I was discussing camps with Mrs. Mudge of the Overseas Children's Committee some time ago and she was trying to get some reduction in rates for war guests at the Y.M.C.A.-run camp, Pinecrest. She telephoned me later that they could not give reductions as the camp is run at cost but told me that the Pioneer Camp was taking 15 English boys and 15 English girls at $10 a week (amazingly cheap!) (they have a camp for girls and one for boys at opposite ends of a small lake). She recommended the camp on the authority of Dr. Mary Northway (on the staff of the Psychology Dept of the Univ.) who has made a special study of camps in Ontario. I know that friends of ours, Dr. & Mrs. Jebb, send their 2 girls to this camp and like it very much. Mrs. Mudge had them send me a prospectus and I found some other friends in the list of parents so telephoned one who sent her 2 small boys last year. She said the boys loved it and came home very fit and well—the counsellors were very conscientious university students and the boys got excellent care in the way of seeing that wet shoes were changed etc. This was the point I was most anxious about for C. & Tom. So many of the camps have counsellors who are excellent leaders of boys but not very good "nursemaids". I never worried about Peter on that score, he has always looked after those things for himself—just out of love of comfort, I think, but C. always needs to be watched—he doesn't like to take the trouble to change wet clothes or put on rubbers or put on a sweater if it's cold or take it off if it's hot. And Tom is always willing to do what is right but never quite sure what is right unless he's told. So it seemed very satis-factory in every way—meals good, etc. I went into the city office to see the secretary and put in applications for the two boys. The Camp is run by an organization called the Inter-Varsity Christian Fellowship which I never heard of before and I find that the camp routine includes a good deal of Bible Study &c, however I don't think it will hurt the boys and I figure that their Bible Study periods work out at about $1.00 an hour which makes it a fairly profitable occupation. (What I mean is, the saving I make by send-ing them to this camp rather than to a less biblical one amounts to that!)[23] I will send you the camp folder. I do hope they like camp—I'm sure C. will and I rather think Tom will too. The only drawback to this camp is that it is for 6 weeks only instead of 8 weeks as most camps are, which brings the boys back Aug. 10. However I am hoping Clare will ask them to her house for the next fortnight.

John has to take his 4 weeks holiday in July. Otherwise I would have sent all 4 children to camp in July, but John rather likes to have some time at home in the summer without the children—he can get so many of his "odd jobs" done after the office when we're alone at the house. So we decided to send Peter & Mary to camp just for the last 4 weeks of the 8 that their camps run (July 25—Aug. 22, I think) and take them somewhere with us in July. We couldn't possibly go to a summer resort because of the expense and finally hit on the idea of renting from John's sister Emily the apartment which she has made out of a wing of her house in Burlington. She rents it furnished to a high school teacher who of course is not there in the summer. It is right on the lake, just outside Burlington, right in the midst of the fruit and market garden country so the housekeeping should not be hard for me, and it is a very small place to look after (just a sunroom—living room with kitchen off, a little sitting room and, upstairs, bathroom, bedroom, sleeping porch and verandah). If the weather's not good for "sleeping out" Emily will let us have one of her bedrooms which can be made to adjoin by unlocking a door.

Peter is through school June 12 and Emily has asked him to come out then and stay with her and take a job picking strawberries at Bell Brothers fruit farm near by. I think it would be very good for him and he is quite anxious to go. There is a desperate need for farm help and fruit pickers this year. He would like to earn some money, too, towards a bicycle for which he is longing (of course it is pretty difficult to get them now even if you have the price). When we go out, in July, Peter can keep on with the raspberry and currant picking if he wants to. It will be nice for John to be in Burlington for a time. He grew up not far from there and has so many old friends round about whom he never can manage to see on our usual visits there, for part of a day only. I expect he will spend a good many days, too, helping his 2 brothers on their small fruit farms near by. He likes that kind of thing if he can have it in not too large doses and with pleasant company. There are 7 brothers and sisters in his family, all very devoted, but he does not see much of them in the ordinary way.

We had a very exciting piece of news on Thursday—Peter has won a scholarship to Trinity College School in Port Hope. I have always felt that Peter was the kind of boy who needed boarding school, and 3 or 4 years ago I got the prospectuses of all the good boys schools and T.C.S. was the one I wanted to send him to—also it offered the best scholarship, $400 a year for two years, open to boys not over 12 ½ on May 1. So I made up my mind he should write for it in 1942, but by the time 1942 came, what with mounting taxes and prices and the prospect of a long war, we felt that we couldn't even make up the difference if he did win the scholarship and rather regretfully gave up the idea. However, all of a sudden about May 1 we decided that it was not fair to the child not to give him the chance to try.... So I wrote off post haste to the headmaster, Mr. Ketchum, not even knowing whether the exams were over. As it happened, they were in 2 days time and though Peter should have applied weeks before, he was awfully kind about it and sent up the papers to Dr. Lewis who let Peter write at U.T.S.... Last Thursday Peter came home almost speechless, with a telegram which Mr. K. had sent to Dr. Lewis, asking him to tell Peter he had won the Old Boys Memorial Scholarship, and I had a very nice letter from Mr. K. next morning congratulating Peter on his good work. He got an average of 1st class honours and did especially well in the English paper. I am awfully glad he is going to have this chance—and through his own efforts, too. In 2 years time he can try for an entrance scholarship to the Senior School (this he has won is to the Junior School)—there are 2 of them, good for $500 a year for 4 yrs. (The fees in the S. School are $750.) ...

JUNE 2

John is in Chicago most of this week at some meetings—he was away part of last week too. Clare is coming down to-morrow to help me with mending and marking the children's clothes and getting things in order for the summer. It has been like a cloud hanging over me and there never seems a minute to get at it! However it is not as bad as if they were all going to camp the first of July. In fact we may not send Peter to camp at all this summer, now that he is going away to school in September. We consider that camp (besides its own pleasures and a rest for mothers!) gives children a much-needed time "on their own" away from home, building self-reliance, which they don't need if they go to boarding school....

I told C. & Tom about the camp plans to-day (I waited until I had confirmation of my applications) and they were thrilled. Tom has read the prospectus from cover to cover and I showed them the approximate spot on the map. They are full of discussions as to whether or not they'll be allowed a canoe trip—they have to swim and handle a canoe for that, so it all depends on how quickly they learn. I think the "covered wagon" overnight trips serve as outings for those who don't qualify for canoe trips. I think they should learn to swim quickly—camp is the best place for that. I struggled for 3 summers to teach Peter and by the time he'd been at camp 2 weeks he could swim well.

I do hope those pictures of the boys that I sent arrived safely. I am so anxious to hear that they did—particularly the film.

Dear Margaret

I had a letter from you this week written April 30, enclosing one for the boys. The post is mixed up, as last week I had one from your mother written May 12....

You will know by now that the letters you wrote Vivien and me in the holidays arrived safely. The parcel from your mother has come and we have a notice that another parcel for Tom is being held in the customs. John has been away all week and I haven't had a chance to go to see about it but now that he is back he can send the messenger from the office for it. I hope you have heard from Bill. I know Vivien has been rather worried all this year because she felt he was not writing you very frequently but she thinks he should be treated as a responsible adult and allowed to manage these things himself so all she could do about it was write to you oftener herself so you would be kept informed about him. He is very well, working rather hard now that his exams are approaching (he never seems to need to work at all during term). John saw Col. Cline, head of the physics Dept. at U.T.S. (he is a cousin of John's) recently and he says Bill has a splendid brain—never needs to be told anything twice but grasps everything instantaneously.

John had Bill come down to the Canada Life one afternoon and showed him around the building, particularly the actuarial dept. and all their multifarious calculating machines, Hollerith system etc. He said Bill seemed very much interested and enjoyed it. I don't suppose he had ever had the opportunity of seeing a big business office before.

It does seem rather strange about the clothing coupons. However I wouldn't worry as I'm sure 20 each would cover the list I sent—I hope it arrived safely. If you have to leave out anything I would omit the socks, and if you want to add, send one more of the underpants and pyjamas....

I told you at length in my last letter of our summer plans. The boys seem quite keen about the idea of going to camp—I do hope the weather improves. We've had nothing but rain for weeks—downpours and cloudbursts and steady slow rain and drizzles and fog. It's most depressing. We had one fine day this past week and the boys got the grass cut....

On the night of the 19th, Tom's birthday, Mary is playing in a piano recital, so I said to Tom "You know, I don't really suppose you would think Mary's recital a suitable birthday treat." Poor Tom, who never knows when you're joking, looked positively scared—as well he might, having heard

Mary play her "piece" at least a thousand times at home! So I quickly added that we'd have Bill come over for dinner and the boys could go to the movies while John, Mary & I go to the recital. Boys of that age don't go in much for parties, they seem to prefer a treat of some kind.

Mary is also playing at the school piano recital on the 12th and she and another girl were chosen to play a duet at the huge Public School concert held annually at the Toronto Exhibition. The "Ex" has now been cancelled on account of the war (the first time missed in about 66 years) but the concert is being held anyway....

I should also like to see your friend Mrs. Whittaker—whether I could cheer her up I don't know but perhaps we could commiserate with one another! I do feel awfully sorry for a lot of the English women who brought their children out. The average Canadian housewife of modest prosperity, even in normal times, has a much harder and more trying life than her pre-war English counterpart. This is due to an accumulation of circumstances—lack of domestics, high cost of labour, the smallness of the houses (because of the high cost of central heating) the fact that few children go to boarding school etc. etc. Few mature Englishwomen can adapt themselves easily to life here in normal times—women like Edith Wilkinson who make such a perfect success of it I greatly admire. And the evacuees have so much more to contend with—the complications of war-time living, the worry in connection with the war, the great difficulties over funds and the separation from their husbands. A good many of them have returned to England from Toronto, which seems a pity....

Food is beginning to be more of a problem. Meat is getting very scarce, especially beef, and may be rationed soon. The sugar ration has been cut to ½ lb. week and tea to ½ what we formerly used and coffee to ¾ what we formerly used. These rations are voluntary but there are stiff penalties for infringement. However, how anyone can check on the tea and coffee I don't see! Personally I think it's an unsatisfactory system because there are always people who will ignore it while the conscientious ones like myself do the saving for all. However, I don't see that disapproving of the regulations relieves one of the duty to carry them out. I am the only one in our house who drinks tea or coffee—I've always had 2 cups of tea a day and 2 or 3 of coffee and have reduced them as requested. I really think the Govt. is waiting until there are a sufficient number of articles to be rationed to justify the expense of issuing coupons. The voluntary sugar rationing did cause a tremendous drop in the sugar purchased.

Shopping is getting difficult—with the shops constantly "out of" what you want—whether due to hoarding or short supplies, I don't know—probably mostly the latter as all manufacturing and processing of food is pretty strictly controlled. The price control system has worked surprisingly well so far, although even so of course the cost of living has gone up a good deal.

Your mother tells me you have a particularly heavy term on your hands. I am glad the Saturday Nights are useful and hope they all arrive. I'm afraid I let them pile up and then send them in a heap. I do hope you get a good holiday in the summer.

P.S. We have so many birds around this house—whenever the rain lets them show themselves—cardinals, bluebirds, orioles, finches of all kinds, hummingbirds, flickers, thrushes etc. The baby robins are learning to fly all over the place. One perched on our window sill at 6 A.M to-day and plaintively cheeped at us....

[23] *[Presumably lost at sea]*

[24] 90 DUNVEGAN ROAD
TORONTO, JUNE 21

Dear Margaret

Your letter of May 27 arrived June 15, when Tom also had one from his father. Tom's parcels arrived from his father, both grandmothers and Auntie Phyl. I told you last week one parcel was held in Customs but the others came through all right. His father had told him he was posting 3 books in separate parcels, one from him, one from Auntie Phyl and one from mother, meaning, I suppose, Mrs. Sharp, but apparently Tom had taken it to mean you, as he told me in some anxiety yesterday that your parcel must have been sunk, as he couldn't find anything from you among his presents. However I explained it to him and told him of your inability to send presents and he quite accepted it without concern—Tom always accepts regulations. If you are permitted to send presents provided you don't exceed the £10 limit you don't need to deny yourself that pleasure, because I'm sure there is no need to send anything like £10 worth of clothes—not for some time to come anyway. (I hope you got my letter going into the clothing situation so you can see we are getting on very well and with little outlay for new things.) However, if the ruling is not clear on that point, you naturally don't want to run foul of regulations, and the actual present isn't at all necessary for their happiness—Tom was thrilled with your cable, and felt I'm sure, that he did <u>very</u> well with the amount of "loot" he garnered in. So I hope you will not worry, one way or the other.

This has been quite an eventful week for the children. Monday Mary had her "party." The boys were all 3 very helpful, arranging games in the garden, helping to carry out and serve the food, etc. I had asked all the mothers please <u>not</u> to send presents but one father who called for his daughter brought a tiny turtle which Mary has been mothering with enthusiasm ever since. She named it Reddy but later changed her mind and though Vivien urged her to call it Myrtle, she decided on Toots, for some unknown reason.

On Tom's birthday I let him choose his own dinner—it was sausages, bacon, potatoes, cabbage, ice-cream with maple syrup and birthday cake. He invited a boy from school, William Leigh-Clare, an English war guest, from Guildford.... He was an extremely nice boy and I think Tom shows very good taste in choosing so suitable a friend—I had not seen any of Tom's friends before. We had dinner early as I wanted the boys to get to their movie before 7 and I had to take Mary and the little girl who shares her duet down town to their recital by 7.45. The children go to movies so very seldom and I had hoped that Captains of the Clouds or Sergeant York or something similar would be at one of the local houses but it always seems when you want them to go, on a special occasion, every movie in the vicinity is showing "Lady of the Tropics" or murder films or something equally unsuitable! However there was an Abbott & Costello picture within walking distance and they are at least funny, so I think they enjoyed it.

Mrs. Fairfoul, my morning charwoman, and mainstay of my life, brought favours as her contribution to both birthdays—for Mary they were little fans made of paper doilies, with bright coloured gum drops on the end of each fan-sticks—for Tom little boats full of sweets, made of heavy red paper. They were very attractive and I thought it was sweet of her.

Peter went to Burlington on Tuesday. He is staying with his Aunt Emily and is presumably to pick berries or do something equally useful to earn money for a bike. I don't know how hard he is working, but we've impressed on him that the bike depends entirely on his own efforts—he is being provided with a golden opportunity to achieve it. His report arrived Wednesday and he was first in the class again—all 3 terms this year. I was surprised this time as he did not work at exam time but I guess he knew his work pretty well....

To-day is "Father's Day," an American institution of a kind I find most revolting. There has been a "Mother's Day" for years—in May. I have more or less had to submit to it as children don't recognize the commercialism of such ideas and the sentimentality rather appeals to them (it's not that I don't love my mother but I do object to being exhorted by bill-boards and advertisements to love my mother on the second Sunday of every May!) but as it always falls about the same time as my birthday they've usually been merged. The florists and confectioners have made such a good thing out of mothers that the haberdashers etc. have tried their hands at fathers. Mary apparently heard about it from the little girl next door and one day they went off after school and bought presents for their fathers to be presented on June 21. One day, later on, I had Tom with me while shopping and we went into a stationer's. Tom said "You know June 21 is Father's Day and I think that I would like to get a present for Uncle John." I was really very much touched and particularly when, after nosing about by himself, he proudly showed me his purchase—a pad for listing telephone numbers. "I think Uncle John will like it" he said "in fact, I rather think it <u>looks</u> like Uncle John, if you know what I mean." I did know what he meant—it looked businesslike and mannish. John was as pleased as I at his thoughtfulness and the proof of his affection.

I am so glad the snaps arrived safely—I hope the film did too. I think the boys appreciate your letters being printed. It must take more of your time but I think it's worth it—you could make the letters shorter if you find you haven't enough time—I don't think the length of them matters so much if it's a choice.

We had C. go down to Dr. Stock yesterday. He had been coughing a bit more this week—mainly early in the morning. (Of course the weather has been bad for that sort of thing—so damp and heavy.) He [Dr. S.] says his chest is absolutely clear and unaffected.... Of course a cough with C. always worries me more than with the other children and I hesitated about sending him to camp to sleep in a tent or cabin without the doctor's sanction. I gave his history on the application form provided and advised that if he should catch cold he should be put to bed under the nurse's care and the cold should be taken more seriously than in the case of the average child. Dr. S. did not view his head-jerking very seriously—it is not an involuntary twitch, just a movement. I have asked C. about it and he says he knows when he does it and thinks he can prevent it when he thinks about it. I am not going to worry about it, at least until we see what the summer does for him. It is worse (naturally) when he is excited and he gets excited rather easily. The blinking and facial contortions have improved greatly.

In view of the advice about Latin from the Ulverston head master, I think Bill should do whatever he decides himself. The reason Viv. and I urged him to continue it was that we thought, if he had been in England, it would be indispensable to his course and we wanted him to follow as closely as possible what he would be doing, were he in England. Your mentioning that the B.Comm. degree is not as socially desirable in England is undoubtedly true and it is exactly those kind of differences (of which we are conscious) that made us hesitate to do much advising of Bill as to his future. It would take a whole long letter to go into this and <u>then</u> none of us would be much further ahead. It is dangerous to make general statements about a whole country but I think one <u>can</u> say that here a man's future and opportunities depend more on what he <u>is</u>, <u>himself</u>, than in England. Also, in this country the tendency is to choose one's educational course with the object of fitting one to earn one's living in one's chosen line. This may be all wrong—a lot of people think so, but nevertheless, it's the case....

JUNE 24

I have just thought of something that you might include if you're sending clothing—a dressing gown for Christopher. The one he has has got to be a standing joke between us—I darn it periodically—I think there are <u>balls</u> of mending cotton and <u>skeins</u> of wool in it—every time a new gap appears I give him a mock scolding on being so hard on his clothes. That would be a great help—I think I'd get one for a boy of 14 and I can take up the hem and sleeves temporarily, if necessary. I think C. is approximately 4 ft. 10 in. tall.

You must be having a most trying term and to be <u>cold</u> would make it 10 times worse. We did not let our furnace out until June 15 and I know how miserable I'd have been all through the spring without it, and no fires. I don't wonder you have had colds and I do hope by now you're getting summer weather. I suppose school continues until the end of July....

We have had 2 blows this week (besides the awful war news, which I won't discuss—what's the use?—but has depressed us all). The income tax people have told John that they can't allow him exemption for the 2 boys. He had claimed in 1941 and it is those returns they're correcting now, so he'll have to pay that up (about $150) and will also have to change his 1942 returns (made April 30) and pay an additional $225 on them (the rate went up in 1942). (We could not have claimed in 1943 anyway, as you are contributing.) It seems very unfair, as they allow exemption for the children brought out under the govt. scheme. The man who talked to John was most sympathetic and felt it was unfair, but naturally had to follow Ottawa's regulations. The odd thing is that the University Com. for Brit. Overseas Children is listed as an authorized war charity, so if we gave them a cash donation (such as they get to help look after the women who brought out their families and are provided with houses) we would get exemption on it as a charitable donation! However there's no use fretting over it—there it is and I'm sure lots of people are suffering much greater hardships and injustices, in these days of blanket regulations.

On top of that the new budget was brought down last night with a sharp rise in taxes. Of course it is necessary and we expected it—we'll just all have to cut corners a little more carefully. I don't think I shall even try to get a maid in the fall. I find that, though I only paid Mary Murphy $30 a month (she came for that low wage on condition I had a woman in the mornings as Mary is not very strong) I am saving about $50 a month by not having her—reduced laundry, light, food bills, gas and Hydro. I don't mind the work at all and I think our meals are better when I do the cooking. The hard part is the being tied but I think I can arrange with Clare to "take over" for an afternoon and evening every so often. Peter being away next year will make one less, too, so I don't think it will be hard. I don't think we realize here quite how lucky we are and if those of us without men in the forces can go through this war with no more hardships than financial ones and food restrictions we are very fortunate....

We get our first food ration books—for sugar only, on July 2. It is a temporary coupon book for 10 weeks, when new ones will be issued and I rather expect by that time the rationing will include a good many other foods. There is a possibility meat will be rationed—it is very very scarce. However I expect we'll be very well fed, and from now to October we should have an abundance of fruit. I am so glad that your boys are here—a lot of English children have gone back home at their parents' request—most unwisely, I think. Naturally the parents miss them but in every other respect it is infinitely better for the children and for England, to have them here. I shouldn't worry too much over growing out of touch with them. I'm sure, from what I know of the children, that, while they seem quite cold-blooded and not in the least homesick, that the minute they are back with you they will just slip back into the old relationship. I think they are fond of us and like being here but they could leave us and Canada without a thought of regret and go joyfully home just as they left England and came here, full of anticipation and desire for fresh fields. It is a most comfortable philosophy of life that they happen to have.

I can't deny that it does take a lot of my time to write to you but I would not think of giving it up, though I may occasionally miss or shorten one. I do think I owe it to you to keep you in touch with the boys and their doings. I try so hard to get them to write more newsy letters about their daily doings but they simply can't realize that you can write about anything but "what happened this week"—that is, something unusual.

Clare was here the other day and remarked to me with surprise how C. had completely stopped his blinking and screwing up his face. I was glad to hear it—I knew he had improved but when you see a child every day it is hard to tell how much. She also thought he was not moving his head as much.

By the way Bill has just got the Engineering prospectus off—he said he did not understand that he was expected to send it. I think he did, at the time, but probably forgot the arrangement.

I'm sorry you're worried about my health—I am really <u>very</u> well indeed—a bit impatient and short-tempered at present but I hope the summer will put that straight.

P.S. Since writing this I have been talking to Vivien and mentioned the dressing gown for C. She says that Bill's is in excellent condition but is too small for him and could come on to C. in the autumn. So it might be better to send the new one for Bill—I think Vivien sent you his measurements. Tom's is getting pretty skimpy but I think will do him through next winter....

[25] BURLINGTON, ONT., JULY 1

Dear Margaret

All last week excitement mounted higher and higher as the end of school and beginning of camp loomed nearer and nearer.... School closed Friday June 26 (not to reopen until Sept. 8—an over-long holiday I think). The children got their reports Friday afternoon and we were proud of them all. C. passed with honours, 3rd in his class, and Tom also with honours (about 82% I think) 4th in his class. Mary was first in her class. I don't know why, but no marks are filled in on their reports this term—just a note to say they passed. Mary was frightfully thrilled because this year she won a bronze medal—each year Honour Certificates are awarded Public School pupils who have maintained a perfect standard in punctuality and regularity (except for illness or good reason) combined with good conduct and diligence. When they've won an Honour Certificate for four years they get a bronze medal and after 8 years, a silver medal. The boys got Hon. Certs. this year....

I had a wire from Mrs. Anthony Friday asking if William could come Saturday evening instead of Sunday as she wanted to get off on her own short holiday. (She had written earlier that Paul is not going to camp for another fortnight.) I wired back to send him, so he arrived Sat. eve. George and Clare came down to stay at the house while I met the train, John being away. The boys and Mary were busy all day Saturday—tidying their rooms and book cases, cutting the lawns, putting away the cricket stumps and garden tools. We were very much taken with William A.—he is a very attractive child and not the least trouble. Bill came down Sunday afternoon and all 4 boys went off to the Museum where Wm. wanted to see the Indian exhibit.²⁴ Mary played with the little girl next door and I was able to get every single thing packed except the boys' hair brushes, but left little spaces for them to go in on Monday morning. They had each a large suit-case and a dunnage bag. We got off in good time Monday morning for which I patted myself on the back, as there were 4 camps taking off by the same train on which they travelled, and more on other trains and soon after we got down the Union Station was a seething mass of parents, children and counsellors. I really thought my staff work was rather good—I'm becoming experienced in handling children en masse and C. was very helpful—carried all the baggage to the checking office, and helped the woman ahead of me (who was also sending two English children to Pioneer Camp) with hers. We got everything attended to expeditiously before the real assault began, then I "checked in" the 3 boys with the Pioneer representative who was gathering his flock in a corner of the station. I had intended to leave them at that point, but stayed to look at the boys as they arrived and they were a very nice looking lot. C. nosed about in the crowd by himself and emerged just before time to go to the train announcing triumphantly "I've found a friend already." I don't think C. had ever seen him before but he seemed a very nice alert, competent sort of boy, so the 4 went off together. I tagged along to see them safely in the "Pioneer" coach—they were almost the first on the train so had their choice of seats and were in high spirits. They had nothing to carry except their lunch in a cardboard box so there was nothing to worry about losing. In the gathering at the station I talked to 1 or 2 people whose boys were going back for the 3rd summer and heard nothing but praise of the camp.

I was very appreciative of C's attitude of willingness to help all during the days of preparation—doing what he was asked cheerfully and constantly asking if there was anything he could do.

Mary and I came back from the train and I then started to get us ready for our hegira. Mrs. F. and I got the washing and ironing all finished by Tuesday noon and I had been working on the packing as well so we got away early Tuesday afternoon. We are very comfortably situated here in Emily's apartment—a small sitting room, dining room and kitchenette downstairs, with two bedrooms and bath upstairs, a glass-enclosed sleeping porch off my room for Mary and a cot on the veranda off John's room for Peter. The front door is only about 12 feet from the steps leading down the low cliff to the lake and all the rooms have lots of windows, looking out over the lake and across to the lift bridge into Hamilton Harbour where the big freighters come in with iron ore to the steel works. The lake is beautiful all day and all night. John's brothers both have fruit farms a few miles away and bring us fresh picked fruit and vegetables every day if we want them. We are just on the edge of Burlington and so have easy access to shops etc. and all deliveries....

I expect the boys will be required to write one letter a week home—that is the rule in most camps. I thought if that letter was written to you, I should not hear from them for the whole 6 weeks (knowing their love (?) of letter-writing). So I told them to write their compulsory weekly letters to me and I would send it on to you and they went off with the firm resolution to write an extra one each to you. I gave them envelopes all ready, addressed to me and told them to enclose the ones to you with mine—I find if they address them themselves they are quite likely to omit vital parts of the address. They asked to postpone the letter they usually write to you on Sunday until Monday after they got to camp. I gave them an envelope addressed to you and stamped and reminded them of it just before they left, but the excitement of arrival may put it completely out of their heads—I hope not.

I do hope you can get a good holiday this summer—you must have had a very trying term.

P.S. The weather has turned over a new leaf and it has been proper summer—fine and hot. I was so glad it came in time to give them a good start at camp.

[26] BURLINGTON, ONT., JULY 16

Dear Margaret

You must be looking forward with longing to the end of term after such a strenuous 3 months. I do hope you get a good holiday....

We are enjoying it here by the lake very much. John goes out nearly every day to his brothers' fruit farms and hoes, weeds and picks fruit for 3 or 4 hours. They are desperate for help this year and John feels better about his 4 weeks holiday if he is doing something to help. He takes the children too, to pick berries and their uncles pay them the current rate. Peter is doing quite well, and has also painted his aunt's new wire fence, so is well on the way towards his bicycle. I have had to stop Mary going to pick berries as she has developed a little hay fever—a very prevalent disease in this ragweed ridden province—and there is ragweed in the raspberry patches. We are revelling in all kinds of vegetable and fruits—the black cherries, red cherries, all kinds of berries and now the early apples and peaches and tomatoes. It makes us feel quite guilty to think of how curtailed you are in England. We can get plenty of sugar for canning and jam—that is, we get it by voucher—½ lb. sugar for every lb. of fruit we bottle and ¾ lb. sugar for every lb. of fruit we make into jam. Actually I use more than that for some jams but our ration of ½ lb. each a week allows quite a bit for jam, as we don't use much sugar (since being maidless I have not done any baking)....

I don't think I told you before of the rather interesting incident while William Anthony was here. At the table one day something Wm. said caused me to ask him "Will you be glad to go back to England?" He gave a most emphatically affirmative answer, to which Tom made some remark, whereupon Mary asked Tom the same question. "Well" reflected Tom, " I don't rightly know. You see I'd like to be in England and yet I like to be here." "I know" burst in Christopher, very definitely "what I'd like! I want England to come out here." "Oh yes!" said Tom joyfully "that's it! If my mother and father and all the family could come out here, that would be perfect!"

You will have heard from Vivien and Bill that Bill's tonsils and adenoids are safely out. It was a very anxious time for her—one feels dreadfully responsible, making decisions for children not one's own, but in the end Dr. Smith simply took it out of her hands, made all the arrangements, and said it simply had to be done.[25] Aside from the benefit to his health, it is sure to improve his appearance and speech to have all that tissue removed, which the surgeon said was blocking all the nasal passages—also they told her at the Dental College that unless the adenoids were removed, in time the work on his teeth which was so successful, would be largely undone again. She discussed with me whether she should cable for your permission, but we both thought you had already given sufficient sanction—also whether she should cable as soon as the operation was over, but I thought that would only give you cause for worry over after-effects during the long wait for letters. I felt badly, being away when it was done, but I suppose I could have been of very little help anyway. Vivien stayed all day with him in the hospital and gave him the greatest care. John had to go to Toronto the following week, for a day, and saw Bill on his way to the doctor's for a final check-up before going north. Everything must have been all right as I understand he left for Cochrane last Monday (July 13). Paul Anthony came from Ottawa on the Sunday and stayed with Vivien over night and went to camp with the other boys (Pioneer) travelling on the same train with Bill. I think Vivien went on that train too, to spend a few days at a friend's cottage on Peninsular Lake. I wish she could be away longer. She has had a very strenuous year and Judy's and Bill's tonsils were rather a strain on top of everything. However, she sends the 2 girls to camp on July 25 (Judy is going to Cedarnook with Mary), so she should have a few free weeks....

I shall number this in [Margaret]'s sequence, 27.

Dear Cousin Mary[26]

Your delightful long letter (no. 3) of June 16 reached me here a few days ago and I must confess that 1. and 2. are still unanswered, though I did enjoy them both so much.... I am so glad the photographs arrived safely and I do hope Mt. got the film of the 3 boys. I knew you would all find that a very good one, and it must be difficult for you to believe that is really Bill! Mt. said it made her feel slightly afraid of him! It is very hard lines on Margaret missing these years out of the boys' lives and feeling, as I'm sure she must sometimes, that they are growing away from her. But I hope she doesn't worry too much over possible difficult readjustments when they come back. As I told her in my last letter, they are such matter-of-fact little mortals and accept things as they come. They are perfectly at home here and do not seem in the least homesick but I'm sure that when the time comes to go home they will have no regrets at leaving and will "settle in" at home with her just as though they'd never been away. It must bother her, too, to think that while we are trying hard to give the boys the best character training we can, according to our ideas, these may not be her ideas and our methods of handling them not hers! She is very sweet about expressing and repeating her confidence in our judgments, so there is no use worrying about it on either side of the ocean! We can only do our best, as we have been doing, to try to make them self reliant, co-operative, pleasant citizens of whatever country they may live in.

Vivien has mentioned to me many times the great change in Bill's attitude during the past 4 months or so. He has been so much friendlier, less sulky, more co-operative and altogether an "easier" sort of person to live with. She does not know why—previously, on 2 or 3 occasions, such as when he came home from the Burns', he has quite obviously made an effort to "turn over a new leaf"—as Viv. said, as though he kept saying to himself "I must be a good boy"—but, being a conscious effort, each time it didn't last—this seems to be a quite unconscious development and is probably due to a combination of causes. I think it has gradually "seeped through" without his consciously realising it, that the Ratcliffes are worthy of respect and affection and that life among them is a very pleasant life, quite apart from its material advantages. Then, too, I think he has become quite satisfied about his schooling arrangements—feels he is doing work hard enough for him, and with good teachers, and feels assured of a suitable university course, whatever one he decides on. All sorts of little happenings and stray remarks show that he is gradually identifying himself with the Ratcliffe family and with Canadians in general. I don't mean by that that he is growing away from England—Bill will always be an Englishman and I doubt very much whether he would ever want to live here permanently.[27] Of course, Bill is self-centred and resents any inconvenience to himself, while remaining oblivious to other peoples' convenience—I expect he will always be somewhat like that, but he is in the very best home environment to bring out the best in him, and he has many good qualities.

When I spoke of the material advantages of the Ratcliffe household, I did not mean that they are wealthy, far from it, but they have every comfort and a well-ordered, delightful house. Bill has complete privacy when he wants it, everything necessary and some luxuries in the way of food, clothing, amusements, spending money etc., and he has perfect freedom of action in all his comings and goings and interests and activities. He is inclined to be rather secretive about his affairs but this does not cause Vivien the slightest concern, it only affords her amusement—the mystery with which he loves to surround his little expeditions seems to foster his childish self-importance and does no one any harm. Vivien realises that he is completely trustworthy—even to the extent, so unusual in boys, that he is very careful to get sufficient sleep—and so asks no questions.

90 DUNVEGAN ROAD, JULY 29

I am sorry about this delay, but the fact of being officially "on holiday" did not seem to give me any more time for letter-writing. John had his 4 weeks holiday from June 27, so he went straight to Burlington, to his sister Emily's, where Peter had already been for two weeks. Mary and I stayed here to get C. & Tom off to camp on June 29 and then followed. We rented from Emily the apartment (as you know, an "apartment" with us equals a "flat" in England), which she made out of a wing of her house by the lake, and rents in term to a high school teacher. It was small but quite adequate, and very pleasant. I slept in a glassed and screened sleeping porch of which the windows could all be lifted to the ceiling, by hinges, making it completely open, and it seemed to be positively hanging over the lake—it was beautiful at all times of day, and at night, looking as it did, across to Hamilton Harbour with the city beyond. At night the sky over there was lit up from the blast furnaces and other lights of the steel mills—not beautiful close at hand but lovely from afar. The big freighters laden with ore from the head of the Great Lakes moved constantly in and out of the harbour. (I do hope the censor won't object to that sentence!)

John was able to see a good deal of his brothers and sisters which was nice for all of them. He and Peter spent a lot of time at the fruit farms of his 2 brothers about every 2nd day hoeing, weeding and helping to pick the fruit. They are pretty desperate for help this year—his brothers' places are not big enough for them to need help constantly and it is almost impossible to get temporary workers for the rush season. They were very grateful and John felt more justified in having a holiday [in] these days of hard work and long hours for every one. Peter proved himself a very good workman—he has been trying to earn money for a bicycle and his uncles paid him for the work he did—he also cut his aunts' lawns, painted a fence for Emily, etc. and made in all $17.00, of which he is quite proud. The difficulty now is that there is scarcely a bicycle to be had! New ones can be got when they come in, a few at a time, but they are $40.00, so he wants to get a used one. Even Mary went out several days and picked raspberries and collected about $3 or $4—she says she's saving for a bicycle too!

The weeks slipped past unbelievably and on July 23 I brought Mary back to Toronto, spent a day washing her clothes and packing her up, and sent her off to camp on July 25. Then I went back to Burlington and got the rest of us packed up and we came home on Sunday, July 26. I am trying to get the house straightened up a bit and am looking forward to the return of my morning woman, the beginning of next week.... I gather Christopher and Tom are having a very good time at camp.... C. and Tom will come back Aug. 10, when the camp closes, but they will still have 4 weeks before school opens Sept. 8....

On re-reading your letters 1 and 2, I am again overwhelmed, as I was when I received them, with humiliation at your appreciation of the little parcel of maple cream. It makes us feel like perfect pigs to be so little restricted that we don't even realise how much you are all so cheerfully doing without, and it's just sheer lack of imagination on our part that has kept us from seeing how much even a small "extra" of sweets means when one has been rationed for so long, or we would certainly have sent it more often. We still have compulsory rationing for only gasoline and sugar (½ lb. week) and a 20% tax on sweets and voluntary rationing of tea (50% ...) coffee (75% ...) and bacon and pork and cheese (50% of what we formerly used). But of course a great many things are unobtainable or very scarce, or sold only in small quantities. I expect by next year rationing will be in full swing, though we do not expect clothes rationing for some time (people like ourselves find our flat pocket books more effective clothes rationers than coupons!) ...

I am sorry to hear of your having domestic upheavals to deal with and hope you have been able to get someone in Betty's place. What a treasure Elsie must be to M. and you! There just don't seem to be any of that kind here—or any of any kind just now! I don't think there is the slightest use my looking for any one and any that I have heard of who are available by some chance, would not consider a household with 4 children, and anyway want $50 a month, which I simply can't pay. So we'll just have to get along as we have been doing and it's not so bad, except that it takes all my time and energy and keeps me tied securely to the house. The children are really a great help and I feel it's very good for them, as training in personal responsibility. For I do not look on the performing of required tasks as an end in itself—rather as a means towards making the child feel himself an integral part of the family <u>just as responsible for the comfort and happiness of the others as they are for his</u>. The attainment of this end covers far more than doing little household jobs—self-control, sympathy, appreciation, the conquest of greediness and bad temper, respect for others' feelings, rights, comfort and property, all these are far more important factors in being a pleasant family member than actually helping to "wash up" though I suppose if one had all these qualities one would naturally help wherever and whenever help was needed! Therefore I think the concrete, self-evident tasks like "washing-up" are as good a way as any for children to start training in citizenship, and the willing giving of time and effort in a common cause is a sign that the child is on the right path. The other less tangible attributes are of slower growth and much more difficult—goodness knows I've made very little progress in them myself! Your letters are so encouraging but make me feel a hypocrite—you give me credit for so many good qualities I haven't got! I can only say honestly that I do my best but I know I am often impatient and "edgy" when I'm tired. This is a long dissertation and I feel I haven't expressed what I mean very well but perhaps you can read my mind?...

You will have heard from my letters to Margaret of Peter's scholarship to Trinity College School in Port Hope, which has pleased us so much! I have always wanted Peter to go to boarding school—he needs to learn how to live in a group of his contemporaries on a common basis, with no special consideration or privileges for anyone—but we had felt it was entirely beyond our means unless he <u>could</u> win this scholarship.... Of course, academically I still don't think any school in the Province equals U.T.S., but Peter is the kind of boy who needs the other aspects of boarding school life. From my own point of view, it will make the housekeeping that much easier, having one less in the house, especially the "one" being Peter, because his hours were different from the other 3—he left earlier, did not come home to lunch, and came home earlier in the afternoon.... C. will miss Peter in some ways, but may be happier on the whole, feeling he is the "big boy" of the house....

I hope Margaret will not mind sharing this letter with you, as I expect she will be home on holiday when it arrives—it has grown to such lengths I'll probably not get another off to her. I can't remember whether the July 1 draft had arrived before I last wrote. If not, I would like to acknowledge it now, with thanks. I am enclosing the boys' letters of the last 2 weeks. As you see, Tom has faithfully written both to me and to her each week, sending both to me, to forward. I am also enclosing the note I had from C's tent leader—I sent his earlier one in my last, and had replied to it, asking how C's swimming was progressing....

[28]

No. 27 I sent to your mother last week

90 DUNVEGAN ROAD
TORONTO, AUGUST 12

Dear Margaret

... The boys arrived home Monday looking <u>very</u> well and brown. They have not even had colds while away, C. gained 3 lbs. and Tom 1 ½ lb., they say, and they apparently had a marvellous time. They eventually both managed to swim 25 yards—Tom adds emphatically "with <u>great</u> difficulty"—which C. just as vigorously denies—whereupon Tom says "Oh you <u>know</u> C. we tried about 10 times before we did it!" which C. will not allow. However I am delighted that they did it....

When we were on our way out of the station on Monday, C. said in a very heartfelt way—"<u>Gee</u> I had a <u>swell</u> time!" and it is obvious they both had. I think perhaps C. did not get enough sleep—he needs a lot more than most boys. He has of his own accord, been going to bed early since he came back and I am going to see that he keeps it up. He has been in bed with light out by 8.30 or 8.40 and when we call him at 7.30 in the morning he is so sound asleep we have to go in to waken him!! He is twisting his head about a good deal which may be partly due to excitement at returning home but I think rest is definitely indicated. But I don't think either of them has ever looked so well since they came to Canada....

Mary is to come home on Aug. 22. She writes the most astonishingly good letters, informative & interesting. She has apparently developed a great interest in swimming and is learning to dive. When she wrote to tell me she had her 25 yd. side stroke badge she said "After I come home I wish we could all go for a swim so we can see how well we can all swim"—which <u>of course</u> meant "so everyone can see how well I swim"!

As I told you John, Peter and I came back from Burlington on July 26. The Anthony boys arrived July 27 and stayed with Vivien a few days, so we showed them about a bit, and since then I have been working like mad to get some housecleaning done while I was fairly free, with only the 3 of us to cook for and look after. Of course, I did not get half what I wanted to do, done, but like everyone else I'm getting to be philosophical about dust "and sich." The help problem gets worse and worse. When Vivien was canvassing for the Red Cross not far from me she used to drop in to "rest her feet" and tell me funny stories of the palatial homes she was calling at where they hadn't even so much as a char any more. When she called at the Archbishop's (Primate of all Canada) Mrs. Owen had to ask her to come back in an hour as she was busy getting some lunch ready for her son and had to go to an out of town engagement with her husband in the afternoon.[28] She hasn't a maid of any sort and naturally her husband's duties involve her a good deal so she said they only got something to eat whenever she had a few minutes to spare! We amused ourselves speculating as to whether she launders his lace cuffs in the evenings before she gets to bed!

We are just floundering through our first week of tea and coffee rationing. It is a bit drastic—1 oz. tea or 4 oz. coffee per week—either quantity is supposed to make 12 cups. However we can get used to doing without. There is a lot of guessing as to what will come next on the list, with the betting on butter, beef and soap. I think I should find butter and soap the very worst—they are my two greatest extravagances—I mean I use a lot of them. However if butter is rationed they will have to let us have margarine (the manufacture and sale of which has always been prohibited in Canada except during the last war).

My brother Bob got his calling-up papers to-day for the Army. He does not mind going in except that he is worried about what Besse and the baby will do—they can't live on alone in the house, with a furnace to look after, etc. However perhaps something will work out....

The news is so bad I hate to look at a newspaper. We are hoping to hear some good news from the Solomon Islands but everything else is black.

[29] 90 DUNVEGAN ROAD
TORONTO, AUGUST 23

Dear Margaret

I shall have to stop sending Sat Night as the new regulations forbid sending newspaper or periodicals to Britain. Sorry.

... I received the July draft, which was welcome, as the 6 month total (about $159) just covered C. & Tom's camp expenses (fees, fares and incidentals) with a few dollars over.

I wish I had mentioned a dressing-gown for Tom in the list of clothes you might send. I expect it's too late now as whatever your opportunities for shopping will have passed. It's not really necessary as his present one is still whole, but is creeping up his arms and legs!

I'm afraid I have no time for more—I often wish there were 6 of me so I could get done what I have to do. Peter's school opens Sept. 14 and I've not started to do anything about his clothes, which is rather preying on me.

[30] 90 DUNVEGAN ROAD
TORONTO, AUGUST 30

Dear Margaret

Your letter of Aug. 3 arrived yesterday and I am so glad you are having a real holiday and complete change.

[Tom] made a friend at camp, Jimmie Armour, whose mother ... took him with her own children to see "Mrs Miniver." They went directly after an early lunch and Tom went home with them for dinner after.... I was much touched by your plea to neglect your boys while getting Peter ready for school but fate always seems to take a hand in my life, to see that whenever I have a job to get done I have to manage it with one hand, as it were—or half a hand! However Clare came down for the day on Tuesday to help with the mending (which was almost bursting out the sun room windows!) and came again on Wed. afternoon, when I took Peter down town and did what buying I needed to have him along for. Then I sent him home and stole 2 hours to see "Mrs Miniver" myself—came out completely exhausted but I wouldn't have missed it for anything....

I'm afraid you will think I am simply hounding you, but I really do implore you to try to write oftener to the boys. I know how busy you are and as far as letters to myself go I quite understand if they are infrequent. But the children are quite another matter. I suppose it's hard for you to realise from your end that, while nothing on earth could make you forget them, they have nothing on earth to make them remember you except your letters. For a time I did feel, as perhaps you did, that, as they (especially C.) seemed rather indifferent about your letters, it didn't really matter whether they received many. But lately I have been rather concerned about it and have thought about it a good deal. I am sure that the reason for their indifference was their inability to read your writing, because any letters that were printed they always read. And if they <u>are</u> becoming indifferent to, or forgetting you, I think it is all the more imperative for you to keep yourself constantly before them. I can understand the typewriter difficulties but the letters need <u>not</u> be long—it doesn't seem to make any difference <u>what</u> is in them. Tom always passes over his father's letters for me to read. They are seldom more than 10 or 12 lines, often less—perhaps just one bit of information—he has seen a certain film, or taken a walk to such and such a place—but they seem to find them perfectly satisfactory and look forward to them because they come regularly.

I wrote to them every week when they were in N.H. last summer and this year while they were at camp I wrote twice a week, as I do to my own children (they love to get mail at camp) and I used much the same technique—in fact I usually write much the same kind of letters the children do themselves—and I find that I don't even have to use my brain to do it and I can run them off in 5 or 10 minutes. Of course I usually print like this and after some practice it is almost as quick as writing, but I know some people don't find it so easy. But I <u>do</u> think it is important enough for an extra effort. I was rather taken aback by Tom last week—he gave me the letter to read which he had just received from his father, so I read it aloud just to be sociable. One sentence began "I have not had a letter from mother for a long time" and to my surprise Tom burst in quite bitterly "Nor have I!" It is so seldom that Tom shows any strong feeling that I was the more surprised, and I hastened to make him feel better by saying "Oh but Tom, don't you remember, you got a letter from your mother at camp not long before you came home." In any other circumstances, if Tom is 'set straight' in that way about anything he <u>always</u> says "Oh! yes yes!" almost before one has finished speaking (we call him our yes-man) but to my amazement Tom countered just as vehemently as before "I know! But that must have been 2 or 3 weeks ago!" Of course I explained then how dreadfully busy you were and told him I was sure you would write when the holidays came. I must confess it gave me quite a jar—I had not realised that either of them felt neglected—though of course if C. did he would never say so. It brought back to my mind, too, a remark Tom made long ago when he said he thought he should ask his mother to send him her photograph so he would remember what she looked like and be able to recognise her when he went back to England.

I do hope all this won't make you feel badly but it has worried me—after all they have been here more than 2 years and the war will certainly last for years more, and one may as well face the fact that mother love or no, children's memories <u>are</u> short. This does not mean that I retract what I said in a former letter—that I was sure when they went home their adjustment would be no more difficult than when they came to Canada but they may never regain the close relationship which they must have had with you formerly unless it is maintained and nourished. I am awfully sorry, and hope you will forgive me, if all this sounds rather brutal, but I feel that I <u>have</u> to give you the hard facts as they exist at this end.

Nobody in the house, not even Tom, was happier than Mary at Tom's recovery [from a cold]. They play out in the sun all day—sitting at a table with a game or playing with Mary's tiny turtle, taking him for 'a run' or a ride in the wagon, or just being happily silly together, laughing their heads off! I had a chuckle at matter-of-fact Tom when I was discussing 'Mrs Miniver' with him. I said "I cried, Tom, did you?" "No" said Tom, "but (evidently as a sop to me) I felt rather sad at the end." "Well" I said "I felt completely worn out at the end. Did you feel very tired when it was over?" "We-e-ll" considered Tom, "my legs <u>were</u> a bit stiff, but then that usually happens when I go to the movies." I <u>must</u> get to bed now—a new week to-morrow.

SEPTEMBER 1

... I forgot to say, when speaking of the boys' letters, that I would advise writing them separate letters—they don't need to be in separate envelopes, but if the letter is a joint one I have to watch—I've found that if Tom gets it first, it's all right, but if C. gets it first he usually forgets (?) to hand it on to Tom.

[31] 90 DUNVEGAN ROAD
TORONTO, SEPTEMBER 7

Dear Margaret

School tomorrow, thank heaven! And of course Mary is now developing a cough! And her concert on Saturday—and the final rehearsal Wednesday!— oh well, there is no use worrying, what will be, will be!

Sorry I've no time to write a proper letter—am really rather tired, my char was ill all last week and though Peter heaved to and scrubbed the kitchen and pantry floors and cellar stairs it has been a bit heavy—also the kids have had too long a holiday and are bored stiff with idleness and the bickering and squabbling and I find this more tiring than the hard labour.

Your air mail letters of Aug. 23 arrived Sept. 2—the ones sent by sea have not yet come. I gave the one to the boys to them—they were playing together outside and they sat on the steps and read it together. I said as I gave it to them—"Will you be able to read it?" C. took a look and said "Oh yes! It's <u>print</u>!" as though he were saying "Hurrah." They seemed to have a lot of enjoyment reading it. At dinner I made some comment on your letter to me and mentioned some of the news you had given and C. said "In my letter mother mentioned a new puppy. I hadn't heard anything about new puppies so there must have been some letters lost." Of course I said nothing—obviously he has completely forgotten neglecting to read those letters last winter. Then Peter spoke up "C. thinks if there is <u>one</u> puppy there must have been more to start with and they were probably done away with"—to which C. agreed, though with no apparent sorrow—just interest....

[32] 90 DUNVEGAN ROAD
TORONTO, SEPTEMBER 16

Dear Margaret

As I expected, I'm rather late with my letter this week. The past two weeks have been a nightmare and now the extra rush is over it is hard to "collect" myself—I am pretty flat and the hot weather—the air so damp and heavy one can scarcely breathe—doesn't help.

Mary, C. and Tom got off to school last week—on the 8th—to their great delight—they even admitted it! Tom is with Mr. Pugh, whom C. had last year. Mary has been put in a combination Grade 4 and 5 (similar to the one Tom was in last year which was a combination of 5 and 6, enabling those who are capable, of doing 2 yrs. work in one). I am not altogether pleased—I'd just as soon she took the slow way but she is so thrilled one can't discourage her. The first 2 days of school there were torrents of rain and Mary developed a cold (it had really started before) and with the Public Schools Concert coming off on Sat. 12th I <u>was</u> in rather a state. I kept her in bed Thurs. and Fri., getting her out for the rehearsals and driving her to them—which took a maddening lot of time and also "arranging"! However, the concert finally came off successfully and I spent Sunday doing Peter's packing comfortably....

Peter had a job all that week—he had canvassed several shops the week before to see if they needed a delivery boy, but without success. On the Tuesday morning that school opened, when I telephoned my butcher he said he had no way of delivering the meat—his truck drivers have been called up so he has laid up his two trucks and the boys on bicycles he had been employing had gone back to school that day.[29] The minute I told Peter this news he dashed for a spanner, fixed the carrier on his bicycle and was off like a shot to get the job. He worked until Saturday night and we were simply delighted over it. We were prouder of that achievement than of his winning the scholarship—that he had the ambition, independence and enterprise to get the job (he had found he needed a new fountain pen and one or two things and wanted to make the money for them) and the guts and endurance to stick with it.... It did Peter a lot of good to feel he was being of real use to someone in an emergency, and, incidentally, to find how much effort goes into the earning of money.

On Monday (14th) John and I took Peter down to his school and spent the afternoon there with him, meeting the masters and exploring the buildings. He was tremendously pleased with everything about it—particularly the Junior School common room library, to which he kept dragging me back to show me some further "find" on the shelves—"all the books Henty ever wrote, mother, and look! all the Ransomes, and this book I've always wanted to read, and the Book of Knowledge—why you could spend a whole rainy day just reading a volume through, etc. etc." John and I were very much pleased with the whole set up and impressed with all the staff—masters, wives, matron, etc. The Junior School (60–65 boys up to 14) is entirely separate from the Senior School (185 boys) and they seem to have a very busy, well regulated, and, I'm sure, happy life. I am anxiously waiting for Peter's first letter.

SEPTEMBER 20

... On Wednesday evening there was a wiener roast for the boys of the choir which Tom enjoyed very much, but Thursday afternoon after school he came and told me he thought there was something was wrong with him, he had had a sore throat and a headache all day. I put him to bed and took his temp. and to my horror it was 103°. (I don't know why he didn't tell me about the sore throat in the morning—usually he rather "enjoys poor health" when he has the chance and reports eagerly the minutest symptom.) Of course I did not let him know I was alarmed but put in a call for the doctor and gave him drinks, bathed his face and hands frequently and kept cold wet cloths on his forehead—meanwhile doing the ironing, getting the dinner and willing the doctor to come and call me, while visions of infantile paralysis, septic throats etc. whirlpooled through my mind. By the time the doctor called I had the temp. down to 101°, and he sent me sulfathiozole and told me to keep on as I was doing. I discovered Tom was constipated so John gave him an enema. He slept well all night and by morning his throat scarcely hurt, even to swallow, but in spite of the sulfathiozole and gallons of fruit juices his temp. climbed to 102°, so the doctor got in to see him and promptly diagnosed it as tonsillitis which of course relieved my mind immensely. He recommended that I try lots of aspirin instead of sulpha and by Sat. morning (the next morning) his temp. was normal and has been ever since. His throat is still red but not sore and I have him gargle, keep up the drinks, and am giving him only soft foods—soup, eggnogs, milk, custard, a little milky porridge etc.—he doesn't want much, which is natural....

I guess I was just borrowing trouble when I worried about the result of Peter having a bike. C. did not seem at all concerned—he rode it a tiny bit at Peter's invitation but Peter himself didn't use it much except the week he was working. Now it has been put away to preserve the precious tires. I did laugh a bit at your concern over C. and the different rule of the road here. I think you forgot for a minute that they've been here more than 2 years and would now find the English traffic much more perplexing than ours!

My brother Bob called in Friday evening to say good-bye. He is being sent away somewhere (either Saturday or to-day) but has no idea where and won't be told until he arrives there! He is in the artillery and, with one other man, has been picked to do some special work—he hasn't been told what, except that it involves maths. and he'd better brush up his trig. and algebra (I can imagine how aghast he felt at that as I'm sure he hasn't thought of either since his Honour Matric. years ago—but the officer gaily assured him that it would "all come back"). Besse has taken little Janet to her mother's and spends part of the day there (though she sleeps at home) and is looking for a job in her own line of work (operating some sort of book keeping machine—I think a comptometer). They are both very gay and optimistic and take it all in their stride.

The gasoline ration is being cut on Oct. 1 to what amounts to about 40 miles a month. However that is more than we have been using under the old regulations. I know John would like, if possible, to get to see Peter once, as he can't come home until Christmas (they've done away with midterm weekends) but aside from that I only use the car for transporting the children in emergencies and to simplify the housekeeping by doing a lot of shopping about once a week. The shops can still deliver once a day, an order of $1.00 or more—if they have any means of delivering but sometimes what you order at 9 A.M. arrives at 10 P.M. or not until the next day, and then not what you ordered! So it's simpler if you can go and get a stock once a week or so. Of course at present there are heaps of vegetables and fruits—peaches have not been so cheap for years—6 qt. baskets 35¢!—I have been trying to bottle some but have not much time. There is almost no meat—we are asked not to use any pork or bacon for 7 weeks while our commitments to Britain are being filled, there is no beef at all for sale (I think a lot is being sent to Russia), the sheep raisers are asked not to slaughter in order to raise more badly needed wool, so a great many butchers have shut up shop. However there is still what would seem to you, I'm sure, a fabulous quantity and variety of foods to choose from. We are only just <u>beginning</u> to feel any restrictions. I suppose our real stumbling block in adjusting to war time conditions is lack of man power. After all you can't take a country of less than 12 million (of whom, in peace time 10% were employed by Dominion, provincial or municipal govts.) and

1. Build up a navy, an air force, an overseas army and a home defence army and a women's army.
2. Develop industrially towards a grandiose goal of being "the arsenal of the democracies."
3. Increase food production and all natural products to supply ourselves and a good part of the needs of the United Nations.[30]
4. Man the ever-increasing and expanding Departments to regulate this and that, at Ottawa, and throughout the country without finding that there aren't enough able-bodied people to go around, and most of us having to double-up on our duties. Some of the seasonal activities which suffer have wide-spread results. For weeks the canneries in Ontario have been asking housewives or anyone else who can help to assist in saving the fruit and vegetable crop before it spoiled—particularly the tomatoes. They had to stop their contracts to the farmers and leave hundreds of cars of tomatoes on the railway sidings while their plants operated at half production from lack of labour. In some of the rural communities high school opening is postponed still further, to October, so the students can continue helping.

So I think the best thing we on the side lines can do is not to expect anyone to do anything for us that we're able to do for ourselves, and as long as I can keep well I don't mind doing without a maid (maybe that's sour grapes, when I know I can't get one anyway!) and John is doing all the odd jobs himself—at the present moment he is glazing a storm sash for the new "combination" back door–screen for summer, glass for winter.

Beginning to-night, all outdoor advertising signs are to be cut off and street lighting cut down—that must seem queer to you after years of black-out. This is not for security but because of the serious electric power shortage. Each household is also expected to reduce the monthly bill by 15%. So much of our household mechanism is run by electricity (we cook with it, operate our coal furnace with it, wash, iron, run the vacuum cleaner, sewing machine and refrigerator etc. etc.) that it's hard to imagine life without it, so I do hope that by everyone curtailing non-essential use there will be enough to go around.

Mary has just come to say that she would like to send you something for your birthday so she has got out her paints and is making a card.

Christopher and Bill went on an expedition yesterday to buy your present—you had told me about your pen trouble so I suggested a fountain pen as a joint present from the 3 and I will parcel it to-night and get it off to-morrow. I hope it is all right—they are sure it is exactly the size and shape you like. Neither Vivien nor I had time to go with them and anyway they much preferred to do it themselves. I did notice that it had the old-style filler—the lever on the side. Of course I think fountain pen manufacture has stopped and I suppose the only ones available are what are left in stock. Anyway I do hope it will be a help....

C. is in the cadet corps at school this year and also takes riflery. I think he'll enjoy them both.

I simply <u>must</u> stop and get the family off to bed. I have Tom in Cs bed while he's sick and C. in the empty maid's room (I think he is revelling in its large bed and huge dormer windows) and I have to watch at meal & bedtimes and not let Mary use the bathroom after Tom until I wash the basin etc. with Lysol....

[34]³¹ 90 DUNVEGAN ROAD
TORONTO, SEPTEMBER 27

Dear Margaret

... I <u>must</u> write to-day to give a report on Tom but will not have time for much else. His temp. was normal all day Sat. 19th and Sun. 20th, all soreness gone from his throat, so I thought everything was over though I kept him in bed. Monday morning (midmorning) his temp. was 99°—it rose to 100° in early afternoon, then subsided to 99°.... [On Friday] C. went up and played cards with him—I had previously kept the others rigidly away from him but I thought he could surely not be pestilent still! In a little while C. came down and reported that Tom had found some spots on his arm (Tom, ever since he's been ill, has been looking for spots, expecting measles or something). I went up and found them scattered down his inner fore-arm, from inside the elbow to wrist and a few on the other arm. They were certainly no rash of any kind and the only thing I could think of was impetigo and that was an unwelcome thought! (I don't know whether impetigo is prevalent in England—when I was young it was considered an affliction only of the unwashed but in later years it has lost all respect for the respectable and bathed and is the bogey of mothers and school teachers and the scourge of summer camps.) ...

I had tea with Edith Wilkinson on Thursday.... On my way home I realised that, except for one or two hurried calls at mother's and our weekend at Burlington, that was the only time since mid-August that I have been in any one's house! That is the trying part of being maidless! And especially when there always seems to be <u>one</u> in bed! Let's hope that part will be rectified soon!...

I had a 16 page letter from Peter last Monday after one week at school, and another, yesterday. He had been very homesick & lonely but I could see each day he was feeling better (the letters are written in sections, one each evening) and progressed to "I am having a lot of fun." He does write awfully good letters—so expressive of his feelings as well as his doings and I think he is going to be very happy. They are busy every minute of the day, which is good for him, and he has a year's Latin to make up, so is expected to spend ½ hr. every half-holiday on it. Last Sat. he spent an hour—and found it great fun! Now that he is on better terms with the boys and enjoying school life I am afraid he will find it rather a bore, but he should be able to cover it fairly quickly....

[35] 90 DUNVEGAN ROAD
      TORONTO, OCTOBER 4

Dear Margaret

I got Tom back to school on Tuesday and he seems quite well. I rather got the wind up on Monday evening, when the spots, about which I told you, failed to disappear (though they did not increase). He seemed quite recovered from the tonsillitis and I hated to keep him home from school indefinitely waiting for the spots to clear. So John took him down to see the doctor, who said it was definitely <u>not</u> impetigo, though he was uncertain just what caused them. They might be from the sulfathiozole he took (though I had not given him much, and it was a week before) though they looked like the kind of spots some people get from being near certain plants—such as primulae etc. At any rate, he said there was no need to keep him at home, but to use calomine lotion or zinc oxide on them. I have been using calomine lotion all week—or rather, the last few days I've had Tom apply it himself—he seemed very doubtful whether he'd be able, but found he could manage it quite well when he tried. They seem to take a long time to go, and yesterday he showed me 2 or 3 new ones which had appeared. I will have a good look at them this afternoon and if I'm not satisfied, will take him back to the doctor.[32]

I have a bit of cough on my own chest—it is nothing much but just enough to make me rather weary, and it's been a busy week—though what week isn't? Every minute I could spare from the kitchen I've been working getting the clothes in shape for winter—letting down the legs of trousers and the sleeves of coats and jackets, patching the flannel pyjamas, and all the never ending darning and mending. Tom must have unusually long arms—I find that the sleeves of his flannel shirts come just below his elbow, so that the cuffs will scarcely button. I am trying to lengthen the sleeves by putting in a piece cut off the tail (which is so long, he <u>never</u> gets it all tucked in his trousers anyway). It's rather a long and trying job but I hope will be worth it, as he is just starting to wear these shirts (3 striped ones, size 12, which he brought out but hasn't needed until now).

Housekeeping and cooking are becoming increasingly difficult. Meat is practically unobtainable. There is talk of rationing it but they can't start until there is something on hand to ration, I suppose. We are not to have any tinned salmon or tinned meat any more as it's all being sent to Britain but there is more cheese available as the British quota is filled for this year. We all like cheese dishes except Tom—when we have them, he eats his without complaint but looks as though he were about to be ill all the time he's eating it! All sorts of prepared and tinned foods which we are accustomed to use to save time and labour are no longer being made—due to shortage of ingredients and of labour, so it means one has to do more cooking—and at the same time try to cut down one's electric fuel bills 15%, as we're told we must. It is difficult to get sweet biscuits etc., so I have started baking our cookies and things. However, we are still awfully lucky in the variety and quantity of things available—one gets used to luxuries so easily, that one thinks of them as essentials and feels lost for a short time when they are removed, but it's surprising how quickly we learn to do without what we can't get! Of course it's easier if one can go from shop to shop, as it were, but I don't have time for that!...

Bill is unfortunately in bed with a cold—not serious—all in his head. I imagine he will be subject to them for some months until the benefit of his tonsil removal makes itself felt. Vivien has been very much concerned lately because she felt that he was again neglecting to write to you. Last Sunday she and Harry (who got home for the weekend) went to the country to see Harry's father and as Bill would be home all day with nothing much to do, she asked him whether he had written you lately and when he admitted that he had not written since returning from Cochrane (4 weeks before) she asked him to be sure to write that day. A day or two later she enquired whether he had got his letter off (she does not feel, as a rule, that she should interfere with these matters which Bill is old enough to look after himself, but it does worry her to think of your being neglected). He was rather evasive about it but indicated that it was written but not posted. Yesterday

(Saturday) as he was in bed with nothing to do but read and write, she thought he ought to get it finished, so she asked him about it and he said he thought it was off but he would have to "check up" on it. Finally on Sunday (to-day) she had to insist on his writing it, so I think it is off now. This dilatoriness is a constant worry to her—every so often she tells herself very sensibly and reasonably that it is Bill's own affair for which he should be completely responsible and she sticks to that policy until as time goes on and on and she knows he hasn't written, she begins to think how she would feel in your place and simply has to speak to him about it—though it obviously annoys Bill intensely to be questioned (I suppose the more justified she is in her questions, the more annoying he finds it).

I have not seen Bill since school started and see Viv very rarely, so I have not found out what he is doing about Latin. They have altered the school hours this year so they have ½ hour longer day and Vivien was hoping that he would be able to fit it in but for some reason he is determined not to take it, regardless of whether he has time or not. When she discussed it with him some time ago, he told her very flatly and with some hauteur that the fact of its being required for an English University did not enter into the question, because whether the war ends or not, he intends to complete his university course here—which did seem to presume on the Ratcliffes' hospitality, but then Bill is rarely tactful!...

[36]   90 DUNVEGAN ROAD
          TORONTO, OCTOBER 12

Dear Margaret

Your cable arrived (by telephone) about 11 P.M. on the 10th—I suppose it was delayed—they all are now. They sent it on by post, arriving to-day. I expect C. told you about his birthday—it seemed highly successful and all the presents from England arrived safely and in good time.

There has been no mail from you since the air mail letter and the other posted the same day, which came by sea. That must be nearly a month ago. I had hoped that when you were on holiday the boys would hear from you oftener.

I have had John in bed most of the week with a bad cold which attacked his sinus, always his vulnerable spot—just got him up Saturday and had to put Mary to bed Sunday, where she still is and I expect will remain for some time. She has been coughing off and on for weeks but it has got decidedly worse and she is running a temp of 99–100. I hate having her in bed—she just can't lie still—(I often say if I could shake Mary and Tom up together, so Mary could get some of Tom's aversion to exertion of any kind and Tom some of Mary's aversion to inertia it would be a help). I have begun to feel as though I am "climbing up the ever-climbing wave" and if I can only get all the household on their feet for a while I might get caught up with the mending and cleaning.[33]

Of course John being ill spoiled our plan for a mild celebration of our 20th wedding anniversary on the 10th. Clare was to have come down to see to the children. He has been out in the sun to-day doing a bit of painting etc., feels much better and says he is going back to the office to-morrow. To-day was a holiday (Thanksgiving Day) and the whole 3 days of the weekend have been absolutely perfect autumn weather—the kind that make you long to be in the country. I do hope this good weather will continue.

I enjoyed very much meeting Mr. Clague (a friend of the Burns', who has a place in New Hampshire where, I think, he met you). When he was in town during the American Federation of Labor Convention—he has charge of Unemployment Insurance for the U.S. Govt. and was here to discuss some social security plan with the A. F. of L. He telephoned Vivien and arranged to go there early Saturday afternoon, so I took the boys up,—I wanted to meet him but thought I would stay only ½ an hour and dash back to Mary, whom I had left steaming in Friars Balsam under the care of John, newly risen from bed. However I liked him so much and found him so interesting, that I stayed until about 4.30 so the 3 boys came back with me and I had to scuttle to look after Mary and prepare the birthday supper—which was fortunately very simple. I was sorry John had to miss Mr. Clague but Harry came home while he was there so they had a good talk.[34]

[37] 90 DUNVEGAN ROAD
        TORONTO, OCTOBER 17

Dear Margaret

No time for a real letter but I must say how thrilled we are at Bill's winning the 5th form scholarship! He has done well.[35]

The parcels arrived on Tuesday—thank you very much. The things are all perfect but I felt very badly when I saw the prices you paid for them. They were all more expensive than similar goods would be here—except the flannel pyjamas, and of course when I buy boys' pyjamas I get flannel-ette, which is much cheaper and quite as warm as they need here, where we keep the bedrooms warm all day so the beds are warm and cosy to get into—of course we've been warned our happy days of warm houses may be over for the duration! I think I mentioned, later, a dressing gown for Tom, but if you haven't done any thing about it please don't. The one he has does very well and it is too bad to pay so much for things and then run the risk of their being lost. The socks I bought for Peter this fall are much like those you sent, are Made in England and cost slightly less than you paid! None the less I am very glad to have the things and they will set them up nicely for some time to come. Your cheque also arrived this morning—many thanks....

I am so hoping we can go to Port Hope to see Peter to-morrow. We have saved our gasoline for it and he is looking forward to it—as are we!...

This is a horrible rainy day after a week of glorious Indian Summer. The boys spent part of this afternoon, when the rain stopped, raking leaves in their rubber boots, and are now playing Russian armies—in Christopher's room, with the help of Hugh Innis. C. has made arm bands and hats with hammer & sickle insignia but has a hard time explaining to the others that he is not a Communist!

OCT. 19

We had our day with Peter—such a delightful one!... It was the most beautiful autumn day imaginable and the country side heavenly. We took Peter out for lunch to Cobourg, on the lake. He was glad to see us, and sorry to see us go, but we could tell that he is completely at home and perfectly happy, and we were pleased with everything and everyone about the school. It was a day without a flaw!...

[38] 90 DUNVEGAN ROAD
TORONTO, OCTOBER 26

Dear Margaret

Except for C's airgraph the boys have not had a letter from you since early September. Incidentally the airgraph, sent Sept. 24, arrived the same day as a letter to me from your mother posted Sept. 26!—so perhaps they aren't as quick as we thought!...

The boys are well—they are out now helping Mr. Innis burn leaves in the garden. They have been raking ours up and awfully anxious to burn them, but I wouldn't let them unless there was a man around—it's so easy for the fire to get out of control with so many leaves.

They went to the circus Friday—not together. C. had arranged to go with another boy and I could see was not anxious to take Tom, so I suggested to Tom that he find someone to go with. It never occurs to Tom that he can do things "under his own steam".... I explained to Tom that when boys arrived at the 7th grade they were expected to be able to get places themselves, but suggested that he telephone William Leigh-Clare and arrange to meet him at the street-car. He apparently had no difficulty. It does make things a lot easier when they have learned to get around a bit "on their own"....

No time for more. I hope school is not too hectic.

...

P.S. Bill was here yesterday afternoon.... Vivien tells me he is doing a job for "The Twig" and according to reports which John Ratcliffe hears from U.T.S., doing it very well. She says he is very busy and "mysterious" over it, but so pleasant, agreeable and considerate in every way about the house—I suppose the result of his feeling of self-satisfaction in taking part in a co-operative effort and being able to handle it successfully. I think it's splendid![36]

[39] 90 DUNVEGAN ROAD
        TORONTO, NOVEMBER 2

Dear Margaret

As usual I have no time but I must let you know of the arrival of your letters. The boys have received—Oct. 26—an airgraph to Tom dated Sept. 26, Oct. 28—an airmail letter to C. posted Sept. 30, Oct. 28—a letter to Masters Sharp posted Oct. 7, Oct. 29—a letter to Tom dated Sept. 30, Oct. 31—airgraph to C. from his father dated Oct. 10, Oct. 31– airgraph to Tom from his father dated Oct. 17.

None of these were censored. So it rather looks as though airmail were not worth while—I expect the North Atlantic air mail is discontinued for the autumn and winter.

This past week has been rather particular hell as Mary is still home [having been sick for a couple of weeks] though the doctor is letting her get up part of each day—which at least saves trays for 2 meals!—and to cap the climax my faithful morning char has been ill and could not come for more than a week. I almost fell on her neck when she appeared this morning but she is coughing dreadfully and I don't know how long it will last—her husband is beginning to get very annoyed at her working so hard and may make her stop coming to me. Mary is still coughing dreadfully and is very pale but she feels pretty well and has no temp.—the doctor says the bronchitis is still there. I am <u>so</u> tired of Friars Balsam and mustard plasters and gargles! I don't ever remember so <u>many</u> people having colds as this autumn....

I am enclosing a couple of exam papers—I am very proud of C's spelling paper—both the spelling, and the writing after he got over his initial nervousness.

[**40**] 90 DUNVEGAN ROAD
           TORONTO, NOVEMBER 8

Dear Margaret

On Nov. 4 the boys each had a letter from you, written Oct. 12, enclosing snapshots. These had been opened by censor so apparently there is no ruling against sending photographs. On Nov. 5 came your letter to me enclosing ones to the boys, dated Oct. 4.... As usual, I am rushed to-night but I <u>must</u> tell you how they are enjoying your letters. Their former apparent lack of interest was more or less <u>due</u> to hearing so seldom and <u>much more</u> to the fact that they couldn't read the letters. When they come often and they can read them easily it seems to make you much nearer to them. And you need make no apologies for their contents in comparison with those of their father. I can tell by the way they read yours together, chuckle over them, and discuss them, that they find them much more interesting than his.

Tom's joy at getting the picture of you was very touching—he was simply tremulous with excitement—it was like his birthday and Christmas put together. And Mary was almost as excited as he. He said "You know I <u>was</u> beginning to forget what she looked like." I am going to see if I can get him a little frame for it. Christopher was delighted with his, too....

I also had a letter from your mother this week, dated Oct. 14, enclosing letters to the boys. I think I told you, but will repeat, that a parcel arrived from her addressed to Mary, C. & T. which I expect is for Christmas....

I don't suppose C. ever thought to tell you that I got the Ransome book exchanged for him. I managed to get down to Eaton's book dept. and talked to the Manager—the edition of Missie Lee they have in stock there was exactly the same except that it was on different paper, and he very obligingly took the one sent to C. and let me choose another book instead—I got him August Holiday (I'm not sure of the author, I think it's Atkinson)—he seems to like it very well. It's on the lines of the Ransome books.[37]

Mary's bronchitis is still not cleared up—she was out of bed (though not outside) as the dr. thought her lungs would clear more quickly if she were active, but two days ago her temp. went up a bit so I had to put her back in bed. This makes 4 weeks and is <u>very</u> discouraging. I feel so sorry for her—she loves activity and people and <u>hates</u> to miss <u>anything</u> and though she is very good about it I know she has a frantic feeling that school and life in general is rushing along and she is missing it all. However, we'll just have to resign ourselves to it and as soon as she's well enough I will have her tonsils out. I have intended to do it for 2 years always waiting for a "convenient time" but I've decided there is no such thing!

The boys got their reports on Friday and I am sending photographic copies. As you may imagine, Tom was simply astounded at the comment on his! However, I don't think it will do him any harm. I had thought myself he was coasting along very casually. Anyway, they both have done very well. Tom is as obsessed with the choir as ever. I let him go to Church this evening (he is getting to be one of the bigger boys in the choir now and seems to feel it is expected of him—in fact he offered, if I let him to go to evening service Sunday, to stay away from choir practice Monday evening and go instead to a newly instituted practice on Friday afternoon)....

I am sorry you went to such trouble over the dressing gown for Tom. It seems too bad when you have to pay <u>such</u> a lot for things in England now and obviously the best goods are being exported. Did I tell you a second time about receiving the parcels of clothing? I intended to, in case one letter was lost. They will all be most useful. I am not having to buy much for them this autumn except shoes. Tom's navy blue suit is finally too small and he has stepped into Peter's, and with some passing around, I think there will only be an odd garment or two needed new. Tom is getting Peter's overcoat and C's is all right (they only wear overcoats on Sundays and the short ones I got them last year for school will do again, I think)....

We are hanging on the news to-day and are so thrilled and excited. I can't help feeling dreadfully sorry for the Canadian soldiers in England. They must be <u>wild</u>, having been there inactive for 1, 2 & 3 years, to have the Americans doing this job. (Of course the Americans were the only ones to handle this particular situation but that won't prevent their feeling bitter.) However I can't help feeling their time will soon come. One feels at last that there is a <u>plan</u> and every sector will soon be fitted into it.

No time for more. I do hope this year turns out easier for you than last and that the coal shortage isn't too uncomfortable—but that's a silly thing to say—of <u>course</u> it will be beastly uncomfortable. I feel worse to think of you all being cold than about anything....

My char returned this week, to my joy, and will keep coming as long as her health holds out. Every time she coughs I cross my fingers!

Dear Margaret

... The nice weather kept up very well this autumn but we had a snowstorm Friday night and yesterday was a beautiful sunny day with everything white and Christmas-cardy. C. had a slight sniffle but they were so excited over the snow that I hadn't the heart to keep him in so the boys spent the morning shovelling the snow and sledding. In the afternoon they went into the Innis's next door to celebrate Hugh's birthday. I am keeping C. in to-day, hoping to head off a real cold. If we have any more illness I really don't know what I'll do. Mary is still in bed—to-day makes 5 weeks. The doctor says her chest is now perfectly clear but there is still enough infection left in the back of her nose and swollen neck glands to make her temp. jump to 100° every time I let her up, even for a few hours. It is very discouraging. Just as soon as this clears up we shall have to have her tonsils out.

I got Clare to come in Thursday afternoon so I could go to the "open house" at the school—I'd never had a chance to talk to any of their teachers. Mary's teacher was most comforting about her missing her work and offered full co-operation when she returns—also insists that I send her only in the morning to start with, as long as I feel it advisable. I am keeping up her arithmetic and spelling but the rest she'll have to "pick up." Both the boys are doing very well, according to their masters (and their reports) and it was all most encouraging.

Incidentally I shall not be able to call on Clare any more to help me out, as the Manufacturers' Life, where she worked for about 15 years before her marriage, have asked her to come back, workers being so scarce, so she is to start there to-morrow morning, full time. She doesn't know whether she will find it too heavy but is going to try it. Mrs. Fairfoul is becoming rather spotty in her attendance too, poor soul—her aged father who lives with her, is ill, and sometimes she can't leave him alone, much as she hates to disappoint me. At this rate my Christmas preparations, I'm afraid, will be rather a hit or miss affair, particularly as I've no idea what any of the children want (Mary's hardy perennial "a two-wheel bike" being out of the question!). I am certainly not going to attempt cakes or puddings myself—the ingredients are too hard to get, for one thing. Our latest shortages are butter and eggs—sometimes one has to go to 2 or 3 shops to get them (that probably sounds ludicrous to you, who know what real shortage is!)....

We have just listened to the broadcast of the Church Bells from England, Scotland, N. Ireland and Wales, finishing with the bells of the remaining tower of Coventry Cathedral—rather impressive! This has been a heart-lifting week. May the good news continue!

P.P.S. I <u>had</u> hoped to get proper photographs of the boys to send to you this Christmas but just haven't had the opportunity to arrange about it.

[42] 90 DUNVEGAN ROAD
TORONTO, NOVEMBER 23

Dear Margaret

... I was <u>so</u> relieved to hear that the pen had arrived safely, and was so glad to have <u>your</u> letter—sorry I haven't time to answer it properly this time.

Thank you so much for your offer of entertainment for Canadians—I don't know of any likely recipient at the moment, but may do sometime. Everyone in England seems to be so good to our boys—poor things it must be pretty trying for them sitting about in England with so much going on elsewhere, but their time will come—all too soon for their anxious parents. We are naturally all frightfully bucked over the present good news and prospects. It won't be any "push-over" but it's grand to feel we're on the move towards the ...

[43] 90 DUNVEGAN ROAD
TORONTO, NOVEMBER 29

Dear Margaret

The only English mail this past week was an airgraph to Tom from his father, sent Nov. 9, arrived Nov. 27.

When writing last week, in answering your letter of Oct. 26, I did not at the time notice the P.S. about renewing Punch. Thank you so much—we do enjoy it and then pass it on to Vivien. Some of the recent numbers have been <u>particularly</u> good. I nearly always get a "great kick" out of A.P. Herbert's "little talk."

I have had Mary at school in the mornings all the past week—she was very white and ill looking at first but has steadily improved. We are now in the midst of a soft wet snowfall that started last night and is continuing its steady, quiet, persistent way with no sign of ceasing. C. shovelled the walks this afternoon and has spent the last 2 hours building a snow man, while Mary is sulking because she's not allowed to join him. I am getting hard hearted—I simply <u>can't</u> have more illness....

No time for more now—C. has had an oral comp. prepared for over a week (on the Defence of Calais—he produced a little book of that title which he says his grandmother sent him one time, and got his material from it). He has practised it on me, John & Tom and hopes very much that when he is called on his performance will entitle him to compete in the Oratorical Contest.

Dear Margaret

... I had your cable re birth certificates on Dec. 1 and had a letter from Mrs. Burns telling me she had your cable agreeing to C. going to them. I had not mentioned the proposal in my letters to you until I was sure you had her letter, thinking that otherwise it might be confusing. Mrs. Burns' first letter, suggesting that C. should go to them was rather a bolt from the blue and my feelings on reading it were rather mixed. I am by nature conscientious about fulfilling responsibilities I have assumed and it rather went against the grain not to carry out to the end what I had undertaken. However, there seemed no logical ground for refusing the invitation. The Burns obviously want to have C. and I cannot deny that under present circumstances the situation here is a decided strain. Also I have to remember that the welfare of the entire family hangs on the none too durable thread of my own health and strength and I have no right to refuse a lightening of the load—especially as the change will, I am sure, be to C's advantage. I have said nothing on the subject to C. as yet, but asked Mrs. B. to write to him herself as soon as she obtained your consent. I should prefer it to come to him as a direct personal invitation from her, rather than "retailed" through me lest he should have the feeling that we had been making arrangements over his head to move him about like a piece of furniture. I fully expect that he will be overjoyed with the idea. He is very fond of Mr. & Mrs. B. and was very loath to return from the summer with them. Then, besides, the prospect of going to live in a new city, in a new country, has a great appeal to a child his age, and I am sure the B's will be able to give him material advantages which we cannot.

However, there is no use wasting time speculating on his reactions. Mrs. B's letter should arrive in a few days (mail from Wash. is very slow) and then we shall see. I don't expect being separated from Tom will bother him—they haven't much in common and rarely play together, and I think

C. is a bit lonely here with Peter away. Tom will probably be very downcast at C. going and him not, but once C. has gone I think Tom will not miss him for long and it may help him to achieve the self-reliance he so badly needs.

I have left it to Mrs. B. to set the date of his going, which will probably be towards the end of Jan. as the Wash. school term begins Feb. 1. The only thing I do feel sorry for C. about is having to adjust to a new school system. But he is doing so well in school now and is getting so much self-assurance in his school work that I don't think it will be so much of a trial this time. (And he does make friends quickly.) The boys are having exams now and C. is getting much better marks than Tom, which Tom doesn't like at all!

Peter will be home to-morrow week and every letter I have is full of all he is going to do as soon as he gets here—making Christmas presents (he sends working drawings and descriptions of things he has in mind) and to-day I have a long letter discussing his ideas for the Christmas table decorations and centre-piece (always his responsibility). He has also started a "secret" correspondence with C. involving many long letters from Peter—some Christmas arrangements, I expect. We are going to have the family here—mother, father, Theresa, Leslie, Clare & George, and Irene (Peterkin) and Ruby (McKay). It will be rather an undertaking but the girls will help me, and I do think it's nice for the children to have a lot of people in the house at Christmas. It seems so much more festive than just the same old family....

Tom is very much excited over a carol service on Wed., Dec. 16 in St. George's (another down town church) in which his choir is to take part. He can only sing in it if he goes to 2 Sunday evening practices (last night and next Sunday) so he and I worked out that he should miss the usual Monday night practice for those 2 weeks. I don't like him to have too many late nights but he <u>does</u> love that choir so! It's really extraordinary!

As usual, I have scribbled this at a fearful rate, and <u>must</u> get to bed. I hope it's all intelligible. Thank-you so much for sending the birth certificates—that seems to be the only thing we need for C's entry into the U.S., except forms we fill out at the Consul's Office and papers from Mr. B. which he is sending. The reason John asked for an affidavit in his cable was that we thought it might take some time to get birth certificates from the Registrar General and the Consul said that failing a birth cert. he would accept an affidavit from the child's father.

With love and best wishes for a better New Year.

Mary made a little needle case and sent it to your mother for Christmas. I hope it arrives.

Dear Margaret

... Mrs B. wrote to C. and also to each of the other boys—it was very
thoughtful of her. The letters came Thursday, while C. was in bed and C's
joy and excitement were a sight to behold. He had to read and reread the
letter to make sure he had read it aright. (In the morning when I went in
and turned on his light, his hand went out at once for the letter, to make
sure he hadn't dreamed it.) He just can't get the grin off his face and is in
a state of bliss. To-day, when I let him up, he went through his shelves and
cupboards, sorting out which of his books and treasures he would take. He
has not the slightest qualm at leaving Tom and Bill—in fact when I asked
him if he'd mind leaving them, he regarded it as a supreme witticism on
my part! So you need have no concern as to his happiness at the prospect.

Tom took it much more calmly and philosophically than I'd expected. In
fact, at first he didn't seem greatly interested—of course it always takes him
some time to grasp things. He has given no outward evidence of sorrow,
resentment or jealousy, of any kind. I was with them when they read the
letters enclosed in mine—you had told Tom to try to be as helpful as C. & P.
put together and of course C. jeered, but I chipped in, upholding Tom and
how helpful he could be, pointing out that he had shovelled all the snow this
morning (of course there was only an inch or two but he did it very well)
etc., and I could see Tom was pleased. I think that is the line to take with
Tom now—to let him feel I depend on him—I don't just mean for physical
assistance, but in all ways. Mary, too, has (quite unconsciously and in pure
selfishness) helped Tom by being so unfeignedly pleased that _he_ isn't going.
For the last couple of years (ever since C. learned to control his temper and
gave up his berserk rages, which she regarded with cold scorn) she and C.
have got on _very_ well, but now that C. is older and plays with other boys,
he has moved more or less out of her orbit and she feels Tom is more (as
it were) "available" as a companion. In actual fact I think Tom may be less
lonely after C. goes. Hugh Innis, next door, is only 6 months older than Tom,
but C. claims him as _his_ friend because he "discovered" him and cultivated
his friendship and does his best to exclude Tom from their companionship.
But when C. is ill (as this week) Tom and Hugh are always together and it
did me good to see Tom scuffling about with Hugh and going sledding with
Hugh to-day, when there was a little snow. I think they'll be good friends as
Hugh is a bit like Tom—rather quiet and not boisterous. As for Bill, I don't
know what his reaction is—I rather expected he would telephone C. to discuss it but he has not, nor has C. thought to telephone him.

I do hope the new arrangements will be satisfactory for everyone and in my opinion it is a marvellous opportunity for C. and in every way to his advantage. I am glad to see that there was apparently no trouble with the High Court as your cable of assent was sent only a day after you wrote me.

I can understand your being tempted at times to try to get the boys back, when you hear of so many others returning, but I do think it would be most unwise, unsafe and also unfair to all the thousands who applied to be evacuated and couldn't be. Of course, if, as seems possible, Germany should be defeated before Japan, there would be no reason why they couldn't return then, as in that case both England and the Atlantic would be free of danger. However, Germany's defeat, though inevitable, is possibly still far distant, though it's encouraging that <u>we</u> are now doing the attacking and apparently working in such perfect co-operation with the U.S.A.

I am sorry you went to the trouble and expense of sending another dressing gown. The first one has not arrived though it <u>may</u> just be delayed. I know you feel you want to do just as much as you're allowed for the boys, but it seems to me a shame when things are obviously scarce and expensive and transportation risky, for you to take that expensive gamble and I'd really rather you didn't try to send clothes again.

I shall send this airmail—it may take just as long (though yours were less than 2 weeks) but one is pretty sure of it being safe.

CONFIDENTIAL[38]

I <u>do most earnestly</u> hope that you and Mr. Sharp intend to follow the psychologist's advice not to tell the boys of his marriage. I can see <u>no</u> reason for telling them and <u>every</u> reason for not doing so. I have not the slightest idea how the fact itself would affect them—whether they would be upset at the idea, but it would undoubtedly undermine the sense of security which they certainly have—Tom most markedly. I am reasonably sure that Tom (at least) has forgotten all about the fact that you and his father are separated—about C. one never knows. In all our association with the boys (Bill included—and in Bill's association with the Ratcliffes) there has never been a hint on either side that you and Mr. Sharp are not a perfectly normal married couple. There was no prearrangement and nothing deliberate in this—it just seemed the natural way to act—and you and he—very wisely I think—have furthered this feeling by mentioning one another in your letters—when you see or hear from one another, etc. We just took our cue from the boys in the beginning, and I remember when Bill mentioned to Vivien, soon after he came, that the plan was for "his parents" to come to Canada to fetch them after the war, that seemed a very good cue.

As far as Bill goes, if you or his father should write and tell him about the marriage, I am sure he would mention it to no one, but I don't see how the knowledge could be anything but unsettling. But with "my" two there would almost certainly be all sorts of complications. I would certainly not undertake to tell them and if they were told by letter I don't know what C. would do but I know Tom would come to me in bewilderment about it. If I advised him to keep it a secret it would only increase his feeling of insecurity and if it were "common property" in the household I can imagine my own children's perfectly natural curiosity—after these years of imagining T. & C's parents just like their own. (I've sometimes wondered whether Peter would think it odd that you and Mr. Sharp lived in different places but I suppose if he thought of it he'd put it down to exigencies of war.)

We have quite a few friends who are divorced (and remarried) but none of them have children who are contemporaries of ours and it would be something so new to their experience (like knowing someone whose father kept a lighthouse or was a "mountie" or something equally unusual) that they would be full of questions which couldn't help but hurt T. & C.—who, I'm sure, are loyal both to you and their father. I remember once overhearing Peter and C. discussing something (I've forgotten what—nationality or legal domicile or something) and Peter, explaining, said "Well suppose your mother and father were divorced and you lived with your mother"— "But I do live with my mother" C. interrupted. "Oh I know" said Peter, with exasperation at C. not grasping his meaning, "but I mean, suppose your mother and father were divorced and you lived with your mother, then etc. etc." and C. said nothing more.

I do feel it would be most unwise to tell them about this until after they return home. When they are with you it would be quite different. As I said before, I don't know whether the actual knowledge of their father marrying would upset them but the attendant complications and the fact that it would drag back into their minds the separation in the family, now forgotten or never thought of, could have nothing but a bad effect, while they are away from you.

[46] 90 DUNVEGAN ROAD
TORONTO, DECEMBER 20

Dear Margaret

... Dec. 14 the second birth certificate arrived—the airmail one came last week....

We now have the 2 birth certificates, for which I thank you very much. They came quite quickly. The one John cabled to the Canada Life for has not arrived, so I am glad to have this. C. had new passport photographs taken yesterday, so I think we have everything assembled and when the B's send their papers we can go ahead on the visa. Mr. B. had influenza when she wrote last week, which was delaying one important document. The date for C's going has not been set yet but I think John will go with him as far as Buffalo, thus seeing him through immigration and customs, and put him on the sleeper direct for Washington, where he will arrive in the morning.

We will miss him very much—he has been a part of our family for so long. Peter was very disappointed at the news (which pleased me, if you know what I mean) but they'll have the Christmas holidays together—and are enjoying being together immensely. C. is looking forward with joy to going and it is indeed a marvellous opportunity for him. I dare say he will miss the other children after he gets there but he makes friends quickly and Mrs. B. says the school near them is one of the best in Wash. and the children of several of their friends go there. I don't think you need worry about his health—he is in good shape. Of course they've both had more illness this autumn and winter than ever before since they came here, but that is the experience of almost all people who come here from the British Isles—their first winter they don't feel the cold or catch cold at all, but gradually their blood thins—probably due in part to our overheated (and usually very dry) houses and the second and third winters they catch colds. I dare say Wash. is damp, but of course Toronto is too. Toronto is supposed to be one of the worst cities on the continent for nose and throat troubles, because of the dampness and very changeable weather. Last winter was mostly slush and rain, with occasional sudden drops in temp. This winter we seem in for severe weather—this morning it was 17° below zero!—to Tom's great excitement. (He has a great interest in the weather and always consults the thermometer first thing in the morning and reads the "probs" before the headlines.) It is discouraging having such cold come so early in the winter—also we had 7 inches of snow fall last week.

Also, I don't think there is any danger of his not being as well cared for physically as here. Mrs. B. seems a very practical person, who thinks of everything, and C. has become quite self-reliant and able to look after himself sensibly (I hope). I know she will have his interests at heart, though she may not be as "fussy" about details as I am—which I often think would be a lot better kind of system both for the children and one's self, though unfortunately I'm that kind of person and can't change myself.

Peter came home Wednesday—such excitement! Tom even stayed home from choir practice to be sure not to miss him! That was the night of Tom's carol service at a down town Church and I was sorry not to be able to go, but Peter arrived just at dinner time and John's sister Emily was in town and came for dinner and to spend the night. The house is popping and cracking with activity and preparations for the play and magic show which Peter and C. are planning for Christmas day. Sometimes I wonder how I will struggle through the next four days <u>and</u> get my own Christmas preparations made. We shall have 15 or 16 for dinner but Clare, Theresa and Ruby are sharing in the labour of preparing food. I have a 17 lb. turkey and do hope I can make it eatable!

There has just been an announcement over the radio that butter rationing begins to-morrow—½ lb. week per person. I am awfully glad. There has been a shortage for about a month now—I only had 2 lbs. for 3 weeks. The govt. kept issuing statements that there was enough butter if <u>only</u> people would not be selfish and everyone would cut down consumption by one ounce a week. And every statement just sent the selfish ones out combing the shops for <u>more</u> butter to store in their cellars. The shops get in stocks every once in a while but one never knows when it's coming and I simply haven't time to spend hours looking for butter. We've been getting pretty annoyed—that is, all the decent people who only want their share—and I am so glad it's to be rationed so I'll know where we are. You see the manufacture of margarine is prohibited (anyway there are no vegetable oils available to make it) and we haven't had bacon for months. The meat situation has been quite good for a month or so but we are warned to expect another shortage after Christmas. I wish they would ration it too, in that event.

Bill came in Friday on his way home from school (last day of term for him) and stayed for supper. He is so big and mature looking one would take him for 18! He has been here scarcely at all, all autumn—there was so much sickness here that he wisely didn't risk getting into it and the last time I asked him <u>he</u> had a cold, and then his exams came on. He is so pleasant now with the other 2 boys and there is none of the bickering and the "Bill & Tom versus C." that there used to be—or any there is is on C's part and Bill can overcome it with our help. Vivien has told me for months how much pleasanter, more "comfortable" and more a part of the family Bill had made himself and I can see it too. And I don't think it's confined to the R's and ourselves—it's all part of a broader development—he is identifying himself more with the school and taking part in its activities, showing an interest in people, and making some friends. I hope you realise that re this Yale course—Vivien thinks it neither practicable nor desirable. She thinks

Bill might <u>much</u> better take his university course here—better from every standpoint, financial and otherwise, but she did think that, as Bill was so interested in it, you ought to know about it and give your opinion, as it was not in her sphere at all. I think Bill, too has given up the idea now—not that he really "harped on it," but it did attract him....

I have made an appointment to have Tom's eyes examined during the holidays, just to make sure they're all right. He had the regular physical examination at the school a few weeks ago—I think I told you—and the report was that he was in good condition except for slight eyestrain. I had Mr Pugh put him in a front seat in Sept. (as Dr. Macrae advised me last year) and he seems to see all right, but it will be reassuring to have Dr. Macrae examine his eyes again.

Tom's height—56 ¼" weight 71 lbs. This is 4 lbs. under average but he has small bones, so the dr. considers that all right.

With love and <u>very</u> best wishes for 1943.

[**47**] 90 DUNVEGAN ROAD
TORONTO, DECEMBER 27

Dear Margaret

Christmas has come and gone very successfully. You must miss the boys horribly at that time. As I told you in last week's letter, I'm afraid your parcels must have been lost—it is too bad, but after all it's remarkable that those are the first not to arrive in the whole 2 ½ years. We had the children do without hanging up their stockings this year—when it really came to Christmas eve I was a little sorry about it, but I simply had not the time or opportunity to shop for all the little toys and oddments to fill 4 good big stockings—anyway there aren't any little toys now (I might whisper that they all came from Japan!). However, the kids didn't seem to mind at all. When Tom went to bed Christmas eve he said he'd probably be able to get to sleep quicker than he did other Christmas eves, on account of having no stocking hung up, as formerly the excitement of thinking of Santa Claus coming kept him awake!

We had 15 for dinner on Christmas, and Besse brought little Janet (who is just walking and a darling sturdy little girl) in for half an hour or so in the afternoon. Every body helped, and C. and Peter did all the waiting on table, etc, and it wasn't too hard, and everyone had a good day.

We had dinner about 5.30 to give the children lots of time for the evening's entertainment on which they had spent days of hectic preparation. They did a play, which C. wrote, and Peter and C. gave a show of magic and mind reading. It was very successful—much better than I'd expected. A friend of mine gave Peter a gramophone which they weren't using and a lot of old records, a couple of weeks ago, so they had sound effects and the National Anthem at the end (this caused them a minor worry as it was part of a record of the National Anthems of the allies of the last war, and the Italian one immediately preceded God Save the King, so they had rather a nice bit of judgement, to drop the needle on at just the right place!).

It was 10 o'clock before they got to bed, but Mary said when she was going "Oh! It was a merry merry merry Christmas!" And Tom said "I don't remember a day in my whole life when I've been so happy!" so I felt very satisfied with the whole thing....

The day was saddened for John and me by the death of one of our dearest friends, Dr. "Tal" Cruikshank (it is his brother who is married to your friend Frances Billington). He and his wife have been among our closest friends ever since we lived in the flat above them in a converted house, the year after we returned from England. That was the year I was ill with septicaemia and their kindness to us could never be measured, though Betty was not well herself and when her little girl was born the following spring she discovered she had tuberculosis and spent the next 1 ½ years in a sanatorium. Kindness and thoughtfulness for others simply flowed from them both—they were the most unselfish people I have ever known....

I was so surprised and pleased early Wednesday afternoon when your friend Ian Ponsford arrived at our door![39] The boys had gone to the movies—it was the first day of the holidays and they had a "treat" coming to them to celebrate Peter's birthday so I sent the three off after an early lunch to "One of our Aircraft is Missing." However, he stayed and had tea with me and Tom came in before he left.... I did like him so much—he is so bright and alert and pleasant and friendly—he must make friends everywhere. I asked him to come on Christmas but he was already booked for Christmas dinner so we arranged for him to come Saturday (yesterday) afternoon and stay for dinner and I asked Bill to come. Unfortunately we had to go to Tal Cruikshank's funeral, as it turned out, and were just about to leave when he arrived, but he is the kind of person that one doesn't feel in the least awkward with, so we just left him in Bill's and the boys' hands while we went—came back to find all 5 of them immersed in "Totopoly." ... John and Peter left them to go to Burlington for the weekend ... so Mary took Peter's place in the game and it continued on and on, just finishing as dinner was ready at 6.30. After dinner Bill had to go, but T. & C. did some magic tricks for Ian and then we all washed the dishes and the four had a riotous game of doubles at ping pong, after which Ian had to leave (about 9) to get his kit in order in preparation for his move to California, where he is being sent as an instructor, to-night. He is so adaptable—I think he thoroughly enjoyed playing with the children....

I had a letter Dec. 24 from Dr. Burns with all the necessary papers (I hope) for getting C's visa—they have to furnish sworn statements about every detail of their lives and finances! I expect I shall hear from Mrs. B. in a day or so setting a date for C. to go. C. is fervently hoping it will be an early one—he doesn't want to go back to school here as he said good-bye to all the boys before the holidays and feels it would be a dreadful anti-climax! School here opens Jan. 4—Peter goes back Jan. 6. I shall have to start right away getting C's things ready—I don't know whether his trunk will hold everything, but if not, we have a big old trunk (from John's college days)—which we've intended to give away for years, but when we moved we decided to bring it along, as it would be needed when the boys went back to England, and if necessary I will use that. He has 30 to 40 books alone now and boxes and boxes of treasures which I don't like to ask him to abandon even temporarily....

1943

"[Tom] has changed so much since he came out here that you will hardly recognize him"[1]

[1]   90 DUNVEGAN ROAD
        TORONTO, JANUARY 3

Dear Margaret

There has been no English mail for over 2 weeks—though Punch came yesterday so there may be letters to-morrow. The ships have probably had other uses recently. Your cable to the boys came Dec. 31....

School starts again to-morrow—C. is rather disappointed at having to go back here as he said good-bye to all the boys before Christmas, but it would be silly for him to sit at home for nearly 3 weeks. Fortunately (for the children) we had a huge snow-fall on Wednesday and the weather has been good since, so they've had a lot of fun tobogganing and skiing both morning and afternoon ever since. This afternoon John has taken them to York Downs—quite an event in these days of short gasoline rations but it is the last time they'll all get out on such an expedition together, as Peter goes back to school Wednesday.

John took all the papers to the Consul on Thursday and C. is to go down with him tomorrow morning at 9.30 and I hope there will be no hitches in granting his visa. I have to take Peter to do a bit of shopping for him so I can take C. down and John can put him on the street car which takes him right to the school, after they get through.

We had Leslie here for 3 or 4 days last week as mother was very ill and father had a bad cold. Theresa came up on Friday (New Year's Day) and as mother was much better, and father practically over his cough, and out of bed, Leslie went back with her....

Dear Margaret

... John took C. to the Consul's office on Monday morning. They had an appointment for 9.30 and did not get away until 12. C. had to have a medical examination but finally everything was signed and sealed and all is in order—his tickets are bought and sleeping berth reserved for the night of the 21st. Mrs. B. sent me your cable of consent which I had to pass on to the University Committee for British Overseas Children. They have to submit the parents' consent to the authorities in Ottawa if a child is sent out of Canada.

Bill came down yesterday afternoon. John had taken the children to Forest Hill School to skate but they went early so were back soon after Bill came and he stayed for dinner. He is looking very well.

Theresa starts at her regular teaching job (mornings only) to-morrow. I think I told you she was trying to get it. Mother is somewhat better but is still <u>very</u> flat in bed and very weak and very averse to taking nourishment, so I am going down there in the morning until she is well enough to be left in Leslie's care while T. is gone. I expect to be able to get back by noon to give the children their lunch....

No more now—I am trying to get to bed very early these nights.

Dear Margaret

This week has been rather a nightmare—I have been leaving every morning just as soon as I get the kids off to school, to go to mother's, to look after her while Theresa's at school—when father comes home about ¼ to 12 I dash for home to get the children's dinner ready for 12.20. It makes the rest of the day pretty heavy, as I have to get as much cooking as I can done each afternoon for the next day, besides making custards etc. to take to mother in the vain hope she'll eat them, and doing what cooking I can to take down for the rest of the family, to save Theresa. In addition I had John in bed Wed. and Thurs.—just a bad head cold but he has to be so careful of his sinus. He insisted on going back to the office Friday but is by no means well. Then yesterday afternoon I had to put Tom to bed with laryngitis—no fever, no sore throat, no cold or discomfort of any kind, and an excellent appetite— just hoarseness. I have thermogene bound with flannel around his neck and Friars Balsam boiling by his bed and I do hope it will go quickly. I have never known so much illness as there is this winter—at least among my own friends, and all the doctors tell the same story—and of course in these days, with no domestic or nursing help available, it is all the more distressing.

In between times I have been trying to get Christopher's things in order. I find the clothes much easier than his personal possessions—I had him sort out what he wanted to take (which was practically everything) and spent yesterday afternoon arranging and packing what seems an enormous collection of games, jig-saws, stamps, marbles, crayons, magic tricks and all sorts of oddments. However, I got everything fitted in quite successfully into a fairly level layer in the bottom half of the trunk. I want to get ahead with things when I can, and besides, we have to have his trunk down on Wednesday morning, to have it examined by the Customs before he goes.

I hope to heaven there will be no more illness before Thursday. I want to take them all down and have supper at a restaurant near the station before the train goes at 6.15. They arrive in Buffalo about 9.30 and we hope there will be time for John to put him to bed in the Washington train before it goes, and then there will be nothing at all to worry about. John will speak to the porter and the pullman conductor and Mrs. B. is to meet him on the platform in Wash. The train does not get in until 9.30 A.M. so I am going to give him some food for the morning—he has an enormous appetite (I'm very pleased about that, I think that is why he is growing so fast—he was 1 ½ in. taller than Peter at Christmas, and they used to be the same height—he is about 5 ft. 2 in. and I want to have him weighed before he goes).... I think C. is very excited about his departure, though he keeps such things pretty much to himself. I'm sure he will be happy with the Burns—I hope Mrs. B. won't find it too much for her.

No more now, time is at a premium. I don't know how long I shall have to keep on going to mother's. She is not very ill any more—that is, she has no temp. and her chest is clear and her breathing all right but she's so weak she can scarcely lift her head and has no inclination to try to exert herself or to take enough nourishment to bring back her strength. I do hope she'll pick up soon.

Bill came in Friday afternoon and was to have come for the day yesterday but has a cold (just as well he didn't as Tom went to bed). So he is to come from school Wednesday and stay for dinner.

JANUARY 18

P.S. ... We were in rather a turmoil to-day as I had a letter from Mrs. B. to say that they had had a friend for 3 days who developed mumps just as she left and as neither Mr. nor Mrs. B. have had it they are terrified they may have contracted it and thought I might want to postpone C's coming. John consulted 3 doctors who all thought it most unlikely that they would have it, and as there is a great deal of it in the city, here, we decided after much discussion, that C. would run no more risk there. All the arrangements are now complete and they took such endless time—his trunk is packed—etc. etc.—also he would be <u>sick</u> with disappointment at a postponement. She asked me to wire a decision so I wired to say he would come the 21st as arranged....

[4] 90 DUNVEGAN ROAD
TORONTO, JANUARY 24

Dear Margaret

Well, C. is safely off, and, as we have heard nothing from Washington, I expect safely arrived.... C. was in high spirits but just as we said good-bye and I hugged him he was a tiny bit teary—but most unnoticeably so and it only lasted a minute as John didn't even notice it.

Their train was late getting to Buffalo so John had only 15 minutes to get C. settled in the Washington train, but he showed him the "ropes," got him washed, and left him in his berth, partly undressed, in charge of the porter. John had to stay over night in Buffalo as there was no train back until morning. The only hitch they encountered was that the immigration officer (who makes his inspection on the train en route to Buffalo) had to collect an $8 head tax on C., which had to be in American funds—that rather put John "on the spot" and he had visions of sleeping in the railway station. You see we can only purchase American funds by making application to the Foreign Exchange Control Board, giving all details as to exactly what we want it for. When John applied they allowed him to get $5 for C. himself to take, and $8 to cover John's expenses for the night (taxi, hotel and breakfast). If he had known about the head tax he could have applied for that too and of course it would have been allowed. It is strange they did not tell him about it in the Consul's office—he paid the $11 fee there, for the immigrant visa and thought that was all that was necessary. (Mrs. Burns sent the funds for C's ticket as we are not allowed to buy transportation in the U.S.) However, John managed the $8 by taking $3.50 of C's money and the rest from his own $8, getting the cheapest room at the hotel, and arrived home with 30 cents in his pocket! Of course he had some Canadian money but that was no use. It was rather hard on C., but I will explain to Mrs. B. and I'm sure she will reimburse him though I don't like her to have to.

When I got home with Mary and Tom I found a parcel on my bed—a box of chocolates—with a letter on top addressed to me. C. had left it—it was very carefully and neatly written—his very best writing, and all correctly spelled. He said "I am giving you this little gift to show my gratitude for all you have done for me." I was completely surprised and very much touched. He had had more money than the $5 he was allowed to take, and after buying a box of chocolates to take to Nelly (the Burns' maid) he still had nearly a dollar left and kept talking about the strange position he was in, of having money he didn't know what to do with! I realise now he talked that way as a "blind" so I wouldn't suspect he was spending it on a present for me!

I spent Friday afternoon and Saturday morning cleaning C's room and moving Tom's possessions into it. Tom is quite thrilled to have it and it will save me a lot of stairs, as Tom was on the top floor before, and it means a lot of trips putting him to bed, seeing about his clothes and his room etc.—to say nothing of when he's ill. He says he doesn't miss C. at all except when there are dishes to wash or snow to shovel! Anne Innis had her birthday party yesterday afternoon, to which Mary went, so I suggested to Tom that he get Hugh to come out to play (he never thinks of making any move like that himself). Mary called Hugh for him on the telephone, and they went out and made a snow fort in the garden....

I must stop now—Tom has just come in—he asked to go to evening service to-night as one of the boys was singing a solo—professional jealousy?

[5]   90 DUNVEGAN ROAD
      TORONTO, JANUARY 31

Dear Margaret

Mail still seems to be rather delayed. We have had no letters from you since Jan. 18, when Tom had one written Dec. 14—before that we had letters, received about Christmas, written Nov. 27. I had a letter from Mrs. Beamish (Dec. 28—Jan. 27). I was so glad to hear from her.[2] I hope we can have Andrew here some time. Mid-term weekends have been discontinued because of expense and the necessity for reducing railway travel, but Easter is so late that I hope they will allow Peter a week-end at home sometime during term, as he is so close (65 miles). I doubt whether we shall be able to drive to see him again. The gasoline ration is being whittled down and we are warned that April 1 may end the ration entirely except for essential cars.

I had a letter from C. written the day he arrived in Washington, which I enclose. I was amused at his interest and evident delight in the luxuries (of the stomach!) available in the U.S.A. I feel a little guilty at the impression he must give them of the Spartan life of hardship we in Canada are enduring in the interests of total war! Actually we have only inconveniences and no hardships. Meat of any kind is very hard to come by, which makes fish and poultry equally scarce, but if this is a temporary situation we can manage all right, and if not, rationing will have to be instituted very soon. The butter ration is being reduced by ⅓ for the month of Feb. but it is hoped it will be restored to ½ lb. week by March.

Mother is much better so I have been able to discontinue my mornings there since Wednesday, and I do find my own household much easier with one less child—both in actual physical effort and in the wear and tear on the nerves....

I have discovered a very pleasant and reliable woman living very close who will come in and stay some evenings so John and I can get out occasionally. It will be a great help not to be so everlastingly tied and now that I am not so rushed during the day I expect to have a little more "ambition" to go out in the evening instead of just crawling into bed as early as possible.

I've had only a very brief note from Mrs. B. since C. arrived—she unfortunately had to be in New York the day he came. I expect she will write soon but this must have been a very busy week for her—her big report was to be released with all the attendant bustle and publicity (she is referred to in the press as a "female Beveridge!"[3] I do hope that by no freak of fortune the mumps could have cropped up!

I hope you're not having a severe winter and the coal supply is adequate for comfort.

[6]   90 DUNVEGAN ROAD
      TORONTO, FEBRUARY 7

Dear Margaret

... Not much time to write—this past week, mother being recovered and my own household lightened and having obtained, as I told you, the services (occasionally) of a "sitter-in" in the evenings, we thought we might try to pick up a few of the threads of our own life, all of which we've had to let drop this past strenuous year....

I had a letter this week from Mrs. B. reporting all going well in Washington. I enclose C's letter written the day he arrived. Have had no others but don't expect any.

[7]   [Letter 7, probably mailed on Feb. 15, was lost, but on May 16, when she was able to find a partial draft of the original letter, Marie sent it to Margaret. It lacked pp. 1–2.]

I shall enclose a letter I had from C. this week—I love his explanation of the school system—you have two chances a year to fail! He wrote Tom too, and tells him he does not have spelling, or writing as a subject—what a break for C.!—but I hope all his improvement won't be lost with no necessity to keep working. His mind as usual runs to food—he gave Tom a complete list of every article of food available in the school cafeteria! He does sound quite happy and at home.

I hope you won't let yourself worry unduly over the Mr. Harrison affair.[4] I dare say some people, if placed in the Ratcliffes' position, would feel insulted, but we all find the whole thing rather ludicrous, and are particularly amused at the thought of poor Mr. Harrison finding himself saddled with the launching in a career of an utterly unknown lad—rather like a bachelor who finds a baby on his doorstep!...

FEBRUARY 13

I am glad to hear news of Mrs. Beamish.... I can understand that so many evacuated children going back must turn your mind to the possibility of trying to get the boys back. However, as I have told you, I think it would be most unwise. It may be that there will be no more heavy raids on England and the prospect of an invasion, I should think, is slim, but there undoubtedly is danger, and when they've been here this long it does seem foolish to expose them to it—besides the danger of the ocean-crossing. Also they are infinitely better off here as far as food goes, so far, and I imagine life is much more normal than it could possibly be in England. Then too, though I am not one of those optimists who think the war will be over this year, still one feels now that it's not going to last forever—as it seemed last year. It is a long separation and very hard for you but I do think you would be well advised, having put up with it this long, to have patience until the end. Vivien feels the same way I do.

FEBRUARY 15

Yesterday the temperature dropped all day—by night it was 10° below zero with a howling north wind—what a night! And there was a practice black-out from 9–10! Hard on the poor A.R.P! This morning we got up to find it 20° below so I kept Mary home from school—she doesn't seem to have the resistance she used to, since her illness last autumn. I bundled Tom up well and gave him his lunch so he would not have the extra walk at noon in the cold. He was simply thrilled at being out in 20° below weather! Reported he didn't find it cold at all.

Tom, as I expected seems to be benefitting by C's absence. When he first came here Tom, as you know, was timid and fearful, obedient but very dependent and disinclined (it almost seemed, unable) to do anything for himself, to think for himself, or to make the smallest decision for himself. It did not take many months for him to lose his fears and to stop giving one the impression that he expected a bear to jump out at him from behind every door. We worked very hard to instil in him a sense of security, and we succeeded. But when that was achieved the real work began—he sank, in visible mental comfort, on the pillow of our care and thought for him, and would have gone on indefinitely, perfectly happy to do everything he was told, if we would go on ordering every detail of his life, telling him when to wash his hands and blow his nose, putting everything he needed into his hands, and doing all his thinking for him. To tell the truth, it would have been much easier for me, busy as I have been, to continue life in that way, but I felt I owed it to the child, for the sake of his future, to try to cultivate in him some measure at least of the independence and initiative he so badly lacked. It has been a long, slow, uphill struggle—I can't go into details—it would take too long and I just haven't the time, but our efforts are just recently beginning to bear fruit and we can see a real development in his ability (and, more important, a growing <u>desire</u>) to think for himself. Since C. went we think we can see a decided improvement in this direction, and I don't think it is our imagination. (Clare was here yesterday and remarked on the change in Tom since she last saw him.) C. did bully him whenever he had the chance, and constantly "smacked him down" so that Tom was afraid to use any initiative for fear of C's sneering at him or telling him he was wrong. He seems much more light-hearted and free and there have been a good many signs of increasing independence of thought and action—small incidents in themselves, but all pointing in the same direction. I have always felt that it was the best thing that could have happened, for all 3 boys, that the younger two were separated from Bill, and now I think it an almost equal blessing for Tom that he should be separated from C. It may seem a very unnatural situation, but Tom is a very unusual child....

[8] 90 DUNVEGAN ROAD
        TORONTO, FEBRUARY 21

Dear Margaret

There has been no English mail this week at all.

Tom has given an oral composition on the course of the war in North Africa, to date which he feels was pretty successful (the oral composition, I mean) and has also completed his project on early Toronto. He seems quite well now, after all his colds etc. earlier, and though there is an epidemic of mild flu and 12 to 14 boys in his class have been absent each day for the past 2 or 3 weeks, he seems to be surviving infection.

Bill was here yesterday for the afternoon and for dinner. His cold, which hung on for so long seems much better. He had a delightfully humourous letter from C., just received, which I told him he ought to send on to you as I was sure you would be very glad to read it. He could not possibly be at all homesick, to write like that.

I asked Tom last week if he had mentioned in his letter receiving the book and games from you. He said he had forgotten—I hope he remembers to-day.

[9]   90 DUNVEGAN ROAD
        TORONTO, FEBRUARY 28

Dear Margaret

... We have just come back from seeing Peter off at the station. It was good to have him home for the weekend, but the time went fast. He arrived Friday at dinner time. Yesterday (Saturday) he had numerous commissions to fill for the boys at school—parts and supplies for making aeroplane models (all of which are getting very scarce) and John and I took the two boys to see "In Which we Serve"—a very impressive and moving picture. Fortunately Mary was invited to a friend's for lunch and the afternoon, so it all fitted perfectly. This afternoon, before going to the station we all went to see mother. She is perfectly well again and her hearing almost completely restored—it has been slightly impaired anyway for some years. All Peter's spare time while home he spent in his room building aeroplanes, with Tom as an interested spectator. This is his great interest at the moment (cultivated in all the spare time he had while in the infirmary)—he finished a model for Mary while at home, and brought home (to leave for safety) a most intricate and elaborate one he had made at school. He amazes me by the skill and patience (not one of his outstanding virtues in ordinary life!) with which he cuts out and assembles the tiny parts (he has washers 1/8" in diam.) and the ingenuity and resourcefulness he shows.

I was struck with Tom's excitement at having Peter home—he never left his side while he was here. I think they all had a happy weekend.

After a few warm sunny days when the ice and snow melted amazingly fast, it turned cold and we had a heavy snowfall on Friday. However, it is gradually going again—I suppose it was too much to hope for winter being over so early, but it has been such a long winter that we're all heartily sick of it.

Dear Margaret

There have been no English letters this week.... On Mar. 1 the Feb. 10 number of Punch arrived, though Jan. 27 and Feb. 3 were missing. Of course it may be that the mails are disorganized (as they seem to have been all winter)—probably that is so as the Feb. 3 number arrived yesterday—but it made me think of the possibility of English mail at the end of Jan. having been sunk....

Mary and Tom brought home their reports for Jan. and Feb.—both splendid! Tom tied for first place in his class and Mary was first in hers—but the only teacher's comment on Mary's was "Mary talks in class"—to which Mary airily remarks "what of it?"—and her conduct is B—when I remonstrated with her she pointed out that B, according to the table given, means "Very good"—so what can you do with a girl like that? One can't say much when she comes out top of the class—all one's ground is cut from under one's feet! Anyway she is happy, cheerful and full of high spirits, so I guess I won't worry about the chatter box features. Tom has copied out his report to send you. I had him put in the Dec. marks too, as I think those were enclosed with the doubtful airmail letter.

To-morrow is "Parents Night" at the school, when the children's work is all on view in the rooms and the teachers present for consultation so John and I will have to go down or they will be dreadfully disappointed (the children, not the teachers!) ...

It was lovely to have Peter home last week end. He went back Sunday afternoon and on Monday morning I had a letter from him, written Sunday evening, telling me how he had enjoyed the weekend at home, thanking me for the movie (we took him and Tom to see "In Which We Serve") very heart-warming, as the usual Sunday letter would not be compulsory for him, having just come from home. We had a special treat while Peter was home—bacon for breakfast on Sunday—our first bacon for at least 6 months. It was a present from a friend in the meat-packing business. Seventy-five percent of all the hogs killed have to be sent to Britain and by the time the army camps, hotels, restaurants, etc. have their whack at the remaining 25%, there's none left to the ordinary consumer—except an odd bit here and there which falls to people with sufficient time, energy and perseverance to canvass shop after shop (I'm not one of them!). However, meat has been much more plentiful lately—strange how, after dozens of published statements that there are actually no cattle to be had, beef appears in the shops every time the Price and Trade Board allows a price increase! The beef, as well as being welcome in itself, provides dripping which is a help to the butter ration.

Tom is doing yeoman service with the snow shoveling to-day—John did a good deal of it after the snow stopped last evening but his back doesn't permit further effort of that kind to-day—too much of it last night, I expect....

[11] 90 DUNVEGAN ROAD
TORONTO, MARCH 14

Dear Margaret

This week have come, on March 8—a letter to Tom from you, dated Jan. 31, March 9—a letter to Tom (note enclosed for me) from your mother, dated Jan. 27, March 13—two airgraphs to Tom from his father, of <u>Jan. 30</u> and <u>Feb. 20</u>....

We have not heard from Washington for a month or more but knowing C's aversion to letter-writing I am neither surprised nor disappointed, and I know Mrs. Burns must be desperately busy just now, with her Natural Resources Planning Board report being presented.

The children are well—Tom is the picture of health—he has a good colour and an extraordinary clear, soft complexion and skin. (I am in such a state of anxiety over their health after all these months of epidemics and flu and illness, that I am getting almost superstitious and afraid to say or write anything like the above for fear he "comes down" with something tomorrow!) He and Mary get along <u>very</u> well—better than with C. here—and have so much light-hearted fun and nonsense. Hugh Innis has recovered from his mumps—he was never really ill but was quarantined, of course, for 3 weeks—and he and Tom have been playing together a good deal. Mary, Tom and the two Innis's went to the museum yesterday to a play and Punch and Judy Show for children....

John and I went to the Parents' Night at Brown School last Monday, when the pupils' work was on view and masters on hand for consultation. We had very good reports on the children. As I told you last week, Tom tied for 1st place and Mary was 1st in her class too. Mr. Pugh says there are 4 or 5 boys fairly evenly matched so there is good competition for Tom. I'm glad he reached first place, he has longed so for it, but I hope he won't worry too much about holding it. As long as he has a good percentage and doesn't drop back in any subject I feel he's doing well and try to make him feel the same.

He is as devoted as ever to the choir. They have altered the system of paying the boys and for Feb. he was paid $1.20. I now have more than $17 of his, for safe keeping. He feels so much wealth quite a burden and periodically discusses the advisability of spending some. I always encourage him in the idea but he never gets any further with it because he can't think of a single thing he wants!! Unusual (to say the least) in an 11 year old boy!

I hope the exam papers are cleared away by now and you are enjoying the spring. We shall certainly enjoy ours when it comes!

[12] 90 DUNVEGAN ROAD
TORONTO, MARCH 21

Dear Margaret

... I was thrilled to have Mrs. Burns call me on the telephone from Montreal this morning. She wrote me a day or two ago promising to do so if she had time during a weekend visit to Montreal. I imagine her life is one hectic rush since the publishing of her report. She reports C. very well and apparently happy, had a good school report—one B+, one C and all the rest B, which seems very good, entering a new school in a new country. His ruling passion at the moment is the Scouts, which he has just joined. She says they enjoy immensely having him and he makes friends wherever he goes....

To-morrow morning at 8.30 Mary is having her tonsils out and is in an advanced state of excitement this evening. I don't know <u>when</u> she'll get to sleep! I got so tired of having this operation hanging over me that Dr. Stock and I decided just to go ahead as soon as the surgeon could secure a room in the hospital....

I'm glad to know from your letters that mine seem to be arriving safely, if not in correct order. Sorry to hear of your illness—you <u>must</u> have been relieved to get exam papers <u>and</u> chapel lessons over!

I can understand your problem over what is best to do about Bill. The arguments pro and con are just as you state them and as you say the future is too uncertain to try to decide what is wisest. One needs clairvoyance as well as wisdom to know which course of action would be best for his education, but undoubtedly he would be much <u>safer</u> to stay here.

As for his clothes, as I said before I'd really much rather you didn't send any, though I know you want to do as much as you're allowed. As a matter of fact I've had to buy <u>very</u> little for Tom this winter and I think there are lots of summer clothes for him. The season for summer clothes is pretty short and they always have a good stock to allow for washing etc. so they last a long time and cricket shirts and cotton shorts don't seem to be outgrown so fast....

We have just heard that Bob [Marie's brother] has signed up for over-seas service. He has been in the "called-up" army, which cannot be sent outside Canada, except to Alaska or Newfoundland (where he is now) but I expect he thought when he was in the army he would rather be in the active forces. I don't know whether that will mean that he'll leave Nfld. right away or not....

[13] 90 DUNVEGAN ROAD
TORONTO, MARCH 30

... I am glad to hear you've had a mild winter. We have had a week of lovely mild weather with strong sun and the snow has almost gone. There are crocuses out in front of some houses which face south and Tom is quite worried because our only early flowers (a few scyllas and crocuses) are in a very shady spot under some shrubs where there is still a layer of ice and snow and he thinks we are going to be outdone by everyone else. He tried to shovel off the snow there but found it pretty solid!

He had quite an exciting weekend. On Saturday afternoon I sent him (with Hugh Innis) down to Varsity Arena to see the finals of the Public Schools skating races. The preliminaries were held in various public parks during the winter but the outdoor ice went too soon to have the finals in Riverdale Park in Feb. as planned. The "Evening Telegram" sponsored the whole affair as part of its British War Victims Fund campaign and at the finals they put on a hockey game and some trick and fancy skating to at-tract a crowd of children. There were numbers on the tickets and Tom had one of the lucky numbers and came home with a fountain pen! Thrills!

On Sunday Jo Robinson asked Tom over for the day so he went there direct from church in the morning and came home after evening service, again in great excitement. During the evening service the rector had read out the names of the choir boys (only 2 of them, Tom being one) who had perfect attendance during March, called them to the lectern and hung bronze crosses about their necks—which I suppose they are to wear for a month. What added to the thrill of this was that actually Tom had missed a choir practice (last Thursday evening) but as he had gone to the Ash Wednesday service, which was not obligatory, they counted that instead—so he felt he had won his cross just by the skin of his teeth! He missed last Thursday evening because he forgot all about it until it was much too late to go—the first time he has forgotten choir practice in more than a year—rather an interesting illustration of what I told you about Tom in one of last month's letters—how anything unusual will knock everything out of his head. That was the day that we had the news of Mary being put into Grade 5—(something which ranks in Mary's and Tom's minds in equal importance to the defeat of Rommel)—and he could think and talk of nothing else—apparently it completely drove all memory of choir practice from his mind....

[14] 90 DUNVEGAN ROAD
TORONTO, APRIL 4

Dear Margaret

... This will only be a short letter. It has been a trying week. Mary made a good recovery and was allowed back to school on Thursday, it being a warm, perfect spring day, but I was pretty well exhausted with all the worry and strain. Then Friday morning she was ill again, having apparently picked up a bad throat infection, quite independent of her tonsillectomy. I had a bad 36 hours, keeping cold cloths on her forehead, trying to make her drink, etc., with her temp over 103½°. However, by last evening she was a good deal better and is further improved to-day. I do hope it will clear quickly. It does seem too bad, she has had so much illness this winter....

Will try to write more next time. Tom seems to be doing very well in his exams. I suppose poor Mary will miss most of hers—just when she's been promoted.

[15] 90 DUNVEGAN ROAD
TORONTO, APRIL 11

Dear Margaret

Mary is much better but is still in bed—I have not been able to keep her temp. down to normal for a long enough period to let her up. It is very wearing, especially as I feel so sorry for the child missing so much school and all her April exams—I'm afraid she'll never be able to stay in the advanced grade. However, her health is the important thing. This makes the third week she has been in bed. The tenderness seems to have gone from her throat and her ears now.

Peter came down with mumps a week ago—it had been prevalent in the school for some time and last week even the Junior School headmaster succumbed! I am really not sorry Peter got it as it's a nasty disease to have later in life but it was very upsetting as it will interfere with his going to Montreal for the Easter holiday with one of his school friends....

Tom is in very good health. I am almost superstitiously afraid to say that for fear he comes down with something tomorrow! I am simply longing for warm weather to come so I can escape from this ever-present apprehension of illness which this awful winter has brought on! One of the blessings of having fewer children in the house is that there are not so many to be ill! We have had some lovely sunshine lately but it is still very cold—we have a few scyllas just about to bloom, though how the poor things stand the frost every night I don't know. We even had quite a snowfall during the past week!

Bill came down yesterday to see Tom. I did not see much of him as, it being Saturday afternoon, I took the opportunity of John's being home to get down town to do a little very pressing shopping. However, he stayed for dinner with us, and is looking very well—has been making some marvellous marks in his exams which are not over yet....

[16] 90 DUNVEGAN ROAD
TORONTO, APRIL 18

Dear Margaret

We have had no mail this week except the letter to Tom which went to Vivien's. Bill brought it down to Tom....

We have had wretched weather—snow every day this past week, with a heavy, wet, fall all day Friday—nearly 4 inches! It has been very depressing, especially with Mary slowly recovering and allowed up by Wednesday, as restless as a colt in a stall, but impossible for her to go out until there was some warmth and sunshine. She spent her time "composing" two "pieces" for the piano and the constant strumming did not tend to soothe the nerves! She wrote them out neatly in her music book with M. F. WILLIAMSON 1933—in the upper corner, and is now just <u>living</u> to see them in print![5]

Peter got home yesterday, having had 3 extra days at school to rid himself of mumps. We took Mary to the station to meet him as it was slightly warmer. Tom had gone to the movies with Hugh Innis to see a Hitchcock thriller "Shadow of a Doubt." Hugh goes to the movies just about as seldom as our children (one of the comforting things about having the Innis's as neighbours) but Mary Innis had seen this picture and, Tom said, pronounced it "quite fit" for them to see....

I had a letter this week from Mrs. Burns, reporting C. with a cold—his first illness. She is frightfully busy, speaking here there and everywhere, trying to get articles written and regular work done, though very short handed at the office. She is away about 3 nights a week. I don't expect to hear from C.—he hates writing letters and all the time he was here I don't think he would have written a single letter to you if he hadn't been made to. I mentioned this when a visitor asked me if I had news from C., and added that Mrs. Burns, being unaccustomed to children, might not put as much pressure on C. to see that he wrote you. "Oh I think she would" said Tom earnestly "you know the summer we spent with Mrs. Burns she expected us to write once a week to you." "Well, if so, Tom" I replied, much surprised "she must have been seriously disappointed, because you didn't write me a single letter all that summer." "<u>Didn't</u> I?" asked Tom, the picture of amazement. "No" I said "C. wrote me <u>once</u>, but you didn't write at all." Tom pondered a moment and his face cleared. "Ah!" he said "then it must have been our <u>mother</u> we wrote to once a week"!!

Incidentally, I have told Tom that from now on I expect him to take personal responsibility for his letters. He is not, like C., averse to writing, but though I have had them write every Sunday (unless away for the day) and always at the same time (after dinner) he has never <u>once</u> remembered to write without being reminded. One would think that after well over 100 Sundays it would become a habit—yet when Mary has been in bed and he had time on his hands, he would "put in time" all Sunday afternoon, sometimes utterly bored, until, seeing that he would never think of it himself, I would suggest his writing his letter. I pointed out to him that he has only forgotten choir practice two or three times since he joined the choir—that is something he <u>wants</u> to do, and, more important, that he knows <u>no one will remind him of</u>. So I have told him that I intend to write every Sunday, as before, and if he produces a letter I will enclose it—if not, mine will go without it. I notice that he has written his to-day. It's just the same old evasion of responsibility—if someone else will do the remembering he doesn't bother....

P.S. Your cheque arrived this week. Thank you very much.

[17] 90 DUNVEGAN ROAD
   TORONTO, MAY 2

Dear Margaret

... We did not write last Sunday—I was even more overwhelmed than usual, last week-end—usually I can count on a couple of hours Sunday afternoon—the only free time I have all week—and that is when I write you. Tom was at the Robinsons'—the ever-kind Jo asked him over for the holidays, so he went Good Friday morning and came back last night. Apparently he intended to write you last Sunday—even remembered to take notepaper with him—but he forgot to take your address so did not think it worth while writing. Some time ago I found that he did not have the remotest idea what either your address or his father's was—he did not even know what county Abbotsholme was in! One would think he'd have enough interest and curiosity to want to know, and he has often posted the letters to you, and it's often been on your letters to him, but it just didn't matter to him. However, I thought he ought to know your addresses, so wrote them out on a paper for him to keep in his writing case—but it didn't do him much good! By the way, Tom gave me his father's airgraph to read, in which he mentions having Tom's letter of Feb. 28, so apparently that arrived safely. All mail seems to be very irregular, so I expect your letters have been held up....

Tom got an excellent report for March-April. He is sending you his marks. In practically every subject he has done better than last time and his average is well above last time. But he was frightfully cast down over it and kept repeating he'd done <u>very</u> badly—<u>because</u>, while last time he tied for first place, this time he is 4th! Poor Tom—he <u>does</u> so want to be "the best in the class"—I think he'd <u>much</u> rather be first with 75% than get 100% if some others did the same! However, both John and I took no notice of his laments as to his standing, but were loud in our commendation of his improved marks in so many subjects.

Poor Mary got no report at all, of course, though Miss Watt, I believe, has promised to give her some individual exams after the holidays—presumably to see whether she is able to stay in Grade 5....

Peter's Easter report came in—he was 1st with an average of 82.6—excellent, considering especially, all the time he missed with illness and that he wrote his exams while in bed with mumps. No time for more now. I hope some of your letters come in this week. Punch and Tom's paper came last week after a lapse.

P.S. I am putting this on a separate sheet as I know my letters sometimes go the rounds of the family. In letter [45] (Dec. [12]) I gave my views on the question of telling the boys about their father's re-marriage. In case that letter was lost—I was strongly against telling them. Like you, I can't really imagine them feeling any tremendous personal concern, though one never knows—especially with Christopher. However—I would willingly wager everything I possess that Tom has <u>completely</u> and <u>utterly</u> forgotten the fact that you and his father are divorced, and I can imagine the utter bewilderment of the child and how the earth would be knocked from under him after all my careful and painstaking building up of his sense of security. With Tom, the effect of such an upset would be very far-reaching—it's hard to explain in a letter, but he is such a creature of habit and so slow to grasp any new ideas that any (even slight) upsetting experience, or the abrupt reversal of an idea he has held, or even any change in daily routine throws him into a fog of forgetfulness and indecision affecting every detail of his daily life. So, if there is no good reason <u>for</u> telling him, I don't see why he should be subjected to this shock. And, to speak quite selfishly, I don't see why <u>I</u> should be required to shoulder the task of guiding Tom through such a (to me) unnecessary crisis. It does seem strange that, though Mr. Sharp is convinced that the news will be very upsetting to the boys, yet he is the one who wants to tell them. I wonder whether it occurs to him that whatever bad consequences the news has on the boys will have to be borne, not by him, 3,000 miles away, but by the people now in charge of the boys, who all have already enough to cope with. He seems more and more to me a person who wants all the rewards of parenthood with none of the penalties. Forgive me for being so outspoken, but I do <u>not</u> think the decision should rest with him at all.

[18]   90 DUNVEGAN ROAD
         TORONTO, MAY 9

Dear Margaret

On May 4 Tom had a letter from you written March 15.... Your airgraph to me arrived May 7—also the one to Vivien. We agreed in thinking that you were quite needlessly disturbed over the possibility of Bill's hearing the news of his father. He never sees the Wilkinsons or Mrs. Bland—except to say "How d'you do" at an occasional Parents' Night at U.T.S. As for David Bland—while he was at U.T.S. he was no more to Bill than any other fellow-pupil at a large school—I don't think he and Bill ever "hit it off" and I don't suppose they ever exchanged more than a greeting. Now that David is at University I don't suppose Bill has even seen him since he left U.T.S. last June. And even if he did see them I cannot imagine anything more unlikely than their telling him. I saw Edith Wilkinson by chance yesterday at the reception at the university—she had had your airgraph also, and she corroborated our views.[6] She said on getting your airgraph she at once telephoned Mrs. Bland who said she had not told David (there would be no reason for doing so, as I expect Mr. S. is only a name to him) and if she <u>had</u> she was certain he would never think of mentioning it to Bill. I hope this puts your mind at rest, though of course, as I think I said in my first letter on the subject, my somewhat strenuously worded opposition to telling the boys applied chiefly to the younger ones. If you would rather have Bill know, that is entirely a matter between you and him. I have no idea, nor has Vivien, whether the news would upset him or not, but if it did, I don't think any of us would know about it. He is extremely reticent on all personal matters and as I told you, has never indicated in any way that you and his father were separated. Of course, after the worry that this "false alarm" has caused you, you may think it better to tell him yourself, in case some similar situation should arise again. If so, be assured that I should not oppose your doing so.

I am rather mystified by your reference to a letter to Bill which may have upset him, but "if so he can be reassured that you intend him to remain here"—but I suppose the letter which you say you have sent me will clarify that. However, I can imagine nothing more unlikely than (in the event of his being unsettled by what you said to him) his consulting either me or Vivien about it. I don't remember his ever telling either of us anything you had written him—except at the time of discussing his school work. Neither of us has ever told him that you had (in letters to us) spoken of even the possibility of his going home—and I don't think such a possibility has ever entered his head—he takes it for granted, as do we, that he will stay here until the war's end. Vivien did let him read the letter from the Committee (stating the policy of the Govt. towards evacuees returning—by the way we have wondered whether you received your copy of it as you've not mentioned it) and his only comment was that it didn't apply to him at all as the war was bound to be over before he was 18. I am telling you all this to show you that there is apparently no conflict in his mind over the question at all.

Tom had a letter from C. not long ago which sounds as though he were very happy. I was _much_ impressed by the spelling—all the simple words which he used to get wrong, were right (except "brougther")—I don't know whether it's the result of the U.S. school system, painstaking care, or just chance—probably the last. I will ask Tom to enclose it for you to read....

I have registered Mary for 4 weeks at Cedarnook Camp and Tom for 6 weeks at Pioneer, both starting about July 1. We are applying for a junior membership in the Royal Canadian Yacht Club here for Peter. With that he can go over to the Yacht Club, on the Island, across the harbour, every morning. They spend the day there, learning how to do everything about a boat, and learning to sail—also swim in the big swimming pool. It is not as satisfactory a summer arrangement as in peace time, of course, as they naturally have not the corps of young men as instructors and guides that they would like. However, I hope Peter will enjoy it. When he's been at school all year we don't like to send him to camp, both for financial reasons, and because we'd like to see something of him in the holidays....

Tom asked me the other day if he might play in the school bantam baseball team, if he could get on it. Of course I assured him I could think of nothing more satisfactory and utterly splendid—however they had the practice to choose the team on Tuesday afternoon, when Tom has to go to choir practice, so he had no chance even to try for the team. He simply couldn't conceive of missing choir practice and not wearing the cross on the red ribbon which denotes perfect attendance!

Not content with the choir activities he has <u>now</u> joined the Sunday School! Apparently one afternoon when there was time to spare at choir practice the asst. choir leader, who also works in the Sunday School, was giving one of the boys the S.S. examination. Tom overheard the questions and showed interest so Allan told him that he was conducting an exam in the S.S. on last Sunday afternoon and he could come and try it if he liked. If he <u>liked</u>!—offering Tom an examination is like offering the normal boy a chocolate bar, so off he went last Sunday. I hadn't realised there was any more to it than the exam, but apparently he is going regularly—has his card punched for attendance, envelopes for his collection (they know how to intrigue the children)—perhaps there's a more advanced exam as a bait, I wouldn't know. Any way, it gives him a busy and important Sunday....

No more now—very late.

[**UNNUMBERED LETTER**, *enclosing first draft of the lost letter no. 7, which has been placed in this sequence at Feb. 15.*]

No. 7 must be lost and I find I must have rewritten page 3 on, to send you, and still have the first draft from that point, so am sending it enclosed.

90 DUNVEGAN ROAD
TORONTO, MAY 16
Rehash of no. 7, sent Feb. 14

Dear Margaret

This is the partial copy (from page 3 on) of letter no. 7, which I told you in no. 19 I would send. At the top of page 3 I was apparently into the clothes question. I do hope I have not seemed brusque or unappreciative in my requests to you not to send clothes. I do understand your anxiety to do as much as you are allowed for the boys' up keep, and I appreciate it, but it does seem so dreadful for you to pay high prices for inferior goods—especially when the much superior English made things come out here and sell for less. However, this condition may not last as we are being warned by the authorities to expect a <u>real</u> clothes shortage by autumn (when rationing will probably start) especially in boys' and childrens' clothes. (Incidentally, as part of the standardization program, to curtail waste of cloth, no more short trousers are being made for boys 12 years and over, and frantic mothers, trying to buy shorts for boys of 12, or "oversize" boys of 9 and 10, are advised by the salespeople to buy longs and cut off the legs!) As far as suits and trousers and coats go, Tom is well provided for. I have got Peter some longs for "special occasions" and I expect next autumn he will be into them for good (I don't like it much but he'll be nearly 14 and the others wear them, though I think he secretly prefers shorts as more comfortable). Now I know that in one letter (possibly this same 7 on the page before the one I have), I suggested your sending winter underwear for Tom as his is pretty well done for. Then in a later letter (which, again, may possibly be this same dashed 7) I revoked this request, as I thought it might be advisable, at least for Peter's first winter in longs, for him to wear long underwear, in which case his present stock could come down to Tom. I suggested that what would be more acceptable would be one or possibly two more pullovers of the same style as the one you sent Tom early in the year.... The pullover was size 34 which is right—a little bit large now, but he will start to wear it in the autumn and constant washings do shrink them a bit. He wears a pullover every day to school for at least 8 months of the year, so if you <u>could</u> send 2 more he would be well provided for the coming year (those he has are just getting pretty small and are well darned).... Apparently in letter 7 I enclosed a letter from C.—too bad you didn't get it. It's the last I've had from him.

Most of the news in the enclosed is old now but it's easier to send it "as is" than to copy out the bits I want you to have. One thing I did want you to get was the account of Tom's development, which is germane to the reasoning in the P.S.—I suppose it's not necessary to send this P.S. as you got my previous letter dealing with the same subject but this explains my reasons about Tom a little more fully.

I will enclose Tom's letter with this as it may be a few days before I can get no. 19 off—my regular weekly letter for May 16.

Let's <u>hope</u> this goes safely. Really though, to think of 46 out of 47 arriving in 1942 is remarkable!

Dear Margaret

... Such a long letter, yours of April 20, I feel quite at sea as to where to start. To begin with, I expect my no. 7, of Feb. 14 must have been lost. (If I had foreseen the frustrations and complications of such a voluminous correspondence, in July 1940, I should certainly have made an effort to get a typewriter, so I would have copies in case of loss.) It was a long one, and apparently I rewrote from page 3, and still have my original (from that point), which is probably much like the one I posted, so I will send that to you, but will send it separately, to avoid confusing it with this one.

MAY 17

... I am sorry to hear that (as I feared) C. has defaulted in his letter writing since he escaped from my stern supervision. I found that with C. suggestions or appeals to his feelings fell on absolutely deaf ears—I had to say, each Sunday "Write your letter"—nor could I say "Write your letter sometime to-day" or "When you finish such and such, write your letter," I had to wait until he was quite free and unengrossed and then say "Write your letter now." I can quite understand that Mrs. Burns hasn't the time to do this, nor can she have time to write you often and fully herself to make up for his remissness or the brevity and perfunctoriness of his usual letters, as I have done. However, the old saw "no news is good news" is true in spite of its triteness, though it's cold comfort in your position, I know. When I next write him I will try to impress his responsibility on him though I don't think it will have any effect....

Meat rationing is to start in a week or so, on a basis of 2 lb. a week, which seems a very adequate allowance, though the working out of the system is going to be a headache for the butchers and the authorities, I'm sure. The standard they work on is, I think, meat with $\frac{1}{10}$ bone, and if we buy cuts with less bone we're allowed less than 2 lbs., if cuts with more bone, more than 2 lbs. It does seem complicated—I am glad I have a trustworthy butcher and will have to leave it to him! My difficulty with him is that he's over a mile away and with the meagre gas rationing I can't waste it driving over for the meat. I lugged an 8 lb. joint home by street car the other day and expect I'll have to continue—the only consolation is that after rationing starts they won't be 8 lb. ones! Our present shortage is potatoes which are practically unobtainable and all the other vegetables (which of course at this time of year are imported) are sky high in price, reflecting the inflated U.S. prices. We'll just have to put up with this situation until our own are available which will be very late this year, because of the late spring—scarcely anything is even planted yet.

Also, because of the desperate farm labour situation the farmers are planting much less than usual, though of course a great many people intend growing their own vegetables. We considered doing this, but our garden is all so shady that we decided it would just be a waste of valuable seed. John dug up an old rose bed in the only reasonably sunny part and planted some carrots and lettuce and we are going to fill it with tomato plants as soon as these are available, but I don't think we'll attempt any more. We have some rhubarb plants in the most sheltered spot and hope it will be ready soon. We are allowed an extra pound of sugar per person this spring to use for rhubarb. Actually the sugar and butter rations are more than adequate and the tea and coffee not bad when one gets accustomed to them. We are to be allowed 10 lbs. sugar per person for bottling fruit and making jam this summer. I don't think I can manage to do much more than that anyway, though I can spare some sugar from the rations. One can't help a feeling of necessity to do a lot when we are warned by the Price and Trade Board that there may be no jam or canned fruit for the public next autumn or winter. However, we are not really worrying, we must have much more (both in quantity and variety) than you, and you can manage, so we can too.

I don't think I can contribute anything of value to the solution of the problem of Bill's education and future. You seem to have canvassed thoroughly all the pros and cons but there are so many "ifs" which no one can answer. If he wins a scholarship, as he certainly should do, it does seem logical for him to go to U. of T. for a year anyway. I think you are well advised to investigate the possibilities of a transfer to Cambridge, if, at the end of the year, you should think that desirable.... I don't think there is any danger of him becoming "Canadianised" but I dare say for a youth starting out in the world in England the prestige of an Oxford or Cambridge degree would be much more valuable than a degree from U. of T. Vivien is trying to sound out Bill's own ideas.... Vivien told me to-day that when having this discussion with Bill last night, he told her, quite spontaneously, that he had never in his life experienced such a complete feeling of happiness as he does at present—as though everything were going the right way. I know Vivien is writing you and will have a much more useful contribution than I. I really see Bill very little—he likes to come to see Tom once in a while and we are always glad to have him and he knows he is always welcome. Of course since the Easter holidays he has been very hard at work and has only been once. When he is here he and Tom play games, etc. and I am usually pretty busy so it is a long time since I've had any "serious" conversation with him.[7]

MAY 18

(during the blackout, 9 P.M.–10 P.M. sitting in the telephone cupboard, the only room I can black out) ...

We were awfully pleased to hear from Mrs. Burns that she is to be in Toronto to-morrow. She is to speak at the Annual Meeting, to-morrow evening, of the Canadian Welfare Council, and will telephone me when she arrives and finds what part of her time will be occupied with official duties. It is too bad John went to New York to-night but he hopes to have breakfast with her when she arrives in New York Friday morning. Vivien and I, of course, have never met her and are looking forward to it. We hope she can give us all her free time because we want her to come to our house and to Vivien's, and of course to see both boys. She leaves Thursday (20th) at 6.15, for New York. I will send you the article from our "Globe & Mail" published when the President presented her report to Congress. There has not been much more in our papers about it, though there have been articles in John's insurance periodicals, of course. I hope you got the article I sent you about Dr Marsh, author of our Canadian social security report, which has an amusing reference to Mrs. Burns....

I feel very badly for Vivien just now. She is under a tremendous strain. Her mother had another heart attack about 2 weeks ago and agreed to come to stay for a bit with Viv., but in 10 days was feeling so much better she insisted on going home again. It is a dreadful worry for Vivien, having her living alone, with her heart condition, but she would never be happy in any one else's house and it is so difficult to find a satisfactory person to live with her. Vivien telephones her night and morning but there is always the fear that something may happen during the night. Then John [Ratcliffe] is to enter the R.C.A.F. on July 1. That is hard for any mother but I've heard so many of her friends say that somehow it seems worse for Vivien. I have never known so close a bond between mother and son as there is between Vivien and John, and always has been. Of course he is a son any mother might be proud of "he has everything" as the saying is. She never hints, even, that she feels at all badly at his enlisting—he had to get Harry's consent as he was under age and of course, he would not only have been exempt from military service until graduation, because of the technical nature of his course, but actually had great difficulty in obtaining a release from his course to allow him to enlist.... I do wish Harry could be home—he is such a tower of strength and encouragement, but he is so useful on the National Finance Council that I'm sure they'll never let him leave. It is a long time now—since Nov. '41—he gets home most weekends for 2 days but has to spend most of them at his own business here or having meetings at the house, and answering the telephone interminably. I'm glad the Loan just floated was such a success—the objective was $1,100,000,000 and it is well oversubscribed.

I simply must stop now—and pray that this letter isn't sunk—not that it's of much value to you, but it's taken so much time to write!...

P.S. I've had my mind so on your letters, while writing this that I've quite forgotten the war news though it's all we can think of most of the time. Isn't it grand to have the other fellow surrendering for a change! We simply couldn't believe the sudden collapse in Tunisia—and now the bombing of the two big dams must have had terrific consequences in Germany. We are waiting for more news of Attu—we haven't liked that Aleutian situation and are glad something has been started.[8] Expect to hear Mr. Churchill address Congress to-morrow afternoon....

[20] 90 DUNVEGAN ROAD
         TORONTO, MAY 23

Dear Margaret

... The big event of this week was, of course, Eve Burns' visit to Toronto. John was unfortunately in New York for most of the week, but Eve went on to New York from here on Thursday night, and breakfasted with John there on Friday morning. She arrived here about noon Wednesday and was of course officially occupied for the rest of the day with the Canadian Welfare Council, whose annual meeting she was attending as guest speaker. Vivien, Bill and I went to the meeting Wed. eve. at which she spoke and had a chat after. It seemed very strange to meet, actually for the first time, someone who seemed like such an old friend from all the correspondence we've had.

Vivien and I both "took to her" at sight and the more we saw of her the better we liked her. Quite apart from her brilliant intellect, which goes without saying, she has such a keen, alert mind and eye, so much practicality and sound common sense, a marvellous sense of humour, a perfect sense of proportion and the utmost tolerance—in fact, to use her own favourite endorsation—she is "a swell human being." I do think C. is enormously lucky in his new foster home. I don't know where he could have had such a combination of excellent influences, both intellectual and social.

She reports C. is getting on splendidly, growing like a weed (she brought a suit case full of out-grown clothes also the dressing gown—such a nice one, and it will do Tom beautifully next winter) and fitting into their home on the whole very well. They have a "Victory Garden" outside the city where they spend Sundays and some weekends and she says his back is broad and brown and muscular and he is the picture of health.

She has been away a great deal of late, on speaking trips, sometimes home only one day a week, but you need have no fear for his physical care. For one thing C. is perfectly strong and tough and needs no more care than the average healthy boy—excessive mothering is anathema to him and he is very well looked after in Eve's absence by Arthur and Nelly, the coloured housekeeper. It was Nelly's possible reactions to a child in what has always been an adult home that gave me the most trepidation but Eve says she has entered into the new arrangements with the greatest enthusiasm, is fond of C., and refused any increase in wages because of her added duties, though the household management, of which she is in full charge, is further complicated by shortages, restrictions and point rationing.[9] So that is very satisfactory. C. is doing quite well in school (4 A's in his last report, a disappointing C in English and F in P.T.!) but she feels, as I did that, if he tried, he could do a lot better. They have, of course, had all the same difficulties with C. that we had—like a great many children he will "get away with" as much as he possibly can and a lot of activities which were not allowed in our house have been trotted out again and tried out, in hopes, I suppose, of more leniency from inexperienced "parents." However, I think they are managing him wonderfully and I do hope he repays their generosity and infinite fairness with his co-operation.[10]

To get back to Eve's visit—on Thursday she was through with the broadcasting station by lunch time and we took her in tow for the rest of the day—had lunch, brought her to our house to see Tom, went on to Vivien's for tea and to see Bill, out to dinner, and deposited her at her train at 8.15.[11] We only wished she could have stayed several days. Bill asked Vivien "Do you see what I meant, now, when I said she was the 'happiest' person I had ever known?" And we did know exactly what he meant.... I took it for granted she would know of [Mr. Sharp's] marriage—there would be far more reason for telling her than me, she being an old friend of both of you, and my only interest in the matter being the boys' connection with it. So when she did not mention it all day, I thought it was in deference to Vivien's and my ignorance and just before she left I broached the subject, to her great surprise. She was surprised, not only at the news, but that there should be any secrecy and thought the boys should be told, especially

Bill. Her reasoning was that when they go back home there will be many difficult adjustments for them which should not be further complicated by this one, also that when Bill <u>does</u> know, he may resent not having been told earlier.

I suppose my own view, of not telling the younger ones at least, was a rather selfish one—there have been so many difficulties and problems with Tom that when it seemed that <u>this</u> was one problem which <u>could</u> be shelved until after he was out of my care, I was all for shelving it—and I suppose that feeling was intensified by my resentment (perhaps unfounded) at their father's arrogating to himself the privilege of taking an action which he felt was inimical to their happiness, while evading its consequences. Nevertheless, from Tom's own side of the matter, I can't quite agree with Eve. When they go back, I don't think Tom will have anything like the adjustments that C., with his much stronger personality, will have to face— I expect Tom will slip into the "new old" life easily, and at any rate the comfort and security of his mother's companionship should cushion any shock there may be. Of course we may all be getting wrought up over nothing—perhaps the news whenever it came, wouldn't bother him at all—and even if he got it now and it upset him a lot, I rather think that if he weren't constantly reminded of it he'd have forgotten it entirely by the time he goes back to England. He has enormous powers of forgetfulness!...

[21] 90 DUNVEGAN ROAD
  TORONTO, MAY 30

Dear Margaret

... Edith Wilkinson was here to lunch the other day, with Vivien. David Bland, who, as you know, won the same scholarship at U.T.S. as Bill is now holding, and tried scholarship Matric. last year, as Bill is about to do, and entered Math. & Phys. on a good scholarship last autumn, as Bill hopes to do next autumn, is going to try for a Cambridge scholarship in August. It does seem like a concrete case to get information about, in case you should decide that would be a good thing for Bill to do next year. Apparently David felt himself well prepared by his work here for the exams, except in one subject which he will work on this summer while in England....

We have been working rather hard at the garden (mostly John) and the people across the way are beginning to compliment him on what he has achieved from the awful tangle of shrubbery and spotty plantings which disfigured the front lawn—all a picture of neglect. No more now—hope you're not having too hard a term.

Dear Margaret

On June 4 Tom got your letter of May 8 and on June 5 an airgraph from his father of May 17.

Tuesday was the first day we felt it safe to let the furnace out and by Wednesday the temp. was 84° and we had 3 hot, humid days, which brought the flowers out with a rush. The garden is really very pretty in an overgrown untidy sort of way—so green from all the rain and the huge big lilacs of all varieties in full bloom, also the bridal wreath, honeysuckle, weigelia and several other shrubs. To-day is cold and dull which will help to hold the bloom a little while—it goes so fast when it's hot.

Yesterday was the big annual event at Brown School—the garden fete. In a weak moment I promised to help at the hot dog stand. As you probably know, hot dogs are frankfurter sausages, boiled and inserted in a long soft bun, by slitting the bun almost through. This is then daubed with prepared mustard and is the favourite between meals food of growing boys. It turned out to be pretty hectic as we had only two small temperamental gasoline stoves to cook 100 lbs. [of] frankfurters while at least 100 children were surrounding the booth continuously, brandishing their nickels and begging for hot dogs. I was glad when the last one was sold and I could leave with a clear conscience but by then the rest of the fair was over and everything sold. I think next year I'll engage myself in advance to help Edith Wilkinson, who always runs the book stall! Or perhaps by that time hot dogs will be on the rationed list!...

Last Sunday evening Tom went to some sort of meeting connected with Pioneer Camp. His last year's counsellor came for him and brought him home. I gather it was a sort of party, with the camp movies, and also a meeting of the leaders and counsellors, with a few campers, Tom among them, who were asked to say what they particularly liked about the camp—as an aid in planning the program for this year....

I've had a bothersome throat all week—a sort of laryngitis, which I don't seem able to lose. I hope it won't last.

Dear Margaret

... I was glad to hear from you but sorry you were so overwhelmed with work and had a bad cold. I think having to do desk work without enough heat is pure torture. We are trying to get in our next winter's coal but are by no means sure of it (or of the quality of what we can get)—the coal mining situation in the U.S.A., where we get most of our coal, is so uncertain. We are, at any rate, at last having warm enough weather that we can do without fires—and even hope for some strawberries in a week or two!

John and I went to Peter's school for Speech Day yesterday—it was a beautiful day and we enjoyed it immensely. We have been hoarding our gasoline ever since April 1, when the ration was cut to 10 gal. month (about 180 miles), because he was looking forward so to having us come. This has been a record-breaking year at the school in many ways—the record number of boys (67 in the Junior School, 184 in the Senior School) a record amount of illness, a record for bad weather of all kinds at all seasons, and a record shortage of domestic help. The whole school has always made their own beds but now the Senior School boys look after their own rooms entirely, do all the dining room work, waiting and clearing tables and some of the boys, to make extra pocket money, are doing the washing up. It has been a very trying year for the staff but they have stood the test nobly and the boys have not suffered a scrap in any way from their elders' manifold worries. And in spite of rationing and (which is worse) difficulties of supply, they are marvellously fed. I have the greatest admiration for them all.

I saw Andrew Beamish, looking very fit and chipper, he tells me his brothers are very well and he was off on the night train to join them—is quite blasé about his lone trips to New York now! Peter, to our surprise, won two prizes, the general proficiency for his form and the religious knowledge (!). (I gather the latter is entirely memory work.) We brought Michael Brodeur (whom Peter visited in Montreal) home with us to stay 10 days. He is a dear little boy, rather quiet but not shy. I think the 4 of them have gone off to play cricket this afternoon. (Tom even decided to skip Sunday School!—not, of course without great deliberation, and attempting to put the decision on me, which I dodged by saying Sun. School was entirely his affair.)[12]

Mr. Tottenham tells me that he is going to have Peter try for the Senior School scholarship next year but warned me it is pretty stiff. I can't help hoping so much he can get it, we like the school so much we would like him to be able to go on through the Senior School, and the scholarship means $500 a year for 4 years, without which we might not be able to keep him on but I am trying not to think about it, and above all not to let Peter think we expect him to be able to make it. He has developed into a good student and has lots of common sense and determination and a good sense of proportion. This year has done a great deal for him. He wants to go to Burlington after Michael goes home to pick berries or do anything useful that is available and make a little money.

I had a bad sore throat last week, topped by a lot of tooth ache which is still bothering me, though I have been daily to the dentist—a practically defunct wisdom tooth which I'm horribly afraid will have to come out. I wish it had waited until the children get away at the end of the month!

I have got things pretty well in order for the children's departure to camp—as much as I can do this far in advance. I do hope we have good warm weather for them in July....

[24]

I think your letters have all arrived—there are big gaps and then a bunch.

90 DUNVEGAN ROAD
TORONTO, JUNE 21

Dear Margaret

... Last week was pretty hectic with two [Tom's and Mary's] birthdays, Peter and his friend Michael here, Mrs. Fairfoul collapsing in the laundry just as she started the washing and me having to get her up to a bed and keep running up and down to see that she was all right and to get the washing done (I knew that if I didn't, she'd be staggering down to finish it as soon as she could stand) while I waited for a taxi to take her home—and every-thing complicated by a furiously aching wisdom tooth which the dentist had to keep deadening as I simply couldn't take time off to get it out until after Mike went home (he went to-day and it's to come out to-morrow). Incidentally Mrs. F. couldn't come back for the rest of the week but <u>did</u> turn up this morning, when I had to forcibly restrain myself from falling on her neck. However we sailed through all right and did enjoy having Michael. He is a dear boy.

Tom apparently was overjoyed with his birthday—we went out for the afternoon and picnic supper to the Cruikshanks' place in the country— more of a treat now that the gasoline ration is so slim and they all had a marvellous time. Birthday cakes are hard to come by now but I had deco-rated Tom's myself and it was quite impressive....

To-day Mary and Tom each had a letter from C. enclosing $1 to each for their birthdays. He explained that he intended to send them presents but couldn't understand the regulations and to send money you couldn't send less than a note, so he was now broke! Too bad the poor kid didn't think of sending $1 between them. It's also too bad he couldn't see how impressed they were!

Bill came in Saturday morning to wish Tom a happy birthday and bring a present. He seems to be standing up to the strain of exams well and not unduly worried. I do hope he does well but am sure he will....

Tom is looking forward to going to camp next Tuesday—I only hope he can get his things ready without a scramble. Mary goes on Wed. but I want to send the luggage of both on Monday. The Union Station is a bedlam these days! I don't think Tom will have any qualms at going to camp alone. Some of the boys in his class at school are going—one, who sits behind him, was there last year too and was quite a friend of C's, and of course he knows the counsellors and so will have no feeling of strangeness.

I _am_ sorry that C. does not write oftener but I'm afraid I'm not surprised. I tried the whole 2½ years he was here to inculcate some feeling of personal responsibility in him but he does lack self-discipline and I'm afraid I didn't get far. If ever I asked him to be responsible for one certain thing he would say "O.K." so cheerfully and pleasantly that I would think "Surely _this_ time he really intends to do it"—but no, when the crucial moment arrived it hadn't been done and if I would ask "C., what did I ask you to do to-day?" he wouldn't have the slightest idea! I do think it's quite likely he has written more letters than he posted. I have not heard from him since 2 weeks after he went to Wash., but of course I don't expect him to write to me. If he writes to you and occasionally to his brothers it's all you could expect. I was pleased that he remembered Tom's birthday. I will get Tom to enclose the letter he had from him.

JUNE 22

The postman has just brought your first parcel—what a _lovely_ pullover! And I'm sure Tom will be delighted with the books etc.! I really don't think there is anything else in the way of clothes—unless you sent some summer underwear, though it's not absolutely necessary—I should think size 30 or 32. If it's too difficult, don't bother, and I'm sure there is nothing else.

I hope that by the time you get this the term will be almost over—have a good holiday.

[25] 90 DUNVEGAN ROAD
         TORONTO, JUNE 28

Dear Margaret

Last week there was no English mail, but this morning Tom and I each had an airgraph from you sent June 11....

Now both Tom and Mary are off to camp—Tom yesterday morning and Mary this morning. The house is in a fearful state after a week's utter neglect while I packed, mended, marked and washed but I am too exhausted to know where to start! John starts his holiday to-morrow and I expect will go to his brother's on Sunday for a couple of weeks. Irene Peterkin would like me to come up to her cottage at Honey Harbour (in the 30,000 Islands of Georgian Bay) for a bit while the others are away, but I don't know whether I want to make the effort of going—besides there is so much to be done here, that I've had to keep putting off while the children were home.

I expect Tom told you in his letter that he passed with 79.3%, in second place, into Grade 8. He intends to go all out next year after one of the two scholarships, of $50.00 each, which are awarded yearly to Grade 8 in Brown School—one for general proficiency, including art, music, and woodwork (these subjects do not count for passing from one grade to another, and Tom thinks they will pull him down) and the other for the best marks in the English subjects. Mary's airy unconcern about her school work made me quite prepared to have her kept in Grade 5 next year—she was put on to Grade 5 while home with her tonsils in April, on a month's trial and only got back to school for about 3 days of the probationary month, missing all the exams, so I had no idea how she was doing.... In the morning when she was leaving she stood in the doorway, mock terror on her face, elaborately knocking her knees together and said "Well, here I go to fail!", then, with an impish grin over her shoulder as she started off, she burst into Gracie Fields' song "Wish me luck as you wave me good-bye." I hope she can keep that care-free attitude to exams! After all, she passed with 73%! She was away 61 days out of the 175 school days in the year, so she did pretty well doing two years' work!

I do hope they both have a good holiday at camp—of course I know they will, but everything depends so on the weather, which is so variable this year—we had a dreadfully hot week last week—one day was 94°—but last night dropped to 50°! However it is getting warmer again. They have both been in a fever of excitement for a week.

Bill finished his exams on Friday and went to a cottage at Lake Simcoe with a group of boys from the school, returning last night. He apparently had a beautiful time and tells Vivien they lived as civilised people ought—breakfast at 12.30, lunch at 4.30, dinner at 8.30 and talk till 2 A.M. I think he is to start next week in a chartered accountant's office for the summer. We all felt very strongly that he ought to do farm work this summer—of course he hasn't the muscular development or stamina for general farm work but there is lots of lighter work—fruit, chickens, market gardens etc.—in fact, Mrs. Sandiford telephoned Vivien about a very desirable job on a chicken farm near Parry Sound, with congenial people—she sent a British boy there last summer and was looking for one to send this year—however Bill "doesn't care for manual work" and neither does his friend Bill Morrison and they want to be together.[13] Presumably they think all the Canadian boys and girls who are doing hard work this summer simply love it! It's a bit "hard to take" when we are constantly being scolded by visiting Englishmen, and Canadians returned from England, for the casualness of our individual war effort—and told that while we are complacently leading idle, selfish, peacetime lives, in the lap of luxury, unaware (to use a hackneyed phrase) that there is a war on, every English man, woman and child is working night and day at whatever task comes to hand, with no thought of personal comfort or convenience!

John talked to Bill about the summer and pointed out that not only is food production the most essential work for the summer months, and work in the open the best occupation from the standpoint of his own health, but also that Vivien ought to be considered and she badly needs a space of freedom from family responsibilities. In these days of nervous strain, especially, with added responsibilities, depleted incomes, difficult housekeeping, and the children ever more "on our necks," owing to no, or inadequate, domestic help, it seems essential, if at all possible, to have the children away for at least part of the summer, to give mothers a chance to draw their breath and call their soul their own—that is why we make any sacrifice to send the young children to camp. Bill quite admitted, in theory, the force of John's arguments, but said that he had already spoken to Harry, who had promised when next he was in town to see if he could place him with a firm of accountants he knows. Bill gave John to understand that if John said he had to go on a farm he would do so, but of course when a boy reaches Bill's age (and especially when he is not your own boy) you don't force him, but tell him your views and leave the decision to him—the decision in this case being a foregone conclusion.

Perhaps I should not write all this to you—I don't expect Vivien would like it if she knew, and it would serve no good purpose for you to mention it to Bill—particularly as the summer would be almost over by then. However Vivien told me that you had expressed disappointment to her that Bill was not intending to go on a farm this summer so I wanted to let you know the situation. I might add that some time ago, when Vivien first spoke to Bill about his working this summer she recommended farm work to him and gave the same reasons that John did in his later talk, but Bill told her that he definitely had made up his mind to work in an office—so he knew how we all felt about it. However the Ratcliffes are people of such infinite patience and tolerance that once Bill had made his definite decision (though against their wishes) they accepted it without question and Harry got the job Bill wanted for him and there is, and will be, no hint of disapproval in their attitude but only helpfulness and encouragement....

[26] 90 DUNVEGAN ROAD
TORONTO, JULY 8

Dear Margaret

This will just be a hurried note to accompany Tom's first two letters from camp. To avoid confusion I told him to write to me each week and I would forward the letters to you, but of his own accord he writes to me and also encloses one to you. I am keeping the ones to me until John has seen them and then will send them on....

I had a letter from Tom's counsellor, who seems just as earnest a young man as the one he had last year—praises Tom as an example to the camp in his unselfishness and good manners. He is trying to get Tom really interested in some hobby, in hopes of developing initiative in him, and assures me that he will do his best to teach him to swim.

I have very satisfactory, bubbly letters from Mary—she tells me she got 10 marks out of 10 for tidiness, which sounds fantastic to her mother, after spending 3 days of hard work reducing her room to order now that she's gone! Could it be that she will come home reformed? I doubt it!

I went to Burlington with John on Sunday, to have a look at Peter—he is the picture of health and has been earning fabulous (it seems to me) sums picking berries—he picked 113 quarts one day—$3.39!

John stayed at his brother's and I came back by bus Monday morning and have been getting the house in some kind of order (where it shows) before taking off to-morrow for Honey Harbour, to stay with Irene Peterkin. John and Peter will come back about the middle of next week, and then come on to Honey Harbour to stay with friends who have a cottage a mile or two away by water from Irene's, on another channel. I have a panicky feeling that I ought not to leave home while the children are away—which is stupid because I can't leave home while they're home and they are having the best of care.... I expect I'll lose the feeling when I get there—it is such a peaceful and remote sort of place—a little cottage on its own pine-covered island of about 1 ½ acres, with other cottages on other rocky islands within sight but not sound.

I have nearly gone mad over the ration book problems, with Peter dividing his time between 2 aunts, and having many meals at a third's, John staying with another one, and then we'll be staying in different houses at the Georgian Bay! However, I expect it will work out.

Will try to write there.

[27A]   HONEY HARBOUR, GEORGIAN BAY[14]
JULY 13

Dear Margaret

In this fascinating, remote, peaceful spot, one little dot among the 30,000 islands, we seem utterly removed from the war and all its implications. The battery of the radio has "gone," we have had no newspaper or mail for 4 days, and as Irene reminds me, the second front may have started and we wouldn't know. It is simply heavenly. Supplies are not easy to come by—the supply boat (a small steamer fitted up as a grocery and provision shop) which used to call at the islands twice a week, has been discontinued this year and the unlimited tinned stuff which people used to be able to have shipped to their cottages at the start of the season has now shrunk to practically nothing. However with what Irene could bring up and the little I was able to bring, and the friendliness of all the cottagers in these parts—who shop for one another on their rare trips to Honey Harbour, 6 miles away (gasoline for boats being rationed of course) we are getting along nicely. The blueberries have started to ripen and we picked 4 or 5 quarts this morning in about an hour. I hope I can gather a lot to take back when I go home, to make jam.

I expect John and Peter will be up the day after to-morrow, to stay with our friends, the Faircloths, not far away. They should bring me letters from Tom and Mary, which would go to Dunvegan. I do feel very far away from them all, but I'm sure they are well looked after.

As always when I come here, I expect I'll do nothing but read, and write heaps of letters, and as always, the days fly faster than at home, and I do nothing. However, I do want to get a letter written to you before the cares of home engulf me again, to try to clarify some points about Bill's future which it might be difficult for Vivien to write about.

We all know that you were frightfully humiliated over the whole "Mr. Harrison episode." It was impossible for a sensitive person in your position to be otherwise. (Incidentally, I think Mr. H. has most understandably "ducked" the rather heavy responsibility he was asked to assume, as nothing has been heard from him.) Vivien and I both feel that the effect of this has coloured your subsequent correspondence on the subject of Bill's future course—that you are so anxious to show your confidence in the Ratcliffes that you hesitate to express your own ideas and opinions lest it might seem that in the slightest degree you doubt their judgment. Now this is most emphatically <u>not</u> what they want—they know that you had no part in that affair—in fact were firmly against it—and besides, it caused them nothing but amusement at the time and has since been dismissed completely from their minds. They do want your frank opinion at every turn and I can promise you their feelings will not be hurt! I think we are all adult and worldly-wise enough not to want flattery, however sincerely meant, and <u>we</u> by no means think Canada the greatest country on earth or the University of Toronto a superlative seat of learning! We do think that U. of T. holds an enviable position among similar provincial universities of equal age and circumstances but it would be stupid—and most unreasonable—to expect a young provincial university in a young country suffering constantly from financial strain and difficulty of administration, to hope to rival such ancient and established institutions as Oxford and Cambridge!!—not to mention dozens more!

When Vivien told you, and Bill, that, in the event of his winning a scholarship here, she was willing (unless unforeseen circumstances prevent) to have him finish his course here, even should the war end sooner, she had only one aim—to make things easier for you. She did not urge or advise Bill to follow this plan, but she thought this offer ought to be made clearly, and early, as that assurance might be a help to you in weighing one plan against another (and I know it is <u>dreadfully</u> hard to decide what is best, with all the present uncertainties)—and also, if he <u>does</u> win a scholarship here, that plan would enable him to get 4 years of adequate (if, quite possibly, not the best) education, with probably the least strain on your financial resources, which she knows are limited. Bill seems to have accepted this as the best available solution of his case (though not, of course, to the extent of closing consideration of other solutions) but I think Bill has neither the age nor the experience to evaluate all the factors involved. To him it is very simple—the M. & P. course here offers him 4 years of good hard work, probably with stiff competition—though less of the latter than in peace time of course—which is what he likes, and also life at the Ratcliffes he finds extremely pleasant. In their comfortable, well-ordered home he has every care and consideration, pleasant, easy family relationships, complete freedom to do as he pleases and no responsibilities aside from his own interests. Under these arrangements he is perfectly happy and the future in that respect seems to him secure and rosy. While realizing the value of a Cambridge degree, he thinks that can be looked after by post-graduate work, which, being 4 years in the future, is too remote for a lad of 16 to worry very much over how it is financed.

The only fact about Bill's future of which we can feel reasonably sure is, that when he starts on his career the war will be recently over and, therefore, opportunities scarce and competition keen. I know you realize that Bill has not a prepossessing manner, nor a personality that would impress favourably anyone interviewing him for a post. Bill's big asset is his brain and therefore it does seem logical, in fact, imperative, that he should be enabled to obtain the very highest and most impressive academic standing that he can manage. I am sure he has no thought of making his life in Canada, nor do I think he would fit into business life here. Therefore, he should be as well equipped as possible to make his way in England. If, lacking this, he should fail to secure a satisfactory niche, it would be pretty bitter for Vivien, after having made the necessary sacrifices (of which the financial would be far from the greatest) to feel that she had defeated her own ends, and done you and him a disservice.

This is all very rambling and discursive, but I want to make clear that we all know that Bill and his future are the most important things in the world to you, and you must let no delicacy of feeling prevent your voicing and carrying out whatever plans seems best to you, especially as Vivien prefers not to be responsible for decisions, though she is willing to do anything in her power to further your plans.

Time to swim, this is my last sheet of paper. It is heavenly to drop right off the rock into the deep, soft water—no chill to it, but not too warm—just right! Wish I could be here a month!

[27B]   90 DUNVEGAN ROAD
          TORONTO, JULY 25

Dear Margaret

John, Peter and I returned home 3 days ago after a lovely holiday. The house is in rather a mess and the garden overgrown with weeds but we are getting straightened out and Peter has got started in the Junior Club of the Yacht Club. He felt pretty much out of it the first day—all the 30 or 40 boys have been going over daily since July 1 and Peter is so reserved and shy that it is hard for him, especially as he knows none of them, and as it seems to him that they now know everything about sailing and he nothing! However in a week's time I'm sure he will be quite at home and will thoroughly enjoy the daily dinghy sailing races....

Bill telephoned John on Friday evening to ask his advice about a plan which he and a group of his friends (who are all working at office jobs for the summer and lunch together every day) had, to go out farming on Saturday afternoons. The city is running a scheme to help the farmers in the surrounding districts—anyone with spare time in the evening, weekends, or longer periods, reports to the City Hall and is despatched where needed. Bill apparently thought he ought to have some sanction and as Vivien and Harry were not home (I think they are back to-day) he asked John—who of course told him to go ahead. We were very much pleased that he had decided of his own accord to do this. I asked Bill about his job, which he says has turned out to be perfectly ideal from his point of view. He is obviously enjoying it very much and I am delighted that his first venture into business has turned out so successfully.

John Ratcliffe has been sent back to an air station in Toronto—a surprise to everyone, as, when he went to Lachine, Que., at the start, he expected he would take his whole training there. I do hope this means that he will take all his training in Toronto....

I have been bottling blueberries and making jam—we brought back 8 qts. from the Georgian Bay, where they grow wild in immense quantities. We would have picked more, but it rained the day we left. They will be a great help as the fruit (which is usually so plentiful) is fairly scarce this year and is selling at simply colossal prices—80c (more than 3s. 6d.) a quart for raspberries, black currants, ordinary red "sour" cherries, etc. I am afraid food will be alarmingly expensive next winter. We are fortunate in having got all our coal in—a slightly inferior grade but we expect it will be satisfactory. After July 1 everyone has to take 25% of their requirements in a definitely inferior grade—and will be lucky to get that (result of the U.S. coal strike). However we don't mind any restrictions and deprivations if the good work in Europe can be kept up. Irene & I were so remote that the invasion of Sicily was on for 4 days before we even knew about it! The news from all fronts seems very encouraging. May it continue!

[28] 90 DUNVEGAN ROAD
TORONTO, AUGUST 9

Dear Margaret

I am enclosing Tom's letters of the last week.... An airgraph to Tom from his father came last week, which I forwarded to camp. There is also a post card for Tom from C.

I wrote to C. last week and gave him a reprimand about his responsibility to write to you, but I'm afraid it won't have much effect. I enclose a clipping from "Newsweek" re Eve's [Mrs. Burns's] department. I suppose this will leave her minus a job, though I know she'd have no difficulty getting another. She may use her free period to write the book on social security which two publishers have asked her to do.[15]

Tom is due home to-morrow. He seems to have had a marvellous time. Mary will be glad to have him back, it is a bit lonely for her though Mrs. Fairfoul has brought her little niece two mornings and one or two of Mary's friends from other parts of the city have come to spend the day with her, and she manages to amuse herself pretty well when alone. Peter goes to the Yacht Club every day and is enjoying it....

I do hope we have a better August than last year—which was a nightmare, with Tom & C. both in bed with colds for 2 weeks! It seems as though a holiday in the clear dry climate of the north takes away some children's immunity to germs and when they get back to damp Toronto they come down right away. During the last month I have been so utterly exhausted at times that it made me a little frightened so I hope we can coast along until the end of the holidays with the least possible expenditure of energy.

I do hope you have a good holiday.

[29] 90 DUNVEGAN ROAD
TORONTO, AUGUST 21

Dear Margaret

... I was so sorry to hear of your accident, but glad it was no worse.[16] But how maddening, to have it happen just at the start of your holiday, and spoil your plans! I do hope it would not prevent your going to London. The summer course does sound rather like a busman's holiday but being in London would be a help!...

I think Bill sent you a cable about his exam. results—which have delighted us all—11 firsts! It is very exasperating now, having to wait for the scholarship awards, but he should have a good chance with that record. Tim Templeton, also of U.T.S., had 11 firsts, and one boy at T.C.S. (Peter's school) has the same, but of course the exams cover the whole province of Ontario and one doesn't know what the competition is! However I should think he is sure of getting a good scholarship. He is apparently enjoying his work this summer and finds it very interesting. His contribution to the war effort in the way of "Commando Farming" seems to have stopped short at one Saturday afternoon—slightly ludicrous, after telephoning John to get his permission (!) to engage in it, discussing it with Mr. Roberts, Vivien's friend and neighbour, to get <u>his</u> sanction, and writing to Vivien saying he hoped he had <u>her</u> approval!

Bill came down last Sunday to see Tom, and had supper with him—I have to give Tom his supper early on Sunday so he can go to evening service. The choir is less demanding in the summer—only one practice a week, of about 15 or 20 minutes—not that Tom minds the more frequent and longer ones!—he quite misses them.

John took the children to the "Fair for Britain" (a rather makeshift affair held in one of the parks each summer while the Toronto Exhibition is in abeyance for the duration—the proceeds go to the British War Victims Fund) on Tuesday afternoon, which gave me my one "afternoon off" of the month. I went up to have tea with Vivien and Bill came home while I was there so I was able to tell him of your accident.

Peter goes to the Yacht Club every day except Saturday and is enjoying the sailing. Yesterday the boys of the Junior Club had their swimming meet so I took Tom and Mary over to it. It was a nice afternoon and the Yacht Club is a very pretty spot and we enjoyed the races and the fun....

I do hope that long before this your arm would let you travel, and that you are having a good holiday.

[30] 90 DUNVEGAN ROAD
TORONTO, AUGUST 29

Dear Margaret

The only mail this week was an airgraph to Tom from his father....

On Tuesday Mrs. Cruikshank was going up to the "Honey Pot," her place in the country, 15 miles out, and asked us to come, so Peter skipped the Yacht Club and we took a picnic lunch and had a perfectly lovely day. The children cut milkweed—loads of it, dragged it up to the cabin and stripped off the leaves, which we spread on canvas to dry. The government has been asking for quantities of dried milkweed leaves, to be used for synthetic rubber. The children were much interested in the job, though I expect they will think it's not a very remunerative one at the price of 3¢ pound—by the time the leaves dry there will be <u>very</u> few pounds to show for their day's work. However they had a lot of fun and it wasn't hard work....

There is so much to do, I wish each day had 50 hours—provided, of course, that I had energy to match. The laundry problem has got so bad that I am washing and ironing the bed linen myself—it's almost unbelievable how many such jobs we've gradually had to add to an already overful week. The fruit season is now at its height—a very <u>low</u> one this year—the bad spring and cold winter played havoc with the trees so everything is scarce and expensive but, even so, I'm constantly haunted by the necessity of preserving what I can and I manage to do a little jam or bottling every few days. The sale in shops of jam, jelly, marmalade and honey has been suspended pending the start of rationing of those foods. I am so glad they are to be rationed, but I do wish they had included canned fruit, as I don't think I was able to get more than 6 tins all last winter, and if I were sure of some, under rationing, as we now are of jam and marmalade, I wouldn't feel so pressed to do a supply—just some for "extra."

We took all 3 children to the movies on Thursday—they go so very seldom it was a great occasion. Of course as always when you really want to take them it is hard to find anything suitable, but we went to see Bob Hope in "They've got me covered"—ridiculous nonsense, and a bit "wilder" than I'd expected, but they found it hilariously funny and it was a most successful outing.

The coming week promises to be pretty stiff, as Mrs. Fairfoul is going on a holiday and won't be able to come at all—also I have a mountain of Peter's clothes ready for mending etc. But I guess I'll weather through.

[31] 90 DUNVEGAN ROAD
TORONTO, SEPTEMBER 5

Dear Margaret

You will of course have heard by cable of Bill's thrilling success in the scholarship exams. To have taken first place in maths. in the province is indeed an achievement and when we heard, on Friday evening, from Mr. Petrie, his maths. master, that he had won the First Edward Blake in maths we were overjoyed—but still more so when we saw in the published results Saturday morning that he had won, as well, one of the Reuben Wells Leonard scholarships for students entering University College. You will have all the details of the awards, of course, in the Matric. calendar, which lists all the scholarships and their value. He does deserve great credit, for besides being brilliant, he is an excellent student, with tremendous ability to concentrate and common sense in his study technique. He should do extremely well in his course next year and I am sure he will enjoy it.

However, I do think Vivien merits a good deal of credit for her part in his success. She has given him encouragement and sympathy, cheerful and

Mary and Tom have their pictures in the *Toronto Telegram* for the money they raised for the British War Victims' Fund

relaxing talk when he wanted it, and privacy when he wanted that. She has smoothed his path in every way, protected him from the slightest disturbance or inconvenience and left him free of the slightest responsibility of any kind so that he could do exactly as he wished at all times. When the nervous strain of approaching exams has made him tense and edgy and accentuated his self-absorption and sense of self-importance, she has sacrificed her own sensibilities to his. I do hope that sometime he will realize all that she has done for him and what it meant in infinite patience and forbearance. She is a marvellous person![17]...

After almost 2 weeks of waiting Mary and Tom finally achieved their goal of seeing "their pictures in the paper" the other night! I think I told you they earned in various ways $3.05 and took it down to the office of the "Toronto Evening Telegram" for the Telegram-sponsored British War Victims Fund. There their pictures were taken and they were promised they would appear soon! It was a red-letter day for them! This yearning for publicity used to make me squirm but I've discovered it's a normal quality in the young!

I must get on to bed—had to spend this afternoon making plum jam as I found the plums my sister-in-law gave me yesterday were not going to keep any longer—had a bad moment when I found I had no sugar, though plenty of coupons—and the shops not open until Tuesday—but my kind neighbour Mrs. Innis lent me 5 pounds and saved the day—and the plums! By this evening I was wondering if I hadn't been altogether too ambitious, bringing all those pears home too, but perhaps some morning soon I'll be fired with enough zeal to bottle them.

I was glad to hear from Viv. that in your cable to Bill you assured him that your arm was better. I hope it didn't interfere too much with your holiday.

P.S. We've just started jam etc. rationing—such a comfort! We get 3 oz. jam, marmalade, honey or jelly a week, or 5 oz. tinned fruit, molasses or syrup or 1/4 lb. sugar. Also the tea and coffee ration has been increased by 1/3.

P.S. It may seem rather extraordinary to you that I never mention the war news in my letters!—but it's lack of time, not interest! I'm sure we feel the same way about the present news!

P.P.S. I reminded Tom about his letter this week—I didn't like you to go so long without. I expect, once started, he'll remember.

[32] 90 DUNVEGAN ROAD
TORONTO, SEPTEMBER 19

Dear Margaret

I did not write last Sunday—Tom apparently forgot all about writing and I was having a very strenuous week end getting Peter's things packed to go off Monday. Bill was here most of Saturday and he and Tom apparently discussed your birthday present and made some tentative plans towards getting it—I should rather think that would remind Tom of writing, but I suppose Bill being here put it out of his mind, and he is such a creature of habit that it would never occur to him to write on any day except Sunday!—that being the regular letter-writing day!...

Peter got off to school on Wednesday—slightly disconsolate when it came to the point of leaving, but he wrote me a long letter on Thursday, full of information about the year's arrangements, and I am sure is quite at home. I miss him very much. He has reached the stage now when he is a pleasant companion, not just a child. Besides he is a great help in so many ways—practical, quick and resourceful. I do hope he has a good year with no illness, like last year.

Bill and Tom went down town on Tuesday to select your birthday present. I gave Tom wrapping etc., all ready, and they posted it when they bought it, so I hope it arrives safely and on time. It seems a bit futile for me to wish you a "happy birthday," but I do indeed send my very best wishes, and the news from all fronts is most encouraging....

Vivien has gone to Ottawa to spend a few days with Harry, who is now sharing a flat with a friend who is a staff officer with the R.C.A.F. I am so glad she is able to—it is dreadfully hard on her having him away all the time and besides, she needs a bit of a change. I hope she will find herself able to stay a week.

I hope Tom will remember to write to-day. If not, I'll prod him again next week. I do wish he would remember of his own accord, and from the heart, not just because it's part of his routine, like brushing his teeth!

P.S. I'm glad to say Tom wrote his letter this evening without reminder.

Dear Margaret

... We go on as usual. Mary was home two days of last week with a little cold in the head but aside from that all is well.

Mary and Anne Innis were seized on Friday with an inspiration to hold a Garden Fair on Saturday (yesterday) for the British War Victims Fund. I tried to discourage them without being too much of a wet blanket though it did seem as though the cold weather was reason enough against it. However, when Mary gets an idea one might as well talk to the wind, and when Anne joins her in it it's hopeless so I just left them alone. They were as busy as bees, asked for no assistance or donations and really showed surprising ingenuity in the amusements & games they rigged up and the articles they put up for sale (pop corn which they popped themselves and did up in paper napkins, bunches of parsley from the garden, etc.). Hugh contributed his ideas and by Saturday afternoon Tom was sufficiently infected by their enthusiasm to help with the sales etc. Anne sat behind a table with "Mousekeeper" on it and showed Donnie's mice (now about 50 in number) in their big cage in the garage, for 1¢ a visit.[18] Customers were few, but they made $3.47, and Mary, Anne and Tom are taking it to the Telegram office after school tomorrow. I <u>did</u> think that having their pictures in the paper once would satisfy them, but of course the excuse now is that this is for Anne's benefit, who missed it before! Apparently Hugh feels he has grown beyond the youthful urge for publicity!...

I am afraid Tom has forgotten to write.

Dear Margaret

... Both children are in excellent health, though as usual I have a lot of trouble keeping Mary from "running herself ragged." ... Of course I have none of that trouble with Tom, who is sedate and slow moving and not given to over-exertion. However he is much more active than he used to be and quite often plays with the other children—in fact I think he practically always joins them now if they are playing a game, but would never think of hunting them up and starting a game, himself. He has also been staying at school for half an hour or so in the afternoons, to play with the boys in the school yard.

Anne Innis, Tom, and Mary playing in their fort in the Innises' back yard

The film "My Friend Flicka" was at our neighbourhood theatre yesterday (Saturday) and I wanted Tom to see it, as he was at camp when the other two saw it and I knew he would enjoy it. I had to telephone several times to get the exact hour the matinee ended, as Tom <u>had</u> to be at the church to sing for a choral wedding, at 5. However, they finally assured me he would be out in time, so I had Tom invite Jimmie Armour, the friend he made at camp, to come over in the morning and stay to lunch and go to the movie. It was all most successful and they both enjoyed the day....

[35] 90 DUNVEGAN ROAD
TORONTO, OCTOBER 12

Dear Margaret

Your parcel to Tom arrived about a week ago and your long letter to me, written in mid-September, a few days later. I do implore you not to send any more clothes. I was simply appalled at the price of the underwear, on the customs declaration. There is no doubt it is superlative quality but I cannot bear your spending so much money and then taking the risk of loss, when I could get him some that would do very well, for a third of the cost....

As you feared, the underwear is much too big, but I find it fits Bill, so will be useful to Vivien—in fact it is better that way, as Bill's clothing expenses, now that he is a young man, are many times Tom's. Tom is, I think, an average height for his age, but is of a slight build, with small bones, and though he has much more flesh than he used to, is naturally slender and does not "take up" his clothes as a sturdier-built boy would....

[Peter's] headmaster telephoned John to see if we would like Peter to come home for the weekend—an unexpected treat for him as weekends during term are supposed to be "out" for the war. Of course we said to send him so he was here from Fri. aft. to Mon. aft. and we all enjoyed it. He is so full of ideas and bursting with energy and was so determined to cram as much as possible into his 3 days that it was rather like living in a high wind, being in the same house with him!—he finds an odd spring out of a broken toy, a bit of mirror and a piece of tin, and immediately goes flying to the cellar, calling out en route that he is going to make a submarine that will fire a torpedo at the touch of a button—then it is an electric magnetic motor, which his mechanics magazine says he can build from two nails, a length of copper wire (unwound from some salvaged electric wire) and piece of tin—then it's a huge fort built of fallen leaves in the garden and when that palls the leaves are put in a heap and boxes and boards built up for a runway down which they plunge in the wagon into the leaves. I am much encouraged to see that when his undertakings don't work out (as often happens because he usually attempts things too elaborate and complicated for his tools and equipment and experience) he no longer is bad-tempered or disconsolate over his failure, as he used to be, but philosophically puts away the part he has completed, tidies up the mess, and is off to something new. It was refreshing to Tom and Mary to have him—his ideas give fresh zest to their games, and Tom loves to help him make things, doing bits of sawing for him, etc....

John left last night for a few days in New York, so I parcelled up our birthday presents for Christopher (Bill's too) and John took them to post in New York, to save any possible bother with customs. I had sent C. a birthday card, earlier, telling him they would be delayed. John had written Eve Burns, thinking it just possible that her travelling about might take her to New York at the same time and they could meet. However she writes that it is not possible. She seems busy as ever, reports C. now as tall as she and wearing a 9 ½ shoe!—an awkward stage when they are rationed at 3 prs. a year! She says they had planned to have him wear some of Arthur's, which are now too small for C.! I am so glad you say C. is writing more regularly. I did give him quite a scolding in July, by letter, but had no hope of it's taking effect....

I believe Tom will be just about the average age at leaving Public School—i.e. 13—of course actually a little younger because his birthday is in June, so he'll be just <u>barely</u> 13.... (You understand that by Public School we mean the elementary state school—the secondary schools (also provincially run) are called High Schools, or Collegiate Institutes—synonymous terms.) I think I sent you the program of studies of the Public Schools. It comprises 8 grades with a year to each, with a previous year in kindergarten optional....

Some years ago, when the High Schools were overcrowded, it was arranged to have a first form of the High School (or Grade 9) in some of the city public schools, and Brown School is one of them, so Tom could go on there for another year after this, which would be pleasant for him as not necessitating a break into new surroundings. French and Latin are both started in first form of High School. It is too bad French is not taught in the Public Schools—the omission is due to political causes—too long a tale to go into here, but the result of inter-provincial enmity, jealousy and strife, with intolerance and bigotry on both sides—education in Canada is a provincial matter—that is, it is administered by each province separately. I should not worry if I were you, about Tom's difficulty with these when he goes back to England. The private schools here start both French and Latin much earlier and as children change from public to private schools at all ages (many when they pass their entrance) and seem to get on all right. When Peter went to T.C.S. the boys in his class had had a year of Latin but he managed with some extra work, to catch up in a month or two. Anyway, even if Tom <u>had</u> to take an extra year for his school certificate I cannot feel it would be a bad thing. He is very immature and young for his age and I think he is better to be in a class with boys his own age or a little younger—none of my friends ever take him to be more than 10 and are much surprised to learn he is 12. As for C., I don't think he can be any less prepared to fit into school when he returns to England than he was when he came out here and yet by the time he left us, in 2½ years, he was doing splendidly. (In fact, he was quite well adjusted after 1 year, when he started at Brown.) He has a good mind, but is easily discouraged.

Aside from all this, I think the physical benefit to Tom from having lived in Canada during these years of rationing and deprivation in England, far outweigh any delay he may experience in finishing his schooling. We have many inconveniences and difficulties, and some shortages, but have never yet had any real deprivations of essentials in the way of food. He has had a quart of milk a day, for instance, about ½ lb. butter a week, an abundance of fruits, plenty of meat (there was a shortage last winter, but rationing put that straight and under rationing we have more coupons than we need). The last two months we have not been able to get oranges but the abundance of tomatoes made them unnecessary (for Vitamin C) and I expect they will be coming in again soon when the new crop matures. Of course we may have much greater food scarcities ahead of us, but even so, I am sure we shall continue to be much better off than you in that respect. Therefore, I think it is much better for him to stay here—besides—the most important point—he is out of danger.

OCTOBER 13

On rereading all this, I have an uncomfortable feeling that it sounds as though I were trying to dictate what is best for you to do about your own child. Please don't take it that way. It is agonizing enough to be parted from your children for so long, but it would be intolerable for you to feel that we, because we <u>are</u> at present Tom's guardians, were usurping the control of his movements which is <u>your</u> right wherever he may be living. If, as I gather, you are toying with the idea of bringing him home because of your desire to relieve me of what might be a trying responsibility, I want you to know that we are willing, and would prefer, to have him stay here until he can return without danger—always provided, of course, that no unforseen calamity occurs to make it impossible. <u>But</u>, if you wanted him to come, quite apart from consideration for my welfare, <u>that</u> of course is an entirely different matter and one in which I have no right to interfere or advise.[19]

I am glad to say the other parcel of underwear (containing the Ransome book) arrived this morning and I will pass the underwear on to Bill.

Tom, of course, was delighted to have your suggestions for Christmas, but I'm afraid he won't be able to carry them out, worse luck. Elastic of any kind has been unobtainable for 2 years—exasperating when trying to clothe children—I have been salvaging half-worn bits from old underpants in the rag-bag, etc. and joining them together. However, I must confess I did a little "hoarding" of elastic bands before they disappeared and think I can spare a few as I am afraid they are going to rot before they are all used (which would be disgraceful!). I don't think that solid powder is to be had either—they tell me it is not being made any more. The hair grips ("bobby pins" here) can very occasionally be picked up in some of the little dry goods shops and I will just enquire whenever I am in one, and see if I can't get a few cards. These little things are hard to do without when one has got accustomed to them.

I do feel sorry for you without fires—I think I could stand hunger much better than cold! And if you are feeling under par, it makes it all the worse to bear. The catarrh and headaches and general run-down-ness must make life an awful drag, especially in such a job as teaching, which makes demands on you every minute of the day, with no let-up. I know you are all so courageous and cheerful about your food situation, but I can't help thinking that such severe restrictions (especially of fruit, meat and dairy products) must be hard on you after a time.

The coal situation here is pretty grim—bad enough due to war conditions, but made dangerous by the regrettable coal strikes. We are awfully lucky in not burning anthracite—we have a special furnace which burns a fine "stoker" coal—really a by-product—so we have been able to get our winter's supply. It makes us feel rather piggish when other people have none at all and don't know when they will, but our doing without would not help the anthracite burners. Of course we are as careful as possible in its use and John has spent hours and hours stopping up cracks around window sash and doors, reputtying panes of glass, etc., to try to make the house as wind and weather proof as possible, and so reduce the coal consumption.

I may have "come down on" Bill pretty hard in my letter to you—I suppose I feel more keenly about any deficiencies in Bill, in his relations with the Ratcliffes, than the R's themselves, because I can't help feeling in a way responsible for his behaviour, they having taken him on my recommendation, as it were. Of course it was his <u>attitude</u> toward the farm job that annoyed us, not the actual fact of his not going on a farm—we always had grave doubts as to whether he could make a success of it. However, as it turned out, the accountant's job was much better for him in every way and Vivien is extremely pleased about it. I am sure she has written you all about this, or is doing so—I know she did to your mother, a week or two ago—so I won't go into it, as this letter is getting very lengthy and time-consuming already.

You asked me whether there would be any moral obligation on Bill to stay at the university, having entered on a scholarship. I don't think you should worry about that at all—you have enough problems to wrestle with—and in Bill's position (which is not unique just now) I don't think there would be the slightest criticism or thought of it (this is just my opinion, of course). I should think the fact that they allow boys from outside Canada, who have no intention of settling here, to carry these scholarships, shows that there is no obligation attached....

[36] 90 DUNVEGAN ROAD
TORONTO, OCTOBER 24

Dear Margaret

... I am sorry to learn from your mother's letter that one of hers to me must have been lost en route—the one, evidently written in July, thanking me for the stamps I sent. I never received it, and am so glad she mentioned it again in this last one. I felt guilty at having been so slow in sending the stamps, and am so glad to hear they arrived safely.

The big event of this week was the annual circus at Maple Leaf Gardens. All the school children are allowed an afternoon off to attend—a certain number of schools allotted to each day. Tom went on Friday with some of his school mates. Mary was much to her joy, invited to go with some friends on Friday <u>evening</u>—an entirely new experience for her. The thrill of going out in the evening and not getting home until 11.30 was just as entrancing as the circus.

The children are well and all goes on as usual.

You asked Tom some questions about his schoolwork in your last letter and I <u>suggested</u> that he answer them today. He seemed to think the idea of reading over your letter before he wrote quite an original and rather bright brain-wave of mine! He had never thought of doing such a thing! I do hope he "lets himself go" a bit and doesn't just give a few bare facts. I have tried to give him some ideas of the kind of thing you would be interested in in his letters but it is very hard for him to work from general principles (in any field)—he wants specific instructions. So I guess it is best just to let him go ahead "on his own." ...

I think he is working very hard and conscientiously at school this year—he has his eye on the $25.00 scholarship for Genl. Proficiency awarded annually in Grade 8 at Brown School.

He has started buying War Savings Stamps this year. I rather discouraged his & C's doing so, before, as I thought it might be a bit of a nuisance cashing in the certificates, after they were back in England. But in Mr. Trott's class there is apparently great pressure put on to have the class 100% purchasers each week. They have the record for the school and often the class (42 boys) buys $35.00 or more (stamps 25¢ each). He now lacks only 1 stamp of a $4.00 certificate (redeemable for $5.00 in 7 years) and is very pleased & proud. He gets 25¢ week pocket money and $1.25 to $1.50 month from the choir and never wants to buy anything for himself (though very generous about spending for presents) so he may as well buy the stamps.

[37] 90 DUNVEGAN ROAD
TORONTO, OCTOBER 31

Dear Margaret

... This will not be a long letter—I have just finished rather a long one to your mother, which I am sure she will send on to you. All is going well and as I told your mother, we are all open-mouthed and pinching ourselves at the appearance of a maid!—a real live living-in one—not very bright but very good-natured and strong and willing. It is only to last a month but it is nice while it lasts! I hope to get a breather and John and I will get out a bit before "digging in" for the winter....

Last night was Hallowe'en (the actual day being to-day, Sunday). Because of the scarcity of sweets and fruit (which are "shelled out" by householders to the children, who go from door to door in costume) all the school children were sent a message from Dr. Goldring (I enclose clipping to save writing). Of course this had infinitely more effect on the children than advice from mere parents and we had only one group of 3 tiny boys come to our door. All the children seemed to have little parties in their own homes. Mary and Tom went into the Innis's—I had asked Anne and Hugh to come here but Mrs. I. wanted to have the party there as her husband was away and it was a good opportunity—when he is home he works every evening and the house has to be kept quiet. Mary wore an outgrown pair of white duck trousers of Peter's, a middy blouse and her little round white camp hat (like a U.S. sailor's). With the serene inconsequence of youth she bought herself a mask which represents either a wolf or a dog—no one knows which! Tom could not think of anything to wear and I am not very good at "dressing up" ideas though I did offer a few feeble suggestions, one of which he was going to follow, but at dinner he announced an idea of his own—to go as a little child of about 5, wearing his dressing gown and carrying Mary's old teddy bear. I went up to help him and decided he'd be more effective with pyjamas under the dressing gown—putting woolen underwear under them to make sure he was warm enough. When he was ready I said "Why Tom! Christopher Robin!" and sure enough, he was C.R. to the life! They went in at 7 and had a most glorious time. All the other Innis's entered into the spirit and were agreeably "scared" over and over, had lights turned out, torches flashed on them, etc. etc. Mary I. (15) organized contests and games—they came home and tumbled into bed at 9.30 completely happy....

[38] 90 DUNVEGAN ROAD
TORONTO, NOVEMBER 7

Dear Margaret

... Mary and Tom got their reports this week. Mary's is very poor, as I expected. She refuses to be serious about her work and devotes herself with such high spirits and such a "don't care" attitude, to having a good time that her work is bound to suffer. I honestly don't mind a little of that in her character—it augurs more happiness for her future life than being too serious, but I don't want it to go too far, so that she doesn't get her foundation work firmly in hand, and fails to learn how to apply herself. She can do well if she tries, so I am hoping she <u>will</u> try these next two months.

Tom's marks are good, except for a D in writing. I was rather surprised, and he was rather cast down, at his getting a B in both effort and conduct. He was 3rd in the class and has an average of 76. In the subjects required for Entrance examination he has an average of 78 (those are the academic subjects, excluding crafts, music, art and health)....

Tom got his Christmas parcels off to England yesterday. I will tell you about them, in case any don't arrive. As I told you (and also your mother) he sent photographs of himself to you, his father and his two grandmothers. He wanted to send little gifts as well, so he sent you a parcel of Kleenex, hair grips and a few elastic bands, to his father some razor blades, which fit nicely in an envelope, and to his Granny Sharp two packets of needles, which do likewise. He has not hit on something small for his other Granny (he sent her some needles with her birthday card). To his Aunt Phyl and Uncle David he sent a box of chocolates (we are only allowed to send one pound at a time now). They were sent direct from the shop and he sent a joint parcel to [his cousins] Tony and Mary and a sort of construction set for Tony. To Brian [Tout] he sent the same as to Mary. Toys are pretty scarce here now—though I suppose not to the same degree as with you....

The maid who, as I told you, arrived by a miracle out of the blue, is still here—not very good in many ways but strong and good natured and very pleasant. I do most of the cooking but it is heavenly to get out of the sink and hand over the heavy work, and be able to get out in the evening once in a while. She came to me temporarily, until she enlisted in the Women's Division of the R.C.A.F. but I rather doubt whether the enlistment will come off—she spent 2 half days this week at the recruiting office, and has her application papers, which she keeps telling me are "so hard," she'll <u>never</u> be able to fill them in. She was to have gone down again at 9 A.M. yesterday for her medical, but "changed her mind" as the forms are still "too hard." I offered to help her but didn't press the offer because if her mental equipment is not up to answering two sheets of quite simple personal questions I fancy she would only come to grief when she got a little further on. I rather expect she'll give up the whole idea. However, if she does, I'm afraid it won't mean I'll have her permanently. She came to me at $5 week, just as a stop-gap to tide her over, and as she was getting nearly twice as much, before, I know she would not stay on for that wage. And for that matter, even that is more than I can afford to pay for very long. I pay Mrs. Fairfoul $6 week, and I would certainly not let her go in order to take on anyone like this Bertha, to whose moronic mind a "permanent" job is something that lasts until at any moment on a whim she leaves without notice (as she did her last mistress). Whereupon, of course, Mrs. F. would be comfortably settled in another job and I should be driven to suicide!...

We had Peter home for the night on Wednesday. The T.C.S. Junior Rugby team (on which he is the humblest of the substitutes) came to Toronto to play Ridley (a school in St. Catharines, but to save expense & travel in war time they met here, mid-way, and played on Upper Canada grounds). Peter and Michael Brodeur, his Montreal friend, stayed here, they played their game on Thursday morning, came here for lunch and I rushed them down town and we managed to see a movie before I turned them over at the station to the headmaster, to go back to Port Hope. It was great fun and Peter was thrilled at being allowed to play. It is awfully good for him to play games, it helps him to mix with the boys and make friends and not be so retiring. He is perfectly happy at the school and I cannot be thankful enough that he was able to go there.

Must stop now—it is time to get Tom's supper, which he has to have early on Sundays to get to church—then John's young nephew is coming for supper, too, and Mary must be seen to. No Sunday afternoon work for maids!

[39] 90 DUNVEGAN ROAD
TORONTO, NOVEMBER 14

Dear Margaret

... John and I went to Parents' Night at the school and saw Tom's teacher, who, as I expected, reports Tom to be a conscientious worker, who gives no trouble. I told him of Tom's disquiet at B for conduct and B for effort, and he tells me that, especially at the beginning of the year, he does not give A's for anything less than practical perfection—otherwise they would have no opportunity to show progress. Similarly in the examinations, he says he is marking pretty severely.

I ran into Edith Wilkinson at the school but had only a minute to talk to her. She seems rather to think that Bill ought to go home next summer. Mrs. Bland apparently intends to go back next spring or summer if women and children can travel by then, which they can't now. She apparently rather got the wind up when David didn't do very well in the Cambridge exams, and thought she might be risking Jennifer's whole future by limiting her to a Canadian education so is anxious to get her back to England....[20]

I am beginning to feel quite pampered with Bertha (the maid I told you about) here to do the dish-washing, scrubbing and let me out of the house once in a while. However it's not to last long. She told me on Thursday that she had changed her mind about joining the Air Force and would like to stay on with me but of course could not continue to work for the $5 week I was giving her. So I told her I quite agreed with her on both points but unfortunately could not afford to pay her proper wages so I regretfully have to let her leave.... My good Mrs. Fairfoul offered to leave so I could keep Bertha on but she has been so faithful. I know I can depend on her so I'd sooner depend on her 15 hours a week than take a chance on a full-time one who might not stay.

John was able to get a film last week and got a few pictures of Peter's rugby game. The two pictures left on the film he took of the three children, Mary, Tom, Anne yesterday and I will send you prints. I hope they are decent ones.

We got Peter's mid-term report this week—A's in everything including wood-work—13 A's altogether, pretty good! He has done so well at T.C.S and is so much happier there than he ever was at any school before, and it has done so much for him that it fairly chills my soul to think of his not being able to go on into the Senior School there next year. There is one entrance scholarship to the Senior School, a marvellous one of $500 year for 4 years—$2000 in all!—and of course he is going to try it, but I try not to think about it because it's an open scholarship like the one he won 2 years ago and one can have no idea what the competition will be.... We are terribly afraid that without the schol. we won't be able to afford to keep him on at T.C.S.—since the last income tax jump last year our taxes are higher than on a similar income in England, the cost of living is steadily increasing and of course salaries are "frozen" since the start of the war. The exemption for children was reduced last year to about ⅓ of what it used to be and of course we've never been allowed exemption for Tom and C. So it means constant retrenchment even to go on at our present rate. So I am just hoping for the best but trying not to think of it too much and above all not to count on it, or talk about it. Time will tell!...

NOVEMBER 15

... PS If you want to tell Bill of his father's marriage, please do not think that I would disagree with your decision—as you might well do after my outburst of last winter. Of course at the time it was the younger boys I was thinking of, and I was incensed at their father's utterly selfish point of view, but Bill is an entirely different matter. After all, he is an adult now, and has a right to your confidence and you have a right to his "moral support" and understanding. Besides, as I think I mentioned before, one never knows who will pop in from England these days and it is just possible he might hear about it, which would not be a good thing. Of course it is for you to decide, but if you tell him I think you have every justification.

Dear Margaret

... My brief respite is over—Bertha left yesterday afternoon, and to bring home my responsibilities to me, I put Tom to bed with a sore throat. John's brother and his wife came down from Burlington to bring us some apples and were here for lunch, and when Tom, who sits next me, asked me to give him only a <u>small</u> piece of pie, I was sure there was something wrong. So right after lunch I went up to his room and found him lying down. He complained of nothing but headache and poor appetite, but was very tearful, as he always is when he doesn't feel well and tries to explain what is wrong.... As soon as the people left, shortly after, I went back up and by that time his throat was a little sore and his temp. over 100, so I put him to bed....

I do hope that Tom's throat will get no worse, though it may coast along in its present state for a week or so, I suppose. You may be assured I will give him all possible care and attention.

NOV. 22 EVENING

Tom's temp. has been normal all day though his throat is still fairly red (but not very sore) and the cold has moved up to his nose and head (uncomfortable but less serious than lower down). He is coughing less but blowing his nose a lot to make up! He forgot his letter yesterday, I reminded him last night and he forgot again this morning. When I reminded him again he apparently was carried away by his desire to make amends, to the extent of 11 pages! Is he proud??

Dear Margaret

Yesterday Tom had an airgraph from you dated Nov. 14. There was no other mail all week, except 2 Christmas parcels, apparently from Mrs. Sharp and Mrs. Hamblin, which I have put away....

Tom is up and about again, was out playing for a while yesterday and if all right will go to school to-morrow. He had no temp. after last Sunday but

I kept him in bed until Fri. afternoon. Mary got a cold in her head during the week and has been in bed since Thursday so I feel the winter is settling in around me! It is very discouraging, but there is a frightful amount of flu and many colds about, so I can't expect to escape entirely and am lucky these were slight ailments. Tom still coughs occasionally but I think I caught his sore throat in time to ward off tonsillitis....

No time for more now—what an awful smashing Berlin is getting—may it hasten the end!

[42] 90 DUNVEGAN ROAD
TORONTO, DECEMBER 5

Dear Margaret

There has been no mail this week. The last Tom had, as I told you last week, was an airgraph from you, received Nov. 27, sent Nov. 14.

Mary and Tom seem to be quite recovered, have been at school all week. I took them, and Anne Innis, down to Eaton's Toyland after school on Thursday. I spent all week steeling myself to stand the ordeal of crowds and excitement and though I <u>was</u> pretty tired, it was not nearly as bad as I'd expected. There is such a poor, feeble, uninteresting array of toys this year that they were very quickly ready to come home and there was nothing to interest them to the point of excitement. However, they did get their presents for C., which I think we should send off this week. Mary got him a little trick mouse, and Tom got two conjuring tricks. I got him a copy of "My Name is Frank"—a collection of the B.B.C. talks given by Frank Laskier, the merchant seaman (he now lives in Toronto, I think) on his experiences on ships during the war.

Peter comes home on Dec. 15 and I don't think it's decided yet when the Public Schools are to close—I expect the 22nd, though I have a lurking fear they will use the coal shortage as an excuse for closing the 17th—I hope not! The house full of children for a whole week before Christmas day is <u>too</u> much!...

[43] 90 DUNVEGAN ROAD
TORONTO, DECEMBER 12

Dear Margaret

... I am sorry to hear of your discomforts and overwork. Lack of water added to lack of heat would indeed be trying! We have read of your epidemic of flu in the papers, and are having one ourselves, of a comparatively mild type.

Last week 10,000 children were away ill in the city schools, and offices and shops, already badly understaffed, are having a struggle to carry on....

I am so glad that you hear more often from C. now. None of us have heard from him since he was in N[ew] H[ampshire] in July. I am getting off his Christmas parcel to-morrow, as they expect a terrific crush of Christmas mail, with consequent delays.

Tom has been in a great state of excitement over this morning's anthem—a soprano one sung by 4 boys alone. They had an extra practice yesterday afternoon and then one boy was taken ill so there were only 3 to sing. I was sorry not to be at church to hear it but I kept Mary in bed this morning, so had to stay home. Apparently they did satisfactorily and are to repeat it next Sunday evening....

If the govt. will allow you to send £10 a month for Tom, and you feel you can manage it, I would like to deposit each remittance in the bank, and see if we cannot manage to add to it sufficiently to send Tom to boarding school next September. Of course it is only a rather vague plan and I shan't mention it to Tom and I hope you won't, as I should not want him to be disappointed if it doesn't come off. I think he would be simply thrilled—he evidently considers Peter's school life glamourous in the extreme. It would be awfully good for him as he would get so many more games and communal activities than at High School or U.T.S., and I expect, too, he would get on faster in the smaller classes with more individual attention—also he might have a better chance of making faster advance in French and Latin. There are 3 good schools close to Toronto, where he would not be far from home. I think it is an idea well worth thinking of, and trying to plan for, even though it should later prove impossible—or unnecessary (because, though I try not to be unduly optimistic, I can't help thinking there is a chance of Germany cracking in time for him to go back next summer!)....

I am enclosing a cutting which I thought would interest you, about the new system of repatriating boy evacuees by warship. I have known about it for some time—two of my friends have English boys who are all prepared to leave on a moment's notice—but it was all supposed to be very "hush-hush" so I had never mentioned it to anyone, but like so many "military secrets" which one carefully keeps under one's hat, in due time one is sure to see it published in the papers. Boys and girls of 17 and over can cross by the regular route, but older women and younger children have had to go by the Portugal route, which was outrageously expensive (at least $1000) and since the "jam" in Lisbon when 300 or 352 of them were stranded for lack of planes to England, no passages could be booked that way. So this new system is to provide for at least the boys whose parents are anxious to have them back for some special reason. The boys are thrilled with the thought of crossing in a war ship, and I understand the fare is only $30.

I am also enclosing the report of the U.T.S. prize giving—I think Vivien has sent or will send the program.

I have just reread your airgraph, and I can assure you there is no reason to fear that Tom will feel himself "pushed out" from home. Any danger there might be would be quite the opposite—that he would lose his memory of, and his interest in, home. Of course it has always been taken for granted that he was here for the duration and when boys he knew have gone back he has never raised the question concerning himself. He has always talked of what High School he would go to after the first year, at Brown, hoped he would win a scholarship to the University of Toronto, like Bill, etc. etc. and has never once mentioned anything about "when I am back in England." I had an American friend here a few weeks ago, who had some conversation with Tom while I was out of the room. She asked him if he were anxious to go back home and Tom answered "Well—uh—no, I don't think so, I like it here—oh—of course I'd like to go home, you know, but probably when I'd been back a while I'd wish I were back here, and then I suppose if I came back here I'd wish I were home"—we were rather amused at the picture of Tom's entire future life as one of utter frustration! I think myself that he is quite contented here and never thinks of going home, but when the time comes to go home he will be tremendously excited and pleased and when once he gets home he will be perfectly contented and happy and Toronto will fade from his mind just like Ulverston has now. I think this would hold good no matter how long he were here.

I really must go to bed now, I have so much to do and so many things to think of in the next 2 weeks that my brain spins. I may not write next Sunday but just send Tom's letter, but I will be sure to give you an account of Christmas—I daresay when Peter comes home bursting with plans and Christmas spirit I'll be spurred on in my effort.

[44]

The Christmas cable came Xmas eve.

90 DUNVEGAN ROAD
TORONTO, DECEMBER 27

Dear Margaret

I did not write last week. Tom wrote and sent his letter off himself. Your Christmas airgraph to Tom came last week and mine arrived Christmas eve. Tom also had two airgraphs from his father, one a Xmas one, and another this morning, telling him of receiving his presents. He had very nice letters from his "little Granny" and Aunt Phyl, enclosed with their gifts.

Christmas was a great success—Tom said it was the best Christmas he had ever had. It is usually awfully hard to get things for Tom. There are few things he is interested in, but this year I seemed to be lucky with him and he was thrilled with everything. He gave me 5 spools of coloured thread, a package of needles, an envelope of mending tissue, and a little hook for darning stockings—all very useful and very acceptable. He gave John shaving soap and a big box of assorted nails, for which he had expressed a wish.

We had a very pretty tree this year—the children decorated it Thursday. All the family were here, though Clare and George could not stay for dinner—they went to George's family. Besse brought Janet up for an hour or so in the afternoon. She is a perfect pet and made a dead set at Bill when he arrived. We had dinner about 6 o'clock—twelve of us—were very fortunate in having a beautiful turkey, which are scarce, but John's brother had had a dozen sent down from Saskatchewan, by a farmer he knows. Ruby McKay brought the sweet—a beautiful big mould of jellied fruit. She had brought her films with her and after dinner we had a delightful movie show—she takes very good ones and showed us great variety—all coloured, beginning with some of John, me and the children in 1937, ones of the 4 children skiing in the winter of 40–41, and a selection of ones she took in New Zealand, Australia, the West Indies, S. Africa and England—Devon, Salisbury, the lake district, London, etc. etc. We all loved them.

Christopher sent us an enlarged snapshot of himself mounted—very good, but he looks so old—though Eve tells me, in a note on her Christmas card that he is as childish as ever, though taller than she!

Tom had a letter this morning from his "little Granny" enclosing one to me, of appreciation for the photograph. I am so glad they arrived safely.

Bill was down for the afternoon and for dinner the Saturday before Christmas—his first appearance since early October. He and Peter seemed to get on so well together—since C. is not here there is not the same spirit of antagonism between them—C. used to bristle as soon as Bill appeared & P. always sided with C. so there was usually friction. Bill was interested in the chemistry set which is Peter's ruling passion at present and which he is collecting bit by bit, making what things he can, such as racks, stands, etc. They made a fire extinguisher with which they chased Tom, putting out imaginary fires in his clothing, to his rather fascinated terror!

Bill of course was here on Christmas too, and sent John and me a beautiful cyclamen plant. He apparently had a most satisfactory Xmas—(or 2 Christmases really, with the R's and us) and is enjoying the holidays. Last summer he had planned to return to the accountant's office for the Xmas holidays but 2 of his Xmas exams are to be after the holidays so he thought he should leave the holidays free for study....

1944

"I hope they will be able to spare one ship from the invasion to take me back to England"[1]

[1]   90 DUNVEGAN ROAD
       TORONTO, JANUARY 3

Dear Margaret

... We have been so glad to have John Taylor with us this weekend—unexpectedly and by accident![2] He was being transferred from Winnipeg to Port Albert, Ont., and was to make a close connection in Toronto on the morning of New Year's Day, but his train from Winnipeg got in too late to make his connection and there was no train until this morning, so he came on up to our house. He is such a nice boy and we enjoyed having him and do hope he will come back. He spent most of yesterday at the Ratcliffe's where fortunately John was home on 5 days' leave, as John T. was able to talk to him about the Navigation Course he is just going on.... He looks very well, and very smart in his officer's uniform, and seems to like his life. If I can find time I should like to write a note to his mother to tell her how he is looking, etc....

By the way I must take time to tell you a rather amusing incident—so typical of Tom. He was in a positive flutter of excitement over John Taylor—hovered about him all Saturday, produced his serial maps to entertain him, and never left his side. On Sunday morning (I had told John T. to sleep as late as he wanted to) Tom was off to church before John T. came down, and John T. was off to the Ratcliffes before Tom came home. Tom and I had our lunch alone together ... and when we started to wash up Tom said "There seem to be a lot of dishes for just the two of us." "Well," I said "there are John Taylor's breakfast dishes, too." "Oh! Yes!" said Tom, the light of remembrance dawning in his eyes "Yes, what happened to him?" He had overnight completely forgotten John T's existence! I wanted to make some utterly fantastic reply, such as that he'd been kidnapped by 3 masked men, but Tom is too literal minded for talking nonsense to him to be often successful!

Tom had a note from Eve Burns, enclosing $2.00 as a Christmas present, and a parcel from C. containing a jig-saw puzzle for Tom and one for Mary. C. remembered Peter's birthday on Dec. 8 which I thought was extremely thoughtful of him, with nothing and no one in his new life to remind him of it. I think I told you C. sent us a very good photograph of himself.

I thought John T's visit would have made Tom remember to write to you yesterday, but apparently the slight break in routine life had its usual effect, as he spent the afternoon, after Sunday School, working on a jig saw and forgot all about it. He may remember before I get this off....

[2]   90 DUNVEGAN ROAD
TORONTO, JANUARY 9

Dear Margaret

This has been an uneventful week and there has been no English mail. The children (Tom and Mary) have been at school all week. Tom has started mortgages in arithmetic and has been besieging John and me with questions as to our financing the purchase of this house—to see if our arrangements conform to the ones they have been taught at school. What struck me about it was that all his questions were in the first person plural—"Do we own this house or rent it?" "Did we own our other house?" "Have we a mortgage on this house?" etc. It shows how completely he identifies himself with our family....

I had a very nice letter from John Taylor this week—his course at Port Albert (130 miles from here) is to be 14 weeks so I hope he will be able to come for a week-end some time.

Tom seems to have forgotten to write you again. If this goes on, I'll remind him.

[3]   90 DUNVEGAN ROAD
TORONTO, JANUARY 16

Dear Margaret

We have not had any letters from you since Dec. 22 or 23, when both Tom and I had airgraphs. Tom forgot to write you last week—the week before, he forgot to write when I did, but I think he wrote himself later in the week.

I hope you get the letter—I did not see the envelope and he has a habit of leaving off the most important part of an address (such as the name of the addressee).

I had rather a harrowing day with Tom on Monday—I can tell you about it, now it is safely over. He fell while playing at school and hit the top of his head on a corner of the brick wall. If he had not had a thick woolen toque on, it might have been very bad, but as it was, it bled a very little and he showed it to his teacher, who sent him to the school nurse. She put on a dressing and telephoned me, saying she thought it was not serious but suggesting that he see a doctor, and sent him home, shortly before noon. I had great difficulty getting in touch with the doctor (they are all worked to death now) but finally his nurse told me to bring Tom in at 3.30 and he would see him between patients.

Meantime, Tom himself was feeling perfectly well and comfortable, had no pain, ate a big dinner and at my suggestion lay down until it was time to go. When Dr. Stock examined his head he said it would require a stitch or two and sent us to the Emergency Dept. of the Toronto General Hospital, telephoning ahead to make sure we would get quick attention.

The nurse who took Tom in told me it would take 10 or 15 minutes, but I sat in the sitting room 45 minutes before he returned—of course I knew it would take them time to cut away the hair, etc., but just the same I couldn't prevent my imagination working overtime on all the most improbable and impossible complications that might arise, and I realised to the full the frightening responsibility of caring for someone else's child. The doctor came out and told me he had put in 3 stitches and would remove them in a week's time. Tom emerged in a high state of nervous excitement, announcing that he was "more dead than alive" and "had been through the greatest agony he ever experienced"—in fact he "didn't think any body had ever suffered so much pain."—he never stopped talking all the way home—not complaints or lamentations but a detailed and excited account of every thing that had been done and said to him in the operating room, interspersed with comments and questions. Finally, however he decided that neither his head nor his arm were hurting any longer and "things like this are awfully nice to brag about when they are over and I'll be quite a hero at school to-morrow"....

Tom had no after-effects whatever. On Tuesday morning I went in and asked him if he felt like getting up or would rather stay in bed and after taking an inventory of the condition of all parts of his body he decided that everything was completely normal, and just as usual, so he went to school and to choir practice after school, and as we had a snowfall on Wednesday, has been sledding and tobogganning. I, however, have been in suspense all week, fearing a reaction from the anti-tetanus injection, but when none came I was beginning to think there would be none. Therefore my heart definitely sank, when, first thing this morning, Tom showed me his arm—there was a swelling around the "pin-prick" as Tom call it, and a little soreness. I telephoned the doctor immediately and he told me not to be concerned as it seemed a normal reaction, and not unduly late. He said it might have come still later and might become much more severe. I have been keeping wet compresses of boracic solution on it all day—they soothe the slight itch and soreness and Tom has not found it too uncomfortable. By evening it seemed to have subsided a bit and at least was not sore, so I am hopeful that it will be of brief duration. I shall not be easy in my mind until it is all gone. We go to have the stitches out to-morrow and can see what the doctor says. I will not post this letter until after that.

Tom seems to have a gift for getting things wrong with him which keep you in a state of uneasiness—fearing the outbreak of certain symptoms but not wanting to ask him about them because (he is so suggestible in matters concerning his health) he would immediately <u>have</u> those symptoms or think he had e.g. that eye trouble he had—the boils—the elusive rash of a little over a year ago—and the latest was when he was bitten by a dog last June. I did not tell you about it at the time because of course with a dog bite there is always a <u>faint</u> danger of complications for a long period after, and I did not want you to worry. By the time that period had passed there was no point in mentioning it....

JANUARY 18

Tom's arm was much better yesterday, and when I took him to have the stitches out of his head, the doctor said the reaction was perfectly normal. By this morning Tom reported, after careful consideration, that his arm felt exactly like the other arm, so I think all is over now. Heaven be praised!

We are having weather almost too good to be true—just cold enough not to be sloppy, and bright on the whole. No matter what kind of winter we still have in store it can't last <u>long</u>, as we are now in mid-January—a great comfort!

[4]   90 DUNVEGAN ROAD
        TORONTO, JANUARY 23

Dear Margaret

Tom had an airgraph from you on Jan. 20, sent Christmas Day!—and one from his father on Jan. 22, sent Jan. 3. I expect the heavy pre- and post-Xmas mail from the troops takes precedence over that of civilians, both by air and sea. I am glad you liked the photograph—his father did not mention receiving his—I hope it arrived safely. In an earlier air-graph he told Tom of getting the razor blades, which were sent with a Christmas card. I hope Tom's little parcel to you arrived not too long after Christmas.

You will be glad to know that Tom had no further trouble with his "wound" or his arm. His hair is covering up the clipped spot and no sign remains....

We have not seen Bill since Christmas Day—nor heard from him, for, though he expressed great concern on hearing from Vivien of Tom's accident (the day it happened) the concern was apparently not deep enough to impel him to make any subsequent inquiries, nor, in fact, to prevent his immediately forgetting the whole affair until Vivien reminded him of it 4 or 5 days later, when, as she reported Tom none the worse, I suppose he felt his casual attitude justified. This incident is not surprising, as Bill seems really incapable of any genuine concern for the happiness or welfare of any person except himself. His colossal self-absorption is a bit rough on the Ratcliffes, but they, after a year or so of conscientiously trying to change his attitude, with few results beyond sulks and friction, decided henceforth simply to accept him as he is, selfishness and all, according him the same thoughtfulness and consideration as though he were doing the same to them. This keeps relationships pleasant and makes for an ideal existence from Bill's point of view—having all the privileges of home life with none of the responsibilities. The Ratcliffes are a family in a million and I wish Bill realized how lucky he is, but he takes it all as his due—or slightly less! It is too bad, for the boy has many good qualities.

Tom is full of the new organist and choirmaster, who is vigourously instituting a new regime of hard work and long practises, in place of the former easy going methods. Poor man! he has a real task ahead of him, as the choir is really in awful shape—the men reduced to 4 or 5 and the boys, while numerous, mostly very young with ragged and undisciplined voices. He will find Tom at least a willing and earnest worker.

We have been thinking of C. this weekend—John reminded us on Friday that it was just a year ago he took him to Buffalo. Time does fly (to be very original). We have none of us heard from C. since the summer—except for Christmas presents from him.

JANUARY 24

Your cheque came in this morning's post. Thank you very much.

Dear Margaret

There has been no mail this week....

Bill is coming for supper this evening and going to evening service, as Tom is singing one verse of a carol by himself. Tom will not be here for supper—to-night is the annual candle-light service, which is combined with a Sunday School "do"—the S.S. children have supper & a movie before evening service, so don't come home. I was a little surprised that it didn't enter Tom's head to miss the supper & movie to come home because Bill would be here. It shows he's pretty well emancipated from his old servility and a good thing.

Not much to say, nor much time to say it. We are all well, the weather has been springlike.

Dear Margaret

On Jan. 31 Tom had an airgraph from you, sent Jan. 16 or 18, and on Feb. 1 he and Mary had letters from your mother, sent Jan. 8....

I had rather a bad day on Thursday with Tom—he wakened me at 4.30 to tell me he was feeling sick. I gave him soda & water, etc. but he got no relief but when Mary came down for her breakfast (she had heard the early commotion and lost no time investigating when she got up) she announced that _she_ would soon have Tom feeling right. She said "When you feel sick and can't bring anything up, the thing to do is _read_ and that soon makes you vomit. So I got Tom a good exciting book to read and I got him a glass of water because he'll want to rinse his mouth after!" Sure enough, whether it was Mary's prescription or the orange juice I gave him, he did soon get his stomach cleared....

He was perfectly well Friday morning but I kept him in bed part of the morning, as he'd had practically nothing to eat the day before, and I simply _had_ to have him well for Friday night, as we had tickets to take the children to the "Ice Follies" and they'd been excitedly looking forward to it for 3 weeks! However, he went to school Friday afternoon and even after the late night at the "Follies" was none the worse on Saturday.

The children were simply knocked speechless by the breathtaking beauty of the first number of the ice show and all through they were simply rapt. I don't think they had ever had such an evening. It really is a marvellous production—superlative skating and exquisite costumes, colour and lighting effects. It was on for 5 nights, in the Maple Leaf Gardens, which holds about 16,000 and was sold out far in advance, with hundreds standing. They were both very tired—it lasted from 8.30 to 11 without a moment's pause except for a 15 minute interval—but it was well worth it, they enjoyed it so....

I was rather mystified to receive a cheque, two days ago for £30, having just got one for £9 a week or so ago. I wondered whether there was an error and this second one should not have come until April. However, I expect it will be explained when you write.

[7]   90 DUNVEGAN ROAD
       TORONTO, FEBRUARY 13

Dear Margaret

... We had John Taylor here for this weekend and were so glad to have him come. He is such a nice pleasant, friendly lad and we are very fond of him. Port Albert is an awkward spot to get to and from and the journey takes an endless time considering the distance—only 130 miles or so. He arrived late Friday evening after leaving early in the afternoon, and left at 6 tonight (Sunday) and will not arrive until midnight. This is the first weekend leave he has had—they work them very hard, 7 days a week. I am afraid we are rather dull and middle aged company for him, but Vivien most thoughtfully got tickets for the Saturday night hockey game, for him and Bill. He enjoyed it immensely, as he had never had the opportunity of seeing one of the pro. games before. He went to church this morning, which of course pleased Tom enormously.

We had our first heavy snow of the winter on Friday, to the children's joy, and as it was close to zero, none of it melted. I cut a lot of branches of forsythia a week or two ago, which are now in bloom in the house, and make it seem as though spring were not far off.

Bill was here this afternoon for tea—I asked him for dinner at noon, but he thought he had better do some studying earlier in the day as he'd been out Friday & Sat. evenings and was going out to-night, and Thursday being his birthday he had done no work. He seems to be doing very well, judging by his Christmas exams....

I am afraid Tom has forgotten to write to-day, but I will keep this until to-morrow, to post, in case he remembers later.

Dear Margaret

Your long letter of Jan. 12 arrived Monday, and to-day I had one from your mother (Jan. 17) and Tom one from Mrs. Hamblin (Jan. 20) so it looks as though the mails were getting back to normal....

To begin with the news of Mr. Sharp's marriage—you will have had, long since, my cable, sent yesterday, to tell you I had given Tom your letter. My worry over Tom's reception of the news had been mainly on the point of Mary's unavoidably being "in on" it. She has all the keenness, penetration and active curiosity that Tom lacks, and I was afraid her endless questions would stir up unhappy memories for Tom. So I handed Tom the letter quite casually, as he was doing his homework, just after Mary had left for Girl Guides. I waited downstairs in some trepidation for his reaction and was prepared for almost anything except what actually happened. He came down, trembling with suppressed excitement and said "Would you like to read this, there is news in it," fluttering the letter about. Determined to keep it all on a light note I said "Oh! your mother told you about your father, did she? She told me, too, isn't it interesting?" I think, Tom-like, he was waiting to get his cue how to take it from me, so he burst into smiles and said "If they have children, what relation will they be to me?" Well— the proverbial feather would have done its trick with me, I can assure you! Apparently that was the only aspect that occurred to him or concerned him and all his questions were on the same topic, followed by "It will be impossible now for my mother to have any more children, won't it?" "Yes, unless she should marry again." "But in that case they would be half-brothers and -sisters too, wouldn't they? I can't have any more real brothers and sisters." Assured on this point, he decided to go back to his history, but I was not to get off as lightly as I thought.

He turned back and asked very earnestly "Aunt Marie, do you know why my mother and father were divorced?" "No" I said "I don't exactly. It was a long time ago and I didn't know them. But a great many people get divorced for many different reasons. Lots of people marry, thinking they want to spend the rest of their lives together, but later on they find they aren't as happy together as they thought they would be, and decide that the best thing is to separate." "I see" he said, and then hesitatingly "and perhaps my father's work—he couldn't keep on living in London—" I could see the child was miserable and was groping for a defence, so I backed up his pitiful subterfuge with "Yes I dare say that had something to do with it too," in a bright, "everything's all right" tone of voice. He stood a moment, and I've never seen anything so pathetic—so defenceless, as the memories he had so assiduously buried out of sight and thought relentlessly flooded his mind. Then, turning his head slightly, to hide his working mouth he said in a low tone, with a catch in his voice "I—I—remember—when he left—we were at Southway"—and stopped dead. Then a few seconds' pause, and he briskly threw back his head and asked if he hadn't better go and tell Uncle John the news, which he did with just the same excited cheerfulness he had discussed it with me at first. When he was going to bed he asked me what relation the new Mrs. Sharp would be to him. The next morning he burst out of his room and greeted Mary with "I've got a step-mother!" I was glad he had got the initial surprise over and his mind "settled" with Mary out of the way because, as it was, he and Mary spent their entire breakfast and also lunch discussing Tom's step-mother and potential half-brothers and -sisters. I am sure Mr. and Mrs. Sharp would be surprised could they see how confidently Tom seems to be expecting a large family of "steps" waiting his return to England. The next time he was alone with me, he got back to the divorce by asking "Aunt Marie, doesn't it say in the marriage service 'till death do us part'?" "Yes" I said "it does, but you see there are two parts to a marriage—the religious ceremony, and also a legal contract, and it is the legal contract that is absolved by divorce, because divorce is a legal process. As for the religious ceremony, that is not even necessary in most countries, though it is in Canada, but even if one has that ceremony, those promises are made by two people to one another and after all, if later on they find they will both be happier by releasing one another from those promises that is their own affair." He asked a few more questions and I hope I reassured him. I was really not prepared at all for the discussion and just did my best on the spur of the moment to explain things truthfully, understandably, and so as not to raise more doubts in his mind.

In the afternoon he asked me whether I thought Bill had heard the news. I said I knew you had written him but could not say whether the letter had arrived, so he decided to telephone Bill and find out. However, apparently his sole motive in this was to have the pleasure of springing a surprise on Bill, with no idea of any discussion of the affair for the conversation was limited to Tom "Have you heard from mother?" Bill—"Yes" Tom (disappointedly) "Oh! Then you know?" Bill—"Yes" Tom hangs up the receiver.

Since then (that was 3 days ago) he has never mentioned it again. It seems as though the news of the marriage affected him only as something very unusual and surprising, which gave him some importance for the moment, as making him slightly different from ordinary people (always attractive to Tom). For instance in conversation with Mary he said "If anyone asks me now how many mothers I have, I can say 'Two'"—and was promptly flattened by Mary's matter of fact "And who do you think would ever be likely to ask you how many mothers you have?" But undoubtedly he was pretty shaken by the painful memories evoked when he had to remember the past—in fact, I dare say a lot of the chatter and excitement were a subconscious attempt to prevent himself dwelling on that.

I remember, when I told you that I was sure he had forgotten about the divorce, you asked whether it might not be an "escape mechanism" and I said I doubted it. But I think that much of his vagueness and forgetfulness is a subconscious attempt to escape from unpleasantness of any kind, and his lack of curiosity and penetration have been cultivated to avoid facing inconvenient realities, just as his helplessness and dependence were cultivated to gain attention and escape personal effort.

On the whole it has not proved very upsetting for him and undoubtedly it is best for him to be told at the same time as Bill. As I see it, though, there is nothing to be gained by your mentioning "Agnes" in your letters—naturally his father will, I expect. And I <u>do</u> hope that I have now done with Mr. Sharp—I am rather tired of pulling his chestnuts out of the fire. I wanted to give you a complete account of Tom's reaction (though it does take so long to write) because you were apparently worried by the whole thing and would be anxious to know how he took it.[3]

I have been several days at this letter and it's rather long already, so I think I shall send it off and answer the rest of your letter at the weekend.

However, I must mention one item in your letter which strikes me with horror—your assurance, in the event of Tom's going to boarding school, that you will guarantee £10 a month for him even if it means cutting down on the others! I simply could not hear of such a thing. I suppose I should have made it clear in my letter, when I mentioned my hope of sending him to boarding school, that it was on my own account I was trying to plan for it (I expect I just thought that would be self-evident) and I explained what I thought Tom's views would be, not to show you I was trying to gratify Tom's wishes, but to assure you that I would not take any steps, though designed for my own comfort, unless the scheme would be satisfactory to Tom both in prospect and fulfilment. However, as you know, whatever extra money you can send Vivien she has earmarked for no other purpose than to put Bill in a university residence next year (if they are not all used for barracks) and I know Eve (she sent me a copy of her letter to you of Nov. 11, to save time writing me another letter to let me know about C.) is similarly putting aside what you send her for C's education, so I would not <u>consider</u> accepting more than ⅓ of whatever you can send.

I shall write again in a few days. Tom had a letter from his Grandmother Sharp to-day, sent Jan. 29. Please let me know as soon as you can that you have received this as I know you will be anxious to have it—also I'd like to know when you get no. 9 as it will be an answer to the rest of your long one. And will you please let me know about the old one of Vivien's.

Sorry to say none of us, nor Bill nor Tom have heard from C. since last summer.

[9]   *[Letter 9 appears to have been written to "Cousin Mary" (Mary Tout), and only a summary written by Mary Tout for her daughter survives.]*

[10]   90 DUNVEGAN ROAD
TORONTO, MARCH 4

Dear Margaret

... Since [an airgraph received on Feb. 19] the only mail is a long letter to Tom from his father, written Feb. 13, which arrived yesterday. I had to read this letter to him, and if I might make a suggestion it would be that it would be better all around for him to have used the same amount of time to print a letter a quarter as long. Neither you nor Mr. Sharp seem to realize even yet that unless your letters are typed or printed he cannot read them and as the only tie he has with you is by letter and those are infrequent it does seem too bad that this one link should be weakened (and therefore, his interest in you still more lessened), as it must inevitably be, by having to be transmitted through a third person. I know no one has much time nowadays but I don't think it would take any longer to print a short letter than it does for me to have to read him a written one, particularly as it often has to be done at most inconvenient times, as if it isn't attended to at the moment it arrives, when he is interested, he lays the letter down somewhere and forgets all about it.

His father still does not mention receiving his photograph, but as I gathered from your letter that all four arrived safely, I imagine that is just an oversight. It is rather a pity, as even insensitive Tom, I think, felt a chill of disappointment at the lack of comment.

I hope my letters 8 and 9 in reply to yours of Jan. 12, arrived safely—also no. 42 of 1943, although I don't expect there was much in that one....

The children are well, though I had a scare with Mary last Monday—she got frightfully ill in school and I had to go down and bring her home, looking like death—and feeling it, poor kid. However a day and a half in bed fixed her up.

I'm afraid Tom has forgotten to write again.... By the way, as far as I know he did not mention his father's marriage to Peter so I expect he's forgotten about that too. I only just thought of it this minute, but I expect if Tom had told him he'd have remarked on it to me.

No more now—I have had a nasty sort of arthritis in my wrists and thumbs the last few weeks—fortunately my right hand is not nearly so bad as the left or I couldn't write at all, but it's exasperating.

[11]   90 DUNVEGAN ROAD
           TORONTO, MARCH 13

Dear Margaret

I had not intended to write this week as time presses so, and, besides, my hands and wrists have been giving me a lot of trouble—I don't know whether I ever mentioned it, but all winter I have had a sort of arthritic condition—first in my thumbs, then wrists, and sometimes right up my forearms. As my hands are in constant use from morning till night, it is rather wearying, but I hope the coming of warm weather will help....

There has been no mail since I last wrote. Your last letter to Tom was the one enclosed in the long one to me, which arrived Feb. 14. With letters so infrequent, it is scarcely to be wondered at that, given a memory—or lack of memory—like Tom's, you are fading to little more than a name in his mind. When people ask him if he is looking forward to going back to England he hesitates and says "Well—uh—uh—I suppose so"—I don't think the thought of seeing you again enters his mind at all. One friend, who had not seen him for a year or two, was here the other day and she asked him the same question but used the word "home" instead of "England" and he looked quite bewildered and obviously didn't know what she meant. I helped him out by saying "This is 'home' to Tom now." "Oh yes" he said, with a laugh, "when I go back to England I suppose I'll be homesick."

He had an excellent report on March 1, with an average of 83 (I expect it was receiving his report that reminded him to write you) and his teacher, whom I saw last week, has nothing but praise for and satisfaction with, his work. It is baffling how he can do so well in his school work and yet in everything else his mind is vague, muddled and forgetful and he needs continual and endless reminding, prodding, bolstering and eternal explaining.

His utter lack of any "general knowledge," even of the most commonplace sort, is unbelievable (the only exception to this is the war news, which he follows pretty carefully, though I sometimes wonder whether he really understands it or just memorizes what he reads, because every once in a while he makes a most astounding observation—such as, after he'd been here about a year, reading and discussing the war news all the time, he asked me what was the "axis" that he noticed mentioned so often!).

I suppose it all boils down to the fact that he considers nothing important enough to try to understand or hold in his mind, except school work and the only achievement which has any meaning or appeal for him is represented by examinations. Sometimes when I've been surprised at his knowing something he will say, rather indignantly "But I've been taught that!" He rarely listens to general conversation unless it directly concerns him, or school, or one of his very few interests—he is very unobservant, and though he reads a lot, nothing in his book seems to register on his mind except the story. So he fails to gather all the infinite variety of information which most children pick up almost unconsciously by using their eyes and ears and curiosity (he is the first child I ever knew who had practically no trace of this characteristic).

Everyone says he has progressed marvellously in self-reliance and alertness but after all, he is 3½ years older than when he came here, and sometimes I feel that all our unremitting efforts have done little more than keep pace with his advancing years—that he is almost as backward and dependent on others now, for 12½, as he was then, for 9....

I think I told you Peter was home for 4 days. It was grand to have him home and he enjoyed it. Since going back he has got a place on the 2nd hockey team, and is naturally delighted tho' they've lost both games they have played so far!

P.S. I had a letter from C., apologizing for letters not sent and telling me he is learning to play the clarinet.

[12] 90 DUNVEGAN ROAD
        TORONTO, APRIL 2

Dear Margaret

... Your airgraph of March 11 was the first message of any kind [Tom] had from you after your letter of Jan. 12, telling him the news. It was a rather unfortunate time for a lapse of two months between letters (5½ wks. at this end, the second being an airgraph)—however it is past and gone now and no use worrying. I am still a little puzzled as to why you wanted the cable, but if it put your mind at rest I am glad.

I am afraid the workings of Tom's mind are a complete mystery to me, and while, off-hand, I should say that it would probably not bother him to have C. go back to England, still I hesitate to try to predict, with any degree of certainty, how he would react. On the whole his motto seems "Whatever is, is right," and any event which does not directly affect his personal way of life, slides off the surface of his mind without making an impression, but once in a long while, something, for no apparent reason, excites his interest enough for him really to examine and enquire about it. So, he might accept C's going back as something that was happening to C. and had nothing to do with him, but, if he were stirred up enough to probe into the question and use his generally dormant imagination on it, he might possibly be jealous—not that I'd say he has any desire to go back himself, but he might resent C's "stealing his thunder" by getting back first to enjoy the lion's share of the glory and limelight—limelight does appeal strongly to Tom! So, after all this writing, I suppose it all adds up to "you never can tell"....

I rather think Tom has remembered to write to-day, after forgetting for several weeks—I have not forgotten but I've been so utterly exhausted for the past month I've done nothing but what was absolutely necessary—there's always enough of <u>that</u> to last all day. Mrs. Fairfoul has had a bad knee and was away more than a week and has to be "saved" since she came back, Mary was in bed nearly a week with a cold, Ruby McKay has had a bad case of asthma for 2 weeks and I've tried when I could to go up to relieve the nurse, so Ruby wouldn't be alone during the nurse's hours off— fortunately she is, while far from recovered, well enough that she doesn't mind being alone for part of the afternoon, because, just when Peter got home for the holidays and I thought I might get to Ruby's in the afternoons, by leaving him in charge, I came down with a bad cold and sore throat—the first real cold I've had in 2 years. I think it's from being so tired out, and it is very annoying. It's rather hard on Peter, my being ill on his holiday, but it is a lifesaver for me, because he gets the breakfast and brings mine up, and is my right hand all day, and to-day (Sunday) he got me to go back to bed right after mid-day dinner and not only got the tea for me but cooked a very creditable supper for the family (in apron and chef's cap). I do hope this miserable throat will clear up soon.

John and I managed to get down to the school last weekend for Peter's confirmation (March 25). We were so glad we went—we hadn't realized that the school made such an "event" of it, and practically all the 35 boys confirmed had their parents there. There is always a big reception after the service, with the kind of food that makes a party memorable for boys!

It was a most enjoyable 24 hours though both John and I found it very wearying after the quiet life we've got used to!

Peter came home Thursday, 30th—he has 18 days holiday—the others have from the day before Good Friday to a week after Easter—9 days. I hope I'm well recovered before the holiday begins.

[13] 90 DUNVEGAN ROAD
TORONTO, APRIL 8

Dear Margaret

Very much surprised to receive your cable but after discussion we think it advisable to follow your suggestion and have T. go home with C. Have obtained instructions how to go about applications, from Univ. Committee and have sent them on to Eve. Can't go into details now, but have been worried recently at signs of T's growing insecurity and unsureness of your affection, especially since the news of his father's marriage, followed by long silence. It seems unwise to prolong the separation. He greeted news of C's probable return with moderate interest and replied to the question "whether he wished he could go too" with an unconcerned "Oh I don't know" but when, baffled by his non-committal attitude I said "If it can be arranged for you to go with C., your mother would like you to go too," his face lit up with speechless joy. It seems as though he must have been troubled by vague fears of your indifference and his unconcernedness must have been a more or less conscious pose to hide his real, though hidden, fears. Dealing with your cable has been complicated by Peter being very ill with measles—and the others on holiday from school! I hope we've now reached the peak of the measles but it's been a bad two days and nights. It will be an anxious 10 days watching M. and T. for symptoms. Shan't have much time to write but will try to keep you posted as to developments. I gather that we enter the boys' names for repatriation and then have no control over when they go. They are "summoned" in turn and if you don't take the passage when offered, the name goes to the bottom of the list.

[14] 90 DUNVEGAN ROAD
TORONTO, APRIL 18

Dear Margaret

Tom and I had letters from your mother of March 16, arrived Apr. 7. Last from you were airgraphs to Tom and me of Mar. 18, arr. Mar 30 and then your cables of Ap. 6 and 17. Mails are so slow between here and Washington that only yesterday was I able to get off joint letters from Arthur [Burns] and ourselves to the Ministry of War Transport. Until I hear from them I don't think there is any use answering your second cable, as I expect they will give us full instructions about everything including transfer of funds for passage. If this proves complicated we are quite willing to make the payment ourselves. It is barely possible that transportation may be provided much sooner than expected or convenient. I understand they are trying to handle as many boys as possible before more pressing needs cause a suspension of this type of transportation. However, we shall have to take whatever opportunity is offered and hope it won't make too much of a rush of preparations. Peter had a very bad case of measles, but made a good recovery and was able to go back to school for opening of term Apr. 17. The other 2 had a good holiday tho' necessarily confined fairly closely to home. They are still well and I hope they stay so as I am pretty exhausted—there are 3 days yet of uncertainty. I think T. is much pleased at the prospect of going home tho' he rarely mentions it. He has never written you since he got the news—nor to C., nor has he thought to telephone Bill to tell him! His reactions do seem to me far from normal, which increases the weight of responsibility for him as he grows older and his deviations from the normal therefore more pronounced. Shall keep you informed of any developments and will cable about funds if advisable.

[15] 90 DUNVEGAN ROAD
TORONTO, APRIL 27

Dear Margaret

Your double airgraph of Apr. 15 arrived 24th—very fast. Also airgraph to Tom of Apr. 17 came to-day. So sorry to hear you have been ill. You and Peter seem to have equally bad luck with holidays. Thankful to say the measles danger is now past—I hope! I don't know how I could have stood it if Tom and Mary had taken it. We are working on Tom's passage—there is a lot of red tape and it's all a question of time—waiting for this and waiting for that and it's rather maddening being so tied with the children and house I can't get out much and after things. However I'm sure it will all work out. Your draft for £30 arrived to-day so that with the last one, which I banked, looking to boarding-school next year, we shall have ample funds for all Tom's passage and expenses and also to buy him anything necessary before he goes. I would like to send him home well outfitted. Clothing is far from plentiful but I expect not nearly so scarce as with you—and not rationed. So don't consider sending any money for his passage.

[16] 90 DUNVEGAN ROAD
TORONTO, APRIL 30

Dear Margaret

I sent you an airgraph 3 days ago but thought I had better try to write a fuller letter (which may have to be finished in bits).

To begin with, we have made little progress with Tom's arrangements. As instructed by the committee, we wrote, jointly with Arthur [Burns], to the Ministry of War Transport. They sent us applications for priority passage, which we despatched back to them promptly, and they also sent us an application for an exit permit, which we filled out and sent back to the Immigration Dept. at Ottawa. We are still waiting for this permit and are told that, until it is obtained, nothing can be done about Tom's passport. What we are to do, when we get the exit permit, is send it, with the passport, to the Dept. of External Affairs, to have the passport validated for travel in the U.S. (This may give us another lengthy wait, tho' John intends to send it to the Canada Life manager in Ottawa and see if he can save time by attending in person.) After that is done and we get the passport and permit back, we have to take him to the U.S. consul (2 visits at least) and get a U.S. visa (new photos etc.). Then, when his final notice to leave arrives, we have to take him back to the U.S. Consul for an "in-transit" certificate. All this for possibly 24 hours in the U.S.A.! We will, of course, go ahead with all this, tho' we have not the slightest assurance that a sailing will be forthcoming. However there is nothing we can do about that.

As I told you in my airgraph, there is no need for you to send money for his passage, and as it could only be done at the last moment it might cause complications when time is short. Anyway, the £60 you have sent this year will be ample both for passage and expenses, and to buy him clothes, of which I would like to send a good supply. He will be allowed only 150 lbs. luggage (including trunks and hand luggage). I am a bit hazy as to how much 150 lbs. is, so I am going to pack a trunk and weigh it, to get an idea, but I hope it will allow for all I would like to send. However, I think it may be taken for granted that he won't be able to take such things as his books, his heavy box of minibrix and things like that. I am enclosing a list of the books he has—some of them are now rather outgrown but I dare say you might like them for his smaller cousins. There are also numerous games, jig-saws, etc. etc. The instructions say that surplus luggage may be sent by freight from Canadian ports. I would like to know what you would like me to do about this. I could pack them and send them by freight, as soon as he has gone, or else keep them and send them with Bill, if he goes next year (though he will probably have a luggage restriction and must have tons of similar stuff himself) or send it by freight when the war hazard is past. Of course if the war is over when Bill goes, I dare say there will be no luggage limit, provided one pays extra for the excess weight. Anyway, I should like your opinion. As for clothes, I am picking up shirts etc. as I'm able to find them (everything is scarce)—these are things he'll need whether he goes or stays, but some things I'll have to postpone buying until we know definitely that he's going, and take a chance on being able to get them if the time is short. A suit for instance—he'll need a new one in the autumn anyway, but it would be a different kind if he's staying here, from what I would get him for England—the same applies to coats and some other things. One thing I shall not be able to get is woolen underwear. We never used very much of it here, and since the war none at all has been made. Even the heavy cotton, with a little wool, which our boys mostly wear, was unobtainable last winter—I couldn't get any new for either Peter or Tom, so their old had to be darned and patched and repatched and is absolutely done. The heavy cotton will be available in the autumn and if he is staying on here, I will get him that—we find it quite heavy enough as our houses are so warm, but I expect in England the wool is necessary.

Also with reference to luggage—the boys, as you know, brought out with them 3 trunks. The biggest one went to the Ratcliffes with Bill. When C. went to Washington the second one would not begin to hold his things so we gave him a big square box trunk of John's, which we did not need, and kept the 2 to use for Tom. The small one (which is quite small) is in very good shape but the larger of the two got a few bashes, apparently, on their way out here, and we are afraid it might not stand the journey back to England, even though it contained only clothes and nothing heavy. Of course it is impossible to buy a trunk but we have a much larger trunk, of similar build (we bought it in England to bring home the blankets etc. we had got there) and we may just send that with Tom instead of the other 2—possibly Bill can use the little one when he goes. Using one large trunk instead of 2 smaller would help with the weight problem as it probably weighs little more than either one of the others. John is going to examine them all for stability—he is awfully good at judging that sort of practical thing and we will do whatever seems best—I would hate to have his trunk smashed en route and I imagine the handling is even <u>less</u> gentle (if possible) than in normal times.

Tom has two War Savings Certificates of $5.00 each. They are in John's strong box and I think I'll just leave them there and post them to him after the war when mail is safe. I thought of putting them in his trunk but an envelope could easily be lost in unpacking and I know Tom would never remember them, and I wouldn't dream of letting him carry them. He seemed to feel he was going to have an embarrassment of riches—he has more than $10 in cash and will have money coming to him from the choir and wanted to know whether he would be allowed to take it home. I suggested that he buy some presents to take home, which he thought a good idea, and I suggested that whatever he has left over, when the time comes to leave, he gives me, to apply to his passage, and I will let you know the amount so you can refund it to him in sterling when he arrives. He seems to think this most satisfactory, and I think it's best because he is so vague and forgetful that I don't think he should carry, and be responsible for, anything of value that can possibly be looked after in any other way. I do hope when he goes, that he has an escort all the way to his ship, who can take charge of his passport, papers and money. I understand that as a rule the committee provides an escort for the train trip to N.Y. (overnight) but that the boys are <u>always</u> met in N.Y. and taken charge of and entertained and delivered at the appointed time to the appropriate hotel, where they are turned over to the Admiralty, who take charge of them from then on. When a party of boys leave, a cable is sent, and through some machinery of the C.O.R.B., committees in all the ports are notified.[4] The boys, while en route, or on arrival, are given addresses and telephone numbers of the committee members in the particular port where they are landed and these people see them on their trains for home. The committee is very proud of their organization, which they have perfected over a period of 6 mos. or so and which works smoothly and satisfactorily....

MAY 2

Sorry I cannot write more—my wrists have been giving me a great deal of trouble and by night they ache like a tooth, so I need a good dose of aspirin to get to sleep. Also, I don't know whether I ever told you—for a year & a half I have had an infection around the nail of the middle finger on my right hand. It dies down and is quiescent for a week or so, and then starts up again and is agonizing for 3 or 4 weeks. Just now it is pretty bad, and the combination of the 2, when my hands are of necessity active every minute of the day, wear me out so that as soon as the children are in bed

I creep thankfully into my own bed. I'm afraid poor John has pretty dull evenings—I don't think we've been out together since Christmas, but by evening I am too dead tired to make the necessary arrangements of having someone come in, and the effort of going out. As a matter of fact John has had to bring work home almost every night—they are so short-staffed that he is dreadfully overworked.

[17] 90 DUNVEGAN ROAD
TORONTO, MAY 17

Dear Margaret

Tom and I had airgraphs from you on May 4 (Apr. 24) and May 12 (May 4) and T. had a letter from his father on May 4 (Mar. 26). I'm surprised Tom has forgotten to write since May 2, especially as he got his report—average of over 80, standing 3rd. We have no word regarding his sailing and don't expect to hear anything until an actual passage is secured—we have passport, etc. ready.... Glad to hear about the Gr[ammar] School—as Peter's headmaster said on this subject "Surely the English schools will make allowances for these boys returning. The Canadian schools made all sorts of allowances and special arrangements for them when they came." You must be looking forward to being able to be at home with your own boys again. Will let you have any news that there is. Love Marie.

[18] 90 DUNVEGAN ROAD
TORONTO, MAY 22

Dear Margaret

Just a note to accompany Tom's letter which he remembered to write yesterday. All goes well with us. We have still heard nothing about Tom's passage. I expect Mrs. Bland is home by now. The uncertainty makes summer plans a problem. If Tom does not get away before the end of June I'd like him to go to Pioneer, where he is so happy, but my Scotch soul hesitates to send in an application, with the necessary registration fee, in case he won't be going—while on the other hand the registration is filling up so fast there may not be room for him if the application is delayed! However, I don't doubt things will work out all right in the end.

I have been waging a time-consuming and discouraging struggle to gather together a few clothes for Tom, in case he does go home. I had not realized quite how scarce things had become and how greatly quality has

I'm glad you are now going to be history mistress at Ulverston Grammar school. Does that mean that you will teach me?

Our choir is in rather a mix up now. Our leading I tenor soloist died a few days ago and another tenor left to be organist of another church leaving one tenor. This means that the only anthems we can sing are all boy's anthems To make matters worse our leading boy is sick!

Love,

From Tom.

P.S. Our I hope they will be able to spare one ship from the invasion to take me back to England.

From Tom's last letter to his parents from Canada; the text of the complete letter appears on pages 365–366

___

deteriorated. However I'll do my best because at least one doesn't need coupons here, though purchases are mostly limited to one article of a kind—when you can find an article you want!

Peter comes home in less than 3 weeks now—he seems very well. John went down for the cadet inspection and gymnasium display on May 13. We had not gas enough to drive and I thought 2 railway fares were too much, so as I had been down for it last year I got John to go. It is always a very enjoyable day at the school.

Bill came down on Saturday and took Tom out on an expedition which was apparently a great success.

Will write again when I have news.[5]

Love
Marie

EPILOGUE

by Margaret Sharp, wife of Tom[1]

SO THERE THE CORRESPONDENCE ENDS—ON MAY 22, 1944, JUST BEFORE
the Allied invasion of France (June 6)—with news expected any day of a
summons to New York for a place for Tom on a warship sailing to England.
The date of that summons is not documented, but Tom was still waiting on
June 12 when he wrote to his mother, "I hope they will be able to spare one
ship from the invasion to take me back to England." The summons must
have arrived soon thereafter. Then Tom took a train to New York via Buffalo,
where he was met by Eve Burns and Christopher. They stayed overnight
at the Barbazon Plaza hotel on Central Park (a great thrill), and the boys
embarked the following day on an aircraft carrier that was taking planes to
Britain, all with wings folded upwards so as to pack in as many as possible.
Since the ship was being used as a transport and was not in battle readiness,
the "pilots' ready room" was not needed for its normal purpose (as a briefing
and waiting area for pilots) and could be occupied for the week-long voyage
by some twenty or so boys, all returning evacuees. Tom has no memories of
the passage back, but we inherited from his mother two brass shell cases,
which, he claims, he and Christopher retained as booty.

The carrier docked at Liverpool, where the boys were met by their father,
and spent the night in his home in Didsbury, to the south of Manchester,
meeting for the first time his new wife, Agnes. The next day they were put
on a train to Rocester, a village close to Abbotsholme School, where, as
the letters record, their mother Margaret had been teaching since 1941.
The boys joined her there for the final two weeks of the summer term.
They were, in fact, her last two weeks at that school and it was a hectic
time for her. From Tom's letter of June 12, we know that she had resigned
her Abbotsholme job from the end of that term, having secured a post

Christopher and Tom with their mother, Margaret, soon after the boys' return to England

teaching history at the grammar school in Ulverston, the town south of the Lake District where the boys had lived immediately before the war and to which she had been returning during school vacations. As Tom's letter implies, it was expected that the boys would both attend that school and there was quite a chance, as Tom speculates, that she would be their (history) teacher. However, this was not to be because, at the same time as the boys arrived home in England, an opportunity opened for her of a kind that she had long been waiting for—the offer of a job teaching history at Bristol University. She had had a teaching job at East London College (now Queen Mary College) of London University in the early 1920s and had been trying to get back into university teaching for many years. Now, at age forty-seven, she had achieved her ambition.

As a result, instead of settling back into the house in Ulverston, the summer was spent finding accommodation in Bristol (a flat renovated from bomb damage on the fifth floor of a Regency house in Royal York Crescent, convenient for the university but with no elevator, not very convenient for living) and arranging schooling for the boys. Christopher went as a day boy to Clifton College, a prestigious private school near the apartment, while Tom, with the benefit of a bursary, was sent as a boarder to Abbotsholme. Christopher did reasonably well at Clifton and went on to get a commission in the Royal Artillery during his national service. He then studied history at Bristol University, where he was taught by his mother, among others. He subsequently had two careers, both in the Far East: the first until Malaysian independence in 1963 as a customs officer in Malaysia, and the second, following training in London, as a chartered accountant in Singapore. He retired and came back to England with his family in 1997 and, sadly already suffering from Parkinson's disease, he died in April 2007.

Tom's school, Abbotsholme, was a so-called progressive school, a precursor to the better known Bedales. Founded in the late nineteenth century by C. J. Reddie, it had a tradition of encouraging drama, music, and literature, rather than competitive sports or examinations. The boys had cold showers, wore short trousers (even the eighteen-year-olds), and used outside earth closets—environmentally, just the thing! It was single sex and quite small—about 120 boys aged eight to eighteen. Tom was at the school from September 1944, when he was thirteen, to July 1949, just after his eighteenth birthday. Soon after he arrived, a new head teacher was appointed who began to encourage both public examinations and competitive sports. At the age of seventeen, thanks in part to an exceptional history teacher, Tom gained an open scholarship to study history at Jesus College, Oxford. Before going to Oxford he completed two years' compulsory military service in the Royal Air Force. He did not, like Christopher, gain a commission, but instead became a radar mechanic—a feat amazing to anyone who knew of his almost complete lack of mechanical skills then or subsequently! Much of his time in this post was spent in Germany, helping keep the navigational radar functioning for planes to Berlin.

Intellectually, Tom thrived at Oxford and graduated in 1954 with first-class honours. His success there was due not just to his schooling and hard work (looking back he admits to having been "a bit of a swot") but also to strong family traditions. He valued that background, but it also weighed on him, and when the time came he chose to accept a place in the civil service in preference to continuing in academe. Within the civil service he was allocated to the Board of Trade (later the Department of Trade and Industry). He started in November 1954 as an assistant principal, which was the management trainee grade, and gained substantive promotion to principal (line manager) in 1959.

It was at this point in his career that I first encountered Tom. But before I talk about this, I must tell you a little about myself. I was born in 1938 and am therefore seven years younger than Tom. I lived during the war in Twickenham, west of London (with spells away during the blitz in 1940 and the doodlebugs—flying bombs—in 1944). In 1948 my family moved to Cheltenham in the Cotswolds, and subsequently, when I was thirteen, to the village of Hadlow, near Tonbridge, in Kent. From there I attended Tonbridge Girls Grammar School and gained entrance to Cambridge in 1957. At Cambridge I studied economics, gaining a first-class honours degree in 1960. Like Tom, I considered an academic career and, like him, rejected it in favour of the civil service, and I entered the Board of Trade at the end of September 1960.

I first met Tom in mid-November. This is how it happened. In my final (May Ball) week in Cambridge I had been filmed by a BBC television crew for a "before and after" show. As I was being punted down the River Cam by my then boyfriend, they filmed me talking about my expectations of life in the civil service. Then, in early November, I was called back to the studio to discuss how it was living up to my expectations. Appearing on television, even for an afternoon program aimed at housewives, was at that time a sufficient rarity for it to be considered a rather glamorous thing to do, and word of my exploits got around the younger members of the department. Thus, somewhat to my surprise, I was greeted the following day in the corridor by a tall thin young man with glasses (Tom), who said, "Excuse me, are you by any chance the young lady I saw on television yesterday?" This, it turned out, as he confessed in more or less the next sentence, was totally untrue—he'd merely heard about the show and used the opportunity to chat me up!

The cheekiness, the absurdity, the humour of the situation stuck. I liked the way he laughed at himself and yet the attention he paid to me. The affair proceeded, like any office romance, through a series of parties to which the younger members of the department (some dozen or so) invited each other and their friends. He was soon showing off to me his prized possession of a brand-new white mini (then a new design auto that was much sought after), and I recall his driving me up the recently opened M1 at 80 mph for a walk in Dovedale in Derbyshire. When in May 1961 I declared that I would be visiting relatives in Bath for the spring holiday weekend, Tom responded that he would be in Bristol and would like to collect me to take me over to meet his mother.

The meeting proved seminal in more ways than one. Marie and John Williamson were in England staying just outside Bristol at Badminton, and I was picked up to meet not just his mother but also Marie and John. Years later, Tom's mother told me that after that meeting Marie had said that she did hope that Tom was serious about me because I was just the sort of girl who she thought would make a good wife for him. Well, she was right. We started talking about getting married that September, got engaged in November, and were married on March 24, 1962.

SO HOW FAR DO I RECOGNIZE THE TOM OF MARIE'S WARTIME LETTERS AS
the Tom I've been married to for almost fifty years? There are indeed times
when, reading through the letters, I find myself saying, "Yes, I recognize
this Tom." While his academic and intellectual capabilities are apparent
throughout the letters (he is portrayed—as I am sure he was—as a diligent and attentive pupil, anxious to please his teachers), in the March 13,
1944, letter Marie notes a dichotomy between his prowess at school and
otherworldliness at home. She comments, "He is very unobservant and
though he reads a lot, nothing in his book seems to register on his mind
except the story. So he fails to gather all the infinite variety of information
which most children pick up almost unconsciously by using their eyes and
ears and curiosity (he is the first child I ever knew who had practically no
trace of this characteristic)." This lack of observation—or curiosity about
what he sees—remains a strong feature of the Tom of later years. All his
life he has been oblivious to advertisements and commercials, unaware of
popular fashion and songs. He is the sort of husband to whom one has to
say—"Darling, I'm wearing a new outfit to-day. Do you like it?"

I do not, however, recognize the "vague, muddled and forgetful" person
whom Marie talks about in that same March 13 letter, nor is he "withdrawn
from the world" as Eve Burns described him in a letter to Margaret in late
1942. Within our family life he has been a loving and sensitive husband and
father, and he certainly would not have had the substantial career achieve-
ments in the British civil service (for example, in trade negotiations or the
British Telecom privatization for which he received the honour of a CBE),
had he not shown evidence of a sharp, functioning mind. Indeed, I wonder whether in fact Tom's vagueness in Canada was his way of insulating
himself from the turbulence of his early life. The divorce of his parents,
the moves to different people and places within England, and then leaving
both parents behind and going to (for him) an unknown family in Canada,
may have caused him to create a sort of cocoon to protect himself that only
dissipated in later years.

The letters, especially the early ones, contain many comparisons between Bill and Tom. Bill, the older brother, precociously intelligent and
conscious of his responsibilities in relation to his brothers, emerges from
the letters as self-centred and arrogant. From the start he was seen to be
adopting an unduly superior attitude toward his foster parents, Vivien
and Harry Ratcliffe. Adolescence is not an easy time for anyone, let alone
a new-found family. As a thirteen-year-old in a strange country with
people whom he did not know at all, Bill quite understandably put up
a defensive wall around himself. The Ratcliffes, having to cope with this

highly intelligent but very tense, awkward teenager, were equally challenged and one senses that they found it easier not to interfere but to let
him have his own way.

The contrast Marie sees between the three boys is interesting: "I think
all children are born selfish, and it takes years for them to learn that
thought for others pays dividends in happiness and improved relationships. Christopher's selfishness, like Peter's, is of this natural variety.... But
Bill and Tom seem to have a different kind, springing from complete absorption in self and utter lack of interest in any person or thing or activity
which doesn't directly affect them or appeal to them" (October 28, 1941).
By the time I got to know Tom, and subsequently his two brothers, no one
saw Tom as selfish or arrogant—rather the other way around. He was, if
anything, oversensitive to other people's needs and has remained so all his
life. All three boys—men by the time I got to know them—were socially ill
at ease, but Tom the least, and I have always put this down to the fact that
he had the benefit of having learned some social graces from Marie. After
the war, home life with their mother, Margaret, was not easy. There were all
the stringencies of postwar Britain, with rationing continuing until 1953,
but Tom's memories are of constantly being on the move—every school
holiday meant moving from the flat in Bristol, to the house in Ulverston,
and often also to the grandmother in London and then back to school in
Derbyshire. There was no car, so all the journeys were by train, with all the
luggage and other paraphernalia.

Christopher, as a day boy at Clifton and then a home student at Bristol
University, was the one who was always there and bore the brunt of housekeeping for his mother. He later made it clear that the tension of family life
in England played a part in influencing him to choose a career abroad. Yet
of all the three brothers, the picture that emerges of Christopher from the
letters is of a very normal boy, who enjoyed the rough and tumble of other
boys' company but had enormous generosity of spirit. It was he, not Tom,
who thought about buying the chocolates or the flowers to say a special
thank-you.

Tom was not close to either Christopher or Bill, although instinctively
his interests were closer to Bill's. The issue, discussed at some length in the
letters, of whether Bill should attend the University of Toronto or try for an
English university, implicitly Cambridge, was paralleled later by a similar
debate on whether he should take up his working life in Britain or Canada
after he received his BA (in 1947) and MA (in 1948), both from Toronto,
and then in 1950 a PhD from Princeton. Canada was his clear choice—he
not only refused to return to Britain (wary perhaps, like Christopher, of being too tied up in the tensions of his mother's life) but also rejected an offer

from Los Alamos and made the explicit choice to work on peaceful uses of atomic power at the Canadian atomic research establishment at Chalk River, northwest of Ottawa. He worked there from 1950 until 1960 and then moved into academia as a professor at the University of Edmonton (1960–62) and then at the University of Toronto. When Bill died at the age of forty-five in August 1972 (in a climbing accident in the Selkirk Range in the Rockies), he was professor of theoretical physics and associate dean of the Faculty of Arts at the University of Toronto.

One notable feature of the Tom that I married that does not emerge from the letters is his sense of humour. As I indicated, it was his ready wit, sense of the ridiculous, and willingness to laugh at himself that initially attracted me. After he retired from the civil service, he served for sixteen years as a county councillor and was well known for punctuating the debate with some seemingly senseless but very funny remark, to the amusement of all. He sat as a Liberal Democrat in Conservative-dominated Surrey; however there were many regrets from all sides of the political spectrum when he retired.

Another enduring feature—one that does come through from the letters—has been the friendship and affection shown to the boys by their foster parents. The letters portray well the sense of fun in the Williamson household when all four children were around, tumbling over each other in their various activities. It is amazing today to look back to a world where distant cousins, as the Williamsons were to the Sharps, were prepared to take all three boys, from a different country, into their home for an indefinite period. And although first Bill and then Christopher went off to live with different families, one cannot but be staggered by the generosity of the offer—a generosity that at times one feels Tom's mother failed to appreciate. Having got to know my mother-in-law later, I can only explain it in terms of the intensity with which she lived her own life. Once the boys were gone, her life would have revolved around teaching history at Abbotsholme, and writing letters to the boys or to Marie probably became a bit of a chore, which she would put off if other things seemed more pressing, as I suspect they frequently did.

For Tom, the extended family of the Williamsons has remained real, and Mary, in particular, has remained in many respects a sister to him. Until the late 1960s, travel across the Atlantic was expensive, and visits therefore infrequent. Tom spent one summer vacation from Oxford in Canada, working in a canning factory in Hamilton and then travelling to the West Coast by train with Bill. Mary spent the summer in Europe after her second year at the University of Toronto (1953). She and Tom attended the coronation together and subsequently went on a holiday in France. Marie and John

Tom with his wife Margaret and their daughters Helen and Elizabeth at Cwm Celyn, their cottage in Wales

Williamson made two visits to England after the war, in 1958 and 1961, and it was on the second visit that I first met them. Tom's and my first visit to Canada was in the spring of 1967 and this was the last time we saw Marie. Four years at the British Embassy in Washington in the mid-1970s enabled links to be rekindled. We made several visits to Hanover, New Hampshire, where Peter, a professor at the Tuck School, Dartmouth College, lived with his wife, Sybil, and three daughters, the youngest of whom was the same age as our eldest, Helen. Since then the traffic has been two-way and frequent. Tom and I have enjoyed many a holiday in Canada and the United States when we have seen either Mary or Peter and family.

It was out of this continuing friendship that this whole enterprise arose. It seems a fitting tribute to Marie, a highly intelligent woman who wrote so well and so fluently, that her letters, penned so conscientiously each week over a period of four years, should provide testimony to the generosity and sacrifices made by ordinary Canadians at that time.

Guildford
June 25, 2010

APPENDIX 1

Margaret Sharp to Marie Williamson after putting her sons on the ship for Canada

1 BELMONT, ULVERSTON
JULY 28, 1940

Dear Marie

Your very nice letter written on 11th July arrived yesterday. I've heard a rumour that a boat may be going about Tues. so am sending off a very hasty line immediately in the hopes it will catch it though I daresay it won't. By the time you get this you will I hope have seen the boys. I'm sure Bill will gladly go to Mrs. Ratcliffe's if it is explained to him; it sounds ever so nice & it is very good of her. He may feel a bit its his duty to look after Tom & so on, it would be quite easy to get round that. I'm sure they will all do whatever you think is best, especially as you can say I want them to do what you think most suitable. This letter is your authority and theirs! I do hope they won't be a great trouble & responsibility to you. In the first weeks when we were considering the scheme I was just thinking of your pockets and how dreadful it would be to give you the expense of my upkeep as well as the boys though I loathed the idea of parting with them. Also if I had come I couldn't have started till October as I had examining obligations which it would have been difficult to shuffle out of at this late stage & I didn't want to hold up the boys till then. But it has been gradually dawning on me that I perhaps was considering the financial aspect too strongly & that you might really have preferred me to be there to look after them & make their decisions etc. I'm sorry to have been so woolly. Because of course there is nothing I really wanted more than to feel it was my duty to go with them! Here one has a slight feeling that an able-bodied adult ought to stay and help though if one is a middle-aged female there doesn't seem much that in fact one is able to do. My brother felt very strongly that I oughtn't to leave. Meanwhile the government have stepped in and won't give exit permits to grown-ups between 16 and 60 <u>unless</u> they fall into one of various categories—one is the mother of young children travelling with her children! So you see I have missed my chance of that and I don't see how I could now get any exit permit. The only chances seem to be if they relax the regulations later or if you find the children difficult or too much for you or their health causes difficulty. I suppose there is a chance that a strongly worded request from you for my presence might get some attention. I am however <u>if</u> all goes well and the boys settle all right apart from bouts of the inevitable homesickness—anxious to get some work. I am at present a candidate for a history teaching post at the school here which the elder boys attended. I think my chances are <u>fairly</u> good, unless they can get a man, which they would prefer. But that isn't very probable. So if I got it I'd really only be available in an emergency. I wish Mother would consider coming but she won't as yet. You see life is perfectly normal <u>here</u> except for petty food restrictions and so on. So she sees no real reason to uproot herself yet.

I am missing the post—and there's still hundreds of things to say especially about Bill's education.

With all good wishes and my most grateful thoughts
Margaret Sharp

APPENDIX 2

Katharine Beamish to Margaret Sharp
after visiting the Sharp boys in Toronto

37 STRATFORD ROAD,
MONTREAL, P.Q.
JANUARY 26, 1941

My dear Margaret,

I am just back from seeing your three, and will write while my pleasure
in meeting them again is fresh. They are all three looking quite extraordinarily well, and they all seem very happy. Bill, of course, I hadn't seen
for a good time before the War—he seemed to me to be at least six years
older than when I met him last! He is in absolutely grand form, and talked
quite unceasingly. I start off with this because when you last wrote to me
I think you were a bit doubtful as to whether he was going to enjoy being with these friends of the Williamsons, or whether he'd find them a bit
Philistine. I expect by now you know this is O.K., but it's always nice to
get confirmation, and he struck me as composed and friendly and sure of
himself and <u>bursting</u> with information and opinions in the kind of way that
he wouldn't be if he were having to cope with an uncongenial background.
I really got a completer picture of Bill in the time I was there than of the
other two; actually he dined with us—the others had supped before—but
even when the three and I were on our own afterwards Bill was so entertaining and such very good company that he got away with the limelight
rather. I <u>did</u> enjoy him, and I'm quite certain he's enjoying himself, criticisms of Canadian ways notwithstanding. He didn't shew any sign of having <u>become</u> a Philistine (I was interested in this as A. [Andrew] has had a
tough Canadian "Aw! lessons!" patch!) but he was vivid in his descriptions

of the thrill of ice hockey matches, and when he was all dressed up to go he kept waggling his ice hockey stick in a knowing and wristy kind of way.

Christopher has the beautifully square and sturdy look that I remember him with. Did he lose this in between, or did his looks never pity him? He sat on the sofa and bounced during our conversation—partly I discovered afterwards with annoyance at having to sit on a sofa instead of playing a game with Peter, poor child. He and Peter are a thoroughly good pair, evidently; the latter struck me as a bright little boy, but I think I must have been looking at yours all the time as I find my picture hazy. Christopher still has that endearing bravado. To this is added a faint Canadian flavour which neither of the others has—their speech and manner seemed to me quite unchanged. But C., though he hasn't perfected the speech has adopted the Canadian small boy swagger, which becomes him very well. The fish he lost was far bigger than the black bass Tom caught—he could skate fast as anything, fast as the wind—sure, he could swim, for miles if need be—a kind of fairy tale exaggeration with his tongue in his cheek and the sofa creaking. Bill and he had long discussions on speech and pronunciation, Christopher 'did' Ulverstone for us, and Bill said in the most adult way how lovely it was to hear real Canadians say Ottawa—that he thought the final 'a' was an Indian sound, and Mrs. W. had to oblige by saying it for us. Except by bouncing and being rather pugnacious on the subject of stamps C. never shewed that he wanted to be upstairs playing games, which I thought was very good manners. But the stamp discussion was funny. Jets of the pure cold water of reason from Bill, who wanted to swap some things, flames of passionate non-cooperation from Christopher, quite undamped by elder brotherliness. But all good tempered. Tom is as utterly Tom as ever and a lovely person I think, but then I always did. He is rather rounder cheeked and a good deal pinker. Till the Williamsons left us on our own I was very much afraid I shouldn't meet him properly. I think just because he had known me better it was faintly perturbing to have me cropping up and making a crack in his carefully constructed new world. So while Bill chatted at me and Christopher twinkled Tom went a little pinker and retreated half way into his shell. But he came out when we were sitting on the sofa and gave at intervals, during the others' ceaseless babble, a series of sensible and well considered judgments. The others poured out a flood of good and laudatory description when I asked about Haliburton. Tom said it was a good place, very good even, but there were other places in Canada that he wanted to see more—Georgian Bay, for instance he thought from what he had heard would be better. The others, Bill with reasoned disdain, Christopher explosively, inveighed against hot Canadian houses. I said my view of this had changed considerably since I found how cold outside was. That an oven was very grateful if you came to it from an ice-house. (Montreal in fact is far colder than Toronto.) It was Tom who said 'Yes, but it would still be healthier to get used to a cooler oven and that in any case the Canadians stoked up far too early in the autumn! (Very true.) I think it was Tom who said, in the complete scientist's manner, when we were discussing some Canadian question, 'I should like to stay in Canada for quite a long time, to find out.' His mind and Bill's seem to me to run on rather similar lines (is this so?) Bill's more quickly, but Tom's with a heavenly steadiness. They both seemed to me very good reasoners; I didn't have a chance to see this in Christopher, but Mrs. W. says that his form mistress says that he has a grand faculty for spotting false logic, so it evidently runs all through the family. Mrs. W. says that Tom and Mary are inseparable, though M. teases him sometimes. She is a pretty fair child, quite attractive, but very feminine—a bit of a minx I thought. I should think she could be maddening on occasion, but Tom clearly enjoys her most of the time.

I am not going to have time to tell you properly how enormously I liked Mrs. Williamson. She has exactly that kind of quietness with the family (a warm quietness) that you would hope. She is the sort of unhustling person who is there for them when they want her and doesn't rush things. I loved the way she told me all the stories of them, with a kind of loving imperson-alness. Oh dear that isn't it at all—I'm writing against time and can't get what I mean—leave it that she is a really good person to have them—but you knew that. And the house is so charming, with a small spaciousness, and a good kind of order in it. Margaret I wish there were time for more but I have a cousin flying in the Clipper who can take it and save time. Copy for your husband. We'll get Tom to stay if we possibly can. All very well here I'll write when I can. We think of you a lot.

A great deal of love and take care of yourself my dear. Your family is O.K.

K

APPENDIX 3

Sylvia Anthony to Margaret Sharp after a visit to
the Williamsons where she had time with the boys

229 WILBROD ST., OTTAWA
JUNE 20, 1942

Dear Margaret,

Maybe Bill has told you that I was in Toronto at the end of May, and saw your three boys, thanks to the kindness of Mrs. Ratcliffe and Mrs. Williamson. They all looked fine. I hope it was right for me to go and see them. I had not heard from you after I wrote, when I saw Mrs. Ratcliffe on her visit to this city last March. I think you probably wrote, but I never received it. It makes me very sad to think so, as I so cherish news from friends in England.

I went up to Toronto for only two days and one night, for two simultaneous learned conventions, so there was very little time indeed for visits, and both Mrs. Ratcliffe and Mrs. W. were awfully kind in letting me come just when I could.

I really and truly was impressed with what seemed like the very good adjustment of the children. Bill not only looked very fit and happy (one can of course only judge these things superficially), but what I most liked was that he seemed to take a personal pride in showing the Ratcliffe house and saying what the Ratcliffes did—he seemed to have adopted the Ratcliffes, in a very delightful way, which I felt Mrs. Ratcliffe really enjoyed. I think both she and I were very much amused when she showed me her lovely bedroom, with double bed, and Bill said, after the statement that this was Mr. And Mrs. Ratcliffe's bedroom—"but he hardly ever sleeps here now"!

Frankly, I was quite surprised to see how happy Bill seemed, not because I imagined he would not have made satisfactory personal relationships, but because I thought he would have a superego that worritted [sic] him to get back to England, as he got older. That doesn't seem to be so.

Tom is exactly the same—taller I suppose, but to my eye identical. Christopher looked more like his old self than in a snap I had seen. However, he is obviously much fitter. Of the three of them, he is definitely the most popular with Mrs. W. and (apart from her special interest in Bill) I think with Mrs. R. One small point: could you arrange to type your letters to him? I gather he doesn't like to admit he can't easily read them—he likes to keep them to himself, and so actually misses much of the contents....

Love from all of us
Sylvia Anthony

APPENDIX 4

Eve Burns to Margaret Sharp after a visit to Toronto when she saw the boys

MAROB

NORTH SANBORNTON, N.H.

JULY 28, 1943

Dear Margaret ...

I had a glimpse (not much more) of Bill and Tom when I was in Toronto. Both have grown very much. I was especially struck by the change in Tom who seems much brighter and has more confidence. I spent an afternoon with Mrs. R. and W. Aren't they nice women! Both feel that all three boys are so much better when they are away from one another, and especially Tom who was completely cowed by C. who is much more boistrous, and T. is just a slave to Bill. Incidentally brotherly love doesn't seem very strong at this age. Bill has written once to C. and Tom a little more often while C's reply when I ask him whether he has written to his brothers is a statement that they agreed that he would not write until they did and as they haven't why should he? Also when I went to Toronto I asked him what he wanted me to find out about the other boys and there was absolutely nothing he could think of!

Bill seems to be getting much more human tho' he is still almost as awkward as ever. He was full of his problems about college. I was inclined to think it would be better for him to go through with as much as he can here, partly for economic reasons and partly because he would inevitably lose a good deal of time in the process of adjusting to the English system. Also he is not the kind who would be a big social success at an English university. It's a shame that he seems to be specialising so young, but I suppose that is happening to all his generation.

347

Incidentally the W.'s told me about Douglas' marriage, thinking I already knew. If you did tell me I never got your letter. They also said you had not wanted the kids told. Do you mind my saying that I don't agree with you? So far as Bill goes he is already quite grown up but still at the insecure stage where he wants to be treated as a grown-up. I get the impression that he is very much closer to you in his feeling than he was two years ago, and I suspect he may feel very much hurt if he thinks that you don't confide in him. And in any case the kids are going to have a great deal to adjust to when they return. The W.s think Tom at any rate has no idea even that you are divorced and that your separation is due to the war. We have taken no special pains with C. to hide the fact of the divorce, and in this country it is so common that noone thinks anything about it. I am inclined to think that if when the subject comes up naturally it would be an easier adjustment for C. to be told that his father had remarried—that is unless you want to tell him by letter. For at his age I am sure everything is "normal" and if accepted by everyone else as a matter of course will be similarly accepted by him. When you write tell me who he married and what you think of my ideas. I hope you don't mind my saying what I think....

With all my love
Eve

APPENDIX 5

Eve Burns to Margaret Sharp to describe Christopher's
reaction to the news of his father's remarriage

3206, QUE STREET, N.W.
WASHINGTON, 7, D.C.
MARCH 7, 1944

Dear Margaret:

I had no time last week to write you about C's reaction to the news about
Douglas' marriage. You will be glad to hear that it was very good. Your letter
to him did not arrive at the same time as ours. About a week later came one
from you, which I supposed, wrongly as it turned out, was the fatal missive.
So I asked him what he thought about the news, and he said "What news?"
Knowing how carelessly he reads all letters, I said "Why didnt Mother tell
you about Daddy's getting married?" His face lit up in a great smile, and
he said "What! Well, I'll be—!" He repeated this phrase (very much used
in his group these days) several times, adding once or twice "The old—".
This habit of unfinished phrases is another characteristic. He laughed like
anything and then went to get your letter but found nothing in it. The
actual letter arrived about three days later. He then said "Why, that means
I have a mother-in-law" but finally decided it was a stepmother after all,
and seemed enormously much pleased at the prospect. He badgered me
with questions to know what she was like, which I could answer only in
the most general terms: wanted to know why D. had not written to tell him
"of his engagement," and immediately called up his friend Chippie, and
was evidently much gratified to receive congratulations! We have not seen
him so much interested in anything for a long time, and he even took the
trouble next day to prepare a questionnaire for D. to fill in giving information about Enid.[1] I don't think you have to worry at all, but I do hope D.

will take the time to write him a full description. He is just at the age when he is beginning to get aware of women and sex, which probably accounts in part for his great interest....

As ever

Eve

NOTES

NOTES TO FOREWORD

1 Quoted in Alfred Gollin, *No Longer an Island: Britain and the Wright Brothers, 1902–1909* (Stanford, CA: Stanford University Press, 1984), 2.

2 *Daily Mail*, November 14 and 15, 1906, quoted in Gollin, *No Longer an Island*, 193–94.

3 Vancouver *Sun*, September 8, 1915, 1; September 13, 1915, 1; Toronto *Daily Star*, July 7, 1917, 1.

4 Editorial "The Long-Awaited Air Raid," Manitoba *Free Press*, January 1, 1915, 9; editorial "Reprisals for Raids," Ottawa *Citizen*, July 10, 1917, 12; editorial "A Canadian V.C.," Vancouver *Sun*, June 9, 1915, 4; editorial "German Zeppelin Crews Worse Than Sitting Bull's Scalping Parties," Toronto *Evening Telegram*, February 7, 1916, 10; editorial "More 'Frightfulness,'" Vancouver *Sun*, February 2, 1916, 1.

5 Ben Wicks, *No Time to Wave Goodbye* (London: Bloomsbury, 1988), ch. 1.

6 Matthew Halton, "Has Canada the Key to Britain's Destiny?" in *Star Weekly*, May 21, 1938, 6.

7 Travis L. Crosby, *The Impact of Civilian Evacuation in the Second World War* (London: Croom Helm, 1986), 15.

8 *The Times*, November 6, 1937, 12.

9 Carlton Jackson, *Who Will Take Our Children?* (London: Methuen, 1985), 2–4.

10 Geoffrey Bilson, *The Guest Children: The Story of the British Child Evacuees Sent to Canada during World War II* (Saskatoon: Fifth House, 1988), 2–4.

11 Editorial "Our Duty to British Children," *Globe and Mail*, July 8, 1939, 4.

12 See Ruth Inglis, *The Children's War: Evacuation, 1939–1945* (London: Collins, 1989).

13 Patricia Y. Lin, "National Identity and Social Mobility: Class, Empire and the British Government Overseas Evacuation of Children during the Second World War," *Twentieth-Century British History* 7/3 (1996), 313–14.

14 Sir Geoffrey Shakespeare, quoted in Crosby, *The Impact of Civilian Evacuation in the Second World War*, 106.

15 Bilson, *The Guest Children*, 14.

16 Lin, "National Identity and Social Mobility," 315.

17 Quoted in Ralph Barker, *Children of the* Benares: *A War Crime and Its Victims* (London: Methuen, 1987), 36.

18 See Michael Fethney, *The Absurd and the Brave: CORB—The True Account of the British Government's World War II Evacuation of Children Overseas* (Sussex: Book Guild, 1990).

19 Quoted in Lin, "National Identity and Social Mobility," 313.

20 Quoted in Lin, "National Identity and Social Mobility," 321.

21 Bilson, *The Guest Children*, 18.

22 *The Times*, June 24, 1940, 3.

23 Bilson, *The Guest Children*, 10, 21.

24 Barker, *Children of the* Benares. For a fine fictional account, see James Heneghan, *Wish Me Luck* (Toronto: Groundwood Books, 1997).

25 Lin, "National Identity and Social Mobility," 316. For a superb fictional account of two CORB evacuees in Canada, see Kit Pearson's *The Sky Is Falling*, *Looking at the Moon*, and *The Lights Go On Again*, also published as *The Guests of War Trilogy* (Toronto: Penguin, 1993).

26 Lin, "National Identity and Social Mobility," 327–28.

NOTES TO INTRODUCTION

1 *Globe and Mail*, July 30, 1940. The story from "An eastern Canadian Port" concerned the private exodus from England of two grey-painted ships carrying nearly 3,000 children and mothers—and pets—in first- to third-class cabins. Singled out was "a large group of women and children from British universities bound for the homes of professors of the University of Toronto." The Sharp boys were attached to this group. The masters and officers of the two merchant ships were universally applauded for carrying their human cargo safely to port.

2 Mary Tout sailed to the United States in 1933 to visit her son Herbert, who was teaching at the University of Minnesota. On April 11, the *New York Times* greeted her arrival with a story headed "Finds Gain Abroad in Girls' Education; Mrs. Tout, Arriving for a Visit, Says English Universities Enroll More Women."

3 Unfortunately, none of the boys' letters written from August to December 1940 have survived, except a handful written from the boat to Canada, and we can only speculate on how they reacted to their new lives in the first few weeks.

4   In letters written through the winter of 1943–44 to both Margaret and her mother (not included here), Marie laid out in detail the possibilities for the boys' return. The exchanges were heated: on February 20, 1944, Marie wrote to Margaret's mother: "So much worry and indecision must be hard on you and I find it very upsetting."

NOTES TO 1940

1   Marie to Margaret, July 11, 1940.

2   Until August 1941, when the Williamson household moved, with two exceptions all of Marie's letters were addressed from 118 Hillsdale Avenue West in Toronto.

3   Vivien Ratcliffe had been a close friend of Marie's since high school and also had been with her at the University of Toronto. See Biographical Notes under RATCLIFFE.

4   Clare Jennings was Marie's younger sister. See Biographical Notes under PETERKIN.

5   The "Provincial Lady" was E.M. Delafield, whose *The Diaries of a Provincial Lady* and the series of Provincial Ladies books that followed—"humorous reading based on her own life experiences"—were bestsellers in the 1930s. Margaret Sharp would have been very familiar with the reference.

6   This is the only letter written by Marie for which a reply from Margaret survives (see Appendix 1.)

7   Marie's older sister, Theresa Busby, met the Sharp boys on their arrival in Toronto. See Biographical Notes under PETERKIN.

8   Ethel Bland had brought the Sharp boys to Canada on the *Duchess of Bedford*, along with several other children including her own. See Biographical Notes under WILKINSON and BLAND.

The "University Group" was the University British Overseas Children Committee, chaired by Bette (Mrs. Peter) Sandiford from 1941 to 1946. This subcommittee of the university's Women's War Service Committee was created to give financial aid to foster parents, but its mandate quickly changed to simply assisting evacuee families, in particular those associated with the universities in Birmingham, Cambridge, and Manchester. In common parlance the committee was referred to as "the University Group." The Sharp children, whose evacuation had been arranged privately, were in effect part of the group. Thus they benefited from the medical insurance plan and were able to participate in organized social events. As its headquarters the committee was given the building at 98 St. George Street owned by the Institute for Child Study, and the institute's head, Dr. Blatz, and members of his staff were closely involved in assessing the evacuee children. The committee had nine hard-working subcommittees that assumed responsibility for the evacuee mothers and children: meeting them on their arrival in Halifax, Montreal, or Toronto; handling immigration documents; finding clothes, health insurance, employment for mothers; fundraising; and follow-up in foster homes.

9   Marie signed her first letter "Sincerely, Marie," but thereafter she wrote "Affectionately," "With love," or just "Love, Marie."

10   Mrs. Bland was a sister-in-law of Bertie Wilkinson, who had studied medieval history at the University of Manchester with the boys' grandfather, Thomas F. Tout, and was already a good friend of the boys' mother, Margaret. See Biographical Notes under WILKINSON.

11   Like Bill, Alan Provost (who had come to Canada in the same group as the Sharp boys) was at the local high school, Lawrence Park Collegiate in Toronto. The Provost boys were nephews of Edith Wilkinson and Ethel Bland. See Biographical Notes under WILKINSON and BLAND.

12   Jack McKellar was principal of Lawrence Park Collegiate. He and his wife, Vera, were close friends of the Williamsons.

13   The University of Toronto Schools (UTS) was a boys' high school staffed by the University of Toronto Faculty of Education. Entrance was by competitive examination, but since the exams were held in the spring and all the places already filled, it seemed unlikely that Bill would be able to get in until the following year. Peter, much to the Williamsons' delight, was one of the boys who had passed the entrance exam and would be starting at UTS that September.

14   Norval R. Waddington was the headmaster of St. Paul's School for Boys on Deloraine Ave. in Toronto from 1935 to 1941, when he sold the school to join the RCAF. Charles Hass was a teacher at the school and often drove Christopher and Tom to school. Mrs. (Ruth Mary, née Carr) Underhill, Tom's teacher in 2A and Christopher's in 3A, was the wife of Frank Underhill, a controversial professor of history at the University of Toronto.

15   Canadian National Exhibition.

16   Douglas Sharp wrote on September 23 to Margaret from his home at 9 Queens Gate Terrace, London, SW7, about the extensive bomb damage in the city, but luckily was able to report that "[t]here is no damage within about 100 yds. of here tho' the bomb that fell 100 yds. away shook the house." Douglas was enormously pleased with the first letters received from his boys. On August 19 he wrote to Margaret: "The letters were just grand. Bill has much to express and knows how to express it; Tom, because he finds writing a nuisance, is a model of conciseness; Christopher is just sweetly characteristic. (I think his first four pages were what he sent from Liverpool). I'm just swelling with pride in them.... I write to them in turn once a week."

17   Christopher had lost almost two years of school in 1939–40 because of sickness from pleurisy.

18   There was general all-round concern about Bill as he grew into adolescence. On November 20, 1941, Douglas Sharp wrote to Margaret about him: "What frightens me ... is the possibility that [Vivien Ratcliffe] will try to initiate him into the holy Mystery of Sex. In that field problems will arise which he can't readily answer for himself nor find the answer in books; & he needs to have a sensible person to answer his questions, & even very delicately to prompt

them. I don't trust Mrs. Ratcliffe one bit, but Bill is the one whom she can harm least."

19 Christopher's birthday was the following day, October 10.

20 Christopher had been in 3B at St. Paul's, largely because he was behind in his spelling.

21 Mary Murphy was the Williamsons' cook-housekeeper. See Biographical Notes under MURPHY.

22 "Church"—In 1922 Marie was a member in "full Communion" of the Presbyterian Church in Canada, and John had been brought up a Methodist. They were married in the Avenue Road Presbyterian Church in Toronto, and some time afterwards made the choice to become Anglicans.

23 The "Museum" is the Royal Ontario Museum at Queen's Park and Bloor Street.

24 The "William book" would be one of the books by Richmal Crompton, author of *Just William* and other books published in the 1920s and 1930s about the unruly English schoolboy.

25 The "wild" park was Sherwood Park, a stretch of ravine south of Eglinton Avenue between Mount Pleasant and Bayview avenues.

26 Croquinole, an eight-sided board game said to have been invented in Canada. The board is made of different varieties of wood and the game is played with discs or "biscuits," one set in dark wood and another in light wood. The playing surface has a ring of pegs near the centre, a trough around the outside, and a depression slightly larger than a disc in the centre. The game is played by flicking the discs through the pegs to sink them in the depression and send your opponent's discs into the trough. The Williamsons' board had been made by the children's grandfather, Charles Peterkin.

27 Arthur Lismer was a founding member of the Group of Seven, the Canadian landscape artists whose exhibition in 1920 launched a distinctly national movement of Canadian art. In 1927 Lismer became educational supervisor of the Art Gallery of Toronto (now the Art Gallery of Ontario), where he taught Saturday-morning art classes to students recommended by their schools.

28 Boys and Girls House of the Public Library was located at the foot of St. George Street, next door to the Central Toronto Reference and Circulating Library.

29 Remembrance Day. In her letter of November 11 the following year, Marie repeats her skepticism about Armistice Day (or Remembrance Day) being a school holiday.

30 York Downs Golf Club, on the east side of Bathurst Street south of Sheppard, now Earl Bales Park, where during the winter members could bring their families to ski on the gentle slopes.

31 Margaret may have had misgivings about the Ratcliffes and her ex-husband certainly had. Marie, having detected a whiff of this, wished to express her respect and admiration for her old friends. On September 13 Douglas had written to Margaret: "I agree with you about Marie and Mrs Ratcliffe, and I'm sorry for Bill, separated from the others and landed with such a prim complacent woman."

32 The "Craven Heifer" was an immense Yorkshire beast which was depicted in a widely circulated early 19th century print. The name was chosen for an inn in Toronto that became associated with the rebels of 1837 and in 1855 was destroyed by fire.

33 The children's paper, *The Monthly War Drum*, was a typed newssheet that featured riddles, jokes, stories, etc., but little news. Future references to the paper tell us that Peter was the editor and proprietor, Christopher the assistant editor, Mary the business manager, and Tom the circulation manager. See January 14, 1941, and December 27, 1941.

34 In connection with the Women's Auxiliary of Grace Church on-the-Hill, Marie worked on Fridays at the Canadian Red Cross.

35 Ruby McKay and Irene Peterkin were Marie's aunts. See Biographical Notes under PETERKIN.

NOTES TO 1941

1 Marie to Margaret, April 20, 1941.

2 While at St. Paul's School, when the boys did not eat their mid-day dinner with Mrs. Chalmers, they sometimes went for a full meal at Liggett's drugstore at the corner of Yonge St. and Yonge Blvd.

3 Bill's letters to his "Mummy" at this time rarely mentioned his own activities except his stamp collecting. He wrote mostly about the war, his marks at school, public transport, and federal-provincial relations. On April 4 he did say (to an undoubtedly uncomprehending mother), "The N.H.L. hockey is getting very exciting—it is near the end of the season with Toronto Maple Leafs and Boston Bruins tied for first place."

4 Clare and her husband George Jennings, Theresa and her husband Leslie Busby, Bob Peterkin and his wife Besse, and Marie herself and her husband John. See Biographical Notes under PETERKIN.

5 Katharine Beamish, a friend of Margaret, had taught Tom at her nursery school in England. See Biographical Notes under BEAMISH.

6 Ulverston, on the edge of the Lake District. Margaret Sharp had always been fond of the Lake District, and after the divorce she moved to Ulverston, leaving the family home at 59 Southway in Hampstead Garden Suburb in north London.

7 See Katharine Beamish's letter to Margaret giving her impressions of how the three boys were getting on (Appendix 2.)

8 Miss Kenyon had been Tom's teacher at Lightburn Elementary School in Ulverston. She wrote to Margaret on July 25, 1940, expressing her sympathy with Margaret having to part with her boys. She added: "I myself feel sure that Tom's short period at Lightburn has helped him considerably to overcome his shyness, and no doubt this new and strange experience will turn out to be all for the good. He showed great promise in his work, and provided that he continues to master his nervousness, he ought to do very well indeed."

9   Eve and Arthur (Bobbie) Burns were English friends who had emigrated to the United States in the 1920s. Arthur was Christopher's godfather. See Biographical Notes under BURNS.

10 Elsie Barrow had been the live-in "mother's help" and housekeeper in Ulverston. The Sharp boys were very fond of her. She stayed on as cook housekeeper after the boys left.

11 John (Jack) Gerrard was one of the four boys who had been evacuated from Salford, near Manchester, to live with the Sharps in Ulverston during the winter of 1939–40.

12 Penelope Redford had been one of Margaret's friends at Manchester University.

13 Margaret had been appointed a history teacher at Abbotsholme, a boys' boarding school in Staffordshire. She remained a teacher there until the summer of 1944.

14 Phyllis Hamblin was the sister of Douglas Sharp, the boys' father.

15 Tom too wrote to Margaret about the snow fort. His letter is reproduced on page 82. It reads as follows:

10/2/41

Dear Mother

I hope you are very well. On Sunday I went too Bill's Birthday party though it was not his Birthday. After the meal everybody felt very full. I gave Bill some stamps for his Birthday. We went to Clares where we built a fort with lumps of snow from the crust. Sometime we will send you a picture of it, though it was half wrecked when the photograph Love from Tom

16 The "little boy next door" was William (Bill) Paterson, who later was a classmate of Mary at Trinity College, University of Toronto.

17 Mabel Tylecote (née Phythian, known as "Phiz") was Bill's godmother. She and Margaret had been friends since their student days at Manchester University. She was active throughout her life in Labour politics and in 1966 was made Dame Mabel Tylecote.

18 Marie had sent Margaret a few copies of *Saturday Night*—"our best weekly"— in the hope that they might interest her.

19 Frances Billington Cruikshank and her husband, Douglas, had lived in Beirut, where he was a doctor with the American University. In 1938 Douglas moved to Baghdad, where he was head of gynecology at the Royal College of Medicine. Frances stayed in Beirut as the climate in Baghdad was too difficult for young children. Frances had been a friend of Margaret Sharp and had taught her brothers Herbert and Arthur as young boys. During the war she lived in Canada and the United States with her three daughters.

20 Bill's godfather was Professor Wallace Notestein, who taught history at Yale University. He had known the Sharp/Tout families for many years and had been in touch with Margaret in 1940 about the possibility of her and the boys' coming out to live in Wooster, Ohio, the college town where he was born and raised and his sister still lived.

21 The "Children's Public Library" was the North Toronto Branch of the Toronto Public Library (at 14 St. Clements Avenue), which had a large children's department.

22 An elementary school had a catchment area defined by street address that determined which local school a child would attend.

23 The twelve Doctor Dolittle books by Hugh Lofting were published from 1920 to 1952.

24 The "bricks" are Minibrix, a children's construction game made up of small rubber interlocking bricks.

25 By this date Dr. Norman Shenstone (1881–1970) was an internationally renowned surgeon with a specialty in chest conditions, including the treatment of tumours.

26 Eve and Arthur Burns, had invited all three Sharp boys to their summer place, Marob, in North Sanbornton, New Hampshire

27 Jo Robinson and her family became deeply involved in the lives of the Sharps from this time on. See Biographical Notes under ROBINSON.

28 On June 22 Arthur Burns wrote to Marie to tell her how well the boys were behaving in New Hampshire and that they were off in all directions exploring their new environment. He added, "I unintentionally smuggled the boys into the States and out of Canada because the Canadian guard was too sleepy even to look at the car and told us to go ahead. Later I had to return to hand over the foreign exchange control forms. That meant crossing the white line of the international boundary three times which was a great success. The American authorities made no trouble for me and were very friendly indeed towards the boys. But there were forms to fill in and it was about a quarter past ten before we got away."

29 Marie's brother Bob had married Elizabeth (Besse) Craig on September 20,1940. See Biographical Notes under PETERKIN.

30 Ann and John Wilkinson were the children of Margaret's long-time friends, Edith and Professor Bertie Wilkinson. See Biographical Notes under WILKINSON.

31 Marie's recently widowed sister-in-law Eleanor Blanshard had a pond in her garden on the Lakeshore Road in Burlington.

32 There had been correspondence between Margaret and her divorced husband Douglas about the comparative merits of Marie and Vivien Ratcliffe as surrogate mothers, with Douglas adopting a negative view of Vivien, possibly on the grounds that from his point of view she was insufficiently cultured.

33 Marie is referring to *The history of the Fairchild family, or, The child's manual: being a collection of stories calculated to show the importance and effects of a religious education* by Mrs. Sherwood, published in the 1870s.

34 Judy was the Ratcliffe's youngest daughter. See Biographical Notes under RATCLIFFE.

35 Honey Dew was a sweet orange drink served at the Honey Dew chain of restaurants.

36 The Arthur Ransome books were enjoyed by boys and girls alike. There were twelve books in the series, beginning with *Swallows and Amazons* in 1930 and ending with *Great Northern?* in 1947.

37   Since George Beamish had completed his work in North America, he and
     Katharine were returning to England, leaving their children with family
     friends in New Jersey. Andrew, the eldest, would be attending Trinity College
     School in Port Hope as a boarder, joining his brother Tim in New Jersey dur-
     ing the holidays.

38   Mary was recovering from chicken pox.

39   The Christmas party was hosted by Emily Williamson, John's older sister, who
     lived on Lakeshore Road (then Water Street) in Burlington. See Biographical
     Notes under WILLIAMSON. The Estaminet Restaurant was a one-minute
     walk west of Emily's house, with views over Lake Ontario.

40   William Maxwell Aitken, Lord Beaverbrook, who grew up in New Brunswick.
     In 1910 he moved to England, where he pursued business interests, entered
     politics, bought the *Daily Express* newspaper, and served as minister of air-
     craft production in Churchill's wartime government.

NOTES TO 1942

1   Marie to Margaret, March 1, 1942.

2   The "Dick" test is a test of the skin developed in the 1920s by the American
     physicians George and Gladys Dick to determine susceptibility to scarlet
     fever.

3   Sylvia Anthony lived near the Sharps in Hampstead Garden Suburb in
     London. See Biographical Notes under ANTHONY.

4   A.R.P. = Air Raid Precautions.

5   AA = anti-aircraft.

6   Dr. Samuel (Sam) J. Streight, O.B.E. (1883–1963), when he was associate
     medical director of Canada Life, tended Marie after an operation in 1924 to
     remove an abscess just below the knee.

7   Dr. Robert Inkerman Harris (1889–1966), who distinguished himself interna-
     tionally in orthopaedic surgery, was probably Marie's surgeon.

8   Little Granny was the mother of the boys' father, Mary Sharp. Big Granny was
     Margaret's mother, Mary Tout, whom Marie addressed as "Cousin Mary."

9   Hilda was the Ratcliffes' maid.

10   The wartime recycling program also included cigarette papers, wire, and fruit
     baskets.

11   The Three Little Pigs Shoe Shop on St. Clair Avenue just west of Yonge Street
     was the destination shoe shop for children in North Toronto. Children loved
     to step into the X-ray machine and look at the glowing green image of the
     bones in their feet.

12   Recipe for Emily Williamson's Gum Drop Valentine Cake: ½ cup butter, 1 cup
     sugar, 2 eggs well beaten, 2½ cups flour, ¼ teaspoon salt, 2 teaspoons baking
     powder, 1 teaspoon vanilla, ¾ cup milk, ½ lb. gumdrops chopped fine, ¼ lb.
     seeded raisins.
        Cream butter and sugar; add eggs. Sift dry ingredients, reserving about
     ½ cup flour to mix with gumdrops and raisins. Add vanilla to milk then add
     to first mixture alternately with dry ingredients. Stir in floured gum drops.

Bake in loaf or large cake tin, greased, at 300° for 1 ½ hours or a bit less. As Marie describes it in her letter, the cake should be baked in a heart-shaped tin and decorated with red and white icing and gumdrop hearts.

13 Regarding the sciatica and lumbago, in her letter to Margaret of February 26, Vivien Ratcliffe wrote that she had just seen Marie for the first time "in weeks" and "she looks very frail but has plenty of spirit. The poor girl has just been through a siege of sciatica. This being her third affliction, I do hope it means the beginning of happier times for her."

14 The family doctor was Dr. Valentine (Val) F. Stock (1888–1954), whose office was in the Medical Arts Building, at the corner of Bloor and St. George streets.

15 Jerome K. Jerome's humorous tale "Three Men in a Boat," originally published in 1889, was for many decades immensely popular on both sides of the Atlantic.

16 For Harold Adams Innis and his wife Mary Quayle Innis, and their children Donald, Mary, Hugh, and Anne, see Biographical Notes under INNIS.

17 For Robbie and Jo see Biographical Notes under ROBINSON.

18 On September 18, 1940, *The City of Benares* was sunk by German U-boats while en route from Liverpool to Canada. Seventy-seven of the ninety child evacuees on board were lost.

19 Marie is uncharacteristically forthcoming about her own academic accomplishments. She ranked second in the Province of Ontario in her Senior Matriculation examinations, and because the first-ranked student left the province she was awarded two Edward Blake entrance scholarships to the University of Toronto. Her achievement was reported in *Toronto Daily News* for Sept. 2, 1915 ("Fine School Career of Toronto girl"), where it was noted that she was only 15 at the time and that "she bears her honours modestly."

20 The School of Practical Science was established at the University of Toronto in 1878. Although from 1906 the name was officially the Faculty of Applied Science and Engineering, it continued to be popularly known as "SPS."

21 On May 9, Vivien wrote Margaret: "Yesterday a wonderful opportunity came along for Bill. Mr. and Mrs. Russell Shirley of Cochrane asked him to come to them for the summer. Mr. S. is a cousin of my cousin Helena Shirley,—but he is not related to me. He has a large wholesale business in Cochrane and supplies the various camps thereabouts—as well as some mines, I understand. They are very well off in this world's goods—I tell you this for the sole purpose of reassuring you as to comfortable surroundings for Bill and also his visit will not impose any financial strain on his hosts. They have six or seven children and the kind of home that stretches to accomodate several guests. Two daughters are attending Havergal College (Mrs. Bland has a position there, you know, and Jennifer attends school there). They (I mean the Shirleys) are splendid, kindly and generous people. I am sure a summer in the far north will be a great adventure to Bill."

22 See Appendix 3 for excerpts from the letter Sylvia Anthony wrote to Margaret after seeing the boys.

23 Regarding the "biblical" profile of the camp, today Tom recollects attempts, successful to some degree, to persuade the boys "to be saved." Tom recalls testifying before an assembly of children that he was saved. While he was in that state, which didn't last for long, in his own mind he judged harshly the conventional Christianity of Marie and John. He probably was too embarrassed ever to discuss this with them, and there certainly is no hint of it in Marie's references to Tom's time at camp, or in letters from him at the time.

24 William Anthony and his brother Paul went to Pioneer Camp with Tom and Christopher.

25 Margaret was asked several times over many months by both Marie and Vivien for a response to Vivien's letter regarding the dentist's report on Bill's tooth straightening, and his proposal to remove Bill's adenoids. Finally, Margaret wrote to Bill on August 13, 1942, "I have just sent a cable to Mrs. Ratcliffe to say that I approve of your having your tonsils & adenoids removed if the doctor still thinks it desirable; it's a great nuisance for you but its just one of the things that can't be helped. After having 7 operations myself you see I am pretty philosophic about them. They aren't very nice, but they can be borne and are sometimes necessary. I had my tonsils & adenoids done when I was 17 in Aug. 1914."

26 This letter was addressed to Margaret's mother, Mary Tout. See Biographical Notes under TOUT.

27 Bill did decide to stay in Canada. See Biographical Notes under SHARP.

28 The Most Rev. Derwyn Trevor Owen (1876–1947) was the 6th Primate of the Anglican Church of Canada.

29 The family butcher was Cook's Meat Market at 2029 Yonge Street, just three blocks from the house at Hillsdale.

30 When the United States entered the war in 1942 the term "United Nations"— and sometimes "the Allies"— was used for the countries who fought against the "Axis." In 1945, 51 countries came together to sign the United Nations charter.

31 Letter 33 was simply a note enclosing letters from the boys to Margaret.

32 In the end Dr. Stock accepted Marie's suggestion that either Palmolive soap or demothing chemicals on Tom's flannel shirts had caused the allergic reaction.

33 The phrase "climbing up the ever climbing wave" is from Alfred Lord Tennyson's poem "The Lotus Eaters."

34 Eve Burns was sufficiently concerned about the situation in Toronto that she wrote to Margaret on October 30, 1942, after Mr. Clague's visit: "Two or three weeks ago Ewan Clague had to go to Toronto for a convention and I asked him to look up the Williamsons and Ratcliffes while he was there. He did so and saw the boys as well and had a long talk with Mrs R. as a result of which he brought back some problems. He was very favourably impressed with both sets of foster parents by the way and said he didn't see how you could have been more fortunate. He thought both were doing an excellent job with the kids and that they were very understanding people and highly intelligent in their way of dealing with the youngsters. But a difficulty has arisen over the state of Mrs W.'s health. I have heard in the spring that she was not at all well

and it now seems that an old bone infection which she has supposed had been cleared up years ago has started up again. Mrs R. is very troubled about her and I have recently had a frank letter from Mrs W. in reply to one of mine in which she confesses that both she and her husband are seriously concerned about the drain on her strength of having the four kids without any maid assistance. For apparently its quite impossible to get anyone to help. She is very distressed about it for as she says she hates having to admit she can't carry through something she started out on."

35 In a letter to Mary Tout (Oct. 17, 1942), Marie wrote: "We are all _thrilled_ that Bill has won the 5th form scholarship—it means his tuition for this coming year at U.T.S.—$75. The award is for the boy passing with the highest standing from the lower 6th form to the higher. He _has_ done well! And it does mean a help to Vivien."

36 _The Twig_ was a U.T.S. (University of Toronto Schools) student magazine published from 1922 to 2004.

37 The book purchased by Marie in exchange for the Arthur Ransome book would be _August Adventure_ by M.E. Atkinson (London: Jonathan Cape, 1937).

38 On November 1, 1942, Douglas had broken the news to Margaret of his impending marriage: "As you may have guessed, I am going to marry again. The girl's name is Agnes Holden, 33 years of age, 5'1" in height, blonde, Rossetti face, grey-green eyes, long lashes and the tiniest hands you have ever seen." Soon after, on November 25, he was considering whether to tell the boys about his marriage: "Though the idea is still rather new to me, I'm quite friendly disposed to the suggestion that we shouldn't tell the children, and I've warned the people at Hale accordingly. When the children at last have the news they will at least have concrete evidence that I haven't lost my affection for, and interest in, them."

39 Ian Reginald Ponsford (1922–2006) knew Margaret at Abbotsholme School, where he had taught briefly. With other British pilots he went on from Toronto to Arizona to earn his flying wings, and was retained there as a flying instructor. Back in England in 1945, as a single-seat Spitfire pilot, he brought down record numbers of the German Luftwaffe, for which he was awarded the Distinguished Flying Cross.

NOTES TO 1943

1 Bill to his mother, December 30, 1943.

2 Katharine and George Beamish had returned to England in late 1942.

3 Eve Burns is mentioned in an article on economist Leonard Marsh by Anne Fromer in _Saturday Night_ (March 27, 1943, p. 2) entitled "The William Beveridge of Canada." The British government asked Sir William Beveridge (a Liberal M.P.) to write a report on the best ways of helping people on low incomes. In December 1942 Beveridge published a report that proposed that all people of working age should pay a weekly contribution. In return, benefits would be paid to those who were sick, unemployed, retired, or widowed.

Beveridge argued that this system would provide a minimum standard of living "below which no one should be allowed to fall." These measures were eventually introduced by the Labour government that was elected in 1945.

As the author of Canada's new security document, Marsh was viewed as Canada's Sir William Beveridge just as Eve Burns was Beveridge's counterpart in the United States for her report to Congress, *Security, Work, and Relief* on behalf of the National Resources Planning Board. All three had known each other at the London School of Economics. Looking back, Marsh shared his recollections of Eve Burns with Ms. Fromer: "Studying economics at the London School wasn't always easy. There was a day when old Professor Cannon didn't show up for a lecture. The class waited to see what would happen and it did. A glamor girl walked through the door, brought the class sharply to order, and proceeded to give us a sound lecture on the theory of marginal utility or something like that. I don't think any of us remembered much of what she said, although we hung on to her every word—but before the lecture was over just about every undergraduate had fallen in love with that lecturer. And that was my first meeting with the great economist Evelyn [*sic*] Burns."

4 The "Harrison affair." While Douglas Sharp, Vivien, and Bill all refer to Mr. Harrison over a six-month period, it isn't easy to get to the bottom of who Harrison was or what he was expected to do. Douglas Sharp in England evidently sought to influence the decision about his son Bill's choice of university—clearly preferring Oxford or Cambridge to the University of Toronto—and asked Harrison (probably through an intermediary as he appears not to have been acquainted with the man) to talk to Bill. Bill wrote to his mother on May 19 mentioning that he had had an "interview" with Mr. Harrison.

5 Mary's piano compositions still exist in manuscript, and she is optimistic that some day they will be published!

6 Edith Wilkinson and Ethel Bland were sisters.

7 In a letter to Mary Tout (Bill's grandmother), Marie wrote, "I have no idea what Bill's thoughts on religion are and I doubt if anyone else has. He goes to church pretty regularly with Vivien, without being asked, and Bill does nothing without a personal reason, so he must like doing so and find it helpful. They go to St. George's United Church.... Dr. Brewing, the minister at St. George's is well-known as an excellent preacher—Vivien says she feels cheated if she misses a Sunday—he has a very good mind and appeals to the intellect, never the emotions, in his sermon—which I suppose Bill appreciates and enjoys" (May 24, 1943).

8 On May 11, 1943, the U.S. 7th Division recaptured from the Japanese the island of Attu, the westernmost island of the Aleutians in Alaska.

9 A point rationing system was introduced in the United States early in 1943. The scheme allowed people to make choices among various foods and other items for which there were shortages, and also ensured that basic necessities were distributed fairly to rich and poor alike.

10 In a letter to Mary Tout Marie wrote: "Eve Burns was here last week and it was a joy for Vivien and me to meet her after having known her so long by

letters only. She is like a refreshing breeze and I do think C. is so lucky to be living with them. No, I don't suppose C. will attend church as much there as with us, though to be honest, I must confess that I don't think it was seeking after religion that made C. so faithful here—it was the pleasant sense of importance and authority he derived from carrying the cross and being warden, etc.! However, he has joined the Scouts, which is good ethical training, and also training in Christian principles. I expect, and I'm sure Eve and Arthur will neglect nothing which they feel will help his development in every way. Eve has been away speaking a great deal lately and Arthur (who is rather concerned that C. having a good mind, should be so lazy in the use of it) has been carrying on a discussion with C. each evening after dinner, on all sorts of topics, to get him to learn to think clearly and express his ideas. Sometimes the subjects are religious, such as "Objective proof of the existence of God," etc. If he had stayed here, I think the usual age for confirmation is about 14, but I would not have had him confirmed unless Mt. particularly asked for it, as I know she is not keen on their having religious instruction" (May 24, 1943).

11 See Appendix 4 for Eve Burns's report to Margaret on her visit with Bill and Tom. She tells of how the boys had developed since she last saw them, in 1940, and how the separation from Christopher affected them. Eve was unaware of Douglas's remarriage and speculates on how the boys would react if they were told.

12 Regarding Andrew Beamish, see Biographical Notes under BEAMISH. Michael Brodeur was a schoolmate of Peter from Montreal.

13 Bill Morrison (W.M. Morrison), who was one of a group of evacuee friends at U.T.S., returned to his home in Edinburgh in 1944. He studied mathematics at the university, was called up to serve in the R.A.F. in 1948, and pursued a career as an actuary in that city where he still lives.

14 From 1926 into the 1950s, Irene Peterkin owned Friday Island near Honey Harbour, Georgian Bay. The island was about seven kilometres northwest of Nickerson's dock, a 30- to 40-minute boat ride. Her brother Ernest, a builder in Toronto, probably built the original cottage, which with a few alterations has survived into the 21st century.

15 The National Resources Planning Board had been dissolved by the U.S. Congress. Eve Burns's *The American Social Security System* was first published by Houghton Mifflin in 1949.

16 Margaret had been butted by a cow in a field near Abbotsholme School, seriously hurting her arm. The horn missed the artery and no lasting harm was done. Vivien Ratcliffe wrote to Margaret on August 25: "I was awfully sorry to hear of your misadventure with the cow. I do hope that your arm is entirely better. I always did dislike cows and now evidently I have reason to distrust them if they can be so nasty to poor defenceless females."

17 Writing to Marie on September 14, 1943, Margaret expressed her appreciation of Vivien Ratcliffe. "I am feeling particularly grateful to Mrs. Ratcliffe for all the care and trouble she has taken with him [Bill]. I am sure if it were not for her getting him to U.T.S. he would not have done anything like so well."

18 "Donnie" (Donald) was the Innises' eldest child. The garage was a substantial two-storey brick building. The mice were housed in several cages in the garage and then, as they proliferated, on the roof. The white mice operation possibly began as a profitable venture, but brown field mice infiltrated the brood from outside and very quickly there were hundreds of mice of no commercial value.

19 In a letter to Mary Tout, Marie wrote: "I suppose it is inevitable that she should worry a great deal over the boys. I hope she does not regret having sent them out here—I think that quite apart from their safety the tremendous physical improvement in all 3 has more than justified the decision. The evacuated children have been returning in such numbers that she must naturally wonder about taking the boys back. My own feeling is that having been out here this long, perfectly happy and in splendid health and with the end of the war (European) now looking not so hopelessly far off, it would be unwise now not to wait until danger is over. I hope, in expressing my views (perhaps rather strongly) I have not seemed to Margaret to be trying to dictate to her what she should do about her own children, from whom she has been parted so long (in her place I'm sure I should resent that) but I wanted to reassure her, if she feared I was wearying of my responsibility" (Oct. 28, 1943).

20 For Ethel, David, and Jennifer Bland, see Biographical Notes under WILKINSON and BLAND.

NOTES TO 1944

1 Tom to his mother, June 12, 1944.

2 John Taylor was a former pupil of Margaret at Abbotsholme School and was now serving in the Royal Air Force.

3 For Christopher's reaction to the news of his father's remarriage, see Eve Burns's letter to Margaret, Appendix 5.)

4 The Children's Overseas Reception Board was established by the British government in June 1940 to organize the evacuation of children during the war. Over 1500 children were sent this way through the C.O.R.B. from Britain to Canada.

5 There are no further letters from Marie, but Tom wrote to his mother on June 12:

THOMAS SHARP
90 DUNVEGAN ROAD
TORONTO

Monday, June 12

Dear Mother and Father:

I'm extremely sorry that I haven't written to you for so long. In my last letter I talked about my April report. Now we are waiting our final June exams from which it is decided who of us will be recommended. We have none of our results yet.

Several times during the past few weeks Bill and I have been for walks. We have had lovely weather for it.

Peter just came back from school on Saturday. He received one cup, three books, two scholarships and a bronze medal. Isn't he doing well!

I'm glad you are going to be history mistress at Ulverston Grammar School. Does that mean that you will teach me?

Our choir is in rather a mix up now. Our leading tenor soloist died a few days ago and another tenor left to be organist of another church leaving one tenor. This means that the only anthems we can sing are all boys' anthems. To make matters worse our leading boy is sick!

Love,
From
Tom.

P.S. I hope they will be able to spare one ship from the invasion to take me back to England.

NOTE TO EPILOGUE

1 Margaret Sharp, Baroness Sharp of Guildford, sits on the Liberal Democrat benches of the House of Lords. Married to Tom since 1962, she had a career both as a civil servant and academic, specializing latterly in the economics of science and technology at the University of Sussex, Brighton. In 1982 she was selected by the Social Democratic Party (SDP) to stand for Parliament in Guildford and subsequently fought four general elections for the SDP and its successor, the Liberal Democrats. She went into the House of Lords in 1998.

NOTE TO APPENDIX 5

1 Margaret underlined "Enid" with a note—"Not my doing! M.S."—before passing the letter on to her mother. Enid had been Douglas's girlfriend when he separated from Margaret in 1934, but he married Agnes Holden.

INDEX

riding, 71, 80; snowball fight, 176; wagon-riding, 223

Ponsford, Ian Reginald, 247, 362n39

postal system, 69, 79, 162, 166, 204, 206, 248, 253, 256, 263, 269, 304, 305, 310, 313, 314, 316, 324, 327; disorganized, 107, 153, 258; irregular, 169, 265; lost parcel, 246

Price and Trade Board, 271

Provincial Lady (Delafield), 34, 353n5

Provost, Alan, 24, 354n11

Provost, Donald, 24

public schools, 211, 295, 304; concert, 205, 223, 224; costs, 128; music curriculum, 131; physical examination, 147, 152; political background, 295; skating races, 261

Punch and Judy show, 259

Punch magazine, 5, 69, 78, 81, 107, 125, 169, 238, 248, 258, 265

radio, xvi, 47, 85, 96, 131, 172, 245, 283; church bells broadcast, 237

Ransome, Arthur, 141, 225, 235, 296, 358n36, 362n37

Ratcliffe (family), 7, 9, 22, 23

Ratcliffe, John Henry ("Harry"), xxi, 2, 10, 22, 38, 142, 143, 181, 291, 335

Ratcliffe, John Henry, 22, 38, 181, 286

Ratcliffe, Judy, 22, 139, 192, 214

Ratcliffe, Nancy, 22, 192

Ratcliffe, Vivien (née Chalmers), 2, 14, 15, 31, 34, 38, 39, 42, 45, 47, 62, 83, 117, 120, 132, 133 135, 142, 149, 173, 181, 196, 204, 214, 245, 267, 271, 272, 281, 354n18, 358n32, 360n13, 360n21, 361n25, 363n4, 364n16; career, 22

rationing, 11, 12, 27, 210, 214, 217, 254, 269, 270, 274, 289, 363n9; butter, 245, 254, 259, 271; clothing, 123, 217; coupons, 169, 204, 205, 290, 295; cuts, 205; electricity, 227; gasoline, 127, 169, 173, 185, 192, 217, 226, 233, 248, 253, 270, 277, 278, 283; hoarding, 12, 205, 245; jam, 214, 290; meat, 205, 210, 220, 230, 270; regulations, 205; shoes, 294;

soap, 220; sugar, 168, 172, 217, 271, 290; tea, coffee, 271, 290; tinned fruit, 290; tires, 169; unsatisfactory, 205; voluntary, 205, 226; postwar Britain, 336

Redford, Penelope, 79, 357n12

regulations, currency, xv, 9, 12, 31, 86, 104, 109, 153, 154, 252, 278; imports, 66; manufacturing controls, 186, 206; sending clothing, 94, 96; sending money, 188, 190

repatriation, 15, 214, 242, 255, 267, 305, 322, 323, 353n4, 365n19; arrangements, 325; clothing, 324–26, 329; documentation, 325, 328; English women, 205; fare, 306, 324, 325; government policy, 267; journey, 331; luggage, 325, 326; problems with, 210; red tape, 324; secrecy, 328

Report on Social Security for Canada, 272

restrictions, 274, 286, clothing, 329; electricity, 230; fountain pens, 228; outdoor advertising, 227; railway travel, 253; salaries, 302; street lighting, 227

Ridley College (St. Catharines, Ont.): rugby, 301

Roberts, John, 42, 288

Robinson, George Gates ("Robbie"), 22, 114, 182

Robinson, Joan, 22, 114, 115

Robinson, John ("Jack"), 22, 113, 114, 116

Robinson, Josepha (née Spence; "Jo"), 22, 111, 113–15, 117, 261, 264

Robinson, Meredith, 22, 114, 116

Roosevelt, Franklin Delano, 272

Rowland, Edna, 103

Rowland, John, 103, 106

Royal Air Force, 333, 365n2

Royal Canadian Air Force, 22, 139, 272, 291, 302, 354n14; Women's Division, 300

"The Royal Canadian Mounted Police," 57

Williamson, John Dudley, xviii, xix, xx, 1, 7, 10, 16, 21, 22, 24, 27, 334, 337; birthplace, 4; career, 4, 5; death of mother, 2; education, leisure activities, 26; family, 4, 5; marriage, 4, 25, *and throughout letters*

Williamson, John Peterkin ("Peter"), 1, 5, 17, 25, 27; education, career, interests, 19, 26; electric train, 13; newsletter, 13, *and throughout letters*

Williamson, Marie Curtis (née Peterkin), xviii, xx, xxxiv, 1, 3, 7, 10–12, 17, 20–22, 24–27; academic accomplishments, 360n19; ancestry, 6; appearance, 5; arthritis, 15; daily life, 5, death, 15; department stores, 6; diary, 2; fashion sense, 6; fragile health, 2, 5; frugality, 6; leisure reading, 5; letters, 2, 14,16; marriage, 4; parenting skills, 9; personality, 5, 6; views on nutrition, 9; views on religion, 5, 52–53; visit with Margaret, 16; role in life, 4, sojourn in London, 2, *and throughout letters*

Williamson, Mary Frances, 1, 13, 16, 17, 25–27, 363n5, *and throughout letters*

Williamson, Walker Murray ("Murray"), 27, 162

Williamson, William Edgar ("Bill"), 27

Woolworth's, 126

World War I, x, xi, 4, 94

X-ray, 40, 76, 139, 165; shoe store, 96, 359n11

Y.M.C.A. camp Pinecrest, 201; war guest reduction, 196

York Downs Golf Club (Earl Bales Park), 64, 66, 163, 186, 248, 355n30

zeppelins, x, xi

Books in the Life Writing Series
Published by Wilfrid Laurier University Press

Haven't Any News: Ruby's Letters from the Fifties edited by Edna Staebler with an Afterword by Marlene Kadar • 1995 / x + 165 pp. / ISBN 0-88920-248-6

"I Want to Join Your Club": Letters from Rural Children, 1900–1920 edited by Norah L. Lewis with a Preface by Neil Sutherland • 1996 / xii + 250 pp. (30 b&w photos) / ISBN 0-88920-260-5

And Peace Never Came by Elisabeth M. Raab with Historical Notes by Marlene Kadar • 1996 / x + 196 pp. (12 b&w photos, map) / ISBN 0-88920-281-8

Dear Editor and Friends: Letters from Rural Women of the North-West, 1900–1920 edited by Norah L. Lewis • 1998 / xvi + 166 pp. (20 b&w photos) / ISBN 0-88920-287-7

The Surprise of My Life: An Autobiography by Claire Drainie Taylor with a Foreword by Marlene Kadar • 1998 / xii + 268 pp. (8 colour photos and 92 b&w photos) / ISBN 0-88920-302-4

Memoirs from Away: A New Found Land Girlhood by Helen M. Buss / Margaret Clarke • 1998 / xvi + 153 pp. / ISBN 0-88920-350-4

The Life and Letters of Annie Leake Tuttle: Working for the Best by Marilyn Färdig Whiteley • 1999 / xviii + 150 pp. / ISBN 0-88920-330-x

Marian Engel's Notebooks: "Ah, mon cahier, écoute" edited by Christl Verduyn • 1999 / viii + 576 pp. / ISBN 0-88920-333-4 cloth / ISBN 0-88920-349-0 paper

Be Good Sweet Maid: The Trials of Dorothy Joudrie by Audrey Andrews • 1999 / vi + 276 pp. / ISBN 0-88920-334-2

Working in Women's Archives: Researching Women's Private Literature and Archival Documents edited by Helen M. Buss and Marlene Kadar • 2001 / vi + 120 pp. / ISBN 0-88920-341-5

Repossessing the World: Reading Memoirs by Contemporary Women by Helen M. Buss • 2002 / xxvi + 206 pp. / ISBN 0-88920-408-x cloth / ISBN 0-88920-410-1 paper

Chasing the Comet: A Scottish-Canadian Life by Patricia Koretchuk • 2002 / xx + 244 pp. / ISBN 0-88920-407-1

The Queen of Peace Room by Magie Dominic • 2002 / xii + 115 pp. / ISBN 0-88920-417-9

China Diary: The Life of Mary Austin Endicott by Shirley Jane Endicott • 2002 / xvi + 251 pp. / ISBN 0-88920-412-8

The Curtain: Witness and Memory in Wartime Holland by Henry G. Schogt • 2003 / xii + 132 pp. / ISBN 0-88920-396-2

Teaching Places by Audrey J. Whitson • 2003 / xiii + 178 pp. / ISBN 0-88920-425-x

Through the Hitler Line by Laurence F. Wilmot, M.C. • 2003 / xvi + 152 pp. / ISBN 0-88920-448-9

Where I Come From by Vijay Agnew • 2003 / xiv + 298 pp. / ISBN 0-88920-414-4

The Water Lily Pond by Han Z. Li • 2004 / x + 254 pp. / ISBN 0-88920-431-4

The Life Writings of Mary Baker McQuesten: Victorian Matriarch edited by Mary J. Anderson • 2004 / xxii + 338 pp. / ISBN 0-88920-437-3

Seven Eggs Today: The Diaries of Mary Armstrong, 1859 and 1869 edited by Jackson W. Armstrong • 2004 / xvi + 228 pp. / ISBN 0-88920-440-3

Love and War in London: A Woman's Diary 1939–1942 by Olivia Cockett; edited by Robert W. Malcolmson • 2005 / xvi + 208 pp. / ISBN 0-88920-458-6

Incorrigible by Velma Demerson • 2004 / vi + 178 pp. / ISBN 0-88920-444-6

Auto/biography in Canada: Critical Directions edited by Julie Rak • 2005 / viii + 264 pp. / ISBN 0-88920-478-0

Tracing the Autobiographical edited by Marlene Kadar, Linda Warley, Jeanne Perreault, and Susanna Egan • 2005 / viii + 280 pp. / ISBN 0-88920-476-4

Must Write: Edna Staebler's Diaries edited by Christl Verduyn • 2005 / viii + 304 pp. / ISBN 0-88920-481-0

Food That Really Schmecks by Edna Staebler • 2007 / xxiv + 334 pp. / ISBN 978-0-88920-521-5

163256: A Memoir of Resistance by Michael Englishman • 2007 / xvi + 112 pp. (14 b&w photos) / ISBN 978-1-55458-009-5

The Wartime Letters of Leslie and Cecil Frost, 1915–1919 edited by R.B. Fleming • 2007 / xxxvi + 384 pp. (49 b&w photos, 5 maps) / ISBN 978-1-55458-000-2

Johanna Krause Twice Persecuted: Surviving in Nazi Germany and Communist East Germany by Carolyn Gammon and Christiane Hemker • 2007 / x + 170 pp. (58 b&w photos, 2 maps) / ISBN 978-1-55458-006-4

Watermelon Syrup: A Novel by Annie Jacobsen with Jane Finlay-Young and Di Brandt • 2007 / x + 268 pp. / ISBN 978-1-55458-005-7

Broad Is the Way: Stories from Mayerthorpe by Margaret Norquay • 2008 / x + 106 pp. (6 b&w photos) / ISBN 978-1-55458-020-0

Becoming My Mother's Daughter: A Story of Survival and Renewal by Erika Gottlieb • 2008 / x + 178 pp. (36 b&w illus., 17 colour) / ISBN 978-1-55458-030-9

Leaving Fundamentalism: Personal Stories edited by G. Elijah Dann • 2008 / xii + 234 pp. / ISBN 978-1-55458-026-2

Bearing Witness: Living with Ovarian Cancer edited by Kathryn Carter and Lauri Elit • 2009 / viii + 94 pp. / ISBN 978-1-55458-055-2

Dead Woman Pickney: A Memoir of Childhood in Jamaica by Yvonne Shorter Brown • 2010 / viii + 202 pp. / ISBN 978-1-55458-189-4

I Have a Story to Tell You by Seemah C. Berson • 2010 / xx + 288 pp. + 10 pp. b&w photos / ISBN 978-1-55458-219-8

We All Giggled: A Bourgeois Family Memoir by Thomas O. Hueglin • 2010 / 192 pp. (illustrations) / ISBN 978-1-55458-262-4

Just a Larger Family: Letters of Marie Williamson from the Canadian Home Front, 1940–1944 edited by Mary F. Williamson and Tom Sharp • 2011 / 408 pp. (illustrations) / ISBN 978-1-55458-266-2

Burdens of Proof: Faith, Doubt, and Identity in Autobiography by Susanna Egan • forthcoming 2011 / 180 pp. / ISBN 978-1-55458-332-4